Creole City

A Chronicle of Early American New Orleans

NATHALIE DESSENS

Gene Allen Smith, Series Editor

Frontispiece image courtesy of The Historic New Orleans Collection, 1958.42

Printed in the United States of America on acid-free paper

This book may be available in an electronic edition.

21 20 19 18 17 16 6 5 4 3 2 1
First cloth printing, 2015
First paperback printing, 2016

LIBRARY OF CONGRESS CATALOGING-IN-PUBLICATION DATA
Dessens, Nathalie, 1963– author.
Creole City : a chronicle of early American New Orleans / Nathalie Dessens.
pages cm — (Contested boundaries)
Includes bibliographical references and index.
ISBN 978-0-8130-6020-0 (cloth)
ISBN 978-0-8130-6218-1 (pbk.)
1. New Orleans (La.)—History—19th century. 2. New Orleans (La.)—Social life and customs—19th century. I. Title. II. Series: Contested boundaries.
F379.N557D46 2015
976.3'35—DC23 2014027982

UNIVERSITY PRESS OF FLORIDA
15 Northwest 15th Street
Gainesville, FL 32611-2079
http://www.upf.com

Contents

Figures

Preface

When I first heard about the existence of the Sainte-Gême Family Papers, from Paul Lachance and Ginger Gould, little did I think that those papers would lead me to spend the next decade of my life working on this manuscript. I vividly remember Ginger telling me about this man who had written a long correspondence to a friend who lived in a little French town no one had ever heard of, St. Gaudens. I laughed and answered: "I was born there." The coincidence did trigger my curiosity, of course. I started looking into the manuscript, archived at The Historic New Orleans Collection, and immediately understood the wealth of Jean Boze's correspondence.

Very often, migrants' letters contain little information on the migrants' new abode. In the case of Jean Boze, the letters bear almost exclusively on his new home, New Orleans. Even though the letters were sent to France and kept there for over a century, they definitely belong to New Orleans, a fact not lost on Mrs. La Fonta Saintegême, who entrusted them to The Historic New Orleans Collection.

The wealth of this exceptional correspondence is, alas, beyond the grasp of many New Orleanians, because the almost 1,200 manuscript pages are written in French, and in outdated French at that.

I spent many hours, days, weeks, months reading the letters. What I hope to do with this book is give non-French-speaking readers access—although unfortunately limited access—to their extraordinarily rich content.

Publishing them in their entirety would have been a still better way to open a window onto New Orleans in its early American decades, still an insufficiently studied period in New Orleans's history. However, their format made the task impossible. The letters are too numerous and too long, and they mostly resemble a logbook, dedicating a few lines or a few paragraphs to one event, constantly changing subjects, developing subjects in short paragraphs over several letters, sometimes repeating news and information that has been given in previous letters. There is an appendix to this book, however, which has the transcript of one letter and its translation into English.

I thus decided to introduce readers to these letters through an essay, wandering through them, just as Boze wandered in the city's streets and history for over two decades. The numerous translated quotes will give the readers some measure of the wealth of Boze's writing, although they cannot be true to the picturesque style of the old Frenchman.

I hope this book will stir up people's curiosity and bring many to The Historic New Orleans Collection's beautiful Williams Research Center, in the heart of New Orleans's Vieux Carré.

Acknowledgments

As with any book, there are many people who deserve thanks in these opening pages. My first thanks go to The Historic New Orleans Collection, for many reasons: first and foremost, for harboring this wonderful collection (and many more); but also for granting me a Diane Woest fellowship, in 2006, to pursue my research on the manuscript collection; and for always welcoming me warmly and giving me all the help I needed throughout the many months I spent reading the correspondence. Everyone I have met there has always been extremely helpful and welcoming. My deep gratitude goes to The Collection's director, Priscilla Lawrence, and to Alfred Lemon, Mark Cave, Jessica Dorman, Daniel Hammer, Eric Seiferth, Siva Blake, Mary-Lou Eichhorn, Sally Sassi, Jennifer Navarre, Frances Salvaggio, and all those who, over the years, have always made me feel at home at the Williams Research Center.

If I spend most of my time in New Orleans at The Historic New Orleans Collection, I also want to thank all the others who opened their doors to me and helped me, among whom are Irene Wainwright, at the New Orleans Public Library, and Charles Nolan, at the Archives of the Archdiocese of New Orleans.

I am, of course, grateful to Lucille Albin La Fonta née Winship, Ernest de Puech's granddaughter, who was adopted, after her parents' death, by her uncle and aunt, Henri de Saintegême and Eugénie de Puech, for leaving the Sainte-Gême Family Papers in the trust of The Historic New Orleans Collection. She recognized the significance of the correspondence and did not hesitate to return it to New Orleans and enable future generations to read what it was like to live in New Orleans in the early nineteenth century.

In researching this book, I was also helped by the descendants of the two protagonists of the correspondence. I want to thank, more specifically, Antoine Pagenstecher and Manuel Miguel de Santagema for sharing with me information about their respective families, as well as Frank Deffes and Shirley Manning, Boze's descendants in the United States, for the many exchanges we had, and Nancy La Fonta Saintegême, for opening her doors to me and allowing me a glimpse of the *château de Bagen*, where Boze's letters were received and read.

Among the scholars who helped me in this venture, I must acknowledge Virginia Gould and Paul Lachance for pointing out the Sainte-Gême Family Papers to me, and Frédéric Rousseau and Jean-Marc Lafon, professors of history at the University of Montpellier, as well as Michel Hanotaux and Manuel Guerrero Acosta, for answering my questions about the portrait of Sainte-Gême owned by The Collection. I also want to thank Harry Redman, Professor Emeritus at Tulane University, who volunteered at the Collection for many years, for our many Thursday afternoon discussions and for sharing the information he had on the manuscript.

While working on such a long-term project, good logistics are essential. And here, I am highly indebted to Virginia Gould for everything. She has offered me, over all those years, her friendship, her advice, a roof, and all the help I ever needed. Thank you, Ginger, for making me feel at home away from home, for the many dinners we shared, and for all our passionate discussions when I came back from the archives. Your friendship is very precious.

Working in New Orleans in the summer is a very pleasant punishment. Many friends from New Orleans, Baton Rouge, Minnesota, or France have made my life outside The Historic New Orleans Collection a permanent party. Thank you, David, Randy, Jessica, Erin, Russel, Georgia, Fernin, and all my other New Orleans friends. Thank you, Jim, Smittie, Catherine, and Greg, for the many weekends together in New Orleans, Baton Rouge, or Grande Isle. Thank you, David, Wilfrid, Marie-Claude, Mark, Françoise, and Jeremy for visiting and making my stays even more delightful. A special thanks to my mother, Madeleine, for ensuring most of the logistical organization while I was working in the archives, and to my father, Jean, for doing without her all those weeks. New Orleans is a city of encounters. I have met, over the years, many people, who are now too numerous to name. I am sure they will recognize themselves and hear my thanks.

Along the way, many historians of New Orleans have inspired me and helped me with my many questions or problems. Although I cannot name here all my sources of inspiration, I want to give a special thanks to Ginger Gould and Paul Lachance again; to Sylvia Frey and Emily Clark, who, besides hosting many a great dinner for me, listened to me and advised me when I needed assistance; and also to Ken Aslakson for very inspiring discussions on our favorite topic, New Orleans.

I also want to thank Sheryl Rahal, my colleague and friend, for accompanying me in the writing of three books. For the present book, as ever, she was there for me. Thank you, Sheryl, for your patient editing of my books. It would be very scary to write in English if I did not know I had a careful reader to help me with my many gallicisms.

As always, my gratitude goes to the University Press of Florida for the many years of collaboration, to Meredith Morris-Babb for her renewed trust and patience, and to the readers who helped me improve my manuscript with their extremely interesting, insightful comments.

Finally, I must thank my husband, Patrick, for his love and his endurance. He never protests when I leave for New Orleans in the summer and is always happy to meet me there. He never complains when I spend long weekends writing and is unceasing in his support and encouragement. He always bears with me in my many time-devouring projects.

Introduction

In May 1809, Jean Boze and Jean-François Henri de Miquel, Baron de Saintegême, known in the Americas as Henri de Ste-Gême, set sail on Ste-Gême's corsair *The Beaver* from Santiago de Cuba. Both men had lived through the Haitian Revolution at the turn of the century. In late 1803, both men had fled what was still then called Saint-Domingue—although for only a few weeks more—and both men had found refuge in Cuba. Both men had tried to rebuild their shattered lives in the Cuban *Oriente*,[1] before being forced to flee once more. On May 20, 1809, together they reached New Orleans, where, for the second time, they took refuge from the disturbances of the Atlantic world.

Their epic encompasses two forced flights, one triggered by a major revolution of this Atlantic world and one induced by the European wars that reverberated throughout the Atlantic space. Their adventure also bridges the gap between the colonial worlds of the previous centuries and the American independences of the turn of the nineteenth century. It is also an itinerary—from a French colony to a Spanish one, and then to a new territory of the young North American republic—that shows the porosity of the colonial worlds of the Americas and of the Atlantic space more generally.

Whether the two men had been acquainted in Saint-Domingue is not known, although there is reasonable certainty that they had, Jean Boze being the captain of the harbor of Port Républicain (formerly Port-au-Prince) and Ste-Gême a high-ranking officer in the French expeditionary corps sent by Napoleon to try to regain control of the colony that the French empire was on the verge of losing forever. Maybe their long-lasting friendship only started in Cuba, or even in their last moments on the island. What is certain is that they fled together on Ste-Gême's corsair when the Spanish authorities declared all non-naturalized French people living in Cuba personae non gratae, in response to Napoleon's imperialistic views regarding Spain.[2]

Expelled from their first refuge, with their property sequestered by the Cuban colonial authorities, the two men eventually dropped anchor in New

Orleans. For nine years, Ste-Gême and Boze lived there, manifestly in close proximity. When Ste-Gême returned to his native castle of Bagen, in the vicinity of Saint-Gaudens, not far from Toulouse, in southwestern France, Jean Boze stayed behind. They never saw each other again, and they died, both in the early 1840s, an ocean apart. Their separation was, however, what enables us today to reconstruct their itinerary and get a grasp of what the Atlantic world was like in the early nineteenth century. Indeed, for more than twenty years, from April 20, 1818, to August 6, 1839, Boze wrote 158 letters, covering almost 1,200 pages, to his friend and benefactor, Henri de Ste-Gême.

The story of these two men is exemplary, but it also epitomizes many transatlantic adventures. It reveals the narrowness of the Atlantic space, crisscrossed by incessant movements between Europe and the Americas, but also within the Western Hemisphere, in the Caribbean and between North and South America. The Atlantic was a space of crossroads, a complex network of commercial movements, of departures and returns, of transatlantic families and correspondence.

Much letter writing went on between the colonial Americas and Europe, and there are innumerable testimonies of Atlantic experiences over the centuries. In recent decades, historians have started using these letters as important sources to study the Atlantic world. In Europe and in the Americas, scholars have compiled and analyzed Atlantic letters, devising rich methodologies for the study of correspondence.[3]

Very few sets of correspondence, however, are as rich as Boze's. Few are as voluminous and continuous between two individuals over such a long period of time. And not many emanate from as keen an observer and articulate a writer as Jean Boze. Many reveal more about the function of letter writing in the Atlantic world than about the world the migrants discovered. Most of the time, the world shared by the writer and the recipient was the world the migrant had left behind, and it was the topic most often addressed in the letters, in order to maintain the bond that migration had disrupted.[4]

Not so for Boze and Ste-Gême. Other than their relationship and family stories, what these two men shared was a common epic in the Americas and a shared life in New Orleans. For once, the correspondence is almost entirely about the Americas, not about the country in which both men had been born, where they had no shared history. And what the 1,200 pages reveal is, of course, two individual narratives, those of Jean Boze and Henri de Ste-Gême, but also the narrative of their transatlantic friendship. This is the first interest of the correspondence. The letters are also a narrative history, or rather several intricate narrative histories: the individual narrative of Boze and Ste-Gême, but also the narrative history of the Saint-Domingue refugees and, more importantly, the larger historical narrative of Louisiana in the first three decades after the end of its colonial history.

The early decades of Louisiana's American destiny are a fascinating period in Louisiana history. A period of mutation, evolution, and development, this early American era was also one of increased importance of New Orleans in the Atlantic space, at what Atlantic historians consider a very late period in its history. Although it is an essential period of transition between more than a century of Latin colonial history and the incorporation of the former colony into the fabric of the young American republic,[5] this early American era is surprisingly understudied in Louisiana history.[6]

For a long time, historians have insisted on the radical changes undergone by New Orleans, and Louisiana more broadly, in this period. It is true that the early nineteenth century was a crucial period of development for the Crescent City. It is, however, closer to reality to assert that these decades were further marked by a complex dialectic of continuity and change. Recent historiographical revisions have started insisting on this dialectic and emphasizing continuity more than historians had done in the second half of the twentieth century.[7] There is still much to write about the transitional early American period and the pattern of ethnocultural rivalry often used as the structuring element of the narratives of early American New Orleans, which most certainly needs to be qualified. Although it was a striking feature in early nineteenth-century New Orleans, the modes of interaction between the various groups living in the city were more complex than is usually thought. The web of social, economic, and political relations should probably be assessed less in terms of ethnocultural rivalry than in terms of increasing interaction, mingling, and, ultimately, possibly, Creolization.[8] New Orleans changed much in the four decades following its purchase by the United States, and those years were influential in the formation of what journalist John Popham called "a special South within the South,"[9] and in the shaping of an identity specific to the city.

While New Orleans was becoming the urban core of the South, however, it was also undergoing evolutions that made it resemble more closely the developing cities of the northeastern Atlantic coast of the United States.[10] Boze's narrative clearly shows that the city followed a model of development that was common to the main Atlantic cities of the young American republic. Yet this narrative clearly makes New Orleans a special city of the Atlantic world, turned toward the southern American continent as much as toward Europe. While the Crescent City remained part of the traditional Atlantic world, it also participated in the inauguration of a new Atlantic era, that of the American revolutions and independences, when the Caribbean became a new space of exchanges. People moved back and forth across the Caribbean, initiating networks—including family ones—and favoring transfers of culture and knowledge within this new Caribbean space. This space did not replace the Atlantic one, but it made the Americas something more than the margin of the Atlantic space. New Orleans was pivotal in this recentering of the Atlantic space. This is still largely unknown territory in the historiography of New Orleans. Boze's narrative will open a few windows onto this history, which scholars will need to focus on in the decades to come.[11]

Although it may sometimes read like a piece of economic, social, intellectual, and cultural history, this book is not meant to be a comprehensive history of early American New Orleans, for Boze's letters must be taken for what they really are: an individual perception of New Orleans, a very personal description of what Jean Boze, with his past, his origins, his education, and his experience, saw unfold before his eyes.[12] They are, in fact, an "entry into his mental universe."[13] Although what he narrates can by no means be taken as simple fact, his correspondence has the merit of offering diverse points of view, through testimonies he reports, newspaper articles he paraphrases or quotes, and hearsay he transmits. It also calls the reader's attention to aspects of New Orleans that are very often neglected in the history of the city. It chronicles two decades of life in New Orleans from the vantage point of a foreigner who had made New Orleans his final home and was moving in restricted social circles but was intent on drawing an extremely detailed description of the city for his addressee. The reader will follow him in his meanderings around the city and his wandering through the city's history. The reader will discover how Boze saw New Orleans, will hear the words he used to describe it,[14] and will catch glimpses of the deeply original chronicles he wrote of the Crescent City in the 1820s and 1830s.

The book opens with the narrative of the epic stories of the two protagonists of the correspondence, to situate the two men in the vast context of the Atlantic space in the early nineteenth century and to better understand Boze's very specific perception of his new port of call. It then focuses on New Orleans, at a time when it was still close to being the small colonial town it had been two decades earlier and when it was struggling to enter a new era of modernity within the expanding and developing young American republic. Chapters 2 and 3 examine successively the still rudimentary conditions of the city and the march to progress of the then capital city of the infant state of Louisiana. Chapter 4 broaches the increasing importance of the city in the Atlantic world. Following Boze's chronicle of the advent of the most multicultural era in the city's history, chapter 5 shows how the divisions and alliances between the various racial and ethnic groups debunk the myth of an early American era marked by a binary opposition between Creoles and Americans. The book closes on the progressive blend of the various groups and parallel shaping of a new identity, specific to the city, through a slow process of Creolization.

1

Adventure

Jean Boze and Henri de Ste-Gême met in the first decade of the nineteenth century, probably in Santiago de Cuba, where they had both found refuge from the Haitian Revolution in late 1803. Together, they sailed to New Orleans in May 1809 and settled there, patiently reconstructing their shattered lives and maintaining close connections until Ste-Gême left the Crescent City forever in 1818. Although they never met again, they never lost contact in the two decades following Ste-Gême's departure.

There are two narratives in Boze's letters. The main one, in terms of volume as well as significance, is that of New Orleans in its most ebullient decades. The second interwoven narrative is the story of the protagonists of the correspondence, Jean Boze and Henri de Ste-Gême. It is, of course, more personal than the main narrative in that it is the story of a relationship between two individuals, but it epitomizes a small, although not insignificant, part of what New Orleans then was. It is broader than the main narrative, because it encompasses transatlantic experiences and thus inscribes New Orleans within the Atlantic world at a time when the city's Atlantic destiny was reaching its climax. To understand the New Orleans narrative, it is thus important to understand the narrative of the uncommon experience of the two men who tell it (Boze, who tells it directly, and Ste-Gême, who encourages it indirectly), as well as the peculiar relationship between them. This more intimate narrative is all the more important to examine because it helps situate the perception of the writer of the letters before even starting to read what they tell about New Orleans in the early American period.

If Jean Boze was a Frenchman living in New Orleans, he was not just any Frenchman living in New Orleans in the early nineteenth century, just as Jean-François Henri de Ste-Gême was not just any Frenchman living in southwestern France in the same era. Both the protagonists of this protracted transatlantic epistolary story had lived lives that, although not so unique, epitomize Louisiana's reputation as a land of adventure. Both men had histories that help illuminate the vision they shared of early nineteenth-century New Orleans. To comprehend the broader narrative, it is important to decode their personal narratives. Although the correspondence contains almost nothing about the past—partly because the two men shared it, and partly, certainly, because it was too painful to relate—reconstructing it gives a snapshot of who inhabited the Crescent City at that time. The letters already tell much about New Orleans society and, more importantly, they explain the very specific perspective of Boze's narrative of the city. Although the personal narrative might seem to tell a different story, every part of it highlights what early American New Orleans was. This chapter depicts an Atlantic adventure (Boze's), an Atlantic circuit (Ste-Gême's), an Atlantic epistolary story (the two men's, for more than twenty years), and tells of the way in which these stories connect with the larger story of New Orleans in the first three decades after the beginning of its new national destiny.

Jean Boze: An Atlantic Adventure

Jean Boze was a relatively anonymous actor in the French colonization of the New World. Somehow, his only significant legacy is his correspondence with Ste-Gême. As surprising as it may seem, however, archives, both in France and in the Americas, are full of reminders of his eventful life, which can be traced with relative accuracy.[1] As distinctive as it may seem to a modern reader, his life was not entirely uncommon in the Atlantic world of the time, and describing it shows not only how tumultuous and dangerous, but also how porous, open, and energetic, this New World was.

Jean Boze was born on September 26, 1753, in La Ciotat, near Marseilles, in southeastern France.[2] The son of a sea captain, he entered the French merchant marine and started navigating across the Atlantic.[3] From 1775 to 1784, he served in the merchant marine, including, in the later years, as captain.[4] Like other adventurers of the high seas, he settled in the colonies, in his case, in Jacmel, in the French colony of Saint-Domingue, on March 25, 1784. Saint-Domingue was then the French part of the island of Hispaniola, whose eastern part, Santo Domingo, was a Spanish possession. The richest Caribbean colony of the French Empire in the Americas, Saint-Domingue was then experiencing its last peaceful years before the slave rebellion, which, in the wake of the French Revolution, led the colony to its independence under the name of Haiti, more than a decade later, on January 1, 1804. A paradise for enterprising men, it was, in the late 1780s, an extremely wealthy and productive French sugar colony.[5] In 1785, Boze was appointed interim captain of the harbor of Jacmel, and, in 1786, after heroically saving a royal frigate, *L'Active*, from sinking, he was commissioned head captain, in command of one of the main harbors of Saint-Domingue.[6] In 1789, at the dawn of the French Revolution, Boze had thus been living in the Caribbean for five years.

As seems to have been very frequent in the colonial world of the Americas, at least among people not involved in plantation activities, Boze moved around the Caribbean and conducted extremely varied activities. He left Saint-Domingue and became a royal notary in Castries, Saint Lucia, a profession he carried out for almost two years, from February 1787 to October 1788.[7] He then returned to Saint-Domingue to resume his position as full-time captain of the harbor of Jacmel. The first years of the Haitian Revolution still placed Boze in Saint-Domingue, although apparently in different functions.[8] He is referred to as "resident in Jacmel,"[9] a "merchant in the city of Jacmel, residing in a house located on Rue de la Juridiction."[10]

He was, apparently, well integrated within the colonial society of the island, to the point that, in September 1794, he married Adélaïde Theuret, a native of Saint-Domingue. Adélaïde's was an old colonial family of the island. Her father, Pierre, born at Les Cayes Jacmel, in 1734, was a plantation owner, in command of the militia battalion of Jacmel.[11] Jean Boze, if he was not a longtime member of the colonial society of Saint-Domingue, managed to integrate into this society by marrying Adélaïde, a third-generation white Creole of the island. Adélaïde's family was obviously part of the socially and economically higher classes of Saint-Domingue society.[12] Boze's proprietorship on the island was limited to two pieces of land with buildings, on the heights of Jacmel, qualified, in the terms of the time, as "urban property."[13] His wife's family, however, owned three plantations in Jacmel, one of which, called Marigot in the Fesle quarter of Jacmel, was legally Adélaïde's.[14] Boze was thus, through his marriage, part of the white Creole plantation world of the wealthiest French American colony.

The long process that led to the independence of the colony started in 1791, when a violent slave rebellion broke out in the northern province of the island. Although Boze was still in Saint-Domingue two years later, he apparently left the island the following year. Many of the colonists left the island for good and found refuge in neighboring islands, especially in Cuba and Jamaica, or in the United States.[15] Some also left the island temporarily, going back and forth, mainly within the Caribbean, for the next decade. During Toussaint Louverture's rule, in particular, between 1797 and 1802, many colonists returned to the island, encouraged by the liberal policies Toussaint held, based on his understanding that he needed their expertise to ensure the economic survival of the island. The decade of the revolution was thus marked by incessant movements from and to the island, due to the political situation.[16] Boze is emblematic of this mobility. He took to the sea again, this time in the Caribbean, sometime between November 1793[17] and September 1794.[18] And for the next ten years, he was found privateering in the Caribbean. He married Adélaïde in Curacao, a colony belonging to the Netherlands, on September 7, 1794.[19] Their first son, Jean-François, was baptized there in October 1794.[20] They were still there in May 1798, when their daughter, Sophie, was born.[21] In 1799, however, they were in the Danish island of St. Thomas, where their second son was born.[22] What Boze was doing in the Caribbean colonies of the Netherlands and Denmark is revealed by a register of the Curacao archives. He is found to be captain of a schooner, *Le Poisson Volant*, armed with cannons, sailing under the flag of the Netherlands for the Batavian Republic of Holland.[23] There is nothing more about these activities. He was obviously conducting corsair activities for the Netherlands authorities, which shows both the mobility of colonists in the Americas and the porousness of the European empires there. This already tells much about the American colonial world of the Atlantic space in which Boze lived.

Boze and his family came back to Saint-Domingue in the last years of the revolution. He was there when Napoleon sent an expeditionary corps to try to recapture the island and return it to French colonial rule, in February 1802.[24] Napoleon's armies, under the leadership of Napoleon's brother-in-law, General Leclerc, were then trying to regain control of the island. They captured and deported Toussaint Louverture to France, where he died on April 7, 1803, in his jail at the Fort de Joux.[25] Boze's family was still in Saint-Domingue in February 1803.[26] Jean Boze was then the officer in command of the harbor of Port Républicain (formerly Port-au-Prince).[27]

The French expeditionary corps sent by Napoleon was then totally defeated by the armies of Saint-Domingue and decimated by yellow fever; the French capitulated and withdrew their remaining troops in the last months of 1803. The colonists still living on the island hurriedly fled before the punitive troops, launched by Dessalines, Toussaint Louverture's successor, to purge the island of any French presence, took over.[28] All the flight stories available are terrifying, as is Boze's. And they suggest much about the former colonists' state of mind once they found asylum elsewhere, in New Orleans, for instance, for several thousands of them.

There is no exact known date for his flight.[29] A family narrative, however, told by Boze's grandson, reveals much about the horrors Boze experienced and already helps us understand some of his perceptions of the slave societies of the Americas.[30]

> ... In 1818, one year after the death of his first wife, my father married my mother, née Boze, about whose family I unfortunately do not know too much.
>
> All that my mother has told me about her family is poor and scanty, as she herself was sent by her father to be raised in France in her early childhood.
>
> Jean Boze, her father, a native of France, had participated in the French Revolution (1789) and had seen himself forced to leave his fatherland.[31] He fled to the Dutch island of Curacao in the West Indies, where, in 1794, he married my grandmother who owned several plantations on the island of Haiti.[32] From this marriage were born two children, a son and a daughter, Maria Louise Sophie, my mother, who came into the world there in 1798.[33] In the early nineteenth century, they seem to have moved back to the island of Haiti, to take possession of their plantation property. The island, which was then still called Domingo, was a French colony and the population consisted of French colonists, who were the only entitled citizens, of free mulattoes and blacks[34] and, finally, of a great number of black slaves.[35]
>
> When, in 1801, a formal war broke out between the French colonists and the native free, in which blacks soon participated, the island became the site of the most horrible atrocities. The [...] National Assembly tried to put an end to the raging extermination by granting equal rights to the third class of the inhabitants. But the majority refused to obey and thus gave rise to new outrageous cruelties, by which they themselves were entirely exterminated. My grandparents fled with both their children and escaped with nothing but their lives. When they were already in flight, my grandmother realized that she had left important documents regarding the property of her plantations and she drove back alone to her estate to retrieve these documents and bring them to safety, but she was shot in her carriage by furious blacks while returning, already in possession of the documents, to her husband and children.

There are many historical inaccuracies both about the revolutionary events in Saint-Domingue and about the Boze family history.[36] The narrative, however, is important to explain Boze's traumas and suggest what sorts of traumas were experienced by many of the residents of early American New Orleans, who were natives or colonists of Saint-Domingue.

After this traumatic flight from the island, Boze, together with thousands of other former inhabitants of the French colony, found refuge in Cuba with his two children. He very rapidly sent Sophie to France for her education,[37] but he and his son remained in Santiago, in the province of *Oriente*, the closest to the coasts of Saint-Domingue. Cuba was then one of the refugees' favorite asylums. More than twenty-five thousand of them settled there, mostly on the eastern coast, in Santiago and Baracoa.[38] For about six years, the life of the Cuban *Oriente* was organized around and by the refugee community. Although we know little of Boze's activities there, he seems to have resumed his position as merchant and possibly also engaged again in privateering activities.[39] What is clear is that he was well integrated in the society of Santiago, where he had many acquaintances. He seems to have known people in the legal and political world.[40] He also manifestly knew people among the planter and merchant circles of the city.[41] His network of acquaintances seems to have been relatively wide, including both refugees and "nationals," as he often says, which is to say Cubans.[42] Boze is mysterious about his past on the island, as with every other episode of his life, but he seems to have led a busy commercial and social life in Santiago in the six years he spent there in the late 1700s.

Although the refugees in Cuba rebuilt their shattered lives in very few years, launched the production of coffee in the *Oriente*, boosted the sugar economy in the western part of the island, and made Santiago a modernized town, full of activity, both economic and social, the refugees' ordeal was not over, and their tranquility in Cuba was short-lived. Because Napoleon decided to put his brother on the Spanish throne, in 1809, the island's authorities declared non-naturalized French citizens personae non gratae and forced them to leave the island.[43] This second forced removal brought Boze and his son, together with some ten thousand refugees, to New Orleans. Little is known of his first nine years in New Orleans, for his personal story, as recounted in his correspondence, is that of a man who only lives in the present.[44] What is known, however, is that with Jean Boze also came Jean-François Henri de Ste-Gême, the recipient of Boze's 158 letters, whose past was as adventurous as Boze's, although in a different way. Knowing who he was helps us understand both the kind of city New Orleans was in the early nineteenth century and why Boze wrote what he did in his letters.

Jean-François Henri de Sainte-Gême: An Atlantic Circuit

Jean-François Henri de Miguel, Baron de Saintegême,[45] known in Louisiana as Henri de Ste-Gême, was a French nobleman, whose birth and death occurred at his family's castle of Bagen, not far from Toulouse, in Haute-Garonne, in southwestern France. While Boze stayed in America once he settled in the New World, Ste-Gême's itinerary was an Atlantic circuit. His life was as rich as Boze's and can be considered as emblematic of another type of Atlantic experience that needs recounting here, in order to understand what the colonial world of the Americas was and what the New Orleans fabric was made of in the early nineteenth century.[46]

His family originated in Spain and was an old noble family of Cataluña. It settled in the valley of Aran, in the north of Spain, in the mid-fifteenth century, and was known by the name of Miquel (or Miguel) de Santa Gema. From there, a branch moved north to southwestern France in 1636.[47] Jean-François Henri, who will henceforth be referred to as Henri, as he called himself in the Americas, was born at the Château de Bagen on January 5, 1767.[48]

The years Boze spent in the service of the French merchant marine, Ste-Gême spent in the army. His military career brought him to Saint-Domingue, in the service of the British Hussars, and this marked the beginning of his two decades in the Americas.[49] As he himself writes in a letter to the French Minister of War requesting a military pension, in 1825, he was then caught up in a "series of extraordinary circumstances." Promoted major of the York regiment of Dragoons, he remained in that position until the British evacuated from Saint-Domingue in 1798. With Toussaint Louverture's permission, the British then authorized his transfer as Captain to the First Regiment of the Colonial Dragoons, in 1799, the year that marked his return to the service of France (F 577). In his letter of 1825, he describes at length the horrors in Saint-Domingue and explains his decision to defend this "splendid colony and its unfortunate colonists."[50] Later appointed to the French expeditionary corps, led by General Leclerc and sent by Napoleon in 1802 to try to recover Saint-Domingue, he became Captain of the Second Legion of Gendarmerie of Saint-Domingue, before being promoted to squadron leader, in command of the personal horse guard of General Rochambeau.[51] He was wounded twice in Saint-Domingue, where he remained until the very end of the island's colonial history, when all French troops left the island. His years in Saint-Domingue are already indicative both of the extraordinary porosity of the American colonial world and of the adventurous lives of many of its inhabitants.

Ste-Gême was discharged for health reasons from colonial service and left the island on August 1, 1803.[52] From there, he went to Cuba, where he settled for the next six years in Santiago, in the province of *Oriente*, where most of the Saint-Domingue refugees found asylum, a few dozen nautical miles from their island. An 1813 certificate signed by Simon Faure, in Westphalia, Germany, explains that Ste-Gême resigned from service when the French completed the evacuation of the French part of the island and went to Cuba, "where he became involved in commercial speculation with the neighboring islands, Louisiana in particular."[53] Ste-Gême's activities in Cuba were clearly related to trading within the Caribbean basin, including, of course, Louisiana. In a letter written by François Dupuy, lieutenant of the French marine, who commanded, at the time of the evacuation from Saint-Domingue, a schooner named *Le Masséna*, Ste-Gême is said to have been the owner of the vessel until it was seized by the Spanish government of Cuba, together with all its booty, indicating that he was a corsair in the service of the French Republic, as confirmed on the seizure certificate by the Spanish authorities. The vessel was confiscated in March 1809, together with two ships it had seized, the *Beaver* and the *Nancy*, as were sequestered all the assets of all the Frenchmen expelled from Cuba by the Spanish authorities.[54] From what Boze later writes, the readers catch glimpses at what Ste-Gême's activities had been in Cuba. He was clearly involved in privateering with his ships *Le Masséna* and *L'Impériale* (F 86), which Boze always calls "corsairs."[55] The extent of Ste-Gême's privateering activities is never more detailed, although Boze makes it clear he had been offered the possibility to engage in the illicit slave trade: "I always regretted that you did not immediately return the ship *The Beaver* to Miguel Millan who had asked you to do so, after you disembarked in New Orleans, to dedicate her to voyages to Guinea since your involvement in this property would have granted you benefits you would have enjoyed for a long time," Boze writes, adding that all the ship owners who had done so were enjoying extraordinary wealth (F 97).

Ste-Gême's wealth in Cuba seems to have been significant, since he was the creditor of many planters and merchants, sometimes guaranteeing his credit with mortgages.[56] Ste-Gême also had many friends in Cuba.[57] Despite his prominent position, in 1809, together with Boze and some ten thousand other refugees, Ste-Gême was expelled from the Spanish colony and migrated to New Orleans, reaching the Crescent City, along with Boze, on May 20, 1809,[58] on one of Ste-Gême's ships, a schooner, which apparently carried a larger group of French people—some records say a few hundred people—from Cuba to New Orleans (F 232). Ste-Gême stayed only nine years in New Orleans.[59] Despite his short stay in the city, he is recorded in the Louisiana collective memory.[60] The reasons for his fame are many. First, he immediately became a high-ranking officer in the militia, commanding the Dragons à Pied. He had the title of major and was second in command of the militia.[61] He was distinguished during the Battle of New Orleans, in January 1815, and was officially acknowledged by General Andrew Jackson.[62] In the letter he wrote in 1825 to the French Minister of War, he accounts for his involvement in Louisiana by writing that he thus "paid to its inhabitants the debt and tribute of gratitude owed by the unfortunate colonists of Saint-Domingue, refugees from Cuba, who found amidst them the most generous hospitality."[63] He apparently remained connected with privateering, keeping close connections with the Lafitte brothers, the two best-known pirates in Louisiana history, at the head of the Barataria pirating community. He was involved in an "affair of honor" involving Pierre Lafitte. The connection between Ste-Gême and the Lafitte brothers is also strongly suggested by a letter sent by Boze from Santiago de Cuba in 1818, in which he warns Ste-Gême that, in case he brings to trial his debtor Pepe Lara, the latter intends to retaliate by mentioning Ste-Gême's participation in the activities of the corsairs from Barataria, thus against Spanish vessels (F 18). Later, he announces to Ste-Gême the death of Dominique You, the second of the Lafitte brothers, qualifying him as "the former captain of one of your vessels" (F 174).[64] Despite this connection, Louisiana history has recorded him in the following terms: "St. Gème [*sic*] had no superior in New Orleans as to social position" and, because of his role in the Battle of New Orleans, he "was considered by the whole population as a sort of Bayard."[65] New Orleans was thus, in its early American period, a city where a former officer of the French and British armies, explicitly involved in privateering activities, could occupy a prominent position in society and could even be one of the high-ranking officers of the militia, to the point of becoming one of the heroes of the Battle of New Orleans.

During the years he occupied high-ranking positions in New Orleans, Ste-Gême lived a life not unusual in the Creole societies of both Saint-Domingue and New Orleans. He had a long-term relationship with a free woman of color, Adélaïde Philibert, born at l'Arcahaye in Saint-Domingue, who had followed him in his Caribbean movements. They had three children together, two daughters and a son, all of them openly recorded in the sacramental records of the archdiocese of New Orleans as the children of Ste-Gême, "natif de Bagen, department de Haute-Garonne en France." The two daughters, Joséphine Henriette Fortunée and Adélaïde Hortense, born in 1811 and 1812, respectively, are recorded in the general baptismal books, normally reserved for white people.[66] The son, Louis, born in 1814, is recorded in the baptismal book for free people of color and slaves.[67] In the case of Adélaïde Hortense, the names of the paternal grandparents, Bertrand Ste Gème and Eléanore Larroquan, are even indicated. Although he left his illegitimate family behind when he returned to France in 1818 with his new Louisiana Creole wife, Ste-Gême never neglected his paternal duties to his three children.[68] This is another aspect of Ste-Gême's life that perfectly epitomizes practices in early nineteenth-century New Orleans and sheds light on many of the mentions (or silences) that Boze's New Orleans narrative contains. New Orleans, in the early American era, had a free population of color that distinguished it from the rest of the slaveholding South. The arrival, in the first decade of the nineteenth century, of a large group of free people of color from Saint-Domingue reinforced this unusual feature of the Crescent City in the antebellum South. Not only were the free people of color a numerically important group, they were economically and socially active, too. Their presence and visibility was proof that openly acknowledged racial mixing was not uncommon in early American New Orleans.[69]

Ste-Gême was obviously perfectly integrated in the Creole society of New Orleans. A close friend to the Dreux family, which owned plantations in Gentilly, he was their son Henri Antoine's sponsor when he was baptized in 1809, the very year Ste-Gême arrived in New Orleans.[70] Two years after Margueritte Lefroy de Dreux, née Delmas, a Louisiana Creole, was widowed, in March 1814, he married her, on April 29, 1816.[71] Through this marriage, he entered the world of plantation owners and took charge of managing his wife's plantation in Gentilly.[72] While in New Orleans, Ste-Gême also became the owner of a considerable amount of property in the city, including a house on St. Peter's Street, one on Claiborne Avenue, some property at the corner of "Dorgenois and Bayou," a house at the corner of Franklin and Conti, a house on Calliope Street, a house on Moreau Street (F 674), and a piece of land on Chartres, purchased in 1813 (F 694). Property was readily available to newcomers to New Orleans at the time and money seems to have circulated steadily through trade, in both legal and illicit activities. Adventurers and newcomers in general could thus make their way to the highest society of the city and be well established in a short time.

New Orleans was also a city of movement, even in the very early nineteenth century. Ste-Gême seems to have gone back and forth between France and Louisiana several times during his stay.[73] In 1818, he left New Orleans forever, with his new family, to all his acquaintances' deepest regret.[74] Although all remained in expectation of his return, he died in Bagen on July 28, 1842, leaving several children born of his union with Margueritte.[75] He occupied high official positions in Haute-Garonne, including that of mayor (F 551) and general councilor, and never returned to Louisiana. A December 1823 letter by Auvignac Dorville, the manager of the Gentilly plantation, even mentions his renouncing his U.S. citizenship to become Knight of the Order of Saint-Louis, an appointment acknowledging his noble rank and his services to his country of birth, which was also his country of death.[76]

Ste-Gême's Atlantic circuit is exemplary. It shows the narrowness of the Atlantic space, proving how easily people circulated within it. From the eastern shore of the Atlantic and back to it, Ste-Gême moved within the Caribbean space, from Saint-Domingue to Cuba to Louisiana. This migration transcended nationality, as demonstrated by his involvement with the British, and then French, troops, his settling in the Spanish colonial space, and then in the young American republic, of which he even became a naturalized citizen, maybe to avoid a repetition of the fate he met in Cuba. It also transcended political barriers, as his passage from the armies of the king to the Republican armies under Toussaint Louverture, and then to Napoleon's imperial armies, proves. It transcended occupational patterns, Ste-Gême's military activities in Saint-Domingue and Louisiana easily giving way to a strong involvement in corsair activities, trading, and filibustering, both in Cuba and Louisiana. He went from the French nobility to the plantation world and back to his origins. He did not cringe at the idea of slave ownership, for which he had no original propensity but which he readily accepted as a totally natural phenomenon. All this is central to the New Orleans narrative that this book relates.

The Atlantic space was also narrow enough to allow the formation of Atlantic families, of which Ste-Gême provides two very striking examples. It also created unbreakable bonds of friendship and service, which Boze's letters so picturesquely illustrate: the correspondence tells the story of a personal transatlantic bond, which is central to its New Orleans narrative.

A Transatlantic Epistolary Story

Determining the exact nature of the links between Boze and Ste-Gême is not easy. Somewhere between friendship and service, their relationship was obviously maintained by their long correspondence, a function often attributed to letters in the Atlantic space. That there were strong personal links between them is obvious from their regular correspondence and the news they exchanged. That Boze was Ste-Gême's inferior and debtor is also obvious. Boze addresses Ste-Gême as "Monsieur et Ami" (something that could be translated as "Dear Sir and Friend") when opening his letters. He always concludes them with the mention "Please receive the sincere expression of the high consideration with which I have the honor of being, dear sir and friend, your very humble and obedient servant," sometimes with a slightly different phrasing. This alone perfectly summarizes their relationship.

Jean Boze became acquainted with Ste-Gême in Cuba.[77] His letters from Cuba constantly give news of common friends and acquaintances, which strongly suggests that they belonged to the same social circles there.[78] The two Frenchmen lived in Santiago, among the Saint-Domingue refugees, a fact important to understanding the fabric of early American New Orleans and Boze's perception of his new homeland. They knew the same people and most probably knew each other, although the closeness of their bond at the time is not known. Boze says, at some point: "we have lost so many of our friends, either here or in New Orleans, since you left," thereby suggesting that those friends were mutual friends (F 65). Although they knew each other from Cuba, their closer link dates back to 1809 and their common exile to New Orleans. They arrived together in New Orleans on May 20, 1809 (F 24), on one of Ste-Gême's schooners, commanded by Don Antonio Vinet (F 97).[79] They lived in close personal proximity in New Orleans. The way Boze transmits news and testimonies of affection to the Ste-Gêmes in his letters attests to this.

Boze had apparently resided with the Ste-Gêmes when they were still in America.[80] Many times, throughout the years, Ste-Gême also invited Boze to come over to Bagen. In March 1825, for instance, Boze writes "I thank you from the bottom of my heart for the offer you made me to finish my days in Bagen in the midst of friends. I would really love that but without a single cent, what would I be doing in France after cracking my whip[81] from 1784 to 1794 with a fortune that was consumed by all the turmoil of the revolution and whose remnants stayed in St. Domingue" (F 96).[82] This suggests that solidarity was strong between them, as among Saint-Domingue refugees in general,[83] and their common past forged an unbreakable link between them. Like other Saint-Domingue refugees in New Orleans, Boze depended on his fellow refugees for a living.

Boze was clearly in the service of Ste-Gême, as he several times mentions "the whole time [he] was employed to [his] service, honored by [Ste-Gême's] trust" (F 200). Except for a brief period of time, in 1819, when he became the accountant of a women's college in New Orleans, Boze never seems to have earned a living independently of Ste-Gême's patronage in his Louisiana years, which suggests both the difficulty for older refugees to fit in to the New Orleans economic structures but also the solidarity that existed among them.

Boze appears to have been irregularly entrusted with missions by Ste-

Gême.[84] Although he was wealthy at one point of his life,[85] his finances suffered from the Haitian Revolution, and still more acutely from his expulsion from Cuba.[86] In one of his last letters to Ste-Gême, he thanks him for taking him out "of this destitution in which the revolution put [him], after benefiting from honorable wealth" (F 283). He is very clear about Ste-Gême's assistance, invoking his financial straits "alleviated by [Ste-Gême's] kindness" (F 19).[87] At some point, he enumerates his services after leaving Cuba, saying that he has "served [Ste-Gême] and been useful to [him] as to a boss." Those services were mainly administrative, revealing the way in which Atlantic business was conducted.[88] Having an emissary in the Americas proved fruitful to people like Ste-Gême who ran their American assets from Europe.

Among Boze's tasks, the writing mission indeed seems to have been essential to Ste-Gême. Boze was the latter's designated writer, even concerning the plantation, an organ of transmission indispensable to the good management of financial assets from a distance.[89] Apart from the various official missions he carried out for Ste-Gême, Boze also had that of transmitting messages of friendship to and from Ste-Gême's friends in New Orleans. This might seem anecdotal, but through the brief remarks and greetings Boze transmits, the reader learns much about Ste-Gême's social circle in Louisiana and thus about early American New Orleans social life. Most of Ste-Gême's friends and acquaintances were Saint-Domingue refugees and, even when the origins of people are not immediately identifiable, Boze often gives an indication that they belonged to the refugee community.[90] The family of Jean-Baptiste Labatut seems to have been closest to him (and to Boze).[91] Also clearly often cited as being among the inner circle were Albin Michel (chancellor at the French Consulate), Pierre Lamber, "the gunsmith, your friend" (F 206), Dr Lebeau, "your friend," and Dr. Lemonier (the elder), or John Davis and his son, directors of the most famous theater in New Orleans, all of whom were Saint-Domingue refugees. This clearly suggests closeness in the Saint-Domingue refugee community.

What these transmitted greetings also indicate is that Ste-Gême was acquainted with the best society of the city: the Fortier family, the Cavelier brothers (F 255), Moreau-Lislet, or Père Antoine (F 34), all eminent members of the city's highest echelon. Even from a distance, someone like Ste-Gême, a foreigner whose time in the city had been relatively brief, connected with the world of corsairs and pirates at that, could still be respected and remembered by the high society of the city. This insight into the personal story between the two men already tells us much about New Orleans, where Ste-Gême had left so many assets, friends, and acquaintances, and which was obviously the focal point of his maintained Atlantic ties.

The correspondence also serves to transmit indirect news on both ends of the Atlantic, thus showing how social circles worked in the Atlantic in this age. Boze and Ste-Gême acted as go-betweens connecting two worlds, the European and American ones. In 1835, for instance, Boze asks Ste-Gême to transmit regards from Jean-Paul Boé and Douceil to their respective families (F 253). They are two of three knife grinders coming from the vicinity of Bagen, who had been recommended by Ste-Gême. Later, he sends to Ste-Gême two letters, with bills, from two men from Sauveterre, Eugène Barès and Michel Maylin, requesting that the letters be given to their respective families. In October 1836, Boze also asks Ste-Gême to announce "gently" to Mrs. Gros that her sister's husband, Mr. Constansy, died in Natchichoches on the first of that month (F 271). The link between the two men further connected the two worlds, that of the old empire with that of its former colonies.

Between personal ties and a relation of service, it is clear that the bond between those two men of very different origins, but who had a rather unusual common history in the Western Hemisphere, was reinforced by the correspondence they shared for twenty years. While their relationship could well not have been sustained had Ste-Gême remained in Louisiana, and while it could have ended very shortly after the latter's departure from the Americas, the letters served to reconfigure their transatlantic relationship.

The correspondence is indeed a breathtaking Atlantic narrative that tells much about the people that inhabited New Orleans, sometimes for short periods of time, sometimes forever.

New Orleans in the Atlantic World

Boze's letters recount the daily life of a Saint-Domingue refugee in New Orleans. His life was most certainly not representative of most of the refugee community's, since he was too old to really become integrated in the economic life of the city. Many aspects of it, however, reveal some of the refugee fate and life in New Orleans. First, his life story shows the resilience of the refugees and their readiness to occupy various positions not necessarily connected to their original area of expertise. In August 1818, for instance, Boze was in charge of the financial administration of a convent, which accommodated a hundred girls between ages six and seventeen or eighteen, for a salary of thirty dollars a month, with free bed and board and laundry services (F 23). He abandoned this position when he went to Cuba in 1820, commissioned by Ste-Gême to take care of his assets sequestered there, although Boze might also have been taking care of business of his own while he was on the island.[92]

After returning to New Orleans, in 1828, he never had another occupation beyond taking care of Ste-Gême's commissions. When France indemnified the colonists, using the money collected from Haiti's debt in return for officially recognizing the independence of the country, he received a small compensation for his property in Saint-Domingue.[93] The refugees did not obtain more than 10 percent of the property the ownership of which they could prove, but this nevertheless helped some of them rebuild their shattered economic lives. Although most refugees managed to find their place in the New Orleans economy, life remained difficult for those at the margins.[94] Boze's financing seems to have come exclusively from Ste-Gême's payment for his services. When he became too old to take care of himself, he was taken in charge by Auvignac Dorville, the manager of Ste-Gême's Gentilly plantation, attesting both to the financial hardships some refugees had to face and to the solidarity that existed in the community.[95]

Boze's life also shows how busy the Atlantic space was and how mobile people were within it. He seems to have had several options for his geographic relocation. Partly by choice and partly out of necessity, he decided to remain in New Orleans, a choice many of his peers also made. Boze never went back to Europe, although, in the early years, he several times mentioned his intention to do so. Just after Ste-Gême's departure, he also wavered between settling in Louisiana and going back to Santiago de Cuba to find a position there. He could also have returned to Santiago to stay on a friend's plantation and "finish [his] career in philosophical calm. [He] would have given [his] preference to Gentilly if [he] did not dread the cold but [he] would have made this step with pleasure, had [Ste-Gême] been present" (F 19). He finally chose to go to Cuba, commissioned by Ste-Gême, before returning to Louisiana. Even after his return from Cuba, in 1828, he still mentioned that his twin brother, his daughter, and Ste-Gême repeatedly asked him to visit them. He regularly voices his hesitation, "after the favorable welcome [he] received here from all [his] acquaintances to make it [his] home again, with the promise of helping them with their assistance if [he] intend[s] to devote [him]self to commerce again" (F 135). He probably felt too old to go on such a distant journey and kept expecting Ste-Gême's return to Louisiana (F 143). In 1832, he wrote to Ste-Gême that he could not afford the journey and was too old (F 200). In 1835, he told Ste-Gême that he was too old to handle the freezing climate of Germany and could definitely no longer envision the journey (F 253).

Upon his return from Cuba, in 1828, Boze settled at Mr. Pierre Martel's plantation in Gentilly, halfway between Ste-Gême's Gentilly plantation and the city (F 118, F 127). In 1830, he returned to the French Quarter, giving as his address a house at the corner of Royal Street and present-day Barracks ("encoignure Royale et du Quartier") (F 160). He writes Ste-Gême that, from his room, he sees the Lalaurie house, the infamous house where Mme. Lalaurie was said to have severely mistreated her slaves, which was located at 1140 Royal Street.[96] In a later mention, when the Lalaurie house was attacked by angry New Orleanians, in the spring of 1834, he added that he was about twenty-five steps from the house and that he lived in an upstairs room that overlooked a courtyard. Judge Canonge was his closest neighbor (F 238).[97] His years in the quarter are those that most interest the twenty-first-century reader, because part of the information he gives about the city comes directly from his own eyewitness accounts. This lasted until late 1836, and he finished his life on Ste-Gême's plantation.[98] Crippled by his declining eyesight, which was, to him, the worst infirmity, because his only remaining pleasures were reading and writing to Ste-Gême (F 286), Boze died in Gentilly.[99] In one of his last letters, in the fall of 1838, he bid farewell to Ste-Gême and added: "upon my death, I wish to be buried in the garden of your plantation in Gentilly, so that I recommend the executors of my will to respect and fulfill my last wishes in this matter" (F 283).

Boze's letters also tell us about his family, which, again, may reveal certain aspects of New Orleans social and economic life, as well as the transatlantic character of many families that lived there. Boze's son, Jean-François, had followed his father to Louisiana. In 1828, he had five children, was a primary-school teacher in La Fourche, and was also a judge in that parish. In 1829, Jean-François lost his wife (F 149) and was left alone with four children, a situation that Boze describes as very difficult (F 160). He remarried in 1831 (F 190) "with an orphan from a Saint-Domingue family without wealth and which left her only a meager inheritance," which suggests that the refugee community was still close-knit at that time (F 233) and, in 1833, Jean-François still lived in Donaldsonville, in the Lafourche Parish, and was still lucratively employed, according to his father, which enabled him to provide for his large family (F 233). In April 1834, Jean-François died at age 40, of a "liver inflammation" (F 238), leaving six children behind, four of whom had to be taken care of by their grandfather.

As for his daughter, Sophie, she returned to her European roots. After being educated in Bordeaux, she followed her godmother to Germany, where she married Louis Pagenstecher. In 1818, Boze told Ste-Gême about his daughter's marriage (F 23). In 1828, he wrote Ste-Gême that his daughter lived at Lienen, in Westphalia, and now had six children, three sons and three daughters. In August 1833, he informed him of the death of his daughter's husband, leaving Sophie in charge of eight children, "most of them very young" (F 233). From time to time, he gives Ste-Gême information about his German family, insisting on its international character.[100] What Boze's story suggests is that family ties were maintained by long-lasting correspondence across the Atlantic, that the Old and New Worlds were still strongly connected, and that the borders between the various nations on both sides of the Atlantic were extremely porous. New Orleans had, by then, clearly become one of the centerpieces of this Atlantic world.

The correspondence is also a narrative of yet another aspect of the Atlantic world. Although he was no longer directly involved in New Orleans social life, Ste-Gême indeed still had many assets there and thus remained part of the economic life of the then capital of Louisiana. In Saint-Gaudens, he seems to have immediately gone back to public life, becoming the mayor of the village of Sauveterre, then a member of the General Council of Haute-Garonne (F 198). Although Ste-Gême never returned to Louisiana, he had strong connections with his wife's family, and Boze regularly kept the Ste-Gêmes informed about their Louisiana relatives. Several social networks are thus traced through the letters.[101]

Boze's letters also gave Ste-Gême general information about his Gentilly plantation.[102] In 1828, for instance, Boze told him that the plantation would "soon be established as a sugar plantation" (F 134). He gave regular information about the proceedings of the plantation, the slave population and crops, although he left to Auvignac Dorville "this worthy and honest procurator, the care of keeping [him] informed on the condition of [his] interests in this country since they are in [his] responsibility" (F 208).[103] A landed aristocrat, involved in local political administration, whose leisure activities revolved around horse riding and hunting, Ste-Gême was also, as many of those French and English landed noblemen were, the absentee owner of property in the New World, a custom more frequent in the Caribbean than in North America and which he had probably inherited from his long stay in the Caribbean. This helped maintain close ties between Europe and the Americas, either in the colonial context or, in Ste-Gême's case, in the now independent country of which he was a citizen. The letters also keep Ste-Gême informed about his real estate in New Orleans, a situation that was not uncommon in early American New Orleans, as indicated by several other correspondences that detail similar cases of property holding in America by owners who had returned permanently to France.[104]

More interestingly in the context of a historical narrative of early American Louisiana, the correspondence is also a narrative of Ste-Gême's family of color, most probably the only report he ever had of his children's life after his return to the home of his ancestors. Following this narrative gives insight into the world of the Creoles of color of early nineteenth-century New Orleans and gives a more accurate picture of New Orleans, its inclusion in the Atlantic world, and Atlantic relationships more generally.[105] Although Ste-Gême's family is not necessarily typical of New Orleans, it is far from being a unique example either. The way Boze's letters convey news between Ste-Gême and his illegitimate family clearly indicates that they were never in direct epistolary contact and that their only connection was Boze, which makes his role essential in maintaining Ste-Gême's family ties in the Atlantic space. He visited them regularly, gave news to Ste-Gême, and transmitted his affection to his children and theirs to their father. He apparently also resided with them, at some point, renting part of their house (F 23). The story of this family epitomizes many features of illegitimate families in New Orleans. First and foremost, their existence was no secret, and Ste-Gême's children were all recorded as his. Second, he provided for them and was concerned about their health and welfare. Third, ties were maintained between the various members of these families, even when they were separated by an ocean, although relationships became loose and communication was, at best, infrequent.

Little is known about Ste-Gême's old companion, "*ménagère*" (translated as "housekeeper" in English), as they said at the time, Adélaïde Philibert, whom Boze calls Adèle and who had followed Ste-Gême into exile, from Saint-Domingue, where she was born, at L'Arcahaye.[106] She died of cholera in the fall of 1832 and, in a long list of mortalities, Boze writes: "Miss of the road of Port-au-Prince died the 4 instant of cholera, the *grande* of three natural children who are in very good health" (F 212).[107] The children's itineraries are relatively more detailed. Fortunée, Dorsica, and Gême all lived on Burgundy Street, in a house donated by Ste-Gême, together with a few slaves (F 27). In May 1819, "the three of them are going to school and they are moving forward rapidly" (F 34). In the fall of 1828:

> Fortunée, the eldest, is tall, with a decent bearing, that she enhances with her kindness . . . Dorsica, the younger daughter, has remained slightly dwarfish in size but she is very amiable, more smiling than her sister. Gême, the boy, already tall, will be handsome when he grows older. He is placed as an apprentice to learn a trade and his sisters are set to sewing. Their *grande* takes good care to have them educated and I would visit them often if she did not get me bored to tears, at each visit, with her whining, as is the custom with her ever plaintive character (F 134).

In November 1833, "Fortunée, her sister and her brother are in very good health and live happily, committed with good will to sewing, so as not to risk financial difficulty" (F 233). In August 1833, their house, in bad need of repair, is being restored, using the money collected from the sale of the slave Caprice, "who indulged in evil." They all live in good union "as recommended by the eldest with her common sense and ability for the administration of a household" (F 231). In May 1835, they move to a new house in Faubourg Trémé, behind the college, on Bayou Road.[108] They are respected members of the community of the Creoles of color: "They move in the fashionable circles of their color which makes them enjoy additional respect, esteem, and friendship." (F 231)

While Dorsica was "still a virgin and very pretty although dwarfish in size" (F 234), in 1833, Fortunée married Firmin Peyraut, the son of a Creole family of color residing in the Bayou neighborhood. A marriage contract, under the name of Fortunée Ste-Gême, was recorded.[109]

> On 4 February, the well-matched wedding of Fortunée G. with a Creole by the name of Firmin Peyraut, aged 22, they say. He is a decent young man, of a good behavior, who assembles carriages on sugar plantations,[110] which has enabled him to have a small income. His Louisiana Creole family is comfortably off and enjoys public esteem in this country.
>
> Their goods have been inventoried and evaluated according to conventions by notary public Seghers the younger, who wrote the marriage contract which sets, for the three heirs to their mother's succession, one share each of the estimate of the house and of six slaves comprising two women and four young children.
>
> Mr. Marc Lafitte, the former notary, who enjoys wealth and a high reputation, has been kind enough to be the adviser of that family of orphans and he willingly helped with all the acts, to see them written in conformity with the law and to the satisfaction of both parties, which needed the assistance of an honest and able man in such a settlement. Victoire attended this ceremony as mother, in replacement of her defunct cousin Adèle. (F 216)

These short paragraphs reveal several important elements of New Orleans society. First, they suggest that free people of color had property and access to all legal and notarial services. They were sufficiently integrated in society to call for these services. There was also solidarity among the Saint-Domingue refugees, as retired notary Marc Lafitte volunteers to assist Ste-Gême's daughter. Although Lafitte may have offered his assistance because of his old connections with Ste-Gême, it is still interesting that he assists a free family of color, suggesting a bond that extends beyond racial barriers among refugees.

In 1833, the two sisters still sewed to supplement the money they obtained from renting part of their house as well as renting out their six slaves, two women and four children. In November 1835, Fortunée gave birth to a son, and to a daughter a little over a year later (F 275). In late 1835, Fortunée's husband purchased a property, where they were having a new house built (F 260).

The son, Gême, was taught English, "a language that [had] become indispensable to engage in trade or other activities in Louisiana" (F 143). In 1833, he started being trained as a joiner and cabinetmaker. Once his apprenticeship was over, he could set up his own business. "He is a charming cavalier and behaves with much wisdom, following the example of his good sisters, so that the public likes to talk about them advantageously because of their merit" (F 231). Possibilities were thus relatively open for the free people of color, who were educated and trained so that they would fit in the New Orleans economic fabric more easily. They also apparently enjoyed a relative geographical mobility, including traveling to the old colonial power, another characteristic that is noteworthy. In the spring of 1834, Gême left for France on the American vessel *La Créole* bound for Le Havre, financed by his brother-in-law. Showing, once again, the openness of the illegitimate familial links, Boze writes to Ste-Gême: "I believe he will not return without visiting you in Bagen," (F 238). After receiving a letter from Ste-Gême, Boze tells him: "the two daughters of deceased Adèle, whom I kissed for you, rejoiced extremely that you remember them with paternal feelings. They hope their brother will visit you during his stay in France, which makes them expect his return eagerly" (F 243).

In the fall of 1835, Gême was about to marry a Creole of color from an honest family (F 258) and was having a house built before getting married (F 260). Again, what may appear as a very personal narrative is already a window largely open onto the larger New Orleans narrative. It attests to the socioeconomic position of free people of color in New Orleans, demonstrates the openness of the city toward these racially mixed families, and also shows that intermixing between the free refugees of color and their Louisiana Creole counterparts was not infrequent.

If this narrative gives insight into the very specific social organization of New Orleans, it also shows the importance of correspondence in maintaining ties of kinship and friendship in the Atlantic space. Not only did Ste-Gême never lose contact with Boze but his letters helped him remain in contact with his faraway children of color left in New Orleans. He provided for their needs, made sure they were taken care of, and always had a keen interest in their lives. Whether Gême visited his father in Bagen is not known, but the very fact that it was discussed shows that their existence was not a taboo topic in Ste-Gême's life and that his legitimate family most certainly knew about them, which seems natural since Ste-Gême was a family friend of his wife before she was widowed and married him.

The personal narrative also tells much about the strength of relationships in this Atlantic space, Ste-Gême receiving signs of friendship from his Louisiana acquaintances and sending back affectionate thoughts to his friends, even twenty years after leaving Louisiana. He never saw most of them again, although some apparently visited him in France.[111] Their friendship, however, remained intact despite time and distance. In the early years of the correspondence, Boze and all of Ste-Gême's friends were expecting his return. His wife had, after all, left her closest relatives behind. They had property in New Orleans and a source of revenue in Gentilly. They were attached to Louisiana, regularly requesting that local products be sent to them.[112] At some point, the return date even seemed to have been set and Boze was expecting Ste-Gême's return in the spring of 1819. As late as 1830, Boze still mentioned his friend's return, planned for that year (F 160), although such notes became rarer, before disappearing altogether in the later letters, as if Boze had resigned himself to the idea that Ste-Gême, too old and in poor health, could no more complete the journey across the ocean than he could. The Atlantic was an impassable barrier, at times, but it was also a small space that allowed ties to be maintained.

If Boze's aim was to keep Ste-Gême informed about his Louisiana assets, family, friends, and acquaintances, he also had the mission of "giving [him] news of home [*sic*], which is always pleasant to him who is away from his family" (F 160).[113] Ste-Gême encouraged him in the practice, since, at one point, Boze writes: "as news from this country is pleasant to you, I will continue this attention with accuracy" (F 163). He also sometimes apologized for sending newspaper extracts instead of writing them in his own hand, which would be time-consuming, but which Ste-Gême had "order[ed]" him to do (F 192). In one of his last letters, Boze apologized for not being able much longer to give him news "of this city for which [he] feel[s] a natural attachment" (F 283).

The personal narrative alone highlights many features of early American New Orleans, giving clues on interracial relationships and on connections between various ethnic groups, as it, for instance, also suggests the modes of integration of the Saint-Domingue refugees, their role in New Orleans society and in the socioeconomic dynamics of the city, among others. This in itself is thus worth examining, but it is also complemented by a much more detailed narrative: the story of the Crescent City at a turning point in its history. Knowing who Boze was and whom he was addressing is essential to understanding the perception he had of the particular historical moment unfolding before his eyes. Indeed, while it definitely tells a very personal story, that of two acquaintances living across the Atlantic, the correspondence is also the narrative of a close-knit community (St-Domingue refugees), a larger group (French-speaking New Orleanians), and eventually, a city in the midst of the radical evolution of a period of turmoil—its early American history.

A Narrative History of New Orleans

With an interruption of eight years spent in Cuba (1820–1827), Boze patiently narrated the history of New Orleans between 1818 and 1839. Although there is little detail on the 1820–1827 period, his first letters of 1828 convey the evolution that occurred in his absence. The correspondence thus highlights a very special period in the history of New Orleans. The first four decades of the nineteenth century were indeed a period of intense reconfiguration, a real turning point in the history of the city. The first letter was written fifteen years after the purchase of the colony by the young American republic, six years after the state of Louisiana was incorporated into the Union by an act of Congress. This early American period was institutionally and politically seminal in the history of the young state and its then capital, New Orleans. It was a time of intense political competition between the French-speaking community and the new American rulers, a period of mutation in the city's political stage, and one of formation and reformation of its institutions.[114]

Those two decades were also a clear economic turning point. In twenty years, the city went from a small colonial frontier town to the third-largest city in the United States.[115] By becoming an internal navigation axis to the young republic in 1803, the Mississippi River became the main means of communication of the northwestern United States, transporting both travelers and merchandise to its mouth, New Orleans. The merchant value of fluvial transport went up to $22,065,518 in 1830 and had more than doubled, to $49,763,825, by 1840. With this development of trade and transportation of travelers from the Northwest of the United States, the port became one of the largest in the United States, the largest exportation port in 1836, ahead of New York.[116] Beyond revitalizing trade activities, this economic evolution also influenced the Louisiana economy, inducing, among many other things, a resurgence in agricultural vitality. The cultivation of cotton developed, as did that of sugar cane in lower Louisiana.[117] This boom had dramatic repercussions on the economy and development of New Orleans. Boze's correspondence also covers a period of extraordinary urban expansion, when the population was multiplied by six, when the city's perimeter enlarged to the point that it engulfed the neighboring towns and villages, and when the small colonial frontier town turned into an urban capital of commerce, entertainment, and culture.[118]

The period covered by the correspondence was also one of intense social change. The population widely diversified, bringing important additions to the old French and Spanish Creole population. Between 1791 and 1810, a large flux of about fifteen thousand refugees from the Haitian Revolution had already more than doubled the city's population.[119] The next decades saw a continuing, albeit relatively low, influx of people from France, but also the migration to the city of people from Germany, Ireland, and, most importantly, from the United States. This invasion of their space by new migrants originally induced a defensive attitude among the French speakers, countered by an offensive of the English speakers from the United States, resulting in a period of difficult balance between the two linguistically and culturally opposed communities.[120] The two decades of continuous mixing between populations with very different cultural, religious, and linguistic traditions strongly influenced the culture that came later as well. It was a period of emulation and of intense cultural vitality, often developed separately by the various communities. It was the beginning of the decline of the French cultural domination over the city, but also the first moments of the creation of a new culture, an era of both Americanization and Creolization.[121]

It is this crucial period in the development of New Orleans that is very minutely described by Boze. While the letters are marginally the narratives of two individuals, and of their families and friends, New Orleans is definitely Boze's central focus, increasingly so in the last ten years of the correspondence—when he writes exclusively newsletters, gives less personal information to Ste-Gême, and progressively reduces the part he dedicated earlier on to political matters outside Louisiana.

This minute depiction of New Orleans, although partly informed by the local newspapers, gives a vantage standpoint, that of a stranger to Louisiana, an Old Regime French man with a rich personal history who observed from a relative distance the struggle between the Creoles and the Americans. His narrative is also that of someone who had come to identify with the Saint-Domingue community, in which he had lived in the last years of the colonial period and whose odyssey he had been part of ever since the final loss of the colony by France in 1803. Because of his origins, he paid special attention to aspects that are not often considered in other histories of the city, especially as far as the refugee community is concerned. Boze, who spent those twenty years doing little else besides visiting people, roaming the city, reading the newspapers, and writing to Ste-Gême, in particular after 1828, is thus an incredibly rich source of information about the city in one of its most ebullient periods. He really becomes a privileged chronicler of early American New Orleans. His narrative is naturally biased, as that of any sojourner in the city would be, but it is also documented by many journalistic sources, which are at times extensively quoted and at times even included in his letters. He often compares the different versions given by the newspapers with opposing views, especially in matters of local politics. What he narrates is either from eyewitness accounts or hearsay, but he generally cites his sources, and whenever the news he gives cannot be verified, he says so.[122] In his letters, he tells the little stories and the larger history of New Orleans.

So let us plunge deep into the history of the Crescent City. Let us follow Jean Boze's footsteps along the streets and listen to his big and little stories of New Orleans. Let us listen to his narrative of the tropical city, full of marvels and beauty but fraught with danger and hardship. These chronicles, which will later examine the wonders and beauty, will start with the rudimentary living conditions the city offered to her residents in the early American period.

2

Extremes

If reaching New Orleans was often an adventure in itself, full of promise and opportunity, living there in the early nineteenth century could be an ordeal, one that Boze recounts in very minute detail throughout his letters. Although his narrative often marvels, it also highlights the adventurous, dangerous, and often violent atmosphere of the city. What was to become the major metropolis of the American South at midcentury was still a primitive place, plagued by tropical dangers and marked by dire living conditions and, sometimes, unrestrained violence. In its colonial days, New Orleans was always described as a small frontier town, containing no more than eight thousand people in 1803, the year of the Louisiana Purchase. In its early national years, it was still a very rugged city, where education and culture were relatively underdeveloped, where the urban environment was extremely unpolished, and where living conditions were often difficult. Although the first three decades of American rule were years of extraordinary development, the Crescent City was particularly inhospitable when Boze started writing.[1]

New Orleans was plagued with disease and crime; its economy was subject to the vagaries of the weather and the whims of yellow fever epidemics; poor sanitation made it a hazardous place to live; and its architecture made it easy prey for fires, floods, and hurricanes. The living conditions of the early nineteenth century were rudimentary, and New Orleans was a city of extremes. It was not exceptional in this respect, as similar conditions existed in other developing cities of the young American republic. In the Louisiana capital, however, it mattered more, for several reasons: first, because the city was not as developed as the port cities of the northeastern United States in the early nineteenth century; also, because it was marked by a more tropical climate than many other places, especially the Northeast; and finally, because it was especially vulnerable to the climatic conditions because of its economic options, as was the case in many other cities of the American South. In the next four decades, it nonetheless experienced a development unparalleled elsewhere in the South and, although it resembled other Southern cities in certain respects, its expansion made it similar, in other respects, to the booming cities of the Northeast. To understand the history of New Orleans in the first half of the nineteenth century, it is thus essential to interpret what Boze tells us about the many dangers the residents of the city faced on a daily basis.

Early in his correspondence, he wrote to Ste-Gême that his wife's "native country . . . is covered with all the insects of Noah's Ark, and . . . has become very unhealthy" (F 21). As he aged, he apparently became more sensitive to the vicissitudes of life in the Louisiana capital, and narration of those dangers naturally fills his letters. Following his narrative, this chapter will focus on the hardships New Orleanians faced at the time—extreme climatic conditions, disease and mortality, fires, criminality, violence, and the many accidents the city endured—as a concession to New Orleans's still very recent rough beginnings and as a prelude to its extraordinary development in the early American period.

A Hostile Environment

The dangers of New Orleans's geography are no mystery to the post-Katrina reader. Although the city itself was, at the time, less exposed to the risks of flooding from Lake Pontchartrain, because it was still limited to higher grounds,[2] it was extremely sensitive to climatic changes, mainly because its economy was still largely agricultural. The weather was always watched closely because of the influence it had overall on the life of the Louisiana capital. If its effects were sometimes beneficial, they could also bring ruin and devastation. Although early frosts, for instance, were always welcome, because they meant that yellow fever season was over, their severity could hobble the New Orleans economy for at least a season, a situation all the more troublesome in periods of economic depression.

Boze's letters are full of indications about the climate and its effects on the lives of New Orleanians. He constantly notes whether it is cold or hot, sunny or rainy, and if there is wind and from what direction it is coming. Sometimes the reader can follow daily climatic evolutions, as if s/he were reading meteorological records; this shows the importance of the weather to a nineteenth-century New Orleans resident.

Louisianans naturally feared hurricanes, although major ones were not that numerous during Boze's correspondence. In the 1818–1839 period, only one major hurricane struck, the Great Barbados Hurricane, which made direct landfall in Louisiana, on August 17, 1831.[3] It destroyed many vessels and damaged numerous buildings in New Orleans. It flooded parts of the city, provoked a storm surge in Lake Pontchartrain, and caused hailstorms. In a letter the mayor, Denis Prieur, wrote to the municipal council, he enumerates the "disastrous effects" of this "gust of wind" (*coup de vent*), mentioning the "flooding that has covered the whole back of the city up to the lake, whose waters had risen to the point of overflowing," making "a relatively considerable part of the population suffer considerable losses and inconveniences it is not yet free of."[4] Boze describes the events in detail. "Around 9 or 10 on that same morning of August 16, the weather became cloudy and, during the night, a kind of hurricane broke out, with a storm wind shifting from north to south and from south to north and continuous torrential rain, to the point that some families, fearing great danger, spent the night standing sentry, so as, if necessary, to avoid being dragged into the disaster" (F 188).

The damage that occurred in the countryside, the harbor, and the city was especially devastating. The Gentilly area, where Ste-Gême's plantation was, was covered with a sheet of water, to the point that some people saw deer swimming along the roads, Boze writes. Bayou St. John emptied into the city. From the bayou to the ramparts, the area was totally flooded, down to Burgundy Street, but mainly "in all the new streets established north of the esplanade of that area, behind the college," what is today St. Claude, in the Tremé. People had to evacuate hurriedly and find refuge in the Quarter. Bridges were destroyed, and the only way to come to the city from Gentilly was by pirogue. Every day for at least five days, vessels reached the harbor, badly damaged and filled with shipwrecked persons, and, every day, New Orleanians received reports about new shipwrecks. Among the consequences the city faced was the rarefaction of agricultural products. Although the sugar cane crop seemed not to have suffered too much, severe damage had been done to the cotton crop, as well as to rice, potatoes, corn, and vegetables, "which today occasions an important shortage in vegetables on the markets, making our tables a little meager" (F 188). On August 24, the *Conseil de Ville* passed a resolution allocating 2,000 gourdes to victims of the hurricane.[5] Many fishermen, who were boating in Barataria and along the coast, drowned; the total number of victims amounted to fifty men, women, and children. A second tropical storm swept over the city between August 27 and 29, but it was much less violent and caused only minor damage. The flooding, however, started anew and reached the western banquette[6] of Rampart Street, making all the neighboring streets impracticable and obliging the residents to evacuate again. Citing the newspaper of Baton Rouge of August 27, Boze comments that the episode of August 16 "by the violence of the wind and the amount of rain, had surpassed everything that had been seen in the neighborhood since the famous hurricane of 1812" (F 188). It is the only major hurricane recorded by Boze, who, like all New Orleans residents, kept in mind that the summers and early falls were dangerous, systematically mentioning the risk or the absence of hurricane episodes. Although there was no other such extreme episode in the two decades of the correspondence, Boze mentions many minor tropical storms and important flooding episodes of the Mississippi River that damaged the city and impaired its economy.

Louisianans were also easy prey to droughts or periods of abundant rain or extreme cold. Although these climatic phenomena had no direct effect on the city, they affected the sugar and cotton crops and provoked food shortages that had consequences on the economy and the living conditions of urban inhabitants. In January 1831, New Orleans faced such a hardship: "Since the beginning of winter, it has been freezing without interruption and often humid weather prevails, which makes it seem very harsh this year. As a result, all the plants and all the small trees of all kinds of gardens in the city and, without exception, all those of the countryside, have been destroyed by frost. The orange trees, in particular, have suffered much and there is not one single leaf left on them. It has not killed them, though, and there is hope that in the spring they will perfectly recover" (F 175). In December 1831, Louisianans were "inundated by a shower of freezing rain," and the cold provoked a rise in the price of lumber and caused the death of many old Creoles and Europeans (F 193). In the early 1830s, a series of extremely cold winters made economic conditions disastrous in the city. In early October 1832, for instance, frost was reported to have made the cane less juicy. In mid-November, frost and ice were ravaging the crops and, in late November, "every day, there is frost and ice, and this has caused [Ste-Gême's] pond to be continuously iced over" (F 233). In early January, the snow was making things still harder: "we experienced from the 3rd to the 5th instant a downpour of snow so abundant that I never saw a similar one, even in Europe, and until today, the 7th instant. The city is still everywhere covered with such a thick coat of ice that the shovel can clear neither the banquettes nor the streets and, if we manage to do so, it is only with a sledgehammer, and in the streets we can see only heaps of two-inch thick ice, which increases the cold we are suffering from in the new year; and the sun, in its weakness, only makes it melt very slowly on the house roofs" (F 235). Such extreme climatic episodes could not but have strong repercussions on an economy relying almost exclusively on agriculture and economic exchanges. Because of early frosts or overabundant rains, agricultural production suffered, causing significant shortages on the New Orleans markets. They also damaged the cane, thus contributing to general economic depressions.

Morbidity and mortality rates were also closely connected to the weather, unusual conditions affecting certain population groups to an unequal degree. Old people, for instance, died when biting cold prevailed, a fact confirmed by the multiplication of burials in extreme weather conditions, while an improvement in the weather was clearly positive, as in October 1833, when "the fair weather that has persisted since the 19th instant, has put a stop to burials" (F 232). Humidity, on the contrary, was often fatal to newcomers unaccustomed to such climatic conditions. In late December of that year reigned an "aquatic climate," which was "not favorable to the slaves imported from the North by the Americans" and which was likely to result in new victims (F 235).

The New Orleans economy and general social life was thus often severely disrupted by the whims of nature. Moreover, every year, because of frequent storms, the summer rainy season, misleadingly called "*hivernage*" in New Orleans as in the French tropics, paralyzed the economy of the city by almost emptying its harbor of ships. In July 1831, for instance, there were only four deep-sea vessels in the harbor, an extreme situation for one of the busiest harbors in the country (F 170). In November of the same year, the first boat since July departed for Bordeaux, the "harbor having found itself empty of boats bound for all the harbors in France, due to the *hivernage*" (F 173). Very often, "the city is sad because the weather, with its changes, impedes commerce, and also its architects' work, and still more that of the poor workers exposed to the stings of the air, which makes everything stop all activity" (F 236).

During almost half of the year, the city thus came to a standstill, and its bustling commercial exchanges stopped altogether. Summers were always, in New Orleans, a difficult period. In 1834, for instance, the city was affected by a heat wave, the temperature being in the high eighties for most of July and even reaching ninety-five between August 20 and 22 (F 243). This was, of course, very scary for New Orleans's residents, for summers were always the deadliest season, and the risk of epidemics drove away many city dwellers, leaving the city prey to "melancholia and boredom" (F 258), slowing down commerce, putting a halt to entertainment, and often decimating the population. Deadly epidemics were, indeed, extremely frequent in the Crescent City in the early American decades.

New Orleans, "the Head-Quarters of Death"

In 1831, a British traveler to New Orleans, Henry Tudor, called the city "the head-quarters of death."[7] Almost all travelers and sojourners gave the same account of the city in the summer. From Governor Claiborne to Alexis de

Toqueville and the Latrobes, Benjamin and John, all lost members of their families to the fever and all left accounts of it, Benjamin Latrobe being the one who gave the most accurate descriptions of the mosquitoes that were eventually found to be responsible for the transmission of the disease, although this medical discovery was not made until the very early twentieth century.[8] Disease crippled all the port cities of the Atlantic world, because of their busy sea exchanges, which facilitated the transmission of epidemics. New Orleans was by no means the only city concerned about yellow fever, but it suffered from deadly episodes more often and for many more years than the majority of the other cities.

Ever since the advent of colonization in the Caribbean, all the colonies had been affected. In the age of revolutions, the deadly disease crippled most of the European armies, which had come to defend their colonial possessions. From French Saint-Domingue, in the late eighteenth century, to New Granada, in the nineteenth century, and even Cuba, later in that century, many nations lost their colonies as much to yellow fever as to the revolutionary armies that often used yellow fever against the colonial army, managing to delay attacks until the fever assisted them in their fight.[9] The revolutionaries were even sometimes favored by the climate, as was the case in Saint-Domingue, when the yellow fever epidemic was worsened by a long El Niño event, with longer-lasting and more abundant rains than usual.[10] Everywhere in the Caribbean, the British, French, and Spanish armies lost most of their troops to the fever, especially in the late 1790s, when an estimated 180,000 men died of the disease.[11]

In the late eighteenth century, military and refugee migrations caused the spread of the disease to the Greater Caribbean in general (Guyana, Veracruz, and the Lesser Antilles, but also the Gulf Coast and New Orleans) to the east coast of the United States and even to European ports. Spain and England experienced extremely severe epidemic bouts at the turn of the nineteenth century, giving historians reason to speak of a transatlantic yellow fever pandemic in the 1791–1805 period.[12]

Historians contend that the Saint-Domingue refugees were an easy vector for the disease, carrying with them infected persons but also, most certainly, mosquitoes.[13] All the port cities with frequent exchanges with the tropics were affected, especially in the late eighteenth century. Philadelphia, for instance, was plagued by it regularly in the 1790s, with major bouts of the disease in 1793 (when one in twelve people died), 1797 (causing the death of three thousand), and 1798.[14] The disease struck New York in 1791, 1795, and 1796. The decade coincided with a busy decade in the Age of Revolutions, marked by frequent movements of populations (military and civil) and also by the strongest El Niño event of the millennium. The Southern cities of the Atlantic and Gulf coasts were usually not spared. While the worst epidemics were found in the Northeast in the last decade of the eighteenth century and the first decade of the nineteenth century, the South remained plagued by the disease much longer, to the point that, after the 1820s, the disease was considered a Southern plague.[15] Charleston, for instance, experienced a major epidemic in 1838, long after the disease had been put to a stop in the North.[16]

No city of the Atlantic world was spared, especially in the early periods, but because of its tropical climate and the city's poor sanitation, New Orleans had the highest mortality rate from yellow fever in the United States, especially in the first half of the nineteenth century. This was all the more true because New Orleans received continuous influxes of new migrants, more prone to contracting the disease, and also because of the development of exchanges with the Caribbean. When the city became the second-busiest port after New York, at the turn of the 1840s, it also became more susceptible to epidemics.[17]

The city experienced one of its worst epidemics in 1832, but that was only one of a long list.[18] The first reported epidemic occurred in 1796,[19] and there were many over the course of Boze's correspondence, including severe ones. In 1819, 1822, 1824, 1827, 1828, 1829, 1832, 1833, 1837, and 1839, the fever attacked the city. Some episodes were deadlier than others, such as that of 1819, when 2,190 people, out of a population of 26,183, died.[20] This means that one out of twelve persons died that year, a figure similar to the death rate in Philadelphia during the 1793 epidemic, which suggests that New Orleans then still resembled port cities of the late eighteenth-century Atlantic world.[21] Altogether, between 1822 and 1844, that is to say adding only one more to the epidemics Boze witnessed (in 1841), 9,637 cases were recorded and 3,787 New Orleanians perished, although the figures given by Boze are far higher than these.[22]

Boze witnessed at least six of these great epidemics from within the city itself, the others occurring when he was in Cuba or living in Gentilly. The many mentions he makes of the disease during these outbreaks show the terror and horror it caused in New Orleans. The most detailed outbreaks are those of 1832 and 1833, during which Boze dedicates most of his newsletters to recounting the progress of the epidemic. Even in years not considered to have had epidemics, yellow fever was present. In September 1830, for instance, "yellow fever has begun its harvest, principally among the non-acclimated youth. On the 3rd of September, there are in the city many sick people and, at

Charity hospital, there are 150 men and 12 women." On September 12, 252 sick people are in the hospitals, 169 of them at Charity. On November 1, "yellow fever has resumed its harvest on the Europeans, principally, and several have died in the past fifteen days." "There are still about 200 in the hospitals and 73 have died there in the past month" (F 174).

Boze was no stranger to yellow fever, since he had spent two and a half decades in the Caribbean before reaching New Orleans and had spent most of the 1820s in Cuba. Yet it was ever-present in his letters, and thus in his mind, to the point that, in the years without epidemics, he kept expressing his relief by indicating that yellow fever had not yet appeared. In the summer of 1831, "the yellow fever that terrifies every year all the inhabitants of this state has not yet started to seize its scythe for its harvest especially on the non-acclimated" (F 188). In September 1838, there was still no sign of yellow fever in the city, "which tranquillizes its inhabitants and soothes the foreigners' terror of yellow fever" (F 283). In 1835, there were a few cases of persons affected by cholera and yellow fever, but the bout had been a minor one, killing only a few people in the city, principally foreigners (F 258).

These indications are a clear sign of the traumatic effect the fever had, every summer and fall, on the city's residents, whether seasoned or not. Not even those who had been dealing with the disease for almost a half century escaped this terror. Beyond relaying morbidity and mortality rates and giving a good measure of the terror it caused among the city's residents, Boze's letters also inform the reader of the myths spread about the disease, decades before its mode of transmission was understood.[23]

As the origins and mode of transmission of the disease were unknown, treatments were essentially empirical and, aside from being ineffective, were sometimes dangerous.[24] Although no one could pin down the exact origin of the fever, many conjectures were made, and city authorities attempted to check the progression of the disease. In 1822, the city council passed an ordinance that created boards of benevolence in each ward, to ensure that proper care was taken of the poor.[25] New Orleanians adopted the habit of burning everything that had touched the dead, and a city ordinance of 1833 required that the dead be buried within twenty-four hours.[26] Many ineffective preventive measures were also taken, mainly sounding the cannon and burning tar, in the hope of chasing the miasma.[27]

Another interesting thing shown in Boze's accounts is that not everyone was equal before the disease. People of African descent were the least likely to contract the disease, as were white Creoles, whether from Saint-Domingue or Louisiana. The most exposed were, by far, newcomers to the city, from

Europe or the rest of the United States, especially the North, and especially from places that had not experienced the disease, contrary to people coming from ports like New York, Philadelphia, Baltimore, Norfolk, or Charleston. Although many eccentric theories were circulated for lack of knowledge of the origins and mode of transmission of the disease, New Orleanians were quick to understand that those who had lived in areas exposed to the virus seemed to have developed a resistance to it.[28] Those who died from yellow fever were "principally the un-acclimated" (F 271), to the point that the fever was sometimes called "strangers' disease."[29]

As Boze's narrative often shows, the effects on the city—on its morbidity, mortality, and economy—were far-reaching. Every year, the city was emptied in the summer months, people leaving for safer regions, on the north shore of Lake Pontchartrain, along the Gulf Coast, in Pass Christian or Bay Saint-Louis, in the countryside, or even in the North. This displacement tremendously slowed down economic life and put to a halt any organized social life. The theater, the opera, and most places of public entertainment were closed during these months. The newspapers suspended—or at least scaled back—publication. The harbor traffic, already impaired by the risk of hurricanes, was even more limited. When a bout of yellow fever erupted, the already sluggish economy stopped altogether, a really disquieting situation in periods of economic recession, as in 1819 or 1822, since during epidemics, the farmers from the surrounding areas stopped coming to the city markets to sell their goods.[30] Food shortages ensued, almost systematically. Every year, in June, "the tremblers fearing yellow fever" started leaving the city, and Boze remarked that "soon there will be many houses for rent for the brave" (F 169). The lull lasted throughout the summer and early fall, with most residents returning to the city only in October (F 189).

The worst consequence of the disease was, of course, human, and the many deaths caused labor shortages (although people of African descent were less likely to die from the fever),[31] left children orphaned, devastated families, and totally demoralized the city's population. In the early days of the 1832 epidemic, *L'Abeille* wrote: "the fever has come out of its drowsiness and has taken away from us some of the newly disembarked and others after 3 to 5 days of sickness" (F 211), and the progression of this terrible epidemic soon accelerated. Between September 30 and October 8, 106 persons died, seventy-six whites and thirty of color (F 211). In October, people had started to return to the city, but the fever struck again, "causing the death of 20, 25, 30, and sometimes 40 persons a day." Although late, the fever that year was "pitiless," "without respect for age and sex," and affected "the un-acclimated and the

Creoles." In late October, there were so many deaths "that people say that the authorities have recommended that the newspapers no longer give the mortality figures, to avoid frightening the healthy" and that people were once again fleeing the city (F 211). It is difficult to make out later victims of this epidemic, because the worst epidemic of cholera in the city's history also struck at that point, and it became difficult to distinguish the victims of the two epidemics. The fever returned the next summer, in August, causing the death of "two young skilled physicians from the United States and several other French, American, Spanish, and German foreigners." A few days later, "yellow fever continued its ravages on the un-acclimated." Between September 5 and 11, the mortality figure was between forty and fifty a day. From September 1 to 15, 544 people died from the fever (F 231).

Yellow fever was thus one of the main concerns of New Orleans residents, but it was far from being the only one. Cholera was another ordeal New Orleanians had to face. The greatest epidemic during Boze's correspondence started in late October of 1832. New Orleans was only one of the cities ravaged by the cholera epidemics that year. All the port cities of the Atlantic world were affected. By October, Philadelphia had recorded 2,314 cases, and 935 persons had died. One Philadelphian in sixty was stricken; one in 173 died. One New Yorker in twenty-five died of cholera that same year.[32] The epidemics followed the ships from port to port, reaching Charleston, for example, from New York on the *Amelia*.[33]

From folder to folder, the reader of Boze's letters follows the epidemic as it moves forward, and one could almost draw an epidemiological map of this progression. In early July, Boze reported that cholera morbus was ravaging cities in Canada, especially Quebec and Montreal. Later that month, it reached New York, so "that we tremble here of its visit . . . which makes many frightened city dwellers emigrate, in the trust that, by their estrangement, they will be able to escape its deadly scythe." Newspapers give a good account of the way the epidemic progressed, filling in the blanks of Boze's report. In late July, the epidemic had struck Philadelphia (F 207). In August, the disease was affecting many cities of the Northeast, and in particular New York.[34] By the end of the month, it had reached Albany, Norfolk, and cities of New Jersey and was also affecting England and Ireland.[35] In early September, it was spreading around New York and had reached Boston, Portsmouth, Baltimore, and Washington.[36] These epidemiological reports show how the disease spread from urban centers to the periphery and from port to port along the coast, the arrival of the epidemic in an urban center being almost systematically connected with the arrival of a specific boat carrying infected people.[37] While news of the spread of the disease circulated, New Orleanians, fully informed by their newspapers, were bracing themselves against the deadly fever. People had left for Pascagoula, Mobile, and Pensacola, making "the business of trade motionless, the city being extremely gloomy" (F 207).

By October 27, the disease had started spreading in New Orleans, essentially Faubourg Ste. Marie (F 211). Within ten days, New Orleans had lost one-tenth of its population.[38] Albert Fossier calls it "the worst calamity ever experienced in New Orleans" and maybe "the worst in the history of the country."[39] According to Reverend Clapp, between October 25, when the first two victims were reported, and November 6, physicians' most conservative computations had at least five thousand dead, an average of five hundred a day, although this was, according to them, a low figure, considering that many people were buried without their deaths being reported.[40]

In early November, it had moved to neighboring plantations, causing the death of many slaves.[41] By November 11, it had moved to Pointe Coupée and other parishes upriver (F 212). In late November, the epidemic had ceased in the city but was raging in the country. In early December, it had reached Mobile and the parish of St. John the Baptist (F 213). In December, it was affecting the parishes of St. John the Baptist and La Fourche (F 214). In early 1833, there were still a few cases in the city, and the disease was resulting in many victims on the plantations north of New Orleans (F 216). In March, it crossed the Gulf and raged in Havana, killing an average of 170 to 200 (and even 250) persons a day. In late April, the epidemic had ceased in Havana (F 223), but the disease was still present in New Orleans, although with diminished strength, compared to the first months, and it did not stop until July, when there were no more cases of it in the city (F 229). The countryside was still affected, however, sporadically, until June 1834 (F 240), and a few cases were still reported in the city in May 1835 (F 252–53). In August, cholera hit Barataria, and more precisely Chénière Caminada, and then the Attakapas (F 258). Despite people's fears, it did not return to the city in the fall. In June, Tampico (Mexico) was affected, the disease killing one hundred people a day, out of a population of four to five thousand. It killed the entire crew, except for one, of a French vessel in the harbor (F 227).

As in the case of yellow fever, not all were equally susceptible to the disease, although the victims were different from those of yellow fever, because the mode of propagation was more clearly linked, this time, to sanitation conditions. It did not spare the Creoles, as yellow fever often did. New Orleans natives were no longer safe, and they ran as high a risk as the not yet acclimated foreigners. Boze describes the first victims as "foreigners living in the city, mostly of the lowest class, including a few enslaved house servants" (F 211). But he quickly shows that everyone was affected. In the first week of the epidemic, he writes: "Today died of cholera and yellow fever Americans, Irish, Swiss, and German people, as well as French nationals and Creoles of the white country and of color, followed by several from Saint-Domingue, but the number of blacks has been more considerable." The dizzying enumeration shows that no ethnic or racial group was spared, and later, in the same newsletter, Boze notes that no gender or age group is unaffected, but that the most numerous victims are among northerners from America or Europeans, and black people (F 212), most certainly because the new migrants and the slaves were at a disadvantage due to their difficult economic situation and rudimentary living conditions.

Like the newspapers, Boze is very specific about prevention methods.[42] Everyone started wearing flannel, a plaster of pitch from Bourgogne (Burgundy) on their stomach, and they purchased preservative medicines, to the point that pharmacists ran out, despite their immediate recourse to gouging to try to prevent shortages and for obvious reasons of interest. Some people "with a tender heart," however, advertised in the press that they would deliver free medicine to the destitute, and the city council, as well as the local banks, and even the United States Bank, several times released sums to succor the poor (F 212). Among the preventive measures, physicians advised people to abstain from eating "fish, fruit, shellfish, cabbage, and raw vegetables," to the point that these products were declared harmful and could no longer be sold in the markets (F 212).

The city authorities advocated, as in the case of yellow fever, the burning of tar in front of houses and the sounding of the cannon, in the hope that it would rid the city of its miasma. Boze writes: "On this day of 1st instant, the cannon has shot powder in all the streets and on the Place d'Armes without interruption and fires of tar or other fuels have been lit before every house, to try to soften by this wise precaution the pestilent air, and the result was, they say, that there were not any more cases" (F 212). They also suggested that quick lime be put in stagnant water, that gutters and canals be kept clear of any obstruction, that graves be kept clear of water.[43]

Although suppositions about the mode of transmission seem to have been closer to the truth than in the case of yellow fever, treatments were, here again, tentative. When the epidemic was announced, everybody started buying "preservative drugs" and intended to "rigorously follow the sobriety diet our physicians had the newspapers publish" (F 211). Hospitals and doctors started getting ready for the epidemic, and some people decided to leave the city for the country or the West Indies (F 212). There are some hints, in Boze's letters, at effective treatments and, although no information is given on the specifics of the method, he writes, for instance, that "many sick persons are saved with the treatment of Doctor Alphen which is still working marvels" (F 212). Many people, however, were misdiagnosed with cholera, and the virulence of the cholera treatments killed them (F 223).[44]

As with yellow fever, both myth and truth were circulated, and it was impossible, at the time, to distinguish one from the other. Some controversies, for instance, seem to have agitated the New Orleans people, such as the one about the absence of hygiene as the origin of cholera. In January 1833, people thought that "the disease might become limited to people of color" in a more moderate form, so that if it was treated immediately, people could be cured. They also believed that "it can be observed here that people who usually drink hard liquor do not survive" (F 216). A few months earlier, however, some people had said "that this dreadful disease affects only blacks or whites who do not take sufficient precautions," and Boze had concluded with the following words: "I see, however, that the sober and those who are not suffer the same fate" (F 212). In November, "the *Argus* has put forward that an article of the *Louisiana Advertiser* said that dissolute and dirty persons were the only ones to contract cholera in the city. Has anything more contrary to truth ever been published? Have we not lost many of our compatriots of both sexes, who were models of cleanliness and regularity? Has not the editor of the *Louisiana Advertiser* himself fallen victim to the terrible epidemic, as well as the Secretary of State? Were they dissolute and dirty? And will the *Louisiana Advertiser* say the same of hundreds of our fellow citizens who were attacked by cholera and have recovered their health?" (F 214). New Orleanians, like all people living in infected areas, were still a long way from understanding the origins and modes of transmission of the disease.

Mortality was exceptional throughout the course of the epidemic. On October 30, there was a total of 113 dead, among whom were fifty-six Catholics, forty-four Protestants, and thirteen from the hospital (since the churches and hospitals were the sources of the official figures), whereas before the epidemic, the daily number of deaths was not above twenty-five. By then, every house had incurred losses, either of family or friend or slave (F 212). At times, there were so many dead that "the hearses and carts used to carry the corpses to the cemetery mostly journey without being followed by a relative, a friend, or even a priest" and "on All Saints, the evening before the Day of the Dead, not a single man, woman, or child of any class went to the cemetery to pray for the dead, while in other years, thousands of Christians crowded there to attend the funeral celebration by the Ministers of Jesus Christ, so strong is the dismay today because of the ravages of the diseases on the population of the city" (F 212). A list of daily deaths published in the newspapers for the Catholic and Protestant churches for the period from October 28 to November 4 gives a total of 1,070 persons buried, 626 Catholics and 444 Protestants (F 212). In late November, the figure of five thousand dead "of all classes and colors" had been reached in one month (F 213). In mid-November, the figure was still at about three thousand persons in one month. For November 9 and 10 alone, there were 115 burials at the Catholic and Protestant cemeteries, and 249 between November 5 and 11 (F 214). City authorities had opened a third cemetery just in case, called the Cemetery of the Corporation, where a "bayou" had been dug, in which were now "piled the gold and mahogany caskets," while those in rough wood were covered with quicklime (F 214). Clearly, no class was spared in the city, and the disease took a toll on the richest as well as on the poorest. In May 1833, the deaths recorded by the churches still amounted to 435 (F 226). From June 14 to 21, a daily average of thirty persons died; from June 22 to July 2, there were fifteen to twenty deaths a day, for a total of 199 (F 227). Altogether, 1,575 religious burials occurred between late May and July 7, 1833. In September, there were still about 970 burials. In October, the disease seemed to start receding, and only six hundred burials were recorded, since the fair weather had returned "on the 19th instant," while, at the same time, frost had put an end to yellow fever (F 232). Those counts were always conservative estimates, however, since many victims were not interred at the churches, which gives a good measure of the ravages of this terrifying disease. Cholera returned to the city sporadically in 1834, and it was not until July 7 that the epidemic was over in the city, according to the report of the Faculty of Medicine (F 229), the newspapers no longer giving the daily death count. There are a few cases mentioned, however, from time to time throughout the summer, and even in May (F 252) and July 1835, "especially blacks in greater numbers" (F 253), but the worst was over. Cholera had killed thousands of the city's residents in a mere two years.

As can easily be imagined, the consequences were far-reaching. Planters had to put off or stop altogether the rolling of sugar cane because of the many losses in their slave population (F 212). Boze several times mentions deaths on specific plantations. He tells Ste-Gême that Mr. Lacoste had lost thirty slaves, Mr. Cucullu about thirty as well, and Mr. Regis about twenty, although Ste-Gême's Gentilly plantation had not been affected (F

214). Several times, he alludes to the very high mortality rate among agricultural slaves and domestic slaves in the city. When the epidemic reached a plantation, a sizable percentage of the slave population died. A planter by the name of Proctor, whose property lay on the lake shore, lost eighty slaves all at once (F 226).

The city was totally deserted, and all activity stopped (F 212). The epidemic also caused a drastic increase in the price of certain goods, of medicine or woolens, for instance, whose prices doubled, and then tripled (F 212). The epidemic also completely halted social life. "It should be expected that, this winter, there will be no public entertainment and no balls, since the whole city is mourning the losses they incur every day, without being able to know when this calamity will end" (F 212). On November 15, "bankruptcies are immense" (F 214). The disease had left, of course, many widowed persons and more than a hundred orphans (F 227).

If yellow fever and cholera were the deadliest diseases because of their extreme infectiousness, other diseases made the lives of city residents hazardous. Medicine was still in its rudimentary stages, and, despite steady progress throughout the nineteenth century, people still died of a number of diseases that would be relatively harmless today. In April 1831, Boze writes to Ste-Gême that "the fatalities in this country are still numerous even though the yellow fever season has not yet arrived" (F 183). In September of the same year, he speaks of "a high mortality from ordinary diseases" (F 189). He mentions several diseases, as in late December 1831, for instance, in the heart of a rough winter, when he says that many people were dying of catarrh and many were affected by persistent colds (F 193). In January 1834, he mentions many sick and several dead persons, without further details (F 233).

Thus, even in a modernizing city, while medicine was constantly progressing, natural elements still made life extremely difficult and took a heavy toll on an ever-increasing population. Although New Orleans was no exception in the young American republic, it was affected for a much longer time period and in often much larger proportions than other cities. Natural elements were hard to master and, in many ways, the city was still very much the little frontier town it had been in the colonial period. It was weakened by an extremely rapid urban development, increased exchanges with the Caribbean and Atlantic seaports, and relatively precarious living conditions. It took a very long time for living conditions to really improve, especially since, when New Orleanians did not fall victim to natural disasters and diseases, they still had to face the harsh conditions of the city itself.

The Flames of Hell

Throughout the colonial era and the early nineteenth century, fire plagued all of the cities of the New World. Buildings were constructed of wood, roofs were often made of vegetal materials, open fires were dangerously set inside precarious constructions, and fire spread very rapidly through crowded housing. Water supply systems were inefficient and fires spread, unchecked, along streets, and even through entire blocks. All of the major cities experienced large fires.[45] Fire was always one of the scourges of the Crescent City, probably due in part to the hot climate that reigned for much of the year. In the colonial era, in 1788 and 1794, the city was almost entirely destroyed by two major fires.[46] No such wide-ranging event occurred in the twenty years of Boze's correspondence, but his letters so often mention fires that it is easy to grasp the significance of this hazard for early nineteenth-century New Orleans residents. In March 1830, Boze describes, although in a probably hyperbolic depiction, his house at the corner of Royal and the Quarter as "built of slightly old matches, with a neighborhood of tinder" to the point that he claims to pack a bag every night and sleep in his clothes, in order to be able to flee if there is a fire at night (F 160).

Despite the probable exaggeration, it is true that there were frequent destructive fires. In March 1830, Boze writes: "there is not a single week in which the tocsin is not sounded for assistance to put out a fire, either in the city or in the faubourgs" (F 160). His letters are full of accounts of fires destroying houses or businesses, and almost every other newsletter mentions at least one large fire. No one was protected from it. Expensive houses were burned down just as poor lodgings were. Residential quarters as well as businesses were lost. Black and white people were affected.[47] Creoles, foreigners, and Americans were all victims.[48]

Fires could destroy, one after the other, a wooden house on Royal, between St. Philip and Ursulines (F 233), six wooden houses in Ste. Marie in half an hour (F 239), several houses on Dumaine, a large wooden house at the corner of Royal and Bienville (F 240), and many more. Some months were apparently particularly destructive, especially those of the warmer season, and there seems to have been fire "epidemics."[49] In February and March 1836, for instance, fire raged at the Debuy brothers' cotton press, near Ste. Marie, and there were fires in Ste. Marie, the Marigny, and on the levee.

Although brick buildings were also affected, most of the destruction was to wooden houses and most fires happened at night. Often, "dilapidated wooden houses" (F 258) or "a few old wooden sheds" (F 260) were destroyed.

In August 1834, a fire started at a bakery on Delor Street, between Camp and Magazine in Ste. Marie, and "all the buildings of the block burned except for three," mainly because "almost all were in wood" (F 244). This confirms Boze's fear at night and his mention that he slept fully dressed in case he had to evacuate.

The faubourgs and the Quarter were often susceptible to fire, but they were not the only areas. In November 1832, Mr. L. Colomb's sugar plantation burned up (F 213), and in March 1833, the beautiful house built by Mr. Bienvenu on his plantation burned to the ground (F 218). What is often striking in the city, however, is the expanse of the fires. In April 1832, for instance, a fire totally destroyed ten houses in the Marigny (F 203). In June of the same year, another fire wrought destruction on Royal Street, between Bienville and Customs (F 205). During the night of November 2 and 3, 1832, new brick houses burned down on Dumaine, between Condé and Levee. In the fall of 1833, a fire broke out at 1 a.m. on St. Claude, between St. Ann and Dumaine. It started in a stable full of hay belonging to Mr. Aimé Pignegui and then burned down a little brick building and a few wooden houses, and "the fire would have spread to the houses that face Rampart and Dumaine but its progress was checked, thanks to the American pump number 2 that we are always certain to find facing danger, along with the indefatigable activity of the men in charge of driving it. On the site of the stable, only remained the iron fitments of the carts stored there" (F 232). In April 1835, three buildings burned down at the end of Tchapitoulas Street in Ste. Marie, which resulted in the loss of seven stores on the first floor and the upper floors (F 252). Later that year, the Tchapitoulas block was almost entirely destroyed from Commerce and St. Joseph to Faubourg Ste. Marie. The fire started in a quicklime warehouse and then spread to tobacco and lime stores and warehouses, a dry-goods store, and a foundry. Altogether thirteen multistoried brick buildings were destroyed (F 256). In July 1835, the hardware store of a certain Hopkins (Ste-Gême's neighbor in Gentilly), as well as the food stores of Bernoudy and Dufilho and of James Allen, burned (F 258).

Oftentimes, fire struck stores and businesses and completely destroyed them. In February 1834, Mr. Odgen's beautiful cotton press, with all the cotton it contained, completely burned down, and the owner incurred considerable losses. Later that month, a food store belonging to a certain Medelice was destroyed. On March 14, the bakery of Mr. Bouny on Chartres, close to the stock exchange building, was also lost to fire (F 237). In July 1834, three houses were lost in one fire in Ste. Marie, including Mr. Gamotis's pharmacy, Mr. Canter's printing press, and Mr. Robeson's store. In the same month, the food store of J A Lyle & Co on the levee was destroyed, although many goods were saved, and Mr. Tourné and Decoin's dry-goods store was destroyed in Ste. Marie (F 241). In August, fire caught, fortunately with little damage, at the printing press of *Le Courrier de la Louisiane* (F 244). In the spring of 1834, two stores belonging to a Frenchman and selling scrap iron, hardware, and ropes burned, as well as an American coffee shop on the levee between St. Louis and Conti. The firefighters managed to contain the fire, but there was extensive damage, and the owner of the coffee shop, found to be responsible for the fire, was arrested and temporarily jailed (F 238). During the night of October 7, 1837, fire caught "in the long row of workshops belonging to the company of the Carrolton Rail Road,[50] two leagues from the city," and in less than half an hour, everything was destroyed, including two sheds, fifteen carts, and one locomotive, for a total of two hundred thousand gourdes, only three-fourths of which was insured (F 283). Some months were thus obviously destructive, especially during dry-weather episodes and when the summer heat reigned in New Orleans.

Most often, only buildings and personal property were lost, sometimes for a considerable amount.[51] Generally, few products and personal effects were saved and, most of the time, the furniture was totally destroyed. When the damage was less extensive, the goods stored were often lost because of the combined effects of fire and water. Lives were also unfortunately lost to the fires, albeit infrequently. In March 1833, two children who had been left alone in their house died (F 217). During the previously mentioned fire in a bakery, in 1834, the owner's wife and five small children were saved but, the next day, the remains of a female domestic slave were found in the ruins of the house (F 237). In the spring of 1834, the fire that started at the Bony bakery and raged on Chartres resulted in several victims among people who, "the next day, were smashed by the collapse of the section of a wall" (F 238).

Fires could be accidental, but many seem to have been criminal. Sometimes, the owners were accused of setting fire for insurance money. In one case, for instance, Boze comments that "this property was insured and he might have earned instead of losing," adding that this owner had been three times victim to fire and that he was always away when it happened, punctuating his sentence with two exclamation marks (F 237). In other cases, attempts to deter the firefighters are even mentioned. During a fire that occurred at the corner of Camp Street, the fire hose was reported cut and a reward of 100 piastres[52] was offered to anyone who helped find the culprit (F 240). Several times, fire was connected to criminality, suggesting that arsonists lit the fires, sometimes in an act of vengeance against the owners and sometimes to steal the goods that were kept in the buildings, especially in the stores (F 258). On August 1, 1830, for instance, people suspect the "return of our previous arsonists who set fire to the beautiful building of Mr. Ferret's cotton press" in the Marigny, since the fire caught "so swiftly and in so many different points that just after it was noticed, the whole vast building was ablaze although it was entirely made of brick and slate" (F 174). In June 1836, arson is also clearly mentioned when Ogden's cotton press caught fire (F 268). In April 1837, "because of accidents of such nature so often renewed, the public is right to think that there is a company of arsonists and to exhort the police to fulfill their duty with much more strictness and swiftness" (F 275). When the roof of the exchange building burned at the corner of Chartres and St. Louis, for example, there was unmistakable evidence that an arsonist lit the fire from inside the building (F 275). Later that month, a fire was started at the corner of Rampart and Customs, although it did not spread, fortunately, since "this neighborhood is made of wooden houses and disaster would have been great" (F 275). In one case, the method used by the arsonists is even described: "a package containing combustible matter wrapped in shavings[53] was thrown under a heap of boards and fire was already beginning to throw light, when someone located on the other side of the street noticed it in time and managed to put it out" (F 278).

If fire sometimes made the lives of the New Orleanians very difficult and had dire economic consequences, the advent of modernity also heralded a new economic era in terms of insurance. There were apparently many instances in which the owners were underinsured, as was the case of aforementioned destruction of the Tchapitoulas block, when the losses amounted to about 100,000 gourdes, of which the insurance company covered only about one-fifth, causing Boze to comment on the "negligence and even sordid selfishness of our insurance companies" (F 256). There were cases in which Boze suspected the possibility of fraud, but there were many instances in which the victims were saved by the advent of insurance policies. Several times, fires meant "losses to the insurance companies" (F 250, F 252). More and more often, as time went by, he mentioned what was insured and what was not. Often, the goods were insured but the house was not, as was the case of a building belonging to a wealthy free Creole of color at the corner of St. Ann and Dauphine, in June 1836 (F 268). Even though the system was not yet stabilized, early American New Orleans was already entering the era of the capitalist economy.

Boze's letters also reveal people's reactions to the fires. Fighting fires was a matter of solidarity. Whenever a fire started in the city, the tocsin was sounded and people flocked from all over the city, with their slaves, to help the firefighters draw and carry water, and to assist the inhabitants in saving as many of their personal effects as possible.[54] When the existence of a company of arsonists was suspected, after the suspicious recurrence of fires, the police was often "assisted by the watch of the citizens, determined to establish block watches at night, starting the next night, to try to discover some of the people guilty of such disasters" (F 275), especially in the summer months, since "the utmost vigilance is necessary in time of drought" (F 278).

Fire seemed, with time, to be more easily circumscribed, partly because the city dwellers understood the importance of prevention. The new buildings were made of brick and tiles, less flammable than the traditional wood and shingles, and kitchens were placed in the slave quarters rather than the main buildings. The city also continued to modernize its fire services, purchasing pumps from England, acquiring ladders and other material, and organizing fire brigades appointed and paid by municipal authorities. In the early years of Boze's correspondence, there were only about fifty firefighters paid by the municipality, to whom were later added volunteers, both white and of color. Two brigades of free volunteers of color were indeed organized as well as, in 1829, the first company of white volunteers composed of merchants, civil servants, and professionals, all men of influence in the city. In May 1830, the city authorities had raised the number of firefighters in the city to eighty (F 166). A few years later, a second company was founded.

As time went by, destruction was generally circumscribed more quickly by the firefighters, often described as efficient, another sign of progress in the organization of municipal services. Boze repeatedly mentions the quick arrival of the brigade, their efficiency, and their ability to check fires that could have spread to the whole block, eventually causing much more damage. In 1834, for instance, the city hailed "the prompt assistance of the pumps, fortunately arrived on time to put out the fire that could have spread to the commercial stores of the neighborhood" (F 237). And again, in the spring, the fire that destroyed a house and the former Bank of Louisiana on Royal Street was extinguished very early, fortunately, because it could have destroyed the whole block, causing the loss of many lives, because many of the inhabitants lived on the upper floors (F 238). As time went by, the fire brigade apparently became better organized. When the Debuy brothers' cotton press caught fire, in February 1836, the fire was quickly controlled, thanks to the "prompt assistance of our firemen who never neglect an occasion to distinguish themselves, even at the risk of their lives" (F 265). Later that month, the "prompt assistance of the firemen" managed to contain another fire in the Marigny (F 265). In April

1837, a great fire destroyed respectable stores—a pharmacy and a paper and music store—and a brick house on Chartres. A third store, selling dry goods, was saved, "thanks to the activity of the brave firemen and the calm of the wind" (F 275).

All of this, however, was still insufficient to really prevent the hazard of fire, and the firefighting squads were still too often impotent, although New Orleans was not especially slow in establishing firefighting services. Philadelphia, notably, had been among the pioneering cities, in the early nineteenth century, but most Southern cities were slower to realize the importance of an organized municipal body.[55] Until the late 1830s, there was no general municipal water system, the pumps did not deliver enough water and did not deliver it far enough to be really effective, there were still too many wooden houses in the city, and the number of firefighters was still insufficient.

Nights were thus often animated in New Orleans, and it is easy to imagine that fear gripped many New Orleanians, troubling their sleep. Fire was far from being the only danger New Orleanians had to face. Criminality also took a heavy toll on the city, reinforced by the permanent influx of adventurers to the city.

Crime and Violence

In a rapidly urbanizing young republic, violence and crime were ever-present in the cities of the United States. Many historians of the Atlantic cities of the Northeastern United States have highlighted the close connection between violence and urbanization, generally explained by the breach in civil harmony due to a sudden influx of new residents, but also attributable to many other factors, such as the inadequacy of the police force, insufficiently augmented to face the population increase.[56] Although most cities had paid police forces early in the nineteenth century, their numbers were more often than not derisory when compared with the population they were expected to police.[57]

Although the first two decades of the nineteenth century were generally often described as relatively peaceful,[58] when New Orleans started rapidly expanding in the 1820s, it was often represented as "a refuge of criminals and unscrupulous adventurers from all over the world."[59] The bustling port brought daily crowds of sailors who indulged in all the pleasures the city could offer. Although many accounts from the turn of the 1830s attest to some progress in the safety offered by the city, many newspaper articles and narratives highlight the lawlessness of the sea adventurers and insufficiency of the city police.[60] Giving the figures of the gendarmerie, in 1834, Fossier gives the astoundingly low number of 102 policemen for the whole city (forty-two for City Hall and, for the faubourgs, twenty-three for Ste. Marie, twelve for Tremé, eleven for Marigny, and eleven for Lacourse).[61] Many newspaper extracts and eyewitness accounts of the period attest to the ineffectiveness and increasing insufficiency of law enforcement.[62]

Boze's narrative is a perfect illustration of this development of violence. He often compares the safety of the city upon his arrival, in 1809, to the criminality that he witnesses, essentially in the 1830s, after his eight-year absence. Regularly, he complains that "for some time, it has been rare not to hear about some murder, fire, theft, or fight" (F 273). In the summer of 1838, he writes: "every day, the newspapers tell us of nothing else but assassinations, duels, fires, breaking into stores, and the condemnation of culprits, some to be executed, others sentenced to the galleys for life or to hard labor for a number of years" (F 283). He attributes this outbreak of crime to the immigrant flow that has followed the arrival of the Americans: "This country no longer offers the same tranquility or the same safety that its inhabitants used to enjoy in your time, its population having so radically changed since the arrival of the Americans who were unfortunately followed by a crowd of tramps of all nations that exude crime" (F 188). The American takeover of Louisiana indeed made the state, and particularly its then capital, a place with increased economic prospects, which initiated a great wave of immigration. The new immigrants, because of their shaky economic situations, may well have included a disproportionate share of criminals. The mere population increase, however, may have inflated the crime rate in the city, causing Boze to blame this new development on the newcomers. Whatever the reasons, his explanation is interesting, as it reveals the relative compartmentalization of New Orleans society and the heightened ethnic consciousness that resulted from the growing cosmopolitan composition of its population.

Whoever was responsible for this new trend, New Orleans was obviously dangerous in the 1830s. In January 1835, Boze writes of a litany of horrors that continue to plague the city, "thefts, murders, fires, duels, forged signatures, checks, and notes," although he admits that many of these crimes result in arrests (F 264). There is hardly a letter in Boze's correspondence that does not relate the occurrence of a crime or the punishment of one, which tells us both that criminality was high in the city and that the newspapers were full of crime reports. In addition to arson, murders, thefts, and swindles were common, and a typology of crime in early American New Orleans can be established from Boze's narrations.

Murders were widespread. They occurred in all neighborhoods and in every class of society, and offered various modi operandi. They were often very violent, as shown in the case described by Boze in May 1830: "On the 29th instant, was discovered up in Faubourg La Fayette a corpse whose neck showed the signs of a deep wound made with a saber or some other cutting instrument. The skull had also been horribly smashed. A hat found a small distance away was cut in several places and bore, in the inside, the following words: Souvenir, Huntress, and Rover. This man had presumably belonged, at some point, to a steamboat company" (F 166). The tone is set, and many a page of Boze's letters echo this horrendous description, confirming that New Orleans was plagued by the extreme frontier conditions that historians often describe in the early American period. Although this feature was found in most of the developing cities of the early American republic, it is an element of New Orleans's history that requires highlighting, if only for its relative omission in the historiography of the city.

Many letters mention the discovery of crimes, the arrest of criminals, their sentencing, and, sometimes, the execution of the sentence, the story of a single crime sometimes staggering over several letters, following the various steps of the procedure over the months. Boze's letters are teeming with stories of people beaten to death, shot, stabbed, and killed in every possible imaginable way. The law was not lenient on criminals in these early days. Offenders were sentenced to the galleys, to imprisonment, and sometimes to death (F 231). If many met their fates, some made deals with the state authorities and became witnesses in exchange for their pardon (F 198).

Although this was not uncommon in the early stages of American urbanization, what the reader also learns from Boze's letters is that murders occurred in all of the different classes of society, and he always takes pains to detail who was concerned, if the victim and murderer were white or black, slaves or free people of color, Creoles or Americans. In a single letter, for instance, Boze successively describes the sentencing of a man of color, that of a certain Ramon Gambao, probably of Spanish descent, that of an American, John James, that of a Colonel Taylor, also probably American, and the execution of three Spaniards, showing both the extent of criminal activities and their reach to all of New Orleans society. In July 1835, a Frenchman, Mr. Maupassan, was assassinated by Mr. Bright, an American, in the Marigny. In the same month, a doctor (Martial Solanges)[63] was assassinated, as was a French youngster, Pelletan, by a foreigner "who had taken his place in his housekeeper's bed." The origins of the various victims and perpetrators revealed the extent of New Orleans's cosmopolitanism, as well as the violence of its early society.

Murders abounded in the city in the summer months, probably because the relative emptiness of the city and sanitary risks attracted mostly ruthless adventurers and gave the criminals a feeling of impunity. Boze concludes his account by stating that "there were two lethal murders [*sic*] in one month, according to the newspapers," even adding the surprising remark that it is "more than in Paris or London in one year" (F 257). The next month, three assassinations are reported (F 238). In April 1837 alone, four are mentioned (F 275). In the summer of 1838, Boze recounts several murders "and other dreadful events," as well as two executions on September 22, followed by two more later that month (F 283). Crime spared no one, not even children. In the spring of 1834, Boze even mentions a knife fight between two little boys, James Lyons and William, near the theater on Camp Street, in Faubourg Ste. Marie, ending in the death of one and the flight of the other (F 238). Even people belonging to the most respectable families committed offenses; for example, a group of young Creoles are seen breaking street lamps, while the police remain inactive, not to be "obliged to crack down on them, according to the law, and cause annoyance to their parents" (F 174).

No color escaped murder, and virtually all groups had both victims and perpetrators among their ranks. Several times, Boze mentions Creoles of color among the victims. Blacks also committed murders and, in April 1837, he relates the hanging of an "assassin slave" (F 275). In 1830, he had already told Ste-Gême about the murder by a *nègre*, the slave of Mademoiselle Lize Soulet, of a *mulâtre*,[64] a coachman, himself a fugitive slave belonging to a Creole family of the city (F 161). He sometimes clearly expresses, in his descriptions, that crime had no color, as when he writes that "the inhabitants have to remain on watch night and day, because of the crowd of white and black bandits that have taken refuge here since the arrival of the Americans in this state" (F 174).

Boze's interest in criminal acts obviously led him often to dwell on the topic, giving the impression of a permanent state of war in the city, even if two fatal crimes in a month does not seem like much, considering the relative lawlessness of the early societies of the Americas. Boze's readers are spared no details, not even about executions, of which he gives extremely detailed descriptions that aptly complete—when they do not reproduce verbatim—those found in the newspapers. In 1837, Boze recounts the spectacular hanging of a criminal in a highly dramatized description covering two pages. The man had killed his father-in-law, had been sentenced to twenty years in the galleys, had been pardoned by Governor White, and had committed a repeat offense. Here is a translated extract of the execution scene:

> That same day, was hanged Thomas Tibbitse, American, aged about 27, sentenced to capital punishment for crimes of assassination, &c &c. A very considerable crowd of onlookers had surrounded all morning the street of the prison, squeezing and bumping into each other to see him, and intently eyeing the fatal door through which the convict would come out.
>
> He finally appeared, he said farewell to those surrounding him and leaped, in one vigorous bound, onto the carriage and stood up on the coffin dedicated to receiving his lifeless remains a few moments later. When he reached the place of execution, he went up to the dreadful floor, renewed, in a firm and confident tone, his last farewells to the audience and begged each of them to forgive him the mistakes he had made, then, addressing the executioner, he said: I wholly belong to you, fulfill your duty, put the rope around my neck and tie the knot here (signaling the spot).
>
> People maintain that no other criminal ever displayed more courage and bravery and that no crowd of onlookers was ever more numerous. (F 275)

This vivid account, beyond the specific case, depicts the process of public executions in New Orleans, apparently frequent, judging by their recurrence in the correspondence.

Not all crimes had such dire consequences, however. Some ended with nonlethal wounds (F 203). Fights or vengeful acts often occurred, regularly perpetrated by close relations, as is the case here: "Mr. Macoin, American, former teacher of the Roman brothers on their plantation, who was beaten by them" (F 167). Boze relishes in gossiping about base actions, as when he recounts that "Mme. Dedune, born Moreau Lilet, legally separated, under the regime of separate estates, from her husband for several years, the mother of three daughters" was "beaten and wounded by her latest lover, an apprenticed baker" and that the "apprentice baker hurt himself beating her" (F 167). No social class seemed to be spared this violence that pervaded the city. Citing the *Courrier* on the multiplication of burglaries, in January 1831, Boze reports that several persons had been arrested. Among them were "maroon slaves" but also many whites "coming from several cities of Europe and of this continent," most of whom came from "honorable families" (F 216).

Theft was also a disease of the early American period, and there seemed to be organized gangs in New Orleans, operating more easily in the summer months, when a large part of the population, including, sometimes, the army and militia, had deserted the city for healthier climates. On the night of July 9, 1830, seven robberies took place in the Quarter, and Boze concludes that the police should be more efficient (F 170). Stores were regularly burglarized, sometimes in series. In July 1834, Boze mentions "a gang of arsonists and one of thieves in town" who, every night, break into stores to steal money and goods (F 242). In August, he again mentions the regular occurrence of burglaries and the growing audacity of the burglars, who smash the windows of the shops to get inside and loot them (F 244). In the summer of 1835, for instance, "the thefts are going on, as well as the murders," and there are some even in the "civilized class" (F 257). Burglaries most often concerned houses and stores, but in April 1837, thieves were also arrested for stealing the sacred vases at St. Louis Cathedral. Among this group of burglars was a Frenchmen who worked at the church at the time of the theft (F 275). Thefts were most often perpetrated by people living in dire economic conditions, a fact that probably underlies Boze's earlier comments attributing the increase in criminal activities to the immigrants who were then flocking into the city. They were not the only ones involved, however.

New Orleans was rapidly moving to a capitalist economy, and many of the crimes mentioned by Boze also had to do with forgery of banknotes or checks, or even, in some cases, organized networks of counterfeiters, with the arrest, for instance, in April 1833, of twelve "rascals" in Faubourg Ste. Marie (F 223). In March 1832, a Colonel Taylor was arrested for forging dollar bills (F 201); in May of the same year, another case was brought to the fore (F 204). Sentences were not light for the counterfeiters: "On the 14th instant, the criminal court sentenced Baker, proven to have had in his possession counterfeit notes with the intent of circulating them, to two days in solitary confinement and two years of hard labor. And to paying for the fees of the proceedings (American)" (F 204). Forgery was thus no petty crime in early American New Orleans, and the guilty were often heavily sentenced, like three men, sent to the galleys for two years, one year, and eighteen months, respectively, in November 1833 (F 233).

Slavery was at the core of the economic, political, social, and cultural fabric of New Orleans, and several crimes were connected to the institution. In some cases, people were sentenced for stealing slaves or purchasing stolen slaves, as was the case of John D. Martin, in May 1832 (F 204). For knowingly purchasing stolen slaves and merchandise, he was ordered to pay the procedure fees, do one year of hard labor, and either pay back the cost of the stolen property or serve a second year of hard labor (F 204). There were also appalling cases of slave mistreatment for which the criminals were put to trial, as was the case of Louis Donnet, in May 1832, for whipping a slave to death, a trial that resulted in a not-guilty verdict (F 204), or the infamous Mme. Lalaurie sued for mistreating her slaves in April 1832. In a relatively factual report, although interspersed with judgmental remarks, Boze writes: "Madame Lalaurie (Widow Planque) is reported to have been brought before the criminal court for her barbarous treatment of her slaves, which will occasion, they say, the laying out of another sum to declare herself absent from this complaint, and in the meantime, the martyred *nègre* remains in the custody of the city where he receives the treatment that humanity commands" (F 204).

Other crimes are alluded to, such as tomb desecration, in April, and again in May 1832 (F 203 and 204), which shows the extent of Boze's attention to all matters pertaining to crime. Nothing escaped his vigilance, and his letters can be considered a minute report on criminality in New Orleans, at least in the 1830s. Many persons were also arrested for vagrancy and, in March 1830, for instance, Boze announces the arrest by city guards of "4 vagrants, 5 slaves, and 2 sailors" on the 23rd, "5 vagrants and 3 slaves" on the 24th, "4 vagrants, 4 slaves, and 3 sailors" on the 25th, and "4 soldiers" on the 26th (F 160). Later that year, Boze indicated that "every night the police arrests vagrants and runaway slaves" (F 161). Runaway slaves were numerous, although Boze never dwells on the particulars, as if his long practice living in slave societies of the Greater Caribbean had led him to consider this sufficiently current to be disregarded. He never mentions the existence of slave patrols, although they were common practice, as other narratives of the same period attest.[65] The eyes of the narrator were clearly biased, and Boze's silences are often revealing of his mind-set and, maybe, more largely, of the spirit of the time.

Whatever the nature of the crime, there is no doubt that New Orleans was still relatively "uncivilized," which was quite natural in a city experiencing such quick development and receiving such influxes of very diverse populations. There seem to be accelerations in crime, at times, as when Boze writes, in March 1833: "suicides, murders, drowning, assassinations, thefts, and informing on without proof multiplied in a frightful way." Boze then goes on citing, in his list, unfaithful spouses, and "to cap it all, the hanging of a Spaniard," concluding on the "horrendous overflowing of vice and frantic, hateful passions" (F 218).

From Boze's narration, the frequency of criminal activities thus seem to have accelerated as the city rapidly urbanized to become the third largest in the United States; this is in keeping with the most frequent findings of urban historians of the young republic.[66] Crimes are mentioned throughout Boze's correspondence, and all kinds of criminal activity apparently went on throughout the period. The only perceptible evolution in the crimes, at least in the ones Boze cites, is that they took a more economic turn in the later period. This may have to do with the fact that New Orleans was becoming a more policed city, while developing economically to such an extent that it attracted more ruthless residents, ready to play off the benefits of the new capitalist system that was blooming in the city.

Crime was undoubtedly a fact of life in early American New Orleans, although, throughout the period, the city attempted to improve security in the streets, reinforcing the police force, enacting new laws, and devising ways to dispose of criminals. Oftentimes, the small City Guard was reinforced by groups of citizens and by the militia.[67] The lamp lighters were also used as night watch.[68] Several times in the 1830s, the municipality tried to develop its police force, devising, in 1829, a plan for the creation of a horse guard company, to be called the Orleans Gendarmes, financed through a voluntary subscription by the merchants and residents of the city.[69] They also enacted laws to ensure the protection of the citizens, instituting curfews for slaves and sailors, for instance.[70]

Conscious of the weaknesses of the police force in the fight against crime, the city also kept looking for new ways of reinforcing them. In 1831, for instance, to try to spare the militia from night service, the governor asked the federal government to grant New Orleans two companies, which was agreed upon by the federal government, on the condition that the city provide accommodations for them (F 187). If the people were often critical of the police force, they also often praised them for their efforts, if not for their effectiveness. After a significant wave of crime in March 1833, Boze writes: "we must do justice to our police; it did its utmost to terminate it" (F 218).

Prisons were indeed full, which shows that criminals were numerous, that the police were more effective than often thought, and that the expansive growth of the population created breaches in the management of urban safety. Although the measures taken seem to have often been insufficient, the state of Louisiana tried to catch up with the rapid development of its people. In March 1832, the Senate voted to appropriate funds for the building of a state prison in Baton Rouge.[71] The city of New Orleans also quickly understood the inadequacy of its penitentiaries. In May 1830, for instance, "the city authorities were presented with a plan for the building of a new prison, and they appointed a committee to assist the city surveyor in charge of indicating the most favorable location for an establishment of such a nature, which requires being close to the city and to the police guard corps in charge of standing guard night and day. But for the moment, nothing has been decided for this venture that both humanity and necessity command, and which would alleviate the suffering of those unfortunate prisoners, cluttered in an enclosure which the sun light never reaches" (F 166). Although this extract dwells on the necessity of social reform, a common topic in the country in the early nineteenth century, it also shows the large numbers of prisoners and the inadequacy of the existing infrastructure. In 1834, the city council adopted a motion for the contracting of a police and county jail. The new jail was in operation in 1837, an important addition to the prisons put up by the various municipalities.[72]

Crimes were thus numerous, and the fight against criminality was a difficult one for the authorities of the rapidly growing city. Violence, however, was not limited to the "swarm of ruffians, gamblers, adventurers, men of loose morals and of easy conscience, *chevaliers d'industrie*, steeped in the way of crime and of vice, ready to pounce on guileless victims and spoil them of their hard earned gains."[73] Violence was ever-present in what was, at the time, the first city of the American West, and when ruthless criminals were not the perpetrators, death came from those who were defending their own honor. Boze's letters would be a very rich source with which to study the sociology of duels in the 1830s. They show the importance of the practice in New Orleans, as well as the specificity of dueling in the Crescent City.

Honor Debts: Dueling in Black and White

Dueling was a relatively common practice in the early nineteenth-century United States and still more so in the antebellum South.[74] New Orleans was no exception; or rather it often looked like an exception with its high frequency of dueling in the early American period, although literature on the topic is extremely rare. Boze's letters are firsthand testimony of dueling practices in New Orleans, and they tell us much about the very unusual pattern of dueling in the city, especially in terms of classes and races. Contrary to the rest of the South, indeed, dueling in the Crescent City involved people from all different backgrounds. Ostensibly a gentlemanly practice elsewhere, duelers were of many classes in New Orleans. Reserved for whites in the rest of the South, it also involved the free people of color of the Crescent City. The correspondence thus allows a groundbreaking uncovering of an as yet totally unexplored field of the history of New Orleans.

In the nineteenth-century South, dueling was often described as "epidemic," contrary to the rest of the young republic, where "antidueling legislation . . . won quick acceptance."[75] New Orleans was one of the cradles of this very Southern activity, and was even said to be "the queen city for dueling,"[76] maybe because its Creole residents with Latin origins were especially hot-blooded, maybe also because the Saint-Domingue refugees among them opened fencing schools in the city when they fled the Haitian revolution and had to find a way to make a living.[77] New Orleans was "the educational Mecca for would-be duelists," and, in the 1830s, many dueling academies were founded, teaching either fencing or firearms, and even advertising in the local newspapers.[78] According to Albert Fossier, the number of duels also rose in the 1820s and 1830s because of the increasing heterogeneousness of the population. For him, it was the consequence of "a period of adjustment between the French and English-speaking segments of the population, with all their incompatibility of culture, nationality, morals, and of interest . . . that brought about a large number of encounters on the field of honor."[79] Although we will later see that this is an oversimplification, since duels often opposed people belonging to the same ethnic group, the increase in the practice is attested. The English traveler Harriet Martineau indicated in her *Society in America* "that in New Orleans there were fought, in 1834, more duels than there are days in the year, fifteen on one Sunday morning; that in 1835, there were 102 duels fought in that city between the 1st of January and the end of April."[80]

Although the city constantly tried to enact laws to ban the practice, as in 1818, for instance,[81] the laws were disregarded by the people and ignored by the police and judiciary, since, as an article published in *L'Abeille* on June 29, 1835, proclaimed, "none are disposed to enforce the law."[82] Historians contend that judges did not really push forward the restrictive laws, because they were reluctant to restrict personal liberties, especially in the upper class.[83] This is obvious from Boze's letters, in which many references are made to duels fought in the city. There is hardly a letter without the mention of one or more duels, and Boze regularly ends his letter on dueling, with sentences like "people say that, every week, there are similar fights at the *Cyprières* (Cypress groves) of the Bayou or of the Métairie on which the police seems to close their eyes" (F 208) or "the duels of the whites and people of color are going on and they go on slightly too often" (F 216), or "there are duels almost every week, either among whites or people of color" (F 223). Often, "duels are fought despite the law" (F 243), and, in 1831, for instance, "the fights of such nature have become very common and the champions compete in the very neighborhood of the faubourgs without fearing the law that bans them, for lack of an exemplary punishment against the offenders" (F 188). Not only did people disregard the law, but those killed or killing in a duel were not considered renegades; quite to the contrary, as is the case of Alexandre Bonneval, "the bulldog of Mr. Davis's academies," who, after being killed by Mr. Regnard, the editor of the newspaper *Le renard démocrate*, was buried with military honors as artillery officer in the legion (F 244). Similarly, Agenor Bosque, who was killed in a duel by Havana-born Francisco Sentmante y Sayas, son-in-law of local figure Bernard Marigny, was buried in a slightly "conceited" way. The mortuary convoy was quite large, and he was "followed by his company of the Orleans Dragoons on horseback," since he had been an officer in that company, as well as by many other corps of the legion (F 264). In June 1837, after three duels (a saber duel between a lawyer whose origins are unknown and a Creole; a sword duel between two Creoles; and a pistol duel between two employees of the Théâtre d'Orléans, in which one was seriously wounded), duels are expressly said to "continue in the open" (F 278).

According to the Southern honor code, dueling was a gentlemanly practice, highly codified, and used to settle personal feuds and to avenge insults. Historian Clement Eaton attributes it to "the military-mindedness of Southerners and . . . their code of virility" and to their mistrust for an overly centralized system of courts, while John Hope Franklin accounts for it by the violence inherent in slave societies.[84] According to New Orleans legend, it was a Creole specialty, and many of these *affaires d'honneur* were settled under the Dueling Oaks (also sometimes referred to as "Allard's Oaks") by Bayou St-Jean.[85]

Historians have shown that Creoles were far from being the only ones to practice dueling, and Fossier has an interesting typology of duel weaponry that confirms it. According to him, and to many other historians of Louisiana,[86] Creoles favored the rapier and the *colishemarde*, a long and slender sword, and generally stopped the fight once blood was drawn. The French favored the use of swords on horseback, a bloodier practice, which caused more fatalities. As for the Americans, they generally preferred firearms.[87] Firearm use was indeed very frequent, especially among Americans, but they were not the only ones who used them. A certain Vinot, obviously a French speaker, for instance, used a pistol (F 169), as did "two young Creoles" (F 229). Creoles, however, often used swords of all kinds, like Théophile Bosque and Prospère Leblanc (F 223), Prospère Marigny and Azenor Bosque (F 229), and Damien Augustin and Mr. Grailhe (F 232), among many others.

From what Boze writes, however, there does not seem to be a division as clear as what Fossier describes, since Creoles and people from France also used firearms. Americans, however, seem not to have used swords, unless they fought with non-Americans, who, not being the offender, could choose their weapon and opt for the sword.[88] This was apparently relatively rare. There does not seem to have been a diachronic evolution either, as both types of arms continued to be used throughout the period. The only pattern that is discernible is, among Creoles, a generational gap, with most of the duels fought with firearms being fought between "two young Creoles," while the older generation (the Marignys, Bosques, Augustins) fought mainly with swords. Some duelists, however, also fought with various arms, since, as Boze notes about Mr. Regnard, he had been involved in several honor matters and had "always been victorious, whatever the weapon" (F 244).

Boze's letters are thus a good source of information on the frequency of duels and the arms used. They also give much information about the dueling protocol in practice in New Orleans at the time, probably mainly from the accounts published in local newspapers.[89] From some detailed descriptions, readers learn about the operational processes:

> Mr. Felix Labatut, the son, experienced an event described in the newspaper *L'Abeille* that led to a cartel and, as he had been challenged, he had, according to custom, the choice of arms and it was the sword, his favorite weapon, which slightly disconcerted the officer who had preferred the pistol, not feeling too strong with the blade.
>
> The two officers' witnesses wanted it to be decided that if the sword of one of the combatants happened to escape him or if its point happened to be blunt, the one who remained armed would have the right to charge on his adversary and kill him, but this barbarous proposal not having satisfied the two witnesses of Mr. Labatut, three or four days were spent in negotiations, without reaching a decision. The latter, however, eager to see this matter end, decided to accept their condition, encouraged by his ability with the sword.
>
> On the 23rd, they went to the other side of the lake, outside of the limits, and, after crossing swords and after making a few thrusts at each other, the sword of the officer having met the guard of Mr. Labatut's, it folded so that it could no longer work, which gave the latter the right to complete the agreements which had been decided and signed. But, far from taking advantage of it, he pointed out to him that he was too loyal to benefit from his accident and kill him, and, as proof of the sincerity of his feelings, he pressed him to accept the spare sword he had brought and to get back in position. The latter listened to the wise advice and re-armed, but having been relatively seriously wounded in the first two thrusts, he cried that is enough, I find myself fully satisfied concerning the insult I was complaining about, which ended their quarrel with no more grudge.
>
> I must not forget to tell you that the victor deserved great praise from the very large audience for behaving with such honor and integrity in this fight in which he displayed much consideration and which could have ended up causing the death of the officer if it had been pursued. (F 194)

This rather long narrative—length such as this being relatively common in Boze's correspondence—provides valuable information on the unfolding of such fights. Duels were carefully planned and negotiated. The location, weapons, and rules were defined in great detail. The witnesses were of utmost importance in order to ensure the proper unfolding of the event, although rules were also set to be broken, as was the case in this duel, with the officer asking for mercy, in violation of the rules he had himself set. Quite obviously, the ritual was more important than the outcome of the duel to the duelers, and the only thing that mattered was the satisfaction of the duelers, in terms of preservation of their honor, as if the duels were more cathartic than anything else. In a pistol duel between lawyer Vinot and an unidentified man, for instance, "no one was hurt but they were content" (F 169). Often, "there were several duels between young Creoles but without unfortunate consequences" (F 170). During a duel between two young men in competition for the love of a woman, shots were exchanged, one of the combatants was very lightly wounded and "the witnesses, together with the two parties, went back peacefully to the city, feeling totally satisfied of this fortunate outcome that had ended their difference without a mortal shot" (F 188). In those cases, fighting to redress one's lost honor was more important than the outcome of the duel itself.

Duelists were not always that easily contented, and Boze relates other cases in which one duelist refused to stop before the death of one of the combatants, in a very different staging.

> That same day a duel occurred between Mr. Puchu, a bank clerk, and Mr. Cuvillier, first-class primary school teacher, colonel in the Louisiana Legion.
>
> The latter, who was walking, holding his wife's arm, in the city, was insulted by the former who complained about a recent grievance so that it ended with punches given in the street in broad daylight, which triggered a cartel, assisted by their witnesses, fought with pistols at the distance of ten paces, on the condition that they shot only when numbers one, two, and three were spoken. After agreeing, the parties went to the Métairie, where they immediately stood on guard, but the shots reached neither one nor the other but Mr. Puchu had the back of his coat transpierced by the bullet, although he was not wounded, and Mr. Cuvilier then offered him to move five paces forward and said that he would do the same and that they could touch hands and thus terminate their disagreement with an amicable peace. But the former refused, saying that the death of one of them had to ensue.

> At this response, Mr. Cuvilier opened his snuff-box and took a pinch, uttering the words: it will soon happen.
>
> They went back on guard and the two shots went, and Mr. Cuvelier was missed, but he shot his adversary dead on the spot.
>
> Mr. Cuvelier is a former French military man who seems to have a long practice at that weapon, to have a sharp sight, so that he has the custom of always shooting in the air when he has been missed to avoid disaster. (F 194)

Beyond the different outcome of this duel, the narrative shows how trained some duelists were in the practice and how uncompromising some duels were. Often, indeed, one of the duelists was wounded, in some cases badly so. In one instance, a man almost lost his leg, and suffered for months after the fight. In a duel between two merchants (Soulé and Border) from Bordeaux fighting for their interests, Border was wounded in the foot and, since the bullet could not be removed, he was left with a limp thereafter. In August 1839, a duel was fought with swords between one of the grandsons of the late Jumonville Sr., with a Creole from Martinique, the former suffering three wounds, including a serious one (F 286). Several times, one duelist was killed, as in the case of a duel between two young Creoles of color (F 235), or that of Mr. Mioton, a former confectioner on Chartres, who was killed, in February 1834 by Mr. Tremé, the son of the owner of the land that later became the well-known faubourg (F 237). Another duel, in July 1834, between two Creoles of color resulted in one death (F 242). Apparently, firearms were deadlier, but there are also several instances of saber or sword duels that ended with the death of one of the combatants, while a duel fought with rifles at sixty to eighty paces might end with no victims (F 258). Beyond instructing the readers on the codification of dueling, Boze's narrative also somehow constructs a sociology of dueling in early American New Orleans, showing, among other things, that military men and prominent people could easily challenge their opponents in this way, despite the official anti-dueling legislation. In this respect, among the many instances mentioned by Boze in his twenty years of correspondence, one is especially worth recounting.

> On the 24th instant, Mr. Denis Prieur, our mayor, was beaten up in his cart by the brothers Felix and Chistoval de Armas, public officers (one of them a lawyer, the other a notary), on his way to the lake promenade, in the company of lawyer Grimes, they unexpectedly gave him lashes and for such an insult, there will undoubtedly be a cartel which will be carried out,

people say, outside the limits of this jurisdiction and without informing the curious, impatient of knowing the outcome of the offense.

The motives that occasioned this unfortunate affair are slightly too complex for me to give you accurate details here; but people agree that this magistrate is entirely in his right and that inopportunely, an uncalled-for grudge for interests concerning his administration led these young people to such an offensive affront for this representative who enjoys, in all respects, and very rightfully, public esteem and a high reputation that deserves respect, so that the whole population in general has been strongly shocked and outraged by their scandalous behavior in this respect. (F 258)

The duel was fought the next month, on the other side of Lake Pontchartrain, and the mayor was wounded by a bullet that went through his arm, fortunately without touching the bone. The specifics of the duel are not very important. What is significant is the identity and status of the combatants, since, if the mayor himself fought in a duel against a lawyer, it is not surprising that anti-dueling laws were never enforced in New Orleans. In some cases (such as the aforementioned duel between Francisco Sentmante y Sayas and Agenor Bosque), the two witnesses were lawyers (in the case mentioned, Grimes and Grailhes), which also suggests that the legal bodies were little inclined to try to suppress the practice (F 264).

It is also interesting to examine the reasons why the duels were fought. Two young Creoles fought because of "blows given in society" (F 169). Often, the causes are extremely trivial, and lax morals, such as an immoderate taste for alcohol, were the origin of the fights, as "today's youth indulges much in debauchery" (F 208). Sometimes, the reason was more intimate, as in the case of Mr. Tuyé, a native of Bordeaux, who fought with his brother-in-law because of his wife's infidelity (F 208). Sometimes, competition between two lovers was the cause: "a duel [was fought] with swords between Dr. Ursain Landreau (the son of the former merchant on Chartres Street), of a Creole family of New Orleans, with Mr. John (German), a musician and merchant of music articles (the widower of a *demoiselle* Faury from the Port of Prince)" for the hand of Mademoiselle Hermann (F 243). Amorous competition, dishonor, or any kind of quarrel, possibly even disagreements about business matters, was thus likely to end with a duel.[90] With such a multiplicity of possible causes, the reader can only begin to imagine the total number of duels fought, especially given that there were a few serial duelers in New Orleans.

The just cited Mr. John, for instance, was not fighting his first duel, since he had killed with a pistol, a few years before, an American who had refused to marry Mademoiselle Caroline Faury, his sister-in-law, "after she had given birth to a child from these loves" (F 243). The recurrence of some names mentioned in these paragraphs clearly indicates, indeed, that some men were quick-tempered and easily ready to fight for their honor, or particularly touchy. Bosque, Marigny, and some others, were, like Mr. John, serial duelists.

Most of the examples cited indicate that dueling in New Orleans followed certain rules shared by the rest of the South. For instance, duels were clearly a manly practice, and there is no known instance of women having fought duels in New Orleans, although in the Greater South, some historians give a few—rare—examples.[91] If the gender pattern did not differ and if many duels occurred among the upper classes of society, as elsewhere in the South, there were other features that clearly differentiated New Orleans from the Anglo-American South, where dueling was generally considered to be a matter of class—and even caste—normally reserved for the Southern upper class. Not so in New Orleans, where all classes and all ethnic groups practiced dueling. Several examples show that the middle class and even the working class had adopted the practice. Many duels Boze mentions in his letters occurred among the lower classes of society. They might involve a cashier at the Banque des Marchands (F 273), two actors of the Théâtre d'Orléans (F 278), a scrap merchant (F 280), the son of an auctioneer and that of a bank cashier (F 235), a confectioner, a notary's clerk (F 258), or the bouncer of Davis's theater (F 244), among many others.

If duels were not, in New Orleans, reserved for men of gentlemanly origins, it seems clear, however, that the two duelists were, each time, more or less socially matched. "Mr. Soulé, a lawyer and alderman of the fifth ward, originally from Toulouse," challenged "Bernard Genois, a Louisiana Creole, the city hall recorder" (F 189); "two young Creoles, the son of Mr. Massy, auctioneer, and one of the sons of Mr. Prevot, the cashier of the consolidated association bank" (F 235) fought to defend their honor. Duels occurred between two journalists (F 240), two young sons of wealthy families, two artists of the Théâtre d'Orléans (F 278), two lawyers (F 258), or two merchants from Bordeaux (F 260).

Most often, the combatants were also ethnically matched, a very interesting feature in highly diverse New Orleans society. Most duels concerned two Creoles, or two Americans, or, albeit less frequently, two French speakers of diverse origins.[92] There were some duels between Americans and men of French background, although they were apparently not commonplace. A duel was fought, for instance, in June 1833, between Théophile Bosqué and Martial Gomez, "an American from New York" (F 227). In December 1833, Mr. Prospère Marigny fought with "an American" (F 235). In July 1832, a duel was fought between Mr. Layet, a Creole from Saint-Domingue, and an American (F 207). Cross-ethnic duels thus happened, the constant here being that the social matching between the two fighters was maintained.

More interestingly, a fact rarely mentioned by historians or eyewitnesses, is that duels were not infrequent among free Creoles of color from New Orleans or Saint-Domingue. This is totally undocumented in the rest of the South. In New Orleans, black people dueled in the open, and their practice was as codified as it was for white people, sharing the exact same protocol. In January 1831, Boze writes that "duels are also very frequent among free people of color" (F 175). In the late 1830s, "duels between whites and between people of color are going on" (F 216), and there are duels "almost every week either amongst whites or amongst free people of color" (F 223), the recurrence of such mentions suggesting a frequent occurrence of those events in the free population of color. Although this exception was apparently deeply rooted in the local society, there was a clear segregation between duel fighters. In all the cases involving free people of color, both combatants belonged to the same racial category, the hierarchy of races making the settlement of matters of honor unimaginable across racial barriers. Many duels are mentioned between Creoles of color, sometimes with information about the origins of the fighters ("a Creole, a natural son, and a St. Domingue one" [F 216]), sometimes even with details about their filiation ("the natural son of late Ladevèze, eye doctor" [F 223]). An honor debt could thus be fought (and even had to be fought) by free men of color, and the mere mention of the father's name, in the last case referred to, suggests that the son of a prominent citizen, although illegitimate, felt entitled to redress his grievances in the same way a legitimate son would. Another case, with the mentions that the dueling Creole of color was "a legitimate son," seems to suggest that the free man of color involved was the son of a free man of color as well, since interracial marriages were illegal in New Orleans and thus extremely rare (although some cases are spoken of by Boze). This mere mention indicates that the father did not need to be an eminent citizen of the city to justify the involvement of his son in a duel. This New Orleans exception already tells us much about the very specific three-tiered society that prevailed there.[93]

New Orleans was thus very Southern both in its addiction to duels and in the fact that duelists were exclusively men. It was, however, clearly exceptional, since men of all classes and colors fought there—although the racial and social matching of the combatants maintained the respectability of dueling—while dueling was normally considered to be white gentleman's practice in the Anglo-American South.

A violent society, where people of all classes and races did not hesitate to take up arms over a mere business or sentimental disagreement, New Orleans was doubtlessly a dangerous city in the early American period, partly because of the lingering roughness of its colonial past and partly because of the extremely rapid growth it underwent in the first four decades of the nineteenth century. If murder and duels took the lives of many of the city's residents, as in most of the frontier towns of the American West and in many of the Atlantic port cities that were experiencing similar growth, many people also paradoxically fell victim to progress. The speedy advent of new technology, associated with people's relative inability to deal with it, took a heavy toll on the city.

The Dangers of Progress

Although the oxymoronic character of this phrase is striking, the city clearly was a dangerous place to travel to and walk in during the years of intense early modernization. Like the newspapers, Boze's letters are full of narratives of accidents that reveal how often the safety of New Orleanians was jeopardized.[94] Progress came at a high price for Louisianans, essentially because technology still needed improvement and refinement. The development of steam navigation and of the railroad, in particular, although bringing to the city much prosperity, also resulted, in the early years, in many casualties. Boze's correspondence attests to this. The frequency of accidents of all kinds was very high and, here again, he is so highly committed to exactness and accuracy that his letters give a very good measure of what New Orleanians had to fear when they traveled in or to the city.

There were, of course, isolated accidents that do not really enable us to draw a complete picture of the risk. Boats capsized in storms, as was the case of the schooner *Catiche*, transporting bricks, which was overturned by a gale on the lake, in July 1830 (F 170). Boze repeatedly mentions sailing accidents: that of former district judge, Mr. James Workman, and of a boat from Bordeaux, in October 1832 (F 211), that of a boat belonging to Mr. Pommarède, of one commanded by Captain Joani, and several other vessels, in March 1833 (F 217). Sometimes, Boze refers to more occasional accidents, as when two children perish at a construction site, leading him to comment on the necessity to work toward improved safety (F 193).

This already suggests the dangers of transportation, but there were also, in that era of early modernization, many traffic accidents. The newly built, quickly expanding railroad was frequently the site of accidents. Barely five days after its opening to the public, on April 23, 1831, "the driver of one of the cars of the sliding railroad fell under the wheel of his car when it was leaving and had his head smashed. He died in less than a minute. It is, people say, the third such accident since the opening of this venture" (F 182). In late May 1832, two railroad cars crashed (F 204). In September of that year, the railroad to the lake killed again, this time "a young *nègre* who was playing, jumping from one car to the next" (F 211). In August 1833, it was one of the drivers who had an accident (F 231). In October, a German fell from a car and a *nègre* was crashed by the railroad (F 232). In June 1834, Boze comments on the railroad cars that too often ran over drunkards who had fallen asleep on the tracks (F 240).

The multiplication of coaches in the city was another cause for serious accidents. Mentioning specific cases, Boze comments that these accidents "unfortunately happen too often, by the fault of the police officers who do not get the carters who set their horses at a gallop punished" (F 234). Because people were not used to these new modes of transportation, the gap between the old world and the new was a permanent source of danger.

The heaviest toll was most certainly taken by the steamboats.[95] Steam navigation was in its early days and was rapidly developing.[96] More and more travelers were using this mode of transportation, which still required much technological refinement. Steamboat accidents were both numerous and deadly. "The steam vessels that navigate the river cause slightly too often accidents that cost the life of their passengers, so that they should be discouraged to take passage, despite all the conveniences they provide" (F 187). Most of the time, the accident was caused by the explosion of the boiler, followed by fire, and sometimes the sinking of the boat. People either died in the blast, were burned in the fire that followed, or drowned trying to escape. The losses, in persons, materials, or cargo, were often extremely heavy. In March 1830, such an accident occurred on the *Guillaume Tell*, bound for Natchez, killing five passengers and causing the loss of the entire cargo when the boat sank (F 161). In April and May 1830, three similar accidents occurred—on the *Caledonia*, with seven missing persons, eight seriously wounded, and seven less seriously wounded; the *Huntress*, with two persons killed in the explosion, two who drowned upon jumping off the boat, and eight burned; and the *Tallyho*, which caused the death of an engineer and two other employees, although the vessel was saved, as were the passengers (F 164). Several accidents are mentioned in November and December 1831 (F 192) and several more in February and March 1832 (F 198). A full report is available on a terrible accident on the

Brandywire, in April 1832 (F 202), and on the *Courtland*, in June (F 205). Boze also details several more in the summer and fall of 1833: three boats in late June (F 228); the *St. Louis*, in August (F 230); and four more in October, the *Columbia*, the *New Brunswick*, the *St. Martin*, and the *Black Hawk* (F 232). The next month, the *Caspian* burned and the *Illinois* killed twenty to twenty-five persons when its boiler exploded (F 233). In December, the starboard boiler of the *Missoury* [*sic*] exploded, burning fifteen persons, among whom seven died. Many more accidents are mentioned by Boze in the letters, showing the hardships of the introduction of progress in the old colonial world, which still featured many of the characteristics of the frontier. Throughout the period, however, the authorities seemed intent on trying to improve safety measures and to ensure the protection of both goods and men. In May 1830 already, the multiplication of accidents on steamboats made New Orleanians suggest that "the American government must subject the captains commanding the steamboats to precaution measures" (F 166). Technological progress required important adjustments, of which Louisianans were perfectly aware, but the cost was high and safety still a long way ahead.[97]

Living in New Orleans in the early days after its incorporation within the United States was undoubtedly an adventure and could be an ordeal. The city still possessed some of the characteristics of the small frontier town it had been in the colonial era. Sanitation was still lacking, and the city was prone to extreme outbreaks of a number of epidemics. Buildings were often rudimentary and thus easy prey for fire. Ruthless adventurers, fortune seekers, sailors, runaway slaves, and gangs of criminals crowded into the city. Municipal services were still struggling to keep up with the swift growth of the city, and firefighters and police officers were both insufficient in their numbers and underequipped. Modern medicine had not yet gained momentum, and doctors were often unable to fight epidemics, cure diseases, or properly tend to wounds, and mortality and morbidity were extremely high in New Orleans. To these dangers was added the very Southern practice of dueling, which, if it did not take as many lives as the previously mentioned hazards, left some New Orleanians crippled when they did not die from a duel. New Orleans was thus, in many respects, still very much the eighteenth-century city it had been under French and Spanish rule, and its residents could fall victim to disease, fire, crime, duels, and many accidents. It was hardly exceptional in these matters: all the cities of the Atlantic world experienced such unfortunate situations, spurred by their extremely rapid development, numerous contacts with the outside world, and difficulty in coping with the advent of modern modes of transportation. In New Orleans, however, what was slightly unusual was the later date at which these extreme conditions were still found, in keeping with its late entry into the bustling Atlantic world. This was enhanced by the fact that the city was paradoxically sharing with the other Southern cities a relative backwardness and some specific features, even as it was undergoing a development unheard of anywhere else in the South, only paralleled by the most active cities of the northeastern seaboard.

If those difficult conditions were indicators of the relative precariousness of the city's situation, they were also the first sign of its great vitality. The first four decades of American rule in Louisiana were indeed a period of extremely rapid growth of the city, which expanded demographically and economically at a speed absolutely unheard of in the history of New Orleans and even in the history of the young American republic. The story of this incredible urban development is one worth following through Boze's letters.

3

Progress

The years covered by Boze's correspondence were indeed, in New Orleans, an extremely busy period. The city was at the intersection of two worlds. The old colonial world was still very present, imparting to the city remnants of the rough frontier world that had been hers for almost a century. Modernity, however, was progressively invading the streets of the busy city at the crossroads of the Mississippi River and the Gulf Coast. The two decades of Boze's correspondence are the years in which it underwent the most change. From a small provincial town lagging far behind the eastern cities of the United States in 1820, it had become, by 1840, the third-largest city in the country, behind New York and Philadelphia, and on par with Baltimore.[1] This demographic boom, matched by very few cities in North America, went along with unheard-of economic development, which spurred the modernization of the city and forever changed New Orleans. Several port cities of the United States followed the same pattern, but New Orleans was the only one west of the Appalachians and south of the Mason-Dixon Line. While Charleston and Savannah steadily declined, "the city's growth rate exceeded any other large American city," including New York.[2] This extraordinary growth and development is manifest in Jean Boze's narrative. It was all the more obvious to him since, after several years spent in Cuba, he returned to New Orleans in 1828 and marveled on every page at his discovery of the changing face of the city. It is thus worth following him in his long narrative of the evolution of the city, and tracking its shift from a small colonial city to a major metropolis of the young American republic, through the building fever of the first three decades of American rule, as well as the profound modernization of urban infrastructure.

New Urban Sprawl

Boze gives little precise information about New Orleans's population growth, except in 1828, when he mentions that the city now has thirty thousand souls

(F 134). The twenty-first-century reader, however, knows of this increase, and Boze's many descriptions suggest the extraordinary expansion of the city. In two decades, its population multiplied by six. This increase is accounted for by the arrival of Anglo-Americans from the eastern states but also by a constant influx of immigrants, essentially from Europe, but also from Latin America. When one examines the figures of the arrival of alien passengers in the main port cities of the United States from 1820 to 1860, New Orleans materializes as one of the leading destinations for foreigners. With 555,322 arrivals, it accounted for 10 percent of the total influx (5,457,914), ranking only behind New York, which welcomed 3,742,532 foreigners.[3] This is all the more surprising because the historiography has often neglected New Orleans as an exception within the South, which was, by then, largely isolated from the Atlantic world.

If Boze almost never gives population figures, his letters are full of mentions of the permanent influx of migrants of all sorts into the city. In November 1818, he writes, "this country has changed much since the French peace has vomited foreigners of all calibers and the majority bad." This causes him to exclaim: "Alas, what a difference in mores from the day when we reached this country on 20 May 1809 and even from the years since 1816, 1817 and 1818; if we do not make up our minds to set striking examples, we will no longer be able to walk safely, even during the day, for each week new unfortunate events happen" (F 24). The impression he often gives of New Orleans is that of permanent chaos, provoked by a totally unchecked migratory influx into the city.

Even though many adventurers made New Orleans their new port of call in those years, the Americans flocking into its faubourgs were clearly the ones changing the face of the city. In the fall of 1818, already, Americans "have purchased a great quantity of houses and land in Faubourg Ste. Marie" (F 23). In 1828, "the market displays a great deal of business of all kinds, and which has been increased by the great number of American merchants who have come to settle in it" (F 134). In the final days of 1828, the striking feature of the city was "the Americans of all classes that have come to settle and continue to crowd here, despite their fear of yellow fever. Their number is so high that they will soon eclipse the French population and the Creole one" (F 135). Although there is evidence that this did not happen until the 1850s, contrary to what has long been assumed, Boze's prediction was well grounded.[4]

With this continuous influx of people, the city expanded, from the Carré outward. On all sides, new faubourgs developed and prospered, schematically along ethnic lines. East of Canal Street, Faubourg Ste. Marie, was the first expansion of New Orleans in the late eighteenth century.[5] Mainly settled by Anglo-American migrants after the Louisiana Purchase, it first developed as a residential district. Quickly nicknamed the "American sector," it progressively became a booming economic center in the city. The Marigny, east of the esplanade, expanded from the early nineteenth century onward, after white Creole Bernard Marigny de Mandeville set to developing land that had been part of his family plantation. Mainly peopled by Creoles of color and Saint-Domingue refugees in the territorial years, it also quickly became, although in lesser proportions, a busy area, both demographically and economically. Named after Claude Tremé, a hatter and real estate developer who owned, in the early nineteenth century, a portion of the old Morand plantation, Faubourg Tremé was the northern extension of the city, beyond North Rampart, and was mostly populated, in its early years, by Creoles of color.[6] These faubourgs underwent such an expansion that, in 1836, the Americans, convinced that they were insufficiently represented in the city council, petitioned the legislature to create a separate municipality for Faubourg Ste. Marie. A bill was passed in March by the legislature and approved by the governor, allowing the city to be divided into three separate municipalities, each with its own municipal council, although all of them were placed under the rule of a single mayor. Thus were created the First Municipality, mostly encompassing the Carré, dominated by Creoles; the Second Municipality, comprising Faubourg Ste. Marie, mainly ruled by Anglo-Americans; and the Third Municipality, in the Marigny, with a more mingled population of white Louisiana Creoles and Saint-Domingue refugees and of Creoles of color, from both Louisiana and Saint-Domingue.[7] In her groundbreaking study, French historian Marjorie Bourdelais shows that residential segregation was never strict in antebellum New Orleans. Although most Americans lived in Ste. Marie, there was a slight anglophone presence in the Carré,[8] and Ste. Marie remained predominantly francophone until 1830.[9] She contends that the division into three municipalities was the engine, rather than the result, of residential segregation, but whatever the political implications of this division, which will be discussed later, it attests to the extraordinary expansion of the city in the three decades following its incorporation within the United States.[10] In 1833, Faubourg Lafayette (which is today the Garden District) became sufficiently populated to be given the status of a city.[11] Throughout this period, neighborhoods also became faubourgs, as was the case of Carolton, in the mid-1830s (F 273).

Boze gives constant indications of this progressive change in the distribution of residences and commercial facilities. In December 1828, he writes,

"This country is becoming every day more majestic through the beautiful buildings, of very good taste, that are being built constantly in all areas, as well as by its improvements that strike with surprise and admiration those that return after an absence of a few years" (F 134). "It is now so big, so majestic, so regular in its constructions in all aspects, etc. that if the construction of the beautiful houses and the beautiful buildings continues in force, with all kinds of improvements and embellishments, as useful as pleasant, and in very refined tastes, it will soon be among the great cities of the continent, and even of Europe" (F 135). In January 1831, "this city that we found very beautiful and big when we arrived in the year 1809 was but a faubourg compared with what it is today, much more beautiful and much bigger due to the very numerous beautiful buildings that are being built without interruption, so that soon there will be no vacant lot and it will be able, within a few years, to vie with the capital of this American continent. You will be bedazzled by its majesty, if you return to it, as I still like to think you will, because the faubourgs are new cities, embellished by beautiful public squares" (F 179). Time and again, Boze describes improvements to the faubourgs. In 1829, for instance, "the Faubourg Ste. Marie, that grows each year with splendid buildings, will soon be a new city and its population is so numerous that I have counted about twelve pharmacies in this area alone, with many beautiful churches, Lutheran, Calvinist, Protestant, &, so that the only thing that is missing there now is a synagogue!" (F 144). In 1830, "The faubourgs, with their banquettes, are starting to be in conformity with those of the city and these neighborhoods are elevated by the establishment of several public squares tastefully surrounded and shaded with alleys of already grown willows" (F 174). By then, "a really beautiful square, called Washington Square, has been established in the Marigny. It has, on its side, a tower with a bell for fire warnings, and enhances the neighborhood where the banquettes, 7 to 8 feet wide, are better made than in the city because they have been laid in brick at the expense of the owners and because the others have been entrusted to a company of workers who have been careless in several streets, so that they will often require repair" (F 175). Again in 1830, "Faubourg Ste. Marie now enjoys a beautiful covered market, since this neighborhood has now become slightly too substantial not to be granted this necessary building. Because it is a new town, with a number of magnificent brick buildings with 2 and 3 and 4 stories and highly populated, to the point that you need to be familiar with its new streets not to risk losing your way there in the full heat of noon. It has been increased by several blocks on its front, where customers formerly flocked, which now forms the street called Chapitoulas [*sic*], with beautiful houses and beautiful brick stores" (F

153). In January of 1834, the Marigny was still being developed "every day with a great number of beautiful buildings erected in force and a quantity of tasteful houses. It has grown so much in beauty that it is no longer recognizable" (F 235).

The expansion was so swift that "by 1830 New Orleans had become one of the most important cities in the country and its commercial and retail center had begun to shift from Chartres and Royal streets to Canal and the American area uptown."[12] Another area of intense development was the riverfront. Large houses, hotels, and commercial buildings were built on Levée (today's Decatur) after the city council decided to sell public land along the river. There was a long and bitter controversy concerning ownership of this land (known as the Batture controversy), but the various oppositions only temporarily checked the development of the area, and buildings ended up covering the total length of the riverfront, for both residential and commercial purposes.[13] The increasing commercial importance of the river made this expansion indispensable, as did the ever-growing competition between the Creoles and Americans, which made the Creoles intent on emulating their counterparts, who were prospering in Faubourg Ste. Marie.

In the spring of 1831, "the two faubourgs [Ste. Marie and Marigny] are now two new towns and the streets of the northern esplanade of the city will soon join the neighborhood of the Bayou [Tremé], because building continues rapidly" (F 183). This expansion was favored by the opening of the railroad and, in May, "property in the Faubourg Marigny, in land as well as in houses, sells today at exorbitant prices (we would never have expected) because of the strong desire of the Americans to have, in this neighborhood, establishments that our capitalists envy, leading them to hurry to make acquisitions, and especially the Compagnie des Architectes which endeavors to build nice pleasant houses" (F 185). In 1835, Faubourg Ste. Marie had a handsome theater and a beautiful covered market for meat and vegetables, a bank named du Canal, attractive public squares, a stock exchange, hospitals, orphanages, "beautiful churches for their Protestant devotion," circuses, and "an elegant hall where the legislature meets every year" (F 253).

Several Atlantic cities of the United States, all located in the Northeast of the young republic, underwent parallel evolutions. Urban historians have noted both the expansion of the urban centers and the grandeur of the new constructions. The 1820s, in particular, were a period of important architectural activity, in New York, Philadelphia, and Baltimore. In Philadelphia, in the wake of the sojourn of architect Benjamin Latrobe in the city, Greek Revival rapidly spread over the city, progressively turning it "from brick to marble."[14] When he left Philadelphia, Latrobe sojourned and worked in Washington and then in New Orleans, bringing to those cities the improvements he had first introduced in Philadelphia.[15] Although New Orleans lagged behind the northeastern cities, going from wood to brick rather than from brick to marble, it underwent extraordinary improvements, all the more so because the competition between the Anglo-Americans arriving in the city and the old Creole population entailed "the duplication of everything."[16] New Orleans thus followed a pattern common to the northeastern Atlantic cities, although in greater proportions, due to a specific historical context, progressively becoming an exception within the American South, especially at a time when the South started developing agrarian theories and rejecting urbanization altogether.[17]

Boze's letters give a good measure of this exception. When he returned to New Orleans, in 1828, after his long stay in Cuba, he marveled at length about the changes the city had undergone in his absence: after wondering about the improvements that occurred in the eight years of his Cuban stay, he concludes, "The new banks are today buildings of great beauty, in particular that of the state of Louisiana, next come those of Louisiana, of the United States, and of Orleans. They are all located in the same center, on Royal, at the corner of Conti" (F 134). The city is now so beautiful that it will soon be "one of the wonders of this world, which makes the Creoles swell with pride at this prospect" (F 135).

The 1830s were a period of intense building within the Carré. The vacant spaces were filled in; old houses were demolished, new storied brick houses with wrought-iron balconies were built in their stead. In the spring of 1831, "the wooden house of the late Father Antoine and those of his neighborhood were demolished up to the brick house at the corner of Royal Street where a Catalan had his shop so that now you can see nature on both sides of the parish behind which there is now a square that still has no purpose" (F 182). But these vacant lots never remained long vacant. New streets and alleys were added, to accommodate this building expansion, Exchange Alley, for instance. Row houses were built in many areas, mainly by the Compagnie des Architectes, along Decatur, between Ursulines and Hospital (now Governor Nicholls), but also by the Gurlie and Guillot Company, at the corner of Royal and Orleans, for instance, or by James Gallier on Burgundy, among others.

The early 1830s brought new building techniques and new architectural fashions, as well as a clear acceleration in the construction impulse and, all in all, increased beauty to the city. In the spring of 1831, "the capitalists are still building without respite beautiful storied brick houses with beautiful iron balconies in all the areas, which increases its embellishment" (F 182). In July, "houses in the city and beautiful buildings continue with force and, very soon, there will not be any vacant lot, and they still sell at high prices, whatever the neighborhood." In September, the Ursulines "continue to have beautiful storied houses with commercially adequate stores built on their land" (F 188). In 1832, magnificent constructions are being added to the city everywhere, "castles with two or three stories, in brick, and with iron balconies artistically worked all along the buildings" (F 196), all giving the city great splendor. In the fall of 1833, two- and three-story houses are being built, "so that a time will come when it will be impossible to see in the city the houses and barracks that we found when we arrived." The city is "so changed in grandeur and beauty that you would be filled with wonder and would be obliged to take a guide for a few days, for it would be unrecognizable to you after an absence of some 15 years" (F 232). Progressively, wooden houses became rarer, and "the residents predict that, within a few years, New Orleans will compete with the Capital" (F 238). Building was so swift that, in 1834, within a few months of the sale of the old barracks, there were already many elegant houses with tenants, which "formed a new street starting from the corner of the Quarter to the fire hydrant, across the Rue des Ursulines" (F 239). The mention of new streets is recurrent, as when, in March 1836, Boze describes the new levee that goes from the Mint to the Customs, with "beautiful houses of one, two, and three stories," which "form several new streets and hide forever the shops of the old levee of [Ste-Gême's] time" (F 267). In August 1837, the Compagnie des Améliorations (Company for Betterment), after buying property in the city, created a new street starting in the middle of Rue St. Louis, across the street from the new stock exchange, and expanding to the Rue de la Douane (Customs, now Iberville). "On both sides, there are now brick houses with two stories, with shops on the ground floor" (F 270).

The recurrence of the indication of the swift building of extraordinary houses, making the hiring of a guide necessary to anyone returning to the city after some years of absence, gives a good measure of the change. New Orleans was then becoming a major urban center, and the many aggrandizements and improvements of the city were often attributed to the arrival of the "numerous American population" (F 255). Most structures even tended to be duplicated by the constant competition between the two main ethnic groups present in the city. In the summer of 1835, the Americans started building a beautiful stock exchange at the corner of Rue Royale and Rue de la Douane (F 257). The Compagnie des Améliorations had bought half a block at the corner of Chartres and Royale, as well as the old stock exchange, and was having the old buildings torn down to also build a "majestic new exchange" and a splendid new hotel, which was to have, on the ground floor "all the offices of commerce and brokerage," which would complement "other buildings of a new taste that will, by the grandeur and the majesty of the whole, eclipse the brilliance of the numerous and various buildings that the Americans have erected in Faubourg Ste. Marie, the neighborhood these nationals have adopted by preference" (F 258). Once completed, the stock exchange was expected by the Gallic population to "reach such perfection that it will be placed after the Seven Wonders of the World" (F 267). There were to be four entrances (on St. Louis, Chartres, Bourbon, and Toulouse), and the building was being "built of cut marble and sandstone on each façade," which shows that the move "from brick to marble" was also starting in New Orleans, albeit a few years later than in the northeastern cities (F 268). The whole urban architecture of the city was changing, emulating the already developed Northern cities in the eyes of the residents. In 1835, a new building was being erected (for the Banque des Citoyens) on Toulouse, between Chartres and Royal, right up against the new stock exchange that was being built on St. Louis and Royal. The building was going up very quickly, with "a beautiful dome rising in its middle with a very big rotunda that will have its own belvedere" (F 265).

Although not all of them were carried out, there were plans for permanent improvement and embellishment, causing New Orleanians to dream of a time "when the Northern capital will have to yield before" their city. Among the signs that "New Orleans has been moving forward at such an extraordinary pace in the past ten years" were plans for the expansion of the Théâtre d'Orléans, plans for the demolition and rebuilding of St. Louis Cathedral, "with more majesty, taste, and grandeur" up to the banquette of Rue Royale, and the development of several public buildings. The whole city was seeking magnificence, which sometimes slowed down construction. The stock exchange, for instance, was going more slowly than expected, because the building company had to import from the North the marble and sandstone that reached New Orleans "cut at the right size," as was also the case of the "fluted marble columns of very great height and with the circumference of the mast of a vessel of 74" (F 268). The stock exchange finally opened on January 6, 1838, for ladies and their escorts and, on January 8, for everyone else (F 280).

Everywhere, progress was noticeable, with the organization of new squares that were constantly beautified and improved. The old Fort St. Charles had been, by the spring of 1830, turned into a beautiful public place, with grass, where the city intended to plant trees. Embellishment was pursued throughout the summer, and the city planned the planting of trees around the square and in alignments within the square (F 170). The banquettes were enlarged around the square to enable pedestrians' easy passage. A few months later, in front of City Hall, "the ground has been very well prepared and cambered with a mixture of gravels and seashells, so that the rains can no longer render it muddy" (F 174). Everywhere, the city looked improved and even dignified, as shown by "the beautiful square near the basin which is today elegantly surrounded with rows of beautiful trees, ash trees, willows, including weeping willows, embellished by a plot of lawn where the circus used to be," where the city intended to erect an elegant building for the legislature.

The political context of these early American years manifestly accounts for the vitality of the city. Although New Orleans's expansion was not unheard of and was observable in the northeastern Atlantic cities, the city was definitely a particular case in the American South. Moreover, the building fever meant that the city was in dire need of urban improvements, and New Orleans, here again, proved to be well ahead of her Southern sister cities and rather in keeping with the main northeastern urban centers, New York, Philadelphia, Boston, and Baltimore.

The Dawning of Urban Modernity

With expansion, indeed, came urban evolution, as in other developing Atlantic ports, much earlier than the old Southern capital of Charleston. Throughout the two decades of the correspondence, the city underwent extraordinary improvements in terms of urban infrastructure and sanitation. Boze's letters are a wonderful testimony to that urban improvement, all the more so because of his talents as a chronicler and because of the care he took in narrating minute details of these improvements.

Urban improvement was common among the big cities of the young republic. The fear of epidemics, the rapid growth of the population, and the constant expansion of the urban centers, but also the improved scientific knowledge and techniques, favored this development. The early nineteenth century was also a period of social reform, following the stabilization of the new nation. Interestingly, New Orleans followed the quick pace of the cities of the old British colonial world, instead of lagging far behind, as it had during the colonial period. Its recent inclusion into the young republic did not impair its integration—quite the contrary. Boze's letters contain numerous references to all these urban improvements: the paving of the streets, the development of a sewer system, and the progressive installation of gas lighting and, maybe more importantly, the water system, including in private houses.

In the early nineteenth century, cities and towns had dirt streets, which became muddy at first rain and encouraged the dumping of all kinds of refuse, thereby creating conditions for diseases like cholera to exist. New Orleans was no exception, but the city rapidly undertook improvements and, by 1840, most streets were paved, putting the Crescent City far ahead of most American cities, especially in the South. To give one example, Richmond had very few paved streets in the late 1840s and no street lighting until the 1850s.[18] Boze's letters guide the reader along on the paving of the streets. In the late summer of 1831, "some of the streets are entirely paved, starting with that of the stores of the levee, and some of them are only paved over 3 to 4 feet along the banquettes, but with, in their middle a stripe in seashell, very well made, which gives the carriages and carts a very gentle progress, since they no longer find the mud of before which was so unpleasant to their progression" (F 189). In February 1832, the residents of Ste. Marie signed a petition for the paving of their streets (F 196). In March 1832, Rue Bourgogne was still not paved but was to be by the summer, at the latest (F 202). In May, Levée and Bourbon were paved; the paving of Orléans was starting, all in shell from Barataria (F 204).[19] In March 1833, Rue Royale was entirely paved "from one end of the esplanade to the other" (F 217). In May, the levee of Faubourg Ste. Marie was entirely paved in stone, from the steam cotton press on, with beautiful banquettes, and it was now "very pleasant for pedestrians as well as for carriages which now no longer meet the uncomfortable mud and dust of the past" (F 223).

With the paving of the streets came the building of the banquettes, enabling an easier cohabitation between vehicles, horses, and pedestrians. New banquettes, 7 to 8 feet wide, were built throughout the Carré and progressively expanded to the faubourgs. The municipality paid for the construction work, and the owners of the houses paid back two-thirds of the money to the city, in proportion to the size of their property (F 166). "By the width they have been given, they facilitate the passage of pedestrians who are no longer uncomfortable, even when they walk six abreast" (F 189). In March 1833, "all the streets of faubourgs Ste. Marie and Marigny now have banquettes 8 to 10 feet wide, very well made in brick, and they can now be walked along on dry feet, even in rainy weather" (F 218). By the mid-1830s, most of the Carré and the faubourgs were thus paved and endowed with banquettes, which made the city both more convenient and more pleasant to walk around for its residents and visitors. Wooden stairs were added to access the houses from the banquettes in the Carré, giving New Orleans one characteristic architectural feature that has survived into the twenty-first century.

This improvement in infrastructure already made the city less muddy and healthier, but there was still much to do to eradicate the main sources of the terrible epidemics that ravaged the city in the summer and fall. Many attempts were made by city authorities, in the twenty years of the correspondence, to improve the sanitary conditions of the city's residents. Although they still had not located the origins and mode of transmission of yellow fever, the connection between cholera and poor sanitary conditions was suspected. They thus worked on reducing the sources of stagnant water that were partly the cause of the noxious air propitious to the propagation of disease. The correspondence mentions, several times, the construction of sewers, as in March 1832, when sewers were set all along Claiborne, as well as on Franklin, Tremé, and Jackson (F 202), an extremely early date if one considers that the New York sewer system was begun only in 1849.[20]

Pursuing the sanitation efforts, in the fall of 1835, a company was also established to work on the drainage of the swamps that still existed within the city district. This enterprise was commanded by the necessity of improving health in the city and the countryside around it. Rapidly, the company began surveying all the swampy places, including the plantations of Gentilly, including, of course, Ste-Gême's. City authorities were obviously perfectly aware of the importance of modernizing New Orleans and giving its residents healthier living conditions. The population increase and concerns about the spread of epidemics also led the authorities to open new cemeteries in the faubourgs (F 214, F 231). Despite the addition of those new cemeteries, another one had become necessary in 1834, "because the old ones have long been full of corpses, which makes us fear epidemics in the summer if we do not hurry to make this acquisition of such a pressing necessity" (F 239). New services were thus constantly provided to the residents, whose growing numbers had rendered the existing infrastructure insufficient and obsolete.

In the 1830s, at a relatively early date, the municipal administration also made water available to an increasing number of residents. New Orleans was no pioneer in this respect, since Philadelphia had built the first municipal waterworks at the turn of the century, the project designed by Benjamin Latrobe being completed in 1801.[21] Even in the South, Charleston had already established Charleston Waterworks, although it was much less developed than the Philadelphia water project, which allied a system of public water delivery to a service to private consumers.[22] New Orleans was then still in the final years of its colonial stage, which explains the relative belatedness of the implementation of a city water system, together with its position on the bank of the Mississippi River, which made access to water comparatively easy. An article from the *Courrier* of June 12, 1834, announced the beginning of construction by the Banque du Commerce to provide water to the city.[23] A cartload of earth had already been brought to the block purchased in the faubourg to this effect, to erect a little mound on which the "machine" was to be placed. A large inaugural ceremony took place on the occasion, in the presence of the governor, the mayor, members of the Corporation, and all the authorities of the city, to inaugurate "a work so useful and for so long desired." The pomp of the ceremony shows the significance of the project in the eyes of New Orleanians. A procession started at 5 in the afternoon, on horseback and with carriages (about one hundred of them), and the mayor himself unloaded some of the earth, to provide a safe location for the machinery that had been purchased in Liverpool and was coming down the Mississippi River on board the *William Brown* (F 240). The first plan was to deliver water to the different neighborhoods of the city. In early 1836, the public works to supply the city with water from the river had started. By then, they had "started digging canals in Rue Chartres to place the pipes that will bring the water to the city." At each of the four corners of the streets, there were fountains or pumps, "as well as in the middle of each block, following the example of cities in the North." This new installation was to be both useful and convenient, and people would no longer have to send their servants get the water "by the riverbank, where it is not always clean enough to drink." The pumps were "very well built of cast iron and neatly covered with wood paneling." They were placed as the digging progressed, although they would not be in operation until the connection with the river was made (F 260). Pumps were even being installed on Rue Royale, where the street's residents would have the option to have water in their homes if they paid for it (F 264). In the spring of 1836, the fountains had been installed, although at that point, only the firefighters used them. The city was now ready for an essential expansion of the network.

Indeed, once water was flowing to the various areas, the Carré as well as the faubourgs, the city rapidly started planning a system of water delivery to individual houses. Again, New Orleans lagged behind the Atlantic cities of the Northeast, especially Philadelphia, where, in 1811, "2,127 Philadelphians subscribed for water"[24] and where, by 1836, "1,530 bathrooms were receiving water from the Fairmount Water Works" alone.[25] But it was still ahead of many others, such as Baltimore, where water was supplied to only the richest neighborhoods until the water supply company was purchased by the city, in 1854.[26] In the fall of 1834, a new project was well on its way to circulate water in the entire city of New Orleans, with fountains in individual houses (F 246). The city had committed to paying the Bank of Commerce (as indicated in the bank's charter) the amount of money spent for the introduction of the water to the whole city. The residents who wanted water in their homes had been provided with the service, on the condition that they pay for the entire installation. They paid for the digging (1 gourde per foot), for the pipe running from the banquette to their house, and for the tap, and 30 gourdes a year for the service (F 268). Although the equipment found in the individual houses still left much to be desired, progress was on its way, and water was only one aspect of it.

As in the other main cities of the young republic, New Orleans's City Hall and the Corporation also installed a new system of gaslights, more efficient than the old system of oil street lighting. Although New Orleans was a little late compared to New York, Boston, and Baltimore, its gas system started operating two years before Philadelphia's.[27] An American was entrusted with the task of putting up the new system, and in the spring of 1834, pipes had already been laid in several streets (F 238). In November 1834, Rue Chartres, "which is considered the main street for commerce," was about to be lit by gas lamps. The pipes were already in the ground, and there was a pole of fluted iron at each corner, 10 to 12 feet high, with a spear to place the lamp. The new device was to be much brighter than the old oil lighting. The city had conducted tests at the end of Canal and also in Faubourg Ste. Marie and in several public buildings of the Carré. If it worked on Chartres, they intended to expand the device to the whole city. The city council had granted fifty thousand dollars to the company in charge of the installation (F 246). As was the case for water, residents could also get the gas brought to their homes, on the condition that they paid for their consumption (F 268).

Besides these important infrastructural improvements, the city continued to be restored and remodeled. Public buildings were constantly rehabilitated or replaced. In December 1829, for instance, the general hospital located on the esplanade of Faubourg Ste. Marie was renovated (F 152). A few years later, the old Charity Hospital on Canal was rehabilitated to harbor the legislature while the new hospital was being completed (F 213). In 1834, the city started building a new penitentiary in Tremé, two blocks behind the esplanade, in a straight line from Rue d'Orléans (F 238). In 1837, the prison was ready to open (F 275). In May, the prisoners were transferred to this "extraordinary" building, which had different areas for the various classes and colors, but also for civil and criminal sentences, and offered the convicts "a very humane stay." Because it was vast, well ventilated, and extremely convenient, it was expected "to soften their painful situation in this penitentiary asylum that has been so long desired" (F 278). The movements of reform of the health and prison systems had manifestly reached the faraway western city of New Orleans.

Throughout the period, the city also modernized its transportation system, opening companies of carriages for rent, building canals, and, the most notable improvement of all, building a railroad from the city to the lake. This movement was, again, common to the developing Atlantic cities of the young republic, although at a pace that varied greatly from one city to the next. New York and Philadelphia had led the way.[28] Canals were a priority in New Orleans, due to the importance of water transportation, both fluvial and maritime.[29] In the spring of 1819, already "the legislature has decreed the opening of the Marigny navigation canal, which will bring to a very high price the properties of that area and its district" (F 34). In the summer of 1831, purchases were starting for a new canal project from above Faubourg Ste. Marie to the river that would enable navigation from the river to the lake. With a width of 70 feet and a depth of 14, the canal was to permit the navigation of vessels of "2 to 300 tons which will be able to navigate on still waters until they reach the harbor, which will be, once it succeeds, very advantageous to maritime commerce by avoiding the passage by the river, longer, more difficult because of wind variations and currents, and more expensive because of the steam boats that must be used to cover promptly the 40-league journey from the Balize[30] to the city" (F 189). Several of Boze's letters detail the progress of the construction by "the Irish and German lions" (F 194), completed with the addition of two lighthouses at the Balize (F 196). In keeping with the essential role of New Orleans as a navigation hub, new levees were built, as in March 1832 in the Marigny, with wooden wharfs added along the harbor and new bridges built to facilitate movement. Canals were added everywhere, from St. Bernard, Fanchon and the Marigny to Bayou St. Jean, with new wharfs, although "they are not as beautiful as those of Faubourg Ste. Marie" (F 202). The port that expanded from the Place d'Armes to the cotton press was equipped "with quays solidly and conveniently built both in length and in width for the uploading and downloading." Although it was not really convenient for merchants, because it was relatively far from the business and commercial center located in the Carré, "the road there was entirely paved and established with large banquettes for pedestrians" (F 265).

The other main infrastructural improvement was the railroad. While in most of the other developing cities of the Atlantic, the railroad was dedicated to improving intercity connections,[31] in New Orleans, it was, once again, conceived as a way to better connect the navigation systems, linking the city to Lake Pontchartrain, which, with its opening onto the sea, was essential in the transportation of goods and passengers from the Gulf to the city. In March 1830, the railroad was under construction and, once it was finished, hopefully the following year, it was expected to be "among the marvels" and to "give a greater value to the plantations neighboring this beautiful public path of a new invention" (F 161). The railroad was a symbol of progress, extremely convenient for many activities, especially the recreational activities in the summer at the lake (F 164). With the railroad, New Orleanians planned to establish "a little town on Lake Pontchartrain, as well as a port which will ease commerce through the railroad to transport merchandise into the city, which will then give the new property a great value" (F 183). In June 1830, the railroad was opened on Sunday the 13th for a trial, although it was closed again the next day for more work (F 167). In the summer, the company decided to renew the operation every Sunday to enable people to go to the lake (F 170). A few months later, in April 1831, it was finally fully operational: "On the 23rd instant, the sliding railroad opened to the public and the cars of this service carry about thirty people per trip and others less, according to their size, some are double-decked. . . . Passengers pay 3 *escalins* one way and 3 more for their return. The loading point for this journey to the lake is on the levee near the property of Mr. Marigny and, within a half hour, you reach your destination, drawn by horses until now, while expecting the arrival of the steam mechanisms that are to get here very shortly. By means of this invention, the duration of the same trip will only amount to ten minutes, people say." A huge banquet was given for the opening ceremony, confirming the importance to New Orleanians of "this wonderful venture [which] really is a marvel that honors its director and the shareholders who supported it by their means to see it reach a perfect success" (F 182). The new railroad was indeed a recurrent object of marvel in the city. In August 1832, the railroad was said to cover the journey to the lake in seven to eight minutes (F 209). The arrival of the Pontchartrain steam locomotive was proudly announced, and New Orleanians flocked to enjoy the "sight of progress offered by this wonder" that covered twenty miles in an hour and drew cars carrying three to four hundred persons (F 211). This new means of easy, cheap, and rapid transportation of masses of people changed the face of the city and the lives of its residents.

New Orleans was thus becoming, in every way, a modern city and was losing, little by little, the old frontier atmosphere it had had when it was purchased by the United States. For with demographic and urban development also came the advent of a new society. Although it often appeared to residents less welcoming than it had been in its first years of national existence, the city clearly displayed a society in constant progression. Once again, New Orleans was relatively exceptional in the young American republic, the only Southern town rapidly becoming a leading city, the only modern city in the West. This exceptional aspect of New Orleans was connected to its economic choices. While the Northeast was rapidly embracing the path to industrialization, and while the rest of the South was emphasizing agriculture, New Orleans became the champion of commerce, an obvious choice for a city located at the confluence of the main access to and from the West, the Mississippi River, and the gateway to the Caribbean and Latin America. Almost immediately replacing Charleston, "this once flourishing city,"[32] New Orleans was propelled to second national rank in terms of commercial exchanges and became, in the 1820s, barely two decades after its acquisition by the United States, the uncontested capital of the South.

An Urban Enclave in the Rural South

The growth of the population made the city a much bigger market, a feature common to all the developing cities of the Atlantic world, especially the ports of the northeastern United States. In New Orleans, however, this development was enhanced by the unusual situation of competition between two main segments of the population: the old Gallic group and the newly arrived Anglo-Saxon group. The enterprising Americans, constantly emulated by other ethnic groups, in particular the Creoles, brought wealth and vigor to the city. The development of infrastructure and new means of transportation had opened up the city to the rest of the nation and to Atlantic traffic, turning its harbor into one of the busiest places in the United States. Its location at the crossroads of the Mississippi River and the Caribbean Sea made it an easy connection point between North America, South America, and Europe. Products from the northern Mississippi Basin and Canada went through the city toward southern countries and Europe, while the Caribbean and Latin America sent their more exotic products to the Northern United States. To these hemispheric exchanges were added intercontinental ones, so that, by 1820, the harbor had become the largest employer in the city.[33] In 1836, New Orleans had become the first exportation harbor in the United States, ahead of New York, and the merchant value of river transportation on the Mississippi River went from twenty-two million dollars in 1830 to almost fifty million dollars in 1840.[34] The development of steamboats and the new railroad opened up the city, which, in earlier periods, could be reached only with difficulty.[35] Products from the North thus found their way to the New Orleans harbor, making the city "the *entrepot* of the west and the gateway to the Mississippi."[36] Cotton, in full development in the southern Mississippi Basin, was the first beneficiary of this development of transportation, as were cereals, sugar,[37] wood,[38] and dry goods. The harbor of New Orleans ranked first in the United States for the exportation of flour.[39] This quick development, in less than twenty years, made the overall economy boom, in New Orleans still more than in the Atlantic ports of the Northeast.

Agriculture was, of course, still an important part of the economy, even in the urban environment. Plantations spread along the Mississippi River but also in proximity to New Orleans, along Bayou St. John, for instance.[40] Although some years were less prosperous than others, all in all, agriculture made the city vital. Sugar, of course, despite its hazards, was the flagship product.[41] However successful, cultivating sugar made the plantation economy and the whole New Orleans economy strongly dependent on the weather, with any rainy episode, storm, or period of drought or frost jeopardizing the entire economy of the city. Year after year, Boze's November newsletter gives news similar to what he expressed in 1833, which was that "the sugar crops have suffered so much that the planters guarantee that they will be scanty again, yielding 100 to 150 *boucauts*[42] where they would normally yield 400, and the deficit will apply proportionally to the rest in small or in large." This was all the truer because the recent development of the sugar industry in Louisiana, which required considerable equipment and trained sugar makers, had obliged the planters to incur debts: "the sugar crop in this state is once again this year totally missed, which gives extreme worries to its planters, especially those who must fulfill loans falling due" (F 233). The conversion of Louisiana to a sugar economy was so recent that it was difficult to regulate the market. In January 1834, sugar was impossible to sell in New Orleans "for this commodity is at present without demand, because the levee is packed with *boucaults* and no purchaser is present to buy them. But as the crop was unsuccessful again this year, we hope it will be in demand later and maybe at the price of $7 per quintal, according to demand" (F 235). In May 1831, the situation was so dire that buyers refused to send their boats to the plantation piers and obliged the planters to send the sugar to town so that they could inspect it more easily, "as do the cotton planters who send their bales to the stores of their middlemen in New Orleans" (F 185).

The information Ste-Gême received about his Gentilly plantation is extremely useful to determine the evolution of agricultural activities. Louisiana, in the 1830s, was clearly dedicated to the cultivation of sugar cane, and a number of large plantations were profitably involved in this production. Small plantations of the southern areas were also turning to sugar, as was the case with Ste-Gême's Gentilly plantation. This crop was not an easy one and was vulnerable to the swings of the weather. The reader follows the vicissitudes of sugar planting through the reports from Gentilly that Boze writes. In March 1830, the planting season had started, but the heavy rainfalls of February and early March, as well as a light frost, had been "prejudicial to the seedlings," and Auvignac Dorville, the manager of the plantation, a Louisiana native, had had to "immediately have recourse to the big planters of this crop to obtain new seedlings and manage to replace on time part of the first ones" (F 160). This profitable crop was luring small planters into trying to capitalize on the initial successes, although it was a very fragile crop, risky for plantations of limited acreage. The difficulty of sugar planting lay mainly in the need for a lot of manpower that small planters generally did not have. The manpower on the Gentilly plantation was "so weak that it hardly meets all the needs of the plantation which will remain a petty sugar plantation if [Ste-Gême] does not add the new forces that it highly needs now to enable it to reach the rank of the sugar plantations with high revenues." According to Boze, the plantation needed twenty-five to thirty more slaves since it had turned to sugar. Without an addition that would about double the working force, it would vegetate, despite its great potential (F 163).

The turning of plantations to sugar was costly because of the "great spending for the plantation's establishment into a sugar plantation" (F 171). The yield varied from year to year. More and more land was taken from other crops to plant new cane (F 176), and planters tried to vary the cane seedlings, using, whenever they could, the high "green ribbons," which were about ten feet high, although they still often relied on the "Creole" canes, smaller but also much less expensive (F 176). Whenever the planters could rely on the former for the majority of their crops, the plantations could become "plantations of the first rank or at least of the second" (F 177). The planters were victims of the weather—of drought, heavy rains, or early frosts—which either impaired the growth of the cane (F 201) or flattened the crop (F 173). Sometimes all those factors put the sugar economy at risk, as was the case in 1831, when the cane "perished due to frosts, but also to the abundance of rains and periods of drought during their growth" (F 213). Even when the crop was perfect until late in the season, as in 1833, early frosts could reduce the juice content and thus cut the expected harvest in half (F 233), or heavy rains could delay the harvest, as was the case in the fall of 1834 (F 246). Sugar planters were also subject to mechanical incidents that brought the mills to a halt for a few days (F 177). Boze's constantly reporting on the health of the slaves also shows how dependent the planters were on their enslaved manpower. Several times, enumerating the illnesses of some of the slaves, he insists on the fact that they delayed the harvest. Most of the time, however, he tells Ste-Gême that all the slaves are in good health and taken care of by his manager and overseer, Auvignac Dorville, and by the doctor Dorville calls whenever he is unable to manage without him. Economic conditions were harder on the small plantations than the slightly larger ones, as shown when Ste-Gême's plantation is compared with that of his neighbor Hopkins. The higher acreage and the forty slaves (compared with Ste-Gême's twelve) yielded about 200 *boucaults*, compared to Ste-Gême's 40 to 50 (F 177).

Even when crops were relatively abundant, they still had to be sold, which sometimes proved difficult. Between January and May 1831, Boze repeatedly says that the crop was still in storage and unsold, while Dorville was already planting new sugar cane (F 178–83). The same situation occurred again in 1834 (F 236–38), and the sugar was sold only in late May (F 239), which means that, most years, seedlings had to be purchased before the crop could be sold, leading to indebtedness, or at least a shortage of cash flow. Even if sugar planting was extremely demanding, "the plantation, with the establishment of a sugar activity, has tremendously increased in value compared to when it was reduced to the daily gardening activity" (F 215). And when the year was a bad one for sugar (both the crop and its subsequent sale), as in 1833, Dorville returned to food crops that were then sold in the city's markets (F 222).

Despite this new focus on sugar, small plantations kept on cultivating a wide variety of products, especially in the vicinity of New Orleans. Many of those nearby plantations, far from following the model of the big sugar and cotton plantations, were often dedicated to producing food crops that were sold in the city markets. Ste-Gême's Gentilly plantation, for instance, produced timber and firewood (F 163), fodder and pasture (F 208), as well as corn (F 168) and food supplies (F 176), including peas, pumpkins (F 208), vegetables, and fruit (F 275). Sometimes there are details about the fruit and vegetables produced, because a stronger bout of frost has damaged the artichokes or the orange trees (F 280) or because the slow economy causes the French melons and watermelons to be so cheap that Dorville despairs at the abundance of his crop (F 286). Gardening for food crops was apparently one of the main activities in the vicinity of New Orleans. This reinforced the connection between the agricultural world and the urban marketing activities of New Orleans.[43] When expatiating on the planters who had turned away from sugar, Boze cites Mr. Hopkins, Ste-Gême's neighbor in Gentilly, who had turned to daily agricultural labor and the production of "wood, fodder, dairy products, and vegetables" (F 249).

In the first decades of the American era, cotton was also a rising crop in Louisiana, on the verge of supplanting sugar, for its relatively easier cultivation. In 1833, already the lowering of taxes on sugar was contributing to declining profits, and "our Louisiana sugar planters are considering abandoning it for cotton" (F 225). In 1834, several planters had abandoned sugar "to plant cotton which offers many more advantages," and it was not "the moment to exhibit a sugar plantation for sale" (F 244). In 1835, cotton planters were said to "have become richer this year, with a price between 16 and 20 gourdes per quintal, compared with rates between 10 and 12 the previous year." Cotton sold so well that planters managed to settle their debts that year (F 253).[44] Although there were other less important crops, like coffee, they were never the focus of Louisiana planters' efforts, especially after Congress passed new legislation encouraging Cuban coffee planters to send their products to Louisiana, thereby decreasing demand for Louisiana coffee (F 197).

Like most of the cities of the American South, New Orleans was thus essentially agricultural, and little industrial activity was conducted there, save that connected to agricultural production. First and foremost, sugar required immediate transformation of the crop, which led to the development of the sugar industry. Moreover, due to the rise in cotton cultivation and production, New Orleans witnessed the construction of several cotton presses, such as the one built on Mme. Lalaurie's old plantation in the fall of 1831 (F 189). Connected activities developed, the cotton press establishing, for instance, a paper manufacture in one of its buildings in March 1833 (F 218). A year later, the paper manufacture of the cotton press was very successful, and people "crowd[ed] to visit this marvel and congratulate those who had launched an establishment so favorable for this state" (F 238). Here and there, some manufacturing activities are mentioned in passing, but the scarcity of those mentions is the clearest sign of the backwardness of New Orleans in this sector, compared with the northeastern cities, such as Philadelphia, the "chief manufacturing center of the nation,"[45] which was then developing the manufacture of steel, power machinery, and textiles, and New York, which turned from agriculture and shipping to manufacturing and was on its way to becoming the "first major industrial city" in the United States, and even Boston, which developed textile and shipping industries.[46] Aside from the processing of sugar and cotton and the manufacture of paper already mentioned, there are, in Boze's hundreds of pages of minute detail about the New Orleans economy, hardly more than a few mentions of rope- and cigar-making, a brick factory (F 236), and a gunpowder factory (F 152). Passim, when mentioning the death of Julien Delpit, a Saint-Domingue Creole about fifty or sixty years old, he indicates that the deceased had had a tobacco manufacture on Rue Chartres for twenty-five years (F 252). Besides what was mere transformation of local products, New Orleans was an industrial desert, and when the firefighters' hose got severed, "as the complex mechanics cannot be fixed, an order will be placed in the North to get another hose" (F 240). New Orleans, like most of the South, thus relied heavily on the North or on foreign exchanges for most manufactured products. Louisiana was an agricultural and commercial state.

The highlight of New Orleans's economy was indeed commerce, as can be expected of a major port city, although New Orleans was clearly ahead of most port cities in the United States, save for New York. New York remained the uncontested leader in terms of port activities, but New Orleans bested it in at least two categories: total exports and domestic exports.[47] In 1834, it even ranked first in value of exports and "continued in that position for nearly a decade, winning a place among the seaports of the world."[48] This commercial activity was perceptible throughout the city. Following Boze along the streets of New Orleans, the reader sees the bustling commercial activity in dry-goods shops or in the markets, the profusion of all kinds of products, from clothes and clothing material to tools, hardware, drugs, and much more. There were stores selling basic necessities, and these could produce fortunes.[49] Louisianans were selling all the normal necessary commodities. New Orleans, however, was also a city where commerce went beyond the essentials. Residents could find music stores (F 24), for instance, "stores [specializing] in fragrances" (F 144), or stores selling luxury goods.[50] There were also New Orleans specificities, like tobacco shops and oyster stands on the levee, the city granting exploitation concessions for the season at a price that was set every year when oyster season started, on September 15.[51] Rue du Canal, described as "big and [located] between the city and Faubourg Ste. Marie," starting at the levee and ending at Rue des Ramparts, was one of the main commercial arteries in the city and had "commercial houses on both sides, built in brick, with one, two, three, and up to four stories (belonging to American owners, people say) which provide a majestic sight" (F 253). New Orleans was definitely a very commercial city, and its activity expanded throughout the early period of American rule.

This was the main original trait of New Orleans in the American South. It induced other specificities, which, again, made it more on par with the northeastern Atlantic cities than with its Southern counterparts like Charleston or Savannah. Because of its commercial activity, it became a city in which the professions flourished in the two decades of the early American era. In October 1828, "the number of lawyers has increased so much in the past ten years that, soon, each block will display the plaque of one, that is the name of the practitioner at his door" (F 134). In January 1834, the professions were reaching proportions still more unusual for the South. "When we came to this country in 1809, there were, in the city, including the faubourgs, about ten pharmacies. Well the number is now 50. Lawyers 10, notaries 4, and doctors 12. Well, today the former amount to 20, the second 15, and for the third, doctors practicing medicine, Creoles and French, Americans and Spaniards, we now count about 30 and all make a fortune, making us hope that, with time, all the professions will arrive at the number of cabarets" (F 235).[52] The numbers were high and rapidly increasing to accommodate the fast-growing population, but what Boze's list also suggests is that the important ethnic diversity of the city probably accounted for the multiplicity of professionals. Pharmacists and doctors prospered (F 144).[53] Very often, the reader catches glimpses of these through gossip, for instance, when Boze lists the marriages taking place in the city. Announcing the wedding of the daughters of the pharmacist Grandchamps, for instance, he says that one married a "notary's clerk who is said to be of great means," the other a pharmacist "who does great business" (F 233). The sons of notaries and lawyers often followed in their fathers' footsteps (F 147). There were educators who managed to become relatively rich, such as Charbonnier, who, besides his teaching activities, wrote books, "which help the pupils in their education with the assistance of his new grammar book," enabling the children and foreigners "to learn more easily and quickly" (F 164).

As suggested by the global expansion of the city and general construction fever, real estate, architecture, and all the activities connected to building were in full bloom. In May 1830, informing Ste-Gême of the sale of six pieces of land for 15,000 gourdes by Mr. Sauvinet, "where the old barracks had been," he adds that there had been an offer for the corner facing Ste-Gême's property and that the piece of land where his old house stood was gaining value every day (F 164). In May 1832, Mr. Nabat sold two houses, partly of wood, partly of brick, in the Marigny, for a total of 15,000 gourdes, "despite their great remoteness from the levee." A house was sold at the same corner as Ste-Gême's for 5,360 gourdes, and potential buyers were rushing "to build there at once, in this beautiful area, beautiful storied houses with balconies which will, without any doubt, yield great revenues for their owners" (F 185). For several months in early 1832, for instance, referring to the wish of Mme. Lalaurie to purchase the large piece of land Ste-Gême possessed on the levee, facing the Ursulines' property, he advised Ste-Gême not to sell it and to wait for better days (F 196–97). Rightly so, since another offer, higher by 20,000 gourdes, was later made by Mr. St-Avid (F 200–211). There was much speculation in New Orleans in those years. In late 1831, Boze mentions several times excessive real estate speculation (F 194–201). One piece of land, acquired from Ste-Gême by Americans, in November 1833, for the amount of 20,000 gourdes (F 233), was put up for sale in February 1834 in four lots facing the levee for 7,000 each and one lot on Barracks (Rue du Quartier) was for sale at 4,000 (F 236). Even if Boze thinks that the slowdown in the economy will bear heavily on these sales, land speculation was clearly a way to make money in ever-expanding New Orleans. Many people made fortunes in real estate, such as Mr. Milnes (or Mils), who sold, in 1831, for a total of 259,217 gourdes, land he had purchased from the Spanish government, 30 years earlier, for 105 gourdes. The reader envisions, through these examples, both the present and future expansion of the city, since speculation even concerned land that was, for the moment, unusable, being composed of bayou land "rather often flooded by the rising tide." The buyers saw long-term profit, however, and planned to make this bayou constructible with inputs of soil (F 183).

Entertainment was obviously also a profitable sector, another feature that distinguished New Orleans from her Southern counterparts, although Charleston had earlier on seemed able to compete with the Crescent City.[54] Theaters, opera houses, ballrooms, gambling facilities, and coffee shops were flourishing. The New Orleans stage was among the first in the country.[55] The theaters were typically open every night, except during the summer months, and several shows were performed on a given night, providing a complete stage experience for the viewers, like on November 1829, for instance, when "the Théâtre d'Orléans played *La Caravane du Caire*, a grand opera, followed by a vaudeville play, and between these two plays, our dancers, men and women, performed several dances for one, two, or three, accompanied by a ballet, which has also received the applause of the public" (F 150). The theater staged tragedies, comedies, vaudevilles, and operas, but there was more than theatrical activities, which were supplemented by a number of side activities as lucrative as—or maybe even more so than—the stage, such as ballrooms, cafés, and gambling academies (F 150). There were several such places in New Orleans, all French in the first years. Davis's theater was continually being expanded and embellished (F 148) and Davis's fortune kept increasing with the "gambling academy and his rooms for public recreation" (F 243). In 1830, for instance, beside Davis's establishment, there was another theater on Rue St. Philippe, containing a café, a gambling room, a vast "room for traveling comedians, puppet shows, dancers, as well as balls of all classes and colors, and finally for newcomers with all kinds of new curios to show to the public, be it paintings of great merit or animals belonging to rare species" (F 153). Financial success was achieved by the gambling academies, including "gambling dens" (*tripots*), and their owners were, most of the time, among "the capitalists of this city" (F 166), although these establishments had caused the ruin of many, "especially the Spaniards expelled from Mexico" (F 166). Among those who prospered with these gambling academies, many were Saint-Domingue refugees (F 148). Cabarets were another path to fortune (F 170). Ballrooms were in fashion, and balls were a New Orleans institution, especially, though not only, during Mardi Gras. There were balls for all colors and classes, and each ballroom had its own specific features. Some, like the one on Rue St. Philippe, accommodated lower social classes, both whites and people of color, Boze explains. Others, like Davis's, were, in his judgment, more selective, organizing balls for the best society of both colors. When masked balls were held there, "the direction, in its wisdom, [took] every possible precaution to ensure mothers the greatest respect for their young ladies by granting entrance cards only to known people, honest and of good mores." Those places were supplemented by a quantity of others, public or private, such as, for instance, a beautiful house in which a Frenchman organized balls "for the girls of color *Cordons Bleus* or of relatively good birth" (F 153). Many other forms of entertainment existed, especially those created by the Saint-Domingue refugees, such as music, dancing, or fencing, among others.[56]

New Orleans was also becoming a major tourist and business center, and all the tourism infrastructure was developing.[57] There were also many hotels, ensuring the prosperity of their owners by welcoming strangers who came to town to conduct business or enjoy the bustle of the city (F 188). Throughout the period, many more were built, whether at the lake or in the city itself. In 1836, for instance, at the center of Faubourg Ste. Marie, "the Americans are building, over an entire block, a superb hotel which will possibly accommodate 500 persons, from what I heard, with many services and charms which will make jealous all those the French have built and are building in the Carré. As beautiful as the latter may be, they will never have as much brilliance, good taste, and riches as theirs, according to these proud nationals" (F 268). Once again, the specific ethnic composition of New Orleans apparently created competition and made for the prosperity of the city.

Although by no means exhaustive, the letters are a good survey of the main activities of the city. If New Orleans shared with the rest of the South a primary focus on agriculture and a relative backwardness as far as industrialization was concerned (save for the processing of agricultural produce), it resembled more the urban centers of the Atlantic Northeast in the vitality of its harbor, the bustle of its commerce, and the diversity of its activities. No other Southern city could compete with it in terms of urban commercial and tourist activity, and in no other Southern city could the urban middle to upper-middle classes be encountered in such large proportions. Despite this booming, diverse economy, what Boze's letters also show are the uncertainties of the developing economy and the fragility of the recent capitalist turn of the city.

On the Winding Path to Capitalism

Because this economic development was recent and rapid, it had many vicissitudes, in New Orleans maybe more than in the other cities of the Atlantic United States, due to the continued intermediary status of the city—which had recently ceased to be a small colonial town—and to its very Southern economic choices, despite its increasing commercial focus. Even though commerce was booming and the plantation economy rapidly developing, New Orleans could very well fall victim to the climate, to summer epidemics, to tensions between the United States and European nations, to new banking legislation voted by the federal Congress, or simply to rumors concerning domestic or international politics.

Because the economy had not yet stabilized and because the advent of capitalism favored unregulated speculation, an incipient system of banking and credit, high inflation, and rapid and unchecked economic growth, New Orleans underwent frequent periods of economic depression (in 1822, 1825, and 1834, for instance) and at least one major crisis that verged on panic, in 1837, provoking a total suspension of payment by the banks (with the sole exception being the Citizens' Bank) and many bankruptcies. Although the 1837 panic was not limited to New Orleans and affected the whole nation, its effects were strongly felt in the young developing city, where commerce and finance were the engines of the local economy. The road to economic development and capitalism was clearly fraught with danger.[58]

Some long periods of economic lull plagued the city, which was particularly sensitive to seasonal changes. The summer was the dead season for the economy, once its residents had left for the other side of Lake Pontchartrain and for the Gulf Coast and once the foreigners had stopped coming in, for fear of the terrifying summer epidemics. Every year, the city was almost empty during these months, and commerce came to a complete halt, which was a real handicap for its development, compared to northeastern cities. In August 1818, for instance, although yellow fever had not yet appeared, "those who fear it have already gone away from the city to the other side of the lake and to the distant plantations" (F 23). In July 1832, there were only twelve vessels in the harbor, hurrying to load their cargo to leave the city before the *hivernage* and its lot of hurricanes, tropical depressions, and diseases (F 207).

As a developing market, New Orleans was also exposed to special conditions, and products were difficult to sell when there was a seasonal abundance of them, as seen in the case of sugar. Gouging was also a commonplace economic activity whenever specific conditions existed. Epidemics caused some products to be in high demand, of course, but the seasonality of the city's economy also heavily influenced the market. In the winter of 1834, for instance, the weather was extremely cold, and firewood was in such demand and so difficult to obtain, due to the poor conditions of circulation, that it became extremely expensive (F 235).

Beyond seasonal variations, there were crises that put a halt to commercial activities and caused many bankruptcies in short periods of time. In December 1828, for instance, "although the market displays a great deal of business of all kinds, and which has been increased by the great number of American merchants who have come to settle in it, business is not sufficiently brilliant to render it merry, not even the French because of the competition with those enterprising men who take every risk. You can no longer see in commerce those fortunes of the past" (F 134). In February 1834, sugar was difficult to sell, usurers had rates of 15 to 18 percent a year, despite the legal limit of 6 percent, and real estate was going down, "because this place is today in such financial difficulty that it is impossible to hope that property might find favor again for some time" (F 236). One month later there were such difficulties "in business matters that several merchants have suspended their payments, which makes people fear that their number will increase at the settlement date in April." There were new bankruptcies every day among commercial establishments (F 237). In late May, the situation was still dire. Sugar did not sell, and most planters still had their crops in their cellars. "Cash has become extremely scarce, confidence is lost, bankruptcies are going on, business is dead, and commerce, which shows its distress, has conferred nothing but sadness on the city for 3 months" (F 239). The situation had not improved at the end of the year, with a terrible sugar crop, yielding less than half the usual quantities, and a cotton crop less promising than the year before (F 260). Although most of those financial and economic crises also affected the rest of the country, the New Orleans economy, based almost exclusively on agriculture and commerce, was even more affected by the vagaries of the larger economy.

Epidemics were an obvious contributor to economic depressions. In August 1829, business was slow because of the numerous departures due to yellow fever. Doctors and pharmacists had to treat the sick for free, and the market was extremely slow.[59] People were so indebted that they went bankrupt and had to sell their possessions.[60] The fall of 1832 experienced the usual seasonal halt and was marked by several bankruptcies and a halt to commerce due to epidemics. Since residents feared the spread of cholera and yellow fever, there was a slump in the sales of certain products, considered hazardous, such as fish, fruit, shellfish, cabbage, and lettuce. This also caused gouging in the prices of other products in high demand during epidemics, like woolens, drugs (especially camphor), and even graves. Banks suspended much of their activity, thereby causing new bankruptcies (F 212). After epidemics, there were lingering collateral effects, such as labor shortages due to the deaths of too many employees. In November 1832, for instance, bread was lacking, due to "the death of several *nègres* belonging to bakers" (F 214). The sugar crop was about one-third that of the previous year, because many planters had lost slaves to cholera and were unable to replace them, in particular because of the decrease in the price of sugar, "making it easy for the usurers" (F 218). Business was bad for pharmacists for a few months, for reasons that are not given but may be inferred. Among them is the fact that the weakest had died in the epidemics and the necessity for drugs was thus lower, as well as the fact that pharmacists had fewer products to sell and people moderated their consumption because they had less money to spend in those difficult times, or even the fact that the relief of being saved contributed to their better health (F 232).

International tensions were another cause for economic declines. In the winter of 1830, for instance, relations between France and the United States became so tense that the two countries were on the verge of war. The bone of contention was not new; it dated back to the Napoleonic Wars, during which France had seized or damaged American maritime property. The issue resurfaced when President Jackson decided to claim reparations from France. Although the two countries reached a settlement in 1831,[61] tensions were renewed in 1833, when the French Assembly refused to appropriate the money for the first installment. The United States was ready to go to war, but through British mediation, France eventually capitulated and paid the debt.[62] Those four years of French–American dispute were hard to bear in New Orleans. In the winter of 1830, already no boat flying the French flag had yet been seen in the harbor. "For several months, no expedition has arrived from the places of Bordeaux, Marseilles, Nantes, and Havre [*sic*]. American ships now make those journeys, sent by merchants of that nation who have settled here to take up this commerce. It seems, from the quietness of our French merchants, that they have not conducted brilliant business with New Orleans, or that they fear a breach with the other powers who seem to have already started conducting military movements to get ready for a war" (F 175). In January 1831, there was not, in the harbor, "the number of 500 vessels as in the previous years" because of "the events that have troubled France and other nations" (F 178). This produced a slowdown in commercial movements, creating an economic lull in the city: "The result is that goods are not sought for and even at a price that is not advantageous for the sugar planters, which does not make them decide to sell their crop, always hoping that business will be able to resume to their satisfaction to enable them to empty their stores cluttered with barrels. . . . The freight of sugar to the Northern places is at $8 per *boucaut* [*sic*] and, even at that price, there are no vessels to charter. Such is today the situation of this place. The price of cotton is between $11 and $12 per quintal" (F 182). Despite its special relationship with France, Louisiana was now part of the United States and thus submitted to national politics and policies decided in Washington.

Indeed, new American legislation, or even rumors that Congress was considering legislating, also had effects, which showed both the relative fragility of the Louisiana economy in those years of expansion and its progressive integration into the young republic. In early 1830, Louisianans thought that "copper money may be introduced in this state, as in those of the North, which might well slightly disturb business" (F 157). In early 1831, the decrease of tariffs on coffee (from four dollars to two dollars per quintal, with the prospect of being only one dollar in 1832) had immediate effects on the local economy, boosting the sales of coffee from European colonies, especially Cuba (F 175). The rumors that the Northern states were attempting to have Congress decrease the tariffs on imported sugar also immediately sent tremors throughout Louisiana. "This would doubtlessly bring great prejudice to the sale of sugars in this colony [*sic*], and all its planters have expressed in turn just representations on the issue, asking for the taxes on imported sugars to be maintained for some more time because of the important expenses they have had to establish sugar plantations, in land as well as in *nègres*, mills, and animals, which have not yet been covered, or else this competition would lead them to their ruin." Congress remained undecided, but rumors kept prices low (five dollars per quintal) and there was little demand for Louisiana sugar, while the previous year, it had sold for six dollars for exportation to Europe and the American continent (F 179). The sugar crisis lasted at least until the summer, since, in May, the demand for sugar, even by Northern states, was low (F 184), and, in July, the price again went down, leaving much unsold sugar on Louisiana plantations and New Orleans market (F 188). In the spring of 1834, in the wake of President Jackson's refusal to renew the charter of the Bank of the United States, the situation in New Orleans was again dire. After months of economic depression, the planters in debt found it impossible "to have banks discount or renew their bills" and those who had no liquid assets had to have recourse to usurers, "who are pitiless in front of adversity." Although New Orleanians hoped that the establishment of the Banque des Citoyens would save agriculture and commerce by "providing the resources they need in this time of crisis to avoid bankruptcy" (F 238), the depression was severe in the city. Because of its relatively recent integration into the United States, New Orleans still lacked some of the financial infrastructure that existed in other states, which made it particularly sensitive to any change in national policies and caused a slower adaptation than elsewhere. The young state was also, more than ever, prey to national crises, as in the spring of 1837, when bankruptcies were already numerous and cash scarce, and when the situation of Louisiana was worsened by the crisis affecting "the places of the North which were recriminating against the Union government for not helping the commerce and for not maintaining reasonable taxation" (F 278). The crisis lasted over a year and was felt throughout Louisiana, but apparently more strongly in New Orleans, which was "in such a cruel distress, no business, no money, no one doing anything, no one paying, every day new bankruptcies and, every day, people emigrating without paying" (F 280).

In the city on the path to capitalism, the least difficulty could be almost fatal. Several times, cases of embezzlement, especially among employees, and sometimes even directors, or in the new banks, initiated short-lived panics with repercussions over the entire economy. In the late spring of 1834, for instance, Antoine Foucher, one of the directors of the Banque Association Consolidée des Agriculteurs de Louisiane (Consolidated Associative Bank of Louisiana Farmers) was accused of counterfeiting signatures, embezzling money, purchasing property, and fleeing from New Orleans. For a total of 200,000 gourdes, he had purchased several sugar plantations, mills, and city houses. Three more people were said to have fled, leaving behind them a deficit of 130,000 gourdes (F 239). Although the property was sold to pay his debtors, the amount was lower than the total of the embezzled sums, due to a relative drop in real estate prices. This, in turn, occasioned losses to the merchants, "especially to the usurers' race," and increased the debtors' financial difficulty. Such events could only have strong repercussions on a newly capitalist society, and indebtedness, easily occasioned by bad crops or an absence of demand for agricultural products, naturally increased economic unrest.

Because its general expansion was still incipient, New Orleans could thus be easily destabilized by special conditions—be they local, national, or international—and its economy was strongly influenced by that of the young republic it was now part of. Its new American destiny also made for its wealth and, despite the ups and downs, the story of New Orleans's economy in those two decades is one of overall unchecked progress.[63]

A Flourishing City

In early 1830, "500 ships of all nations fill in the harbor, and its movements of commerce are so important that they can be compared, without exaggeration, to those of the main places of the north, Philadelphia and New York" (F 157). In June 1831, numerous boats had arrived within two weeks, enabling the sale of much sugar at the price of five dollars and even five and a half per quintal for superior-quality sugar (F 183). Commerce was, most of the time, flourishing in New Orleans.

Moreover, after tensions or epidemics had slowed down business, the end of troubles was always marked by a prompt economic recovery. As soon as the yellow fever epidemics receded, for instance, business started anew, boats and merchants returned to the city, fancy dress and masked balls resumed: "the luxury of the fashion clothes is beginning its progress and Davis, who is waiting with his troop every day, will bring festivities to the enthusiasts and the whole city" (F 149). In November 1829, numerous vessels returned to the harbor, the price of daily-essentials consumer products dropped, and luxury products were again sold "for high prices to ladies and young damsels, who can then appear in the splendor of ostentatiousness in public places and wear their rich coats in their strolls in the city" (F 150). In October 1832, a recess in the cholera and yellow fever epidemics was immediately followed by a resumption of commerce. Streets filled up again, construction sites became busy again, and employees were back to the stores of artisans and cigar makers (F 212). In November, the city had "recovered its gaiety" and commerce had "resumed with such acuteness and celerity that the foreigner reaching town would never believe that the pests of yellow fever and cholera have caused to this city the loss of about 3,000 persons, according to the calculations made for the three classes." "The city sings alleluia, alleluia, and alleluia" and "the merchants beam with joy and contentment" (F 214). Economic crises were also followed by periods of economic boom. In December 1828, for instance, "despite all this and the financial difficulties many families are in, luxury is still at its climax, and in particular during the carnival, when women of all ranks and all classes buy at all costs rich fashionable clothes to attire themselves so that they may shine at the fancy dress, masked balls. . . ." (F 134). After the deep depression of 1834, recovery was seen everywhere in 1835. Cotton sold well, and the price of real estate was rising again (F 255). Numerous foreign and French migrants were arriving "with beautiful and rich merchandises in great quantities and of all kinds, and the commerce of this place is now in great movements, giving hope that the fair will be very brilliant this winter, when the speculators from the city, who have gone to France to purchase clothes for the season, will all have returned, making stores for rent scarce, especially those located in the commercial streets." By October and November, those who had returned were unpacking "their treasures of luxury, taste, and Parisian fashion," and women were rushing to find novelties "to be remarked and shine with great distinction in society and with much splendor and brightness at the fashion receptions of the carnival period" (F 258). The reader gets the impression that, as soon as the economy started recovering, people felt the need to make up for lost time, which gave an immediate boost to the city's business. Immediately, the harbor was full of vessels, carrying "passengers of all nations, by groups of 25, 30, 50 and up to 100," full of merchandise "to greatly surpass the number of previous years" (F 258).

Although in less striking proportions, every year, in the fall, once the *hivernage* was over, life returned to the city with renewed vigor. In October 1836, "since the 1st instant, foreigners of various nations have flocked into the city, coming on vessels with rich loads, making the commerce start its great business movements." Every day, people who had left the city for the summer came back to town and "Mandeville, Louisville, Baie St. Louis, and Biloxi will soon be deserted again." People were regaining faith in the future, and "the crisis that commerce has suffered lately and which had disturbed the business of some houses, has only been temporary, and the public, seeing today confidence resume, no longer seems worried about the future" (F 271). Even in years without epidemics, the summer months were always slow, either because people had left for healthier climates or because boats did not come to these shores during the hurricane season. But as soon as the hurricane season was over, the harbor was again full of vessels. In November 1831, for instance, boats had returned to New Orleans, and "they have started to give commerce a great movement of business, giving us hope that the market will be beautiful and rich" (F 174).

All in all, despite the ups and downs the city witnessed, expansion was the general economic trend throughout the first decades of the American period. As solid proof of the city's financial wealth, banks expanded during the two decades of the correspondence, and Boze keeps a very close count of them. In August 1818, "a fifth bank has just been established but it is not yet operational because the house has not been found. They propose to purchase a piece of land and the old houses that stand on it to have this building of significant size erected. The block is the one close to City Hall whose façades are on Rue Royale, vis-à-vis Cadet Mouton, the other Rue St. Pierre, vis-à-vis Grandchamp, and the third one Rue d'Orléans, vis-à-vis Père Antoine's presbytery" (F 23). In January 1832, there were seven banks (F 194), and in April the city counted eight banks: "Louisiane, La Société Consolidée, Orléans, les Etats-Unis, Etat de la Louisiane, du Canal, de la Cité, et de l'Union" (F 203). In April 1833, there were eleven banks, with three new additions to the previous list: "Citoyens, Commerce, et Mécanique" (F 222). In May, the number had risen to twelve, with the opening of a new establishment "for the class of the artisans in difficulty," sometimes nicknamed the "Bank for the Poor" (F 226). In early 1836, a new bank opened, causing Boze to exclaim that "soon their number will be greater than that of the cabarets" (F 265). In June 1837, the city counted twenty banks (F 278). The last count, slightly lower than the previous one, probably on account of the recession of the previous year, is given in early 1838: there are now sixteen banks in the city, a great advance compared with the mere three it had in 1809, when Boze reached the city with Ste-Gême (F 280). Following Boze's mapping of the banking activity in the city is a wonderful indicator of the city's growth, both in terms of population and economic wealth but also of the increasing integration of New Orleans within the United States, since, side by side, are found banks representing each level of the federal organization of the nation. Not only were the banks more numerous, they grew in beauty and majesty as time went. In December 1828, Boze writes that "the new banks today are buildings of great beauty and mainly that of the state of Louisiana, then comes that of Louisiana, of the United States, and of Orléans. They are all located at the same center Rue Royale, at the corners of Conti" (F 134). New Orleans was a major financial center in the South. In the later years, it was largely outdone by New York (which counted 152 banks in 1846),[64] but in the 1820s, New Orleans was no doubt keeping pace with the major northeastern Atlantic cities.[65]

Throughout the first decades of American rule over the city, new stores, new markets, and new facilities were built, both in the Carré, which remained the core of the city's economic life, and in the faubourgs, especially the so-called American Faubourg Ste. Marie. In 1828, the market was flourishing.

"There, there is dealt a great deal of business, increased by the numerous American merchants who have settled in it" (F 134). In 1829, to the covered market for the sale of meat, have been added two more, one for the sale of fish, the other for vegetal products, vegetables, and fruit (F 150). Every month, in New Orleans, new brick multistoried houses were being built, to accommodate both the growing population and increasing commerce. In most cases, the first floor was indeed dedicated to commerce and manufacturing, the second floor to storing merchandise, and the third story was set aside for apartments or boardinghouses (F 275).

Three decades after the Louisiana Purchase, the Crescent City had become a place of opportunity and true success stories. In the early 1830s, it was a place where "Mr. Angaud, a native of Bordeaux, who had been a merchant of fat in Cuba upon the evacuation from Saint-Domingue and, continuing in the same trade here, had made a small fortune that his French heirs will enjoy without prejudice to the share of his natural children" (F 182). It was a place where a lawyer from Toulouse, Soulé, could have a house built, "a very beautiful two-story house on Rue St. Louis, independently from other properties he has already acquired, which attests that this well-known justice officer is managing very well in this country" and where an "immigrant, native of Nantes" had become a very successful dry-goods merchant on Rue Royale (F 232).

Although the Gallic population from Louisiana, Saint-Domingue, or France spurred this new economic development, the Americans were, no doubt, the main engines of expansion, either directly or indirectly—by triggering among the Creoles a wish to emulate them.[66] Rivalry brought on competition, thereby stimulating development in the Carré and in the city as a whole, definitely making for its modernization, improvement, and embellishment. In 1829, already, "this city, since the arrival of American business, has become very wealthy, to the point that in all the stores of all the *quartiers*, we can see but immense riches, with a great movement of business in sales as well as purchases, that will soon make the city vie with the first cities of the North, that you may be surprised when you return here" (F 150). The arrival of the Americans is clearly connected with the incredible development of the economy. Their presence also seems to have introduced competition in elegance. Houses were being built near the cotton press (this "majestic establishment") by the Compagnie des Architectes, whose architects erected "beautiful houses with beautiful stores for commerce, to the point that this neighborhood will become very brilliant with time, to make Faubourg Marigny vie with Ste. Marie, despite the greed of the Americans who pursue its magnificence with their wealth" (F 218). In 1833, two banks (out of the twelve in town at that moment) considered moving to the faubourgs: one to the Marigny, "which would grant still more luster to this neighborhood which keeps growing in businesses and houses," the other, of course, to Ste. Marie (F 228). Throughout the correspondence, the reader witnesses the need for the Americans to emulate their Gallic rivals whenever they show any superiority, and reciprocally, thus making New Orleans a very ebullient city. In the fall of 1835, for instance, the Americans "are building a comedy room [a theater] in Faubourg Ste. Marie" and, once completed, it "will have the beauty of Mr. Davis's" (F 258). This, in turn, led Jean Davis to try to purchase houses at the corner of Rue Royale and Rue d'Orléans to expand his ball and theater rooms to "emulate Théâtre Saint-Charles" (F 267). When the new stock exchange was built in the Carré, although it was very handsome and although it was impossible not to go "to visit it, out of curiosity, and contemplate, in raptures, its shine, although it is slightly flashy," many predicted that it could not "outshine the brilliance, elegance, and taste of that of the Americans on Rue Royale, close to the customs" (F 269). The competition between the two main communities thus made for the improvement and modernization of the city.

By 1840, New Orleans was much larger, much wealthier, much busier, and much more elegant than ever. It had become, in the previous two decades, a major metropolis of the young American republic. From the small provincial town it still was at the time of the Louisiana Purchase, it had turned into a modern city, with largely improved urban facilities and much better infrastructure. It no longer had the feel of the small colonial town it had been when the Americans had purchased it and often resembled, in the eyes of its older residents, an increasingly anonymous big city.

Toward an Urban Society

Boze's perspective is naturally biased. Already an old man, who had lived most of his life in small colonial towns, he saw urban growth as a plague, not unlike most antebellum Southerners. His testimony, however, once cleared of its negative judgmental opinions, reveals the permanent evolutions of the city. The old man often complains about the decline of mores since the arrival in New Orleans of crowds of migrants. For him, the American "invasion" had made it less welcoming and less pleasant, and upon reaching the city, "the foreigner no longer encounters, when visiting the city or living in it, that joy, that affability, that kindness, that obliging quality, or even that pleasant and thoughtful welcome that flattered us so much when we arrived in 1809 from all its nice inhabitants" (F 135).

The small village had given way to a large city, and the values that had been part of its charm when Boze and Ste-Gême had settled were, according to the eighty-year-old witness, vanishing. The city had changed since the years 1809–15, Boze writes, when relations were marked by "affability and frankness," when people "enjoyed doing each other favors," and when concord ruled. By the 1830s, the city was no longer the place where "business was made with Christian good faith, where true friends were numerous, where the foreigner enjoyed a flattering respect which made him congratulate himself every day at finding asylum in it, where misfortune met sensitive souls who consoled it by deeds of charity." Now, everything was but selfishness and there were different mores brought over by "new inhabitants full of pride, who, unfortunately, have been followed by crowds of vagrants of all classes, exuding crime and thus disturbing the city" (F 160). Mutual assistance no longer existed, and Boze elegiacally writes "we have lost the golden age, and forever" (F 164).

In Boze's eyes, mores were in decline and people and rules no longer respected.

> I will not cease to repeat to you that the mores have changed, that this country, with its new population, no longer offers the perfect union of the past, that affability, nor the same charms that we enjoyed in our first years in this country. My surprise is so great that I think I see, every morning, the sun rising on side of the bayou and setting on the side of the Balize!
>
> Now we see families deny their close relatives small assistance when they could oblige them. Hearts have become so hard toward the poor souls that there no longer is good faith or even trust in business and that true friendship which, in the past, procured days of pleasant life to the foreigner no longer exists. It has been replaced by selfishness, to the point that friends only visit politically, and then, people remain buttoned up in conversation. Although I do not suffer from the life I live, this city is becoming sadder to me every day, because of the Great Change I find in it. (F 164)

According to the old man, a general lowering of standards was perceptible, especially among the youth. "Today's youth, French and American and Spanish, is beautiful and numerous but with excited minds and the spirit of the century." Youngsters no longer show any respect for religious practice. They go to church "to have fun criticizing people's outfits, to play mischievous tricks, and to ridicule the modesty of the penitents" (F 161). "The youth of 1830 is no longer that of 1809, which befriended peace at all times," and it now goes armed to the theater (F 164). Young Creoles bear weapons, and there are too many crimes "on which justice keeps closing its eyes" (F 172). "There is not a single week without the condemnation of criminals to the shackles by the criminal court, and for several years, this country has been swarming with so many foreign vagrants" (F 184). To reinforce the charge, he adds "the attitudes have changed, and even the Creoles admit this truth" (F 161).

Crime had spread, but maybe more importantly, justice seemed impotent and unjust. Mme. Lalaurie, the infamous mistress of maltreated slaves, was indicted several times "but with her wealth, she always managed to get out of trouble" (F 238). The director of a bank accused of forgery could walk away unpunished because "the law, which should be strict with everyone, today bends for a rich man guilty of a greater crime because he belongs to a great Creole family, residing here and endowed with a fortune" (F 239). And Boze rants against the Americans. "When we arrived in this country in 1809, we found only wisely established concord reigning among families and among society, which proved that morality is always linked with a civilized population. Alas! Since the day the Americans have taken possession of it, it exudes crime, since there is not a month, sometimes a week, without the narration of murders, suicides, infanticides, duels, drowning, thefts, fires, bankruptcies, forged bills and signatures." Everything attests to the lowering of morals. "Drunkenness is in fashion at all ages" and Creoles are turbulent and no longer "brought up with the care and the decent European style that existed in the old days of the *ancient regime*!" (F 260). The old man—he was between seventy and ninety when he wrote—could not come to terms with the advancing modernity, but his complaints clearly show that New Orleans was becoming a major urban center.

To members of the old colonial population, New Orleans seemed to indulge in ostentatious practices. Interpreted differently, those practices could also be a sign of economic advancement. People erected tombs to "children barely off the breast," with "golden letters engraved in marble" (F 177). Sometimes, Mardi Gras celebrations, "rich with splendor," full of "great luxury," in the fashion of the day, gave the feeling that people were insensitive to "the sufferings of the hospices which cry for help." People, young and old, men and women, now wore glasses "by necessity or fashion," making "old people and the *ancien régime* shrug." Despite the critical undertones, Boze's assessment is clear about the positive evolutions that the city's society had undergone. New Orleans no longer was the rough frontier town it had been during the territorial period. In 1828, upon his return after his long stay in Cuba, he marvels at the progress he witnesses: "The deceased now move in elegant coaches and rest a few moments in the new church built to that purpose on the esplanade, near the basin, where funeral orations are sung before their entering the garden of equality" (F 134).[67]

The descriptions of the houses and public buildings also denote luxury. The stock exchange was considered the epitome of taste, convenience, and decorum; its employees were careful, polite, and prompt; its refreshment room was well supplied; and it was so well decorated that "commerce and agriculture find, to their contentment, everything that can be pleasant and useful" (F 269). The Compagnie des Améliorations even had a public ballroom there, "richly furnished and decorated, to the point that it outshines Davis's in all respects." Everything denoted increasing refinement. The entire stock exchange was heated in the winter; the preservation of order was ensured by a Swiss "armed with a cane that has a great silver knob, similar to that of the drum major of the great army of the Cossacks." The refreshment area had desks, tables, and chairs, where "the public can find all commodities to manage its writing and enjoy the reading of all the newspapers with all the advertisements." The beautiful rotunda room was reserved for auctions. It was furnished with armchairs, and "everything occurs there in the calm and decency that civilization commands" (F 280). The little frontier town of the late colonial period was long gone.

Luxury was to be found in many social events, and the high society of New Orleans could enjoy the privilege of retreat away from the heat of the summer. "The Lake and the Baie St. Louis are, in this fair season, places of rest, of recreation, and of yachting for the rich, and places of entertainment for the idle who love celebrations. Day and night, on Saturdays and Sundays in particular, coaches are in great movement to carry as many men as women and children, and a same number make the journey taking the same route, coming out of the Basin in rowing boats, dinghies, and pirogues drawn with a rope by horses at a gallop which surpass the carriages in speed, all in joy and not seeming to worry about the dead and the dying they leave in town" (F 144). In May 1832, two new leisure establishments opened by the Lake, Hôtel du Lac and Hôtel de Washington, with water baths, and "everything contributes to making this place one of the most pleasant in the Union" (F 204).

Members of the high society continued to rival one another in fashion, "and luxury among women preserves its great brilliance and their outfits are always in the latest French fashion" (F 147). Every year, in late October, the dancing academies reopened. In November, Mr. Davis and his theater company returned to the city, ready to "renew the pleasures of the theater that make this city very joyous, especially with the winter balls in outfits of the latest fashion." The beautiful theaters welcomed "the best Creole society of New Orleans of both colors."

Mardi Gras was always the social season, and "the number of the men and women who enjoy the pleasures of social life is more considerable, especially during the period of carnival, when the shows and the fancy masquerade balls are open to those who enjoyed them" (F 150). Every year, there were "all kinds of beautiful outfits of luxury and fashion for both sexes" that the stores displayed for "those who liked novelty and who are getting ready to attend the balls of the winter and its carnival, extremely brilliant, according to Louisianans' taste" (F 175).

Celebrations were always sumptuous. Among the highlights of the year was Sainte-Barbe, which "our artillerymen have celebrated with much splendor, with the cannon and fireworks on the Place d'Armes, across the parish, at 7 at night, in the presence of many citizens, and on Sunday 5, they had a high mass sung with the music by the orchestra of Davis's theater" (F 175). On January 8, every year, the anniversary of the Battle of New Orleans was also commemorated, along a well-organized pattern: "The legion of Louisiana, infantry and cavalry, appeared on the Place d'Armes in full dress. They performed some military movements and then they went to the parish, where a *Te Deum* was sung in thanksgiving to God" (F 175).[68] New Orleanians, whatever their origins, wanted their city to shine in the new republic.

In the twenty years covered by Boze's letters, the city undoubtedly changed face. From a small colonial town still enclosed within its ramparts, it became a major metropolis, progressively engulfing neighboring towns, to the point that Ste-Gême's plantation in Gentilly no longer seemed unreachable. The city turned into an economically bustling place—its urban development was such that Boze keeps telling Ste-Gême that he would need a guide were he to return to the city. The drainage system kept the newly paved streets clean, pedestrians could walk on the banquettes, away from the mud, the streets were lit at night, and water and gas were available in the city and progressively reaching individual homes. The economic vicissitudes of the colonial era were receding, and the city, at the crossroads of the Mississippi River, the Gulf Coast, and Lake Pontchartrain, was within easy reach, now that the steam era had settled in. The railroad and steamboats made it a place of encounters and exchanges, bringing together men and women that, by this confluence, made the city what many newcomers called the Babel of the American South.

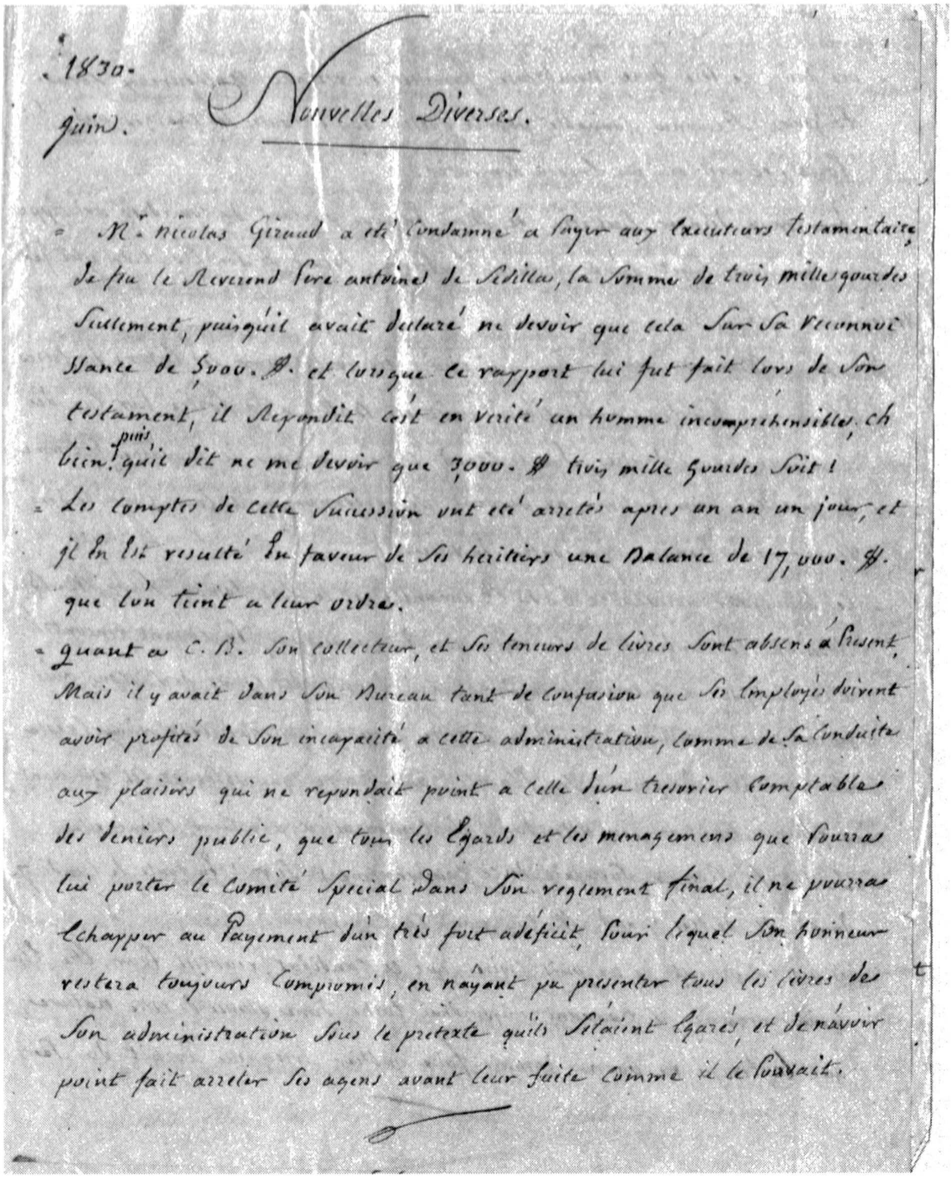

1830.
juin.

Nouvelles Diverses.

= Mr. Nicolas Giraud a été condamné a payer aux executeurs testamentaires de feu le Reverend Pere antoine de Sedilla, la somme de trois milles gourdes seulement, puisqu'il avait declaré ne devoir que cela sur sa reconnoissance de 5000. $. et lorsque ce rapport lui fut fait lors de son testament, il repondit c'est en verité un homme incomprehensibles, eh bien! puis qu'il dit ne me devoir que 3000. $ trois mille gourdes soit!

= Les comptes de cette succession ont eté arretés apres un an un jour, et il en est resulté en faveur de ses heritiers une balance de 17,000. $. que l'on tient a leur ordre.

= quant a C. B. son collecteur, et ses teneurs de livres sont absens à present, mais il y avait dans son bureau tant de confusion que ses employés doivent avoir profités de son incapacité a cette administration, comme de sa conduite aux plaisirs qui ne repondait point a celle d'un tresorier comptable des deniers public, que tous les égards et les menagemens que pourra lui porter le comité special dans son reglement final, il ne pourra échapper au payement d'un très fort déficit, pour lequel son honneur restera toujours compromis, en n'ayant pu presenter tous les livres de son administration sous le pretexte qu'ils s'etaient égarés, et de n'avoir point fait arreter ses agens avant leur fuite comme il le pouvait.

Figure 1. Cover page of letter of June 1830, Folder 167, Ste-Gême Family Papers, MSS 100, Williams Research Center, The Historic New Orleans Collection.

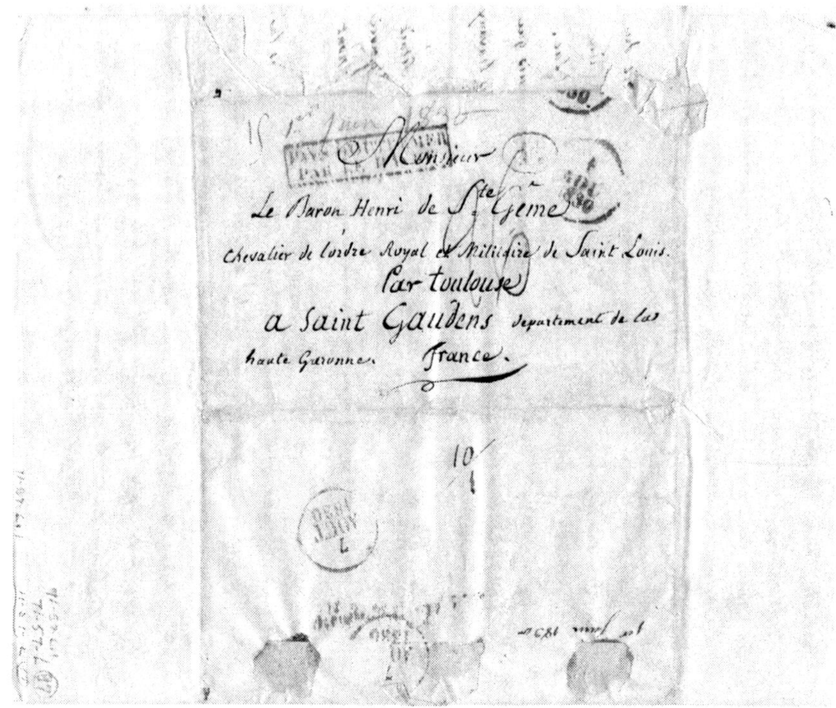

Monsieur
Le Baron Henri de Ste Gême
Chevalier de l'ordre Royal et Militaire de Saint Louis.
Par toulouse
a Saint Gaudens departement de la haute Garonne. France.

Figure 2. Envelope, August 7, 1830, Folder 167, Ste-Gême Family Papers, MSS 100, Williams Research Center, The Historic New Orleans Collection.

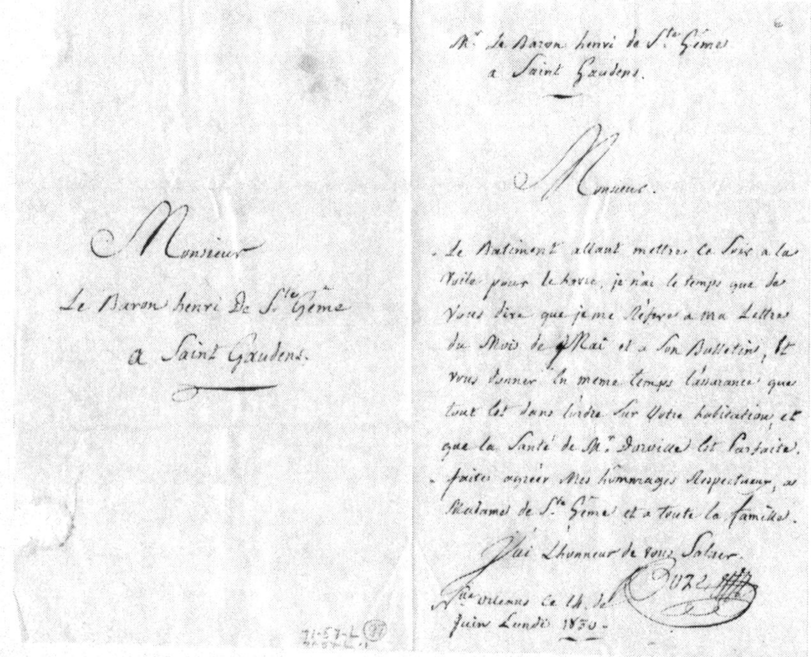

Monsieur
Le Baron henri De Ste Gême
a Saint Gaudens.

Mr Le Baron henri de Ste Gême
a Saint Gaudens.

Monsieur.

Le Batiment allant mettre ce Soir a la Voile pour le havre, je n'ai le temps que de Vous dire que je me Réfères a ma Lettres du Mois de Mai et a Son Bulletin, Et vous donner En meme temps l'assurance que tout Est dans l'ordre Sur Votre habitation, Et que la Santé de Mr [illegible] Est Parfaite. faites agréer Mes hommages Respectueux, a Madame de Ste Gême et a toute la famille.

J'ai L'honneur de vous Saluer.

[illegible]

Nlle Orleans Ce 14. de Juin Lundi 1830.

Figure 3. Page 6 of newsletter of June 1830, Folder 167, Ste-Gême Family Papers, MSS 100, Williams Research Center, The Historic New Orleans Collection.

Figure 4. Portrait of the Baron de Ste-Gême, Williams Research Center, The Historic New Orleans Collection (1976.171). The portrait reproduced here is owned by The Historic New Orleans Collection (1976.171). Although thought by the Sainte-Gême family to be of Henri de Ste-Gême, it has been examined by French specialists of military history Manuel Guerrero Acosta and Michel Hanotaux, who both date it from the mid-eighteenth century, probably under Louis XV, and thus conclude that, although the officer wears the Cross of the Order of Saint-Louis, as Henri de Ste-Gême did, it cannot represent Henri de Ste-Gême, unless he posed in an older uniform. From passports that were delivered to him for travel to Bordeaux, however, we learn that he measured 5 feet 6 inches (or 1.78 meter, as another document puts it), had brown hair, blue eyes, a full face, an "ordinary" nose, a midsize mouth, a round chin, and a covered forehead. A second passport describes his mouth as small, his nose as turned up, and adds that he had a beard and a florid complexion. See Folders 612 and 616.

Figure 5. A view of New Orleans taken from the plantation of Marigny (1803), Williams Research Center, The Historic New Orleans Collection (1958.52).

Figure 6. New Orleans from the Lower Cotton Press, 1852, Williams Research Center, The Historic New Orleans Collection (1959.184.14).

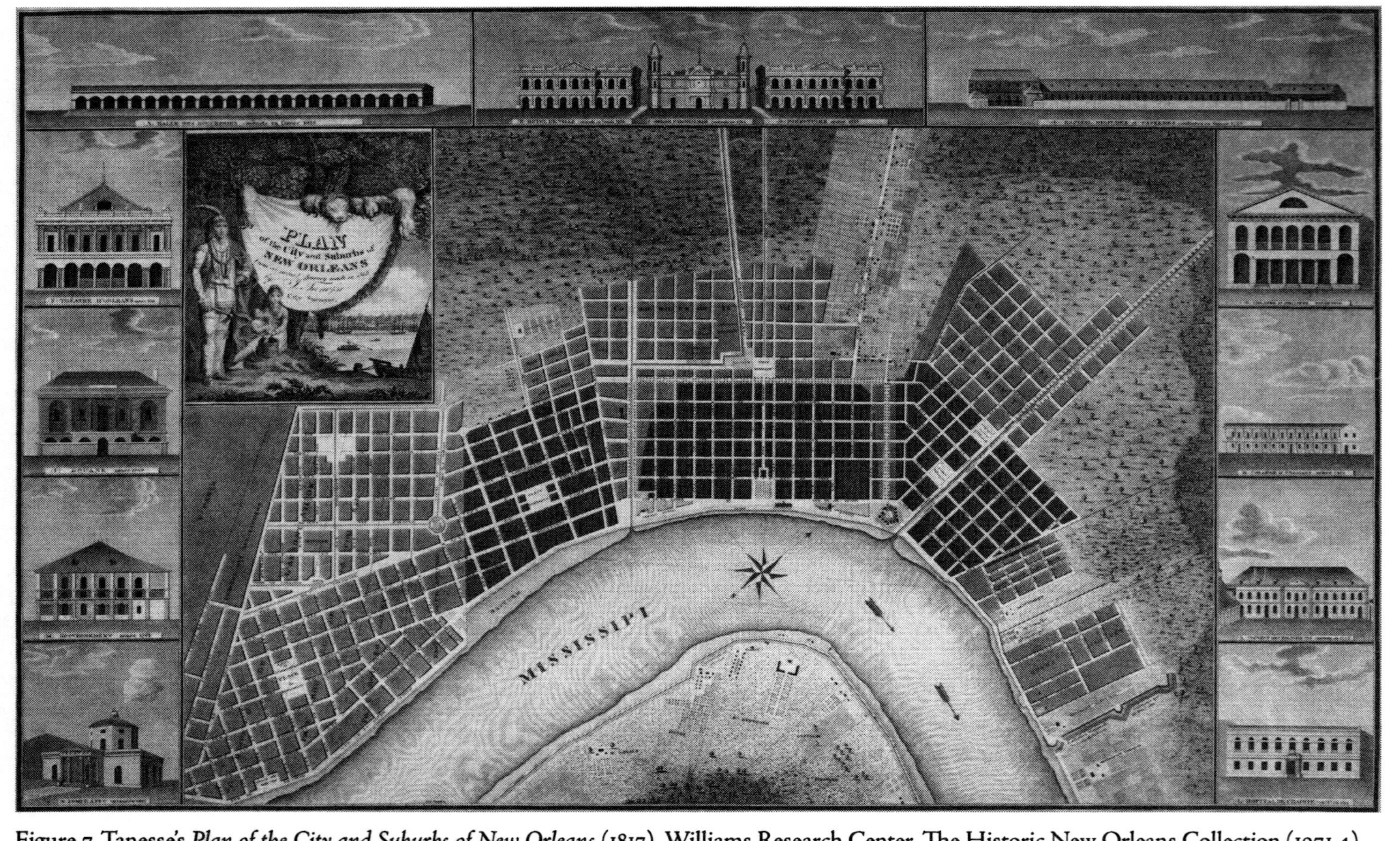

Figure 7. Tanesse's *Plan of the City and Suburbs of New Orleans* (1817), Williams Research Center, The Historic New Orleans Collection (1971.4).

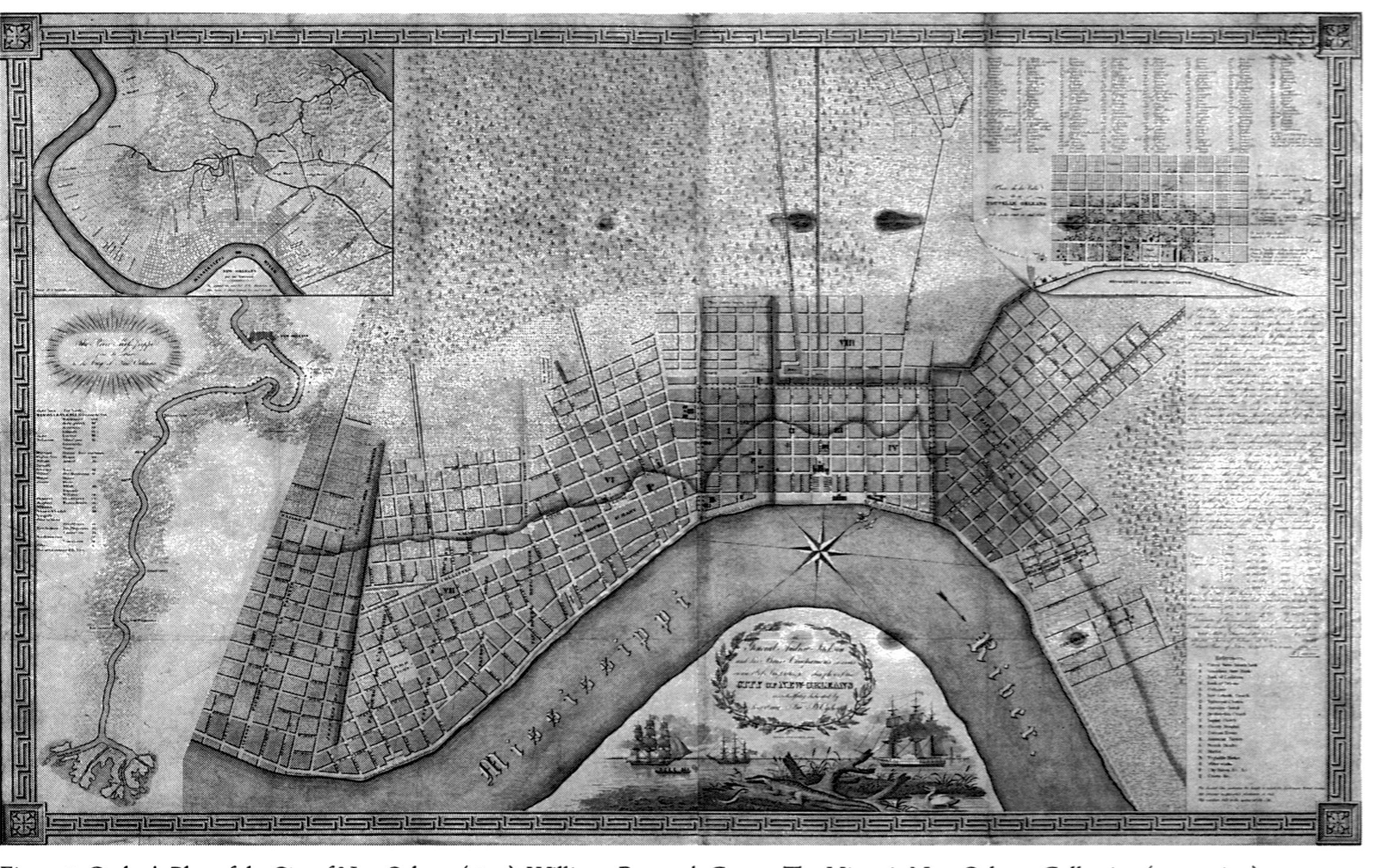

Figure 8. Ogdon's *Plan of the City of New Orleans* (1829), Williams Research Center, The Historic New Orleans Collection (1971.21 i–v).

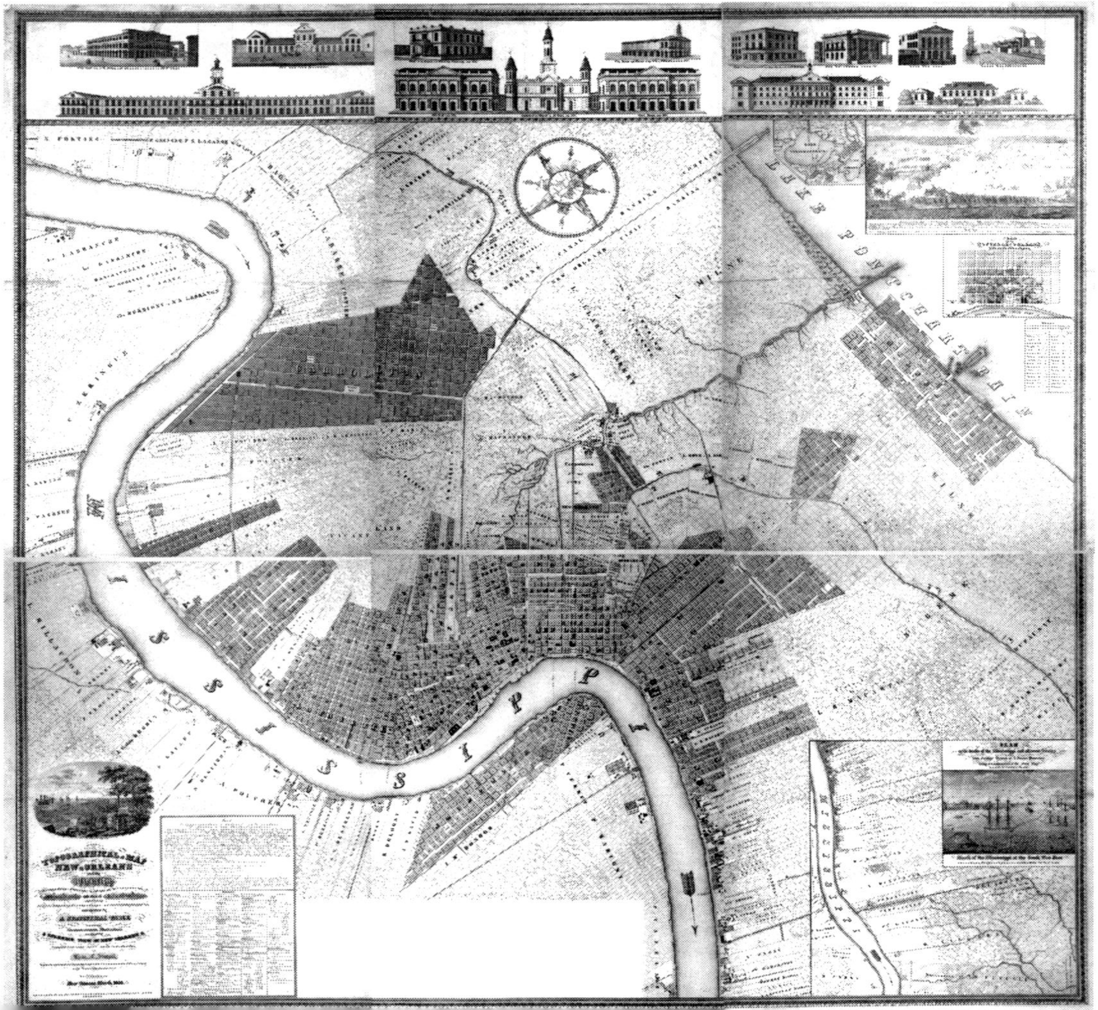

Figure 9. Zimpel's *Topographical Map of New Orleans* (1835), Williams Research Center, The Historic New Orleans Collection (1955.19 a–f).

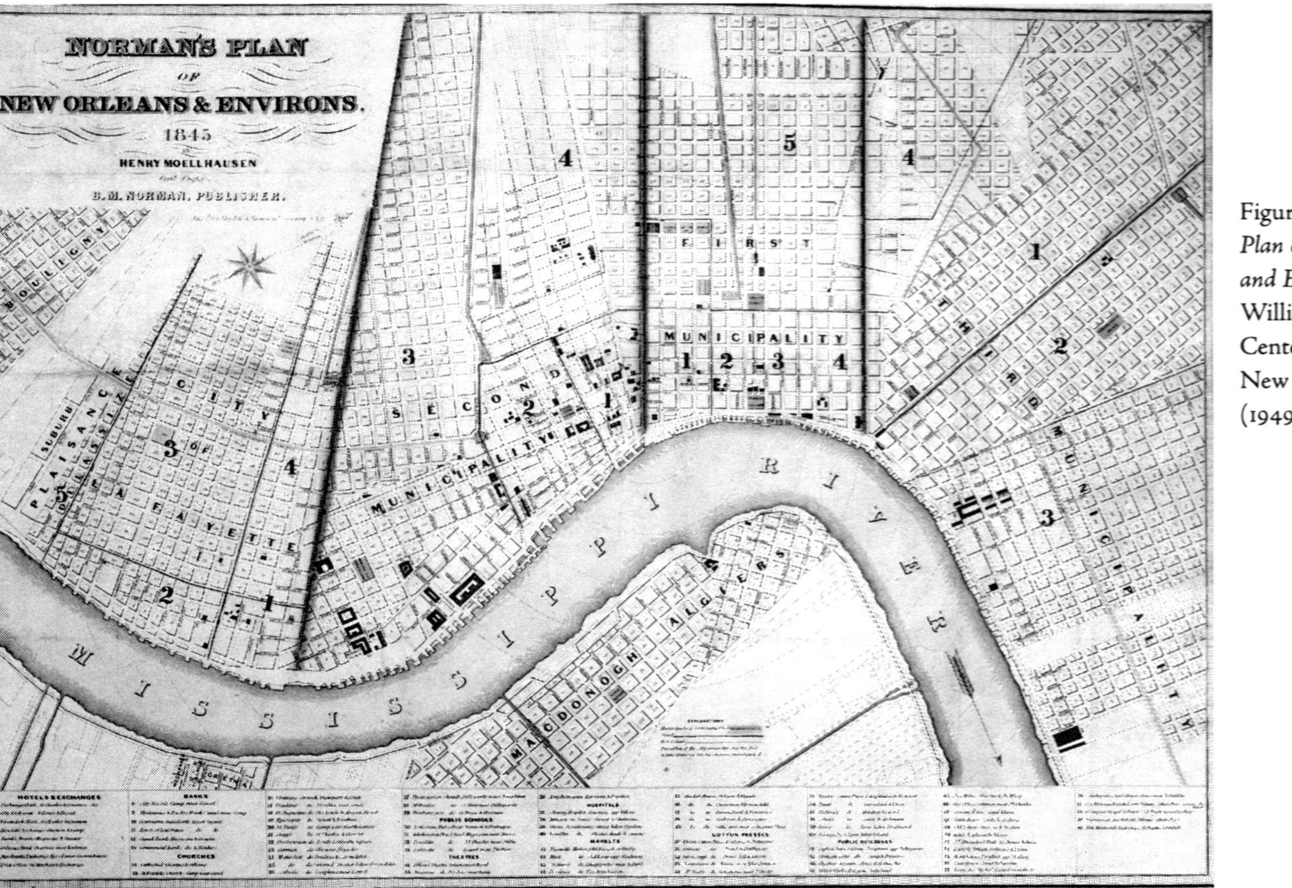

Figure 10. Norman's *Plan of New Orleans and Environs* (1845), Williams Research Center, The Historic New Orleans Collection (1949.7 a, b).

4

Crossroads

Beyond the extraordinary demographic and economic development of the city, what is striking about early American New Orleans as described by Boze is the way in which it was connected to the outside world. At the confluence of the Mississippi River and the Gulf of Mexico, it was a privileged outlet toward Europe, the Caribbean, and Latin America for the ever-expanding United States in the first half of the nineteenth century. It was without a doubt a city of exchanges, and not only in the economic sector. A transit city between the Americas and Europe, it was also a crossroads within the Americas, mixing people, products, and ideas, as well as reinforcing reciprocal influences within the Atlantic and Greater Caribbean spaces. It was the principal port city in the South and was clearly at an advantage, compared to the Northeastern harbors, because of its strategic position in the Americas. Moreover, more than any other city in the United States, it had been influenced by its complex colonial history to remain close to the non-anglophone world. Because it had been French and then Spanish and then briefly French again, it had kept relations with the old European colonial centers and with the rest of the Gallic and Hispanic world of the Americas.

Boze, always attentive to the colonial worlds, probably because he had long been a colonial interacting in several European empires (French, Spanish, and Dutch), often mentions the relations between Louisiana and the rest of the world. And those connections, both numerous and frequent, tell us much about New Orleans in the first decades of the nineteenth century and can help us to understand many of its subsequent evolutions. Although Boze's status as an immigrant, his colonialness, and his persisting connections with France may account for his continual interest in the connectedness of New Orleans with European empires (or former empires), these things also most certainly make him a biased observer. However, numerous New Orleanians were in the same situation. His narrative may be more representative of the experience of the "foreign French" than of the Creoles, but newcomers from Europe or the former American colonies of European empires were so numerous in the city at the time that it is worth examining at length. It is obvious that New Orleans was still very close to her original imperial empire, and the city's links with France clearly did not end with the Louisiana Purchase. Many New Orleanians were still very European, if only because of the increased presence of European immigrants among them, and attentive to what was happening in the world. The relations between New Orleans and the outside world were thus first marked strikingly by continuity. Boze's letters, however, also show that, underlying this continuity, the Louisiana Purchase made the city more American than ever, firmly implanted in the United States and on the American continent. The city was then going through a critical moment of transition between the still strong imprint of its European past and a new American future, fraught with potentialities. This chapter will first address the notion of continuity, insisting on the enduring connections between Louisiana and Europe, and more specifically the ties maintained with France, and the city's place in the Atlantic world, before turning to the potential offered by its inclusion within the Union, the prelude to its repositioning in the Greater Caribbean and, more generally, in the Americas.

New Orleans and Europe

When Boze started writing, Louisiana had been part of the United States for fifteen years and had been a state of the Union for three years. When his correspondence ended, the colonial era was almost forty years in the past, and yet there are clear signs, throughout the exchange, that Louisiana was still interested in European matters and that her eyes were still turned toward the old continent. New Orleans newspapers still carried news of European events, all the more so because, for a long time, Europeans had continued flocking to the Crescent City, despite its new destiny within the young American republic. New migrants from Spanish and French American colonies, but also from France and other European countries—in particular Ireland and Germany—never stopped coming throughout the two decades of the correspondence.[1]

This is not surprising, because those newcomers were still interested in their countries of origin and the newspapers tended to humor them by including numerous observations on events happening in Europe. Boze commented, for more than twenty years, on European politics. It is true that European nations had to face numerous confrontational situations in those years. A number of wars involved European nations (for example, the Russo-Persian War of 1826–28 and the Russo-Turkish War of 1828–29). Several internal wars for independence or wars of succession also involved European nations. This was the case of the Greek War of Independence of 1821–1832 and the Belgian Revolution of 1830, as well as the two main wars that occurred in Spain during the two decades, the French expedition to Spain, decided on by the main European nations, aimed at consolidating Ferdinand VII on the Spanish throne (1823–24), and the Carlist War of 1833–40, triggered by the succession of Ferdinand VII and involving France, the United Kingdom, and Portugal. The European nations were also entangled in many colonial wars, which worsened the national agitation: the Netherlands in Sumatra (1821–37) and Java (1825–30); Britain in Africa (Anglo-Ashanti War of 1823–24) and Asia (Anglo-Burmese War of 1823–26); France in Algeria, a war of conquest that started in 1827 and led to the seizure of Algiers, in 1830, although the 1830s were marked by continuing Algerian resistance; and, of course, Spain and Portugal, caught up in all the wars for independence in Latin America.[2]

Although the interest of Louisianans in the conflicts that occurred on the American continent was logical, because they could be directly affected, either by the migrations these conflicts triggered or by their effects on the overall economy and system of intracontinental exchanges, Louisianans' persistent attention on all things European might seem surprising, at a time when the young American republic was, through its proclamation of the Monroe Doctrine, turning its back on Europe to focus on the Americas. Yet New Orleanians were undoubtedly interested in European matters, as all of the newspapers of the period attest. A glance at any of the main newspapers—*L'Abeille*, *Le Courrier*, *L'Argus*, or any other—reveals the abundance and exactitude of the news coming from Europe. Some reports involved international matters, but others bore on very precise elements of France's or England's domestic politics. Boze's interest in news coming from Europe was constant for its influence on Louisiana life but also, sometimes, because it affected the lives of his family and friends there. Those European events often triggered political comments on his part.

In November 1830, for instance, he lamented "the distressing situation of the states of Europe," suggesting that if Ste-Gême was not coming back to Louisiana, it was for fear of leaving his family unprotected in Europe, for in the early months of the reign of Louis Philippe, "France is today surrounded with volcanoes of insurrection of all the people against the old dynasties." He expressly wished that numerous uprisings would occur, in the hope that "the Kings will submit and give to their peoples, amicably, a liberal constitution to their satisfaction, to avoid making them obtain it with armed hands, which would make them incur the same fate as Charles X, this unhappy prince through his own fault." Although he called for these uprisings, he feared for his daughter who lived in Lienen, Westphalia, very close to Osnabruck, explaining his fears by saying: "I believe they are very close to the fire" (F 177).

In early April 1830, he delved into the French–English relationship. France, to him, was displaying signs of weakness, and England seemed to have allies everywhere. The relationship between the two nations had been difficult in the previous decades, especially in the Napoleonic era. However, the struggle for power had more or less receded in the early nineteenth century, with the two nations being more intent on securing their positions worldwide than on conquering new territories. France conducted cautious foreign policy in those years, remaining Britain's ally in most European affairs. For instance, it refused to annex Belgium when it became independent. It was allied with Britain during the Greek War of Independence.[3] This was probably hard to bear for most New Orleanians, who showed a persistent pro-Napoleon and anti-British sentiment, all the more so because the War of 1812 and its final battle, the Battle of New Orleans, in January 1815, had left strong anti-British feelings in Louisiana.[4] Boze often expressed mistrust in the way France conducted her international policies and voiced the concern he apparently shared with many New Orleanians at the new French–British alliance, if we are to believe the way in which he dealt with the topic. He accused some French ministers of being "Wellingtonian," that is of supporting Napoleon's archenemy, who had become prime minister in 1828 but had faced internal opposition leading up to the fall of his government in the autumn of 1830. Boze especially criticized Polignac, the former French foreign minister and president of the Council after 1829, whom he tremendously disliked and accused of collusion with England (F 166). He feared that England might be plotting to place a king under its rule on the throne of Greece, independent since 1822, and then to fly its flag over Turkey to establish a military place "for its colossal navy to be able, if need be, to impress Russia." Although Britain had avoided wars of conquest in the last years of the reigns of George IV and William IV, England still was the enemy and competitor to New Orleanians. Boze developed at length his vision of the power of Britain, "that proud and ambitious nation," which might end up coveting Algiers, which was so important to France "by the abundance of its grains that it delivers every year according its needs and other goods." In one of his letters, he recalls, in his childhood, "always hearing the elders say that France would need the commerce of three such colonies as Algiers" before concluding in unmitigated terms: "I wish France would take up arms against England" (F 161). France was indeed involved, at that time, in the war of conquest of Algeria. Despite

Boze's fears, its expansion in North Africa went unchecked by Britain, and the war Boze was calling for never happened. If his remarks seem anecdotal, they indicate that the newspapers carried news of European matters, and they show the deep interest that New Orleanians still had in the old continent, as if their colonial past still weighed heavily on them, more than three decades after their integration into the United States.

To Boze, as to apparently a number of New Orleanians, interest in European matters was also often a good reason to comment on French politics, at a time when the French king, Charles X, was being threatened by internal opposition. In the fall of 1831, for instance, Boze lamented the capture of Warsaw by the "Russian barbarians." After an uprising in Poland, in November 1830, the Russians had indeed intervened militarily, and the Polish capital had fallen to Russian troops in September, after France had denied the insurgents the help they had requested. In his commentary, Boze showed his own interest in European politics and his general awareness of the various diplomatic and military moves that occurred there, but he also frequently alluded to the fact that the people of New Orleans shared both his interest and his concerns. The news of the capture of Warsaw had "thrown the population of this city in a great consternation, except for the Carlists" (the king's supporters), which implied that his opinion was shared by some of the New Orleans people but also suggested the existence of opposing political factions in New Orleans on matters of European affairs (F 189).[5] Clearly an opponent of Charles X himself, Boze strongly criticized France's role, pitying "the brave, unfortunate Polish, abandoned by the whole world, who have finally succumbed under the yoke of Russia, because of France" (F 198).

Boze shows that he and his fellow New Orleanians were informed about and interested in what was going on in Europe. Most of the time, however, his considerations about Europe were strongly connected to the interests of France, and it was France that still mattered primarily to him and, apparently, from what he writes, to New Orleans residents. Louisiana's long history with France—inaugurated by the French colonial era and hardly disrupted by forty years of Spanish colonial rule—had left many marks on the relationship between Louisiana and France, and this *relation spéciale* obviously still endured long after the integration of Louisiana within the United States.

New Orleans and France

Although actual possession by France had ended four decades before the Louisiana Purchase, to be resumed only for a short three-year period of unofficial rule after the San Ildefonso Treaty of 1800, Louisianans were still, in the early nineteenth century, extremely close to France. Boze's case is not to be considered the rule, of course. He was, after all, already an old man when he started writing his letters; he had been born in France and had lived most of his life in French colonies. He was also writing to a Frenchman. That he still felt very French is to be expected, especially since he apparently died a French citizen, but reading his comments about French politics does show the proximity of French-speaking New Orleanians to their old metropolitan center.

The early nineteenth century was, in France, a period of relative political turmoil. After a decade and a half of Napoleon's rule, the mid-1810s were marked by the emperor's first destitution (1814–1815), brief return to the political scene (the Hundred Days), and final exile (and death) on Saint Helena. The Second Restoration, which returned Louis XIII to the throne (1815–1824) before placing his brother, Charles X, at the head of the French monarchy, was a period of strong opposition between the kings and the French nation. The struggles between the national guard and the king, in 1827, between the monarchy and the chamber, especially in 1830, between the newspapers and the government, in 1830, and between the people and the executive, constantly threatened the monarchy and gave the impression of a permanent state of insurrection in France. The Second Restoration ended with a real revolutionary movement, the Three Glorious Days, in late July 1830, leading to the abdication and exile of the king and his replacement by Louis Philippe, who became the king of the French under what was known as the July monarchy (1830–1848). This period was, again, marked by political instability. Heirs to the crown were opposed on questions of legitimacy;[6] governments were short-lived;[7] the people rebelled, as in Lyon, during the famous Canut revolts, which saw silk workers violently demonstrate against the monarchy, in November 1831 and again in April 1834; several assassination plots against Louis Philippe were uncovered;[8] and several coups attempted by Louis Napoleon Bonaparte, Napoleon's nephew, were thwarted (in October 1836 and August 1840). In short, France was permanently torn between the three types of regimes that had governed it in the late eighteenth century: monarchy, republic, and empire. Napoleon's popularity was still strong among the French, as the return of his ashes to Les Invalides, in December 1840, shows. The monarchy was still deeply implanted, although it seemed to be constantly jeopardized by republican thrusts.[9] The loyalty of the French citizens was clearly divided among these various regimes, and this division had obvious repercussions in New Orleans.

As a Frenchman, Boze often situates himself on the French political chessboard and shows that New Orleanians took a position in the French debates. Although he says that "popular uprisings are always dangerous" (F 181), he sometimes expresses republican—or at least anti-monarchic—sentiments. Believing that Louis Philippe's government had betrayed the July Revolution of 1830[10] and disarmed France, he praised, for instance, the workers' rebellion in Lyon in November 1831,[11] adding that the people must rebel (F 198). When, in April 1834, the Canuts again rebelled in Lyon, the uprising was repressed, causing the deaths of two hundred people. In the wake of this repression, workers also rebelled in Paris. This time, Boze deplored the incidents organized by the Parti Républicain in Lyon and Paris, adding that they had caused many victims, among the citizens and the military, and would prevent, according to him, the Republicans from ever again attempting to use force to "proclaim the republic" (F 243).[12] He very often expresses his fear that there might be revolutionary uprisings, but the reason for his fear is humanitarian in nature, as he fears that lives might be lost needlessly and that "a revolutionary tremor may bring disorder in the whole of France" (F 164). He never speaks as a staunch monarchist in his New Orleans years, even if he was an Old Regime man who had repeatedly requested royal appointments during his Caribbean years. If his position sometimes seems ambiguous, it is because he speaks more out of pragmatism than dogmatism and because "[his] soul rests" with the "courageous" people of France who refuse to submit to the yoke of tyranny, whoever might be in power (F 183). In the late months of the reign of Charles X, he criticizes the government and some of the ministers, although he still can write a panegyric of one of them, Chateaubriand (F 164). What he constantly regrets is the apparent loss of power of France and her allegiance to foreign powers. Criticizing the weakness of the head of government, Jules de Polignac, he exclaims: "Tell me if our former kings and Emperor Napoleon ever needed the permission of the government of England to attack Algiers or any other power when they wanted to make war!" (F 166). Later, his criticism of the French monarchy can be explained by the fact that he obviously tremendously disliked Louis Philippe and his way of ruling, clearly expressing to Ste-Gême that he does not declare himself "his partisan in any respect," expecting "heavenly vengeance" to strike the monarch (F 255). Yet, in the early days of the July monarchy, he had spoken of "this good king whose virtues are greatly praised by his people" (F 177), "the good government of the King," "the choice of his good ministers," the "good administration," and the "formidable forces animated by the most fervent patriotism and the reunion of all parties which keeps at bay the jealous sovereigns of his new splendor," which had brought France to "resume her rank as first nation"

(F 181). Despite these strong initial hopes, the state of grace did not last. In later newsletters, he repeatedly criticizes the king's administration, his alliance with England, his weakness, and his refusal to hear the grievances of the people of France. He declares his opposition to Louis Philippe's refusal of amnesty to political prisoners, for instance, the former ministers of Charles X who, in 1830, were arrested, tried, and condemned, and describes the trials against political prisoners as "revolting procedures" (F 256). He accuses the new king of being a "tyrant of the people" and of "abolishing the press" instead of delivering on his promises, most certainly referring to the development of censorship in France (F 258).[13] Boze seems already impregnated by the values of the young American republic and committed to the defense of freedom of speech and of the press. Nothing, in his eyes, justifies any form of tyrannical rule. He reproaches the monarch for his "ignorance in politics," his "lack of courage," and his "humiliation in front of all the crowned foreigners for asking them for peace at all cost," weaknesses that he always sets against the greatness of Napoleon, "who showered France with glory" and "who kept at bay all the kings in obedience to him" (F 255). When expressing his dislike of the French king, he concludes: "after all, I speak as a liberal, but without meaning to hurt the opinion of whomever" (F 198), and he leaves it to the "sovereign people," turning, once again, into a firm believer in the decisions of the people.

Despite Boze's sometimes wavering positions, what he seems to have been all his life is a fervent supporter of Napoleon. For him, the emperor was the artisan of the greatness of France, which the French kings were progressively destroying. In February 1832, he complains that "France is no longer that first nation of the past and no longer enjoys the strong government that made all the nations respect her under the reign of the great man who could have flipped them down from their thrones" (F 198). Such laudatory remarks recur throughout the correspondence, and there are whole paragraphs on the wonders Napoleon's administration brought to France, systematically concluding with "the humiliations that [his] homeland is enduring under Louis Philippe" (F 258) and lamenting that, since Napoleon's death, France "has lost this glory and this majesty she enjoyed during the reign of that great man who had made under his arms the emperors and the kings bow down" (F 258). Once more ranting against the debasement of France, which had gone from first to second rank among nations, and against Minister Thiers, who had the nerve to criticize "the policies of the greatest man the most beautiful century has produced," he again praises "the man who preferred to fight alone against the rest of Europe and die as a captive on Saint Helena rather than patiently bear the threats of foreign nations" (F 256). Again, what seems to motivate Boze is more the place of France in Europe and the world than the mode of government itself.

Louisianans, like Boze, were apparently very well informed about events in France. Several times, Boze mentions reading accounts in the New Orleans newspapers, as, for instance, on the occasion of the assassination attempt against Louis Philippe on July 28, 1835.[14] He writes that the newspapers have given all the details, and he mentions nominally the perpetrator and those who lost their lives in the assault (F 258). The New Orleans residents were both informed and interested. From what Boze writes, Louisianans seem to have been as divided in their loyalties as the French were. He mentions various groups, the Carlists (F 189), the "Philippists of this city" (F 258), attesting that groups of defenders of the French kings existed in New Orleans. At the same time, he cites the *Franc Parleur*'s criticizing Louis Philippe, suggesting the existence of a debate among New Orleanians about French politics (F 257). But on some matters, the French of New Orleans seem to have been united. Their heroes were apparently Boze's heroes—Lafayette, "this permanent defender of liberty," whose death "has brought grief to this whole continent" (F 240), or Napoleon, whose last doctor, Dr. Antommarchi, was welcomed to New Orleans as a hero.

In May 1830, Boze includes in his newsletter a long development about French politics and Louisianans' reaction to news from their former empire. Four whole paragraphs are dedicated to the response of the French representatives to Charles X's decision to adjourn the assemblies until the following September. He discusses at length the proposal voted on by 221 representatives in opposition to Polignac's reactionary government, in which they expressed their defiance of the government, asking the king to replace it. He also expatiates on the feared consequences of the king's decision: "it is said that the minds are agitated and in rightful ferment, which makes everyone fear a revolutionary tremor which might bring disorder in France, if the monarchy persists in its unfair views, in the belief that it can, by force and on horseback, return the people to its old enslavement, *libera nos domine*." New Orleans was manifestly informed in detail of what was happening in France, and its residents had opinions about it. Boze was not the only one to comment on French news, since he adds: "The liberals in this city, both the French and the foreigners, have been outraged by the disparate measures taken to obtain the abolition of the charter, the disappearance of which would revive the *Ancien Régime*. Consequently we all expect, with the deepest impatience, the outcome of the struggle between those two powers. But he should be careful not to be thrown down from his mount!" (F 164). The object of the opposition was the interpretation of the definition of constitutional monarchy provided by the Charter of 1814. The king favored a strict literal interpretation of the charter, which allowed him to appoint the ministers of his choice. The liberals, however, tried to move the charter toward the British parliamentarian model, advocating the necessity for the ministers to have the assembly's approval. This question was not solved under the July monarchy. Beyond the case discussed, removed from most Louisianans' preoccupations, what this example shows is that France was still very present in Louisianans' minds and that debates in France also occasioned debates in New Orleans, even when they were of extremely remote concern.

Some news occasionally provoked scenes of public rejoicing. News of the dethroning of Charles X after the Three Glorious Days of July 1830, for instance, was received jubilantly by the New Orleans people. The liberals celebrated the event in the city: "by firing 21 times the cannon, our fellow soldiers of the battalion of artillery have paid homage to the tricolor flag[15] that was flown on several public buildings of the city. Last night, there were many serenades, accompanied by military music. This morning, all the vessels of the harbor hoisted their flag. At noon, a salute was fired and, at 4, the Louisiana Legion and some other elite corps took up arms to celebrate the triumph of freedom over despotism, in the presence of an affluence of people of all ranks and all classes." That the French flag was flown on public buildings is highly symbolic of the enduring ties to the old colonial power. Such signs of support for the people of France were manifested throughout the first half of the nineteenth century. On the occasion of the visit to France by two New Orleanians, Mr. Guillot and Mr. St-Maurice, the two men were entrusted with "a beautiful tricolor flag that the Louisiana Legion sends as a present to the national guard of Paris." This was an occasion for a new display of French patriotism in the city: "This standard was entrusted to the former, in charge of bringing it to Mr. de Lafayette, general-in-chief of the Parisian national guard, in sincere homage of the Louisianans to the heroic events that have just ensured France the guaranty of its liberties. And from the moment the vessel set sail, flying these beautiful colors on its mast, a detachment of the battalion of artillery, gathered on the levee, saluted its departure with 21 cannon shots, with the immense support of a thousand cries of joy from our fellow citizens, who sang the Marseillaise anthem." New Orleanians then organized many banquets and celebrations to show their joyousness (F 174). France was clearly still in all minds, although Louisianans had apparently also become sensitized to the democratic ideals of their new nation.

French events were also regularly commemorated, and the deaths of famous French people—people with American and, even more specifically, Louisianan, connections—were occasions for memorable tributes. The most striking example might be the funerary honors paid to the "illustrious General Lafayette" in July of 1834. Lawyer Jackson delivered, "at the parish," a speech in English, and lawyer Mercier gave one in French. All day, every half hour, the cannon of the Place d'Armes was sounded, and all the shops remained closed. "This ceremony was, for the city, a day of mourning, and in a general silence that expressed the pain felt at the loss of this distinguished apostle of the freedom of the peoples" (F 243).

Lafayette, it is true, was a hero of the Americans as well as of the people of French descent. But other men, slightly less meaningful to the Americans of Louisiana, were also warmly celebrated. Boze recounts the arrival in the city, in October 1834, of Dr. Antommarchi, Napoleon's last physician in St. Helena, who had become famous for his autopsy of the former emperor and his attributing Napoleon's death to stomach cancer. "The news of the arrival of a man to whom are connected so many memories, has occasioned among us the keenest enthusiasm." An improvised delegation of many citizens with, at their head, the honorable Judge Maurian, went to welcome him at John Davis's. The judge extemporized a touching address, giving the hero "the assurance that the population of the city, full of gratitude for the boundless devotion he displayed to the illustrious prisoner, expressed the desire to keep him among them and would eagerly seize the opportunity to pay part of the debt of the French nation." It is true that the connection with Napoleon was meaningful to many, if only for making Louisiana part of the United States. Another address was delivered by Dr. Formento, on behalf of the medical profession of the city. The hero was then temporarily housed at the Macarty Hotel, near the stock exchange, and people continually expressed their interest by sending civil and military delegations. Comedians and musicians gave him a "very distinguished serenade," thereby offering one more bit of proof of the wish "to give him evidence of how much New Orleans is happy and satisfied to have in its midst a person so deserving that the city enjoys celebrating him every day" (F 245). For several days, banquets were organized in honor of "this respectable foreigner so deserving," who has shown "such virtuous behavior in the exile of the great man," and who is an example of "enlightenment," "goodness," and "affability," to such a point that he is eagerly sought out by people "whatever their religion"—*religion* here meaning most certainly much more than religion itself, and suggesting both political religion and ethnic origin. The famous physician was again invited as a guest of honor at the Sainte-Barbe banquet, everyone being "flattered by his company" (F 236). The whole city seems to have been in a commotion at the presence of the honorable guest, who, after a short stay in New Orleans, moved to Mexico, before going to Santiago de Cuba, where he died in 1838. Although he chose not to accept the warm welcome of the city permanently, Antommarchi expressed his gratitude to New Orleanians by presenting the mayor with a death mask of the emperor, which, after being lost during the Civil War, was returned to municipal authorities in 1909 and is now on display at the Louisiana State Museum at the Cabildo.[16]

Surprisingly, people often showed a certain attachment to France and to its symbols, including the flag and *La Marseillaise*, the national anthem, which were often used to pass all kinds of messages in the Louisiana capital. On the occasion of a murder committed by a New Orleans resident, a mob formed and "in the evening, around midnight, it went to the door of his wife's house, vis-à-vis the prison and struck up the *Marseillaise*, pausing with a ferocious joy on the chorus 'let impure blood water our furrows'" (F 271). New Orleanians also often paid respect to the French flag, particularly when the city eagerly anticipated the first vessels showing the French flag after the long period of *hivernage*, enabling the resumption of direct connection between Louisiana and her former empire.

New Orleanians were still very attentive to the fate of the French empire, even though they were no longer affected by it. In 1830, news of the fall of Algiers reached New Orleans. After three years of blockade by the French expeditionary corps, the city had surrendered. "On 16 September instant, we got the important news of the capture of Algiers on this past 5 July, with all the details of the surrender of that Barbaric place which will purge the Mediterranean of those pirates and will forever free Christianity of slavery after so many centuries of suffering. You can well imagine how this delighted the whole population of this city in general, and in particular the French who ardently wished the arms of France to triumph in this conquest after all the great sacrifices the country had made to manage to extinguish this Moorish power" (F 174). The French campaign in Algeria continued, under close scrutiny by New Orleanians. On December 15, 1837, they commemorated the capture of Constantine, which had taken place two months earlier. "All the French vessels which were in the harbor of New Orleans have hoisted the colors today and an artillery salvo was shot at noon sharp on board the schooner *Bastamente* in the middle of the river, to commemorate the victory of the French army in front of Constantine and the capture of this fortress." From noon on, "the cannon was fired every quarter of an hour in remembrance of the loss of General Damremont in that city on 12 October" (F 279).

Although this might seem surprising to the modern reader, who would not expect former colonials to feel a part of their old empire, Louisiana had left the French empire through the decision of the nation's ruler, not through any autonomous claim of its people. There was no rancor to impede popular support of French imperial policies, especially in the eyes of people who had been the spearhead of French colonization in the Americas, be it in Louisiana or Saint-Domingue.

Other topics pertaining to French politics recur in the correspondence, sometimes out of a personal interest of the author of the letters, although this personal interest was apparently often shared by many in the Louisiana capital. This is the case, for instance, of the indemnification of the Saint-Domingue refugees by the French government at the turn of the 1830s. France had eventually agreed to acknowledge Haitian independence, in April 1825, in exchange for the payment, by the Haitian republic, of 150 million francs to compensate the former colonists. The French government had then instituted a complex procedure to divide this indemnity among the former colonists, to compensate for their lost colonial possessions.[17] Because he had a primary interest in the indemnification paid to the Saint-Domingue refugees, Boze often mentions this topic, ranting against the French government. In August 1829, he exclaims: "How can the commission in Paris have paid and be still paying indemnities to many colonists from Saint-Domingue and not care to satisfy the others who have the same rights after handing in their property titles, according to the law ruling this claim, which worries them much." He thinks that the French were probably privileging "protégés while there must be legal uniformity in such a distribution" (F 145). In 1831, he laments the horrendous news of a new diplomatic breach between France and Haiti, exclaiming: "And since this past June, Haiti has broken its alliance with France, which will cause prejudice to the interests of the former Saint-Domingue colonists, who have been suffering, for several years, from the delay in the payment of their indemnification which would alleviate their miseries. They have been eagerly expecting the outcome of that quarrel which can make them know for certain what their fate will be, and may God make it to their satisfaction!" (F 174). Even if these topics may be interpreted as more personal, thousands of refugees shared Boze's interests, frustrations, and hopes. For technical or sentimental reasons, ties with France were thus maintained by people of Gallic origin who had lived in the Americas for decades, sometimes even generations, and by the French people still migrating to New Orleans a long time after the integration of Louisiana within the young American republic. Much of the correspondence indeed broaches the persisting Atlantic migrations to the city.

Atlantic Movements

In the fall of 1835, Boze mentions the arrival in the city of "numerous French and foreign migrants" (F 258). This migratory flux was constant in the first four decades of American rule, and during the period of Boze's correspondence an estimated 8,264 persons arrived from France at the port of New Orleans.[18] Although Boze's remarks often seem anecdotal, his mentions of new migrants from France help reveal the pattern of this permanent immigration. Often, he refers to men, coming from Sauveterre, Ste-Gême's village in southwestern France, bearing letters of recommendation from Ste-Gême (recommendation was common practice at the time and eased newcomers' assimilation into New Orleans life). Boze helped them settle in and they were regularly accommodated in Gentilly, on Ste-Gême's plantation, until they found employment and could thus become independent. In early 1836, Boze writes that one of them was planning to return home in the spring (F 265), showing that those in-migrations were not necessarily final, and that Atlantic movements in both directions between New Orleans and France were persistent—an interesting fact about transatlantic influences. Several times in 1837, he mentions arrivals of such people recommended by Ste-Gême. In a single newsletter, he announces the arrival of several people, all coming from a relatively small area in southwestern France, suggesting not only the existence of an uninterrupted flow of migrants from France, but also that, when migrations occurred, the presence in the French village or town of people having experienced migrations favored the constitution of networks, encouraging the concentration of migrants in some precise locations in the Americas.

The newcomers experienced various fates. One of the men recommended by Ste-Gême is said to have settled in the Attakapas as a blacksmith and locksmith. Another, Michel Maylin, became a coppersmith in an area upriver. Joseph Bon, from Saint-Gaudens, died in the summer of 1837, but his younger brother, François, recovered from his sickness and was able to work for a living. A Labatut from Toulouse, also recommended by Ste-Gême, found a position as salesclerk in a shop. At some point, Mr. Latapie, the brother-in-law of Mme. Latapie, born Celeste Dreux, thus related to Ste-Gême's wife, is said to have arrived in the city three months earlier and to have settled in Gentilly, while trying to secure a position, which he still had not managed to do. People apparently still saw Louisiana as a means to make a fortune in the New World, as a land of opportunity for French nationals. Boze sometimes expresses pessimism about the opportunities offered to Latapie, since, even if the economic depression ended, he thinks that the latter's ignorance of the city, of commercial business, and of English would make it difficult for him to find a position (F 282). Later that year, however, he says that the two Frenchmen, Labatut and Latapie, had managed to find positions. Labatut was selling "tats" in the faubourgs and on plantations upriver and Latapie was employed by "a company of capitalists" for "excavations at the Barataria Canal" (F 283). Later, Boze adds that "Latapie has a position as supervisor of a canal that is being built between New Orleans and the Attakapas." As for Labatut, he had borrowed some money, had started a partnership with a young man from Bordeaux, and was selling goods, using the pirogue they had purchased for coastal navigation. His business did so well that he refused a position that was offered to him at a college at a salary of eight hundred dollars (F 283). In most cases, thus, the migrants came to New Orleans by choice. In some, they were even invited there for their expertise. Several times, for instance, John Davis's son, Toto, is said to have recruited French actors for his father's company. There were thus cases of invited migrants who had expertise that was needed in the Crescent City, although Boze never says if they stayed long in New Orleans (F 267). Some instances are also given of migrants who came to Louisiana to make a fortune and returned home once they had met with success. In April 1837, Boze mentions Mr. Farès, a "Creole [*sic*] of [Ste-Gême's] birthplace," who was a "good man, and is very deserving by his wise behavior and his love for work" and who "returns in the midst of his family with some thousands of *escalins* that his honorable industry have made him earn" (F 275). Movements were thus numerous and apparently normal in the Atlantic space and thus permanently renewed the interest of Louisiana in whatever was happening in the former colonial power.

Moreover, the commercial and personal ties between New Orleans and France were still very close. Numerous boats permitted exchanges between New Orleans and the port cities of Atlantic France, mainly Le Havre and Bordeaux. Boze constantly mentions transatlantic connections, and the regularity of the departure and arrival of letters to and from France attests to these links. Such arrivals were always sources of rejoicing among New Orleans residents. A long-expected boat from Le Havre, for instance, reached New Orleans on April 29, 1830 (F 164), bringing, to the great relief of the people, French newspapers, which enabled the city's residents to be informed about the main political events taking place in Paris (in this case, the March 1830 opposition between the king and the French Chambre des Députés). The long hurricane season, which put a halt to all movement in the harbor, made New Orleanians eager for the return of the unfading links with its former empire. In November of 1830, for instance, Boze writes Ste-Gême that there were still no boats coming from France because of the *hivernage*, which was apparently hard on Louisianans. "The youth is already making preparations to celebrate the Captain commanding the first vessel that will arrive with the French flag," he writes, using the very French expression "tricolor" to refer to the flag (F 177). It is amazing to imagine the endless transatlantic crossings the people were willing to endure. The *Zelia*, for instance, took seventy-five days to cross the Atlantic from Bordeaux, arriving in New Orleans on February 7, 1831 (F 181).

Products were regularly exchanged, and New Orleans was still very fond of French goods. French ideas, trends, and fashions were constantly brought into New Orleans, and Boze keeps mentioning clothing fashions imported to the city, particularly for the various festive events there, either during the Christmas season or during Mardi Gras. In November of 1832, several boats arrived from Le Havre, bringing back many New Orleans residents after a sojourn in France, and "luxury and fashion tats for the lovers of Carnival balls" (F 212). In the fall of 1835, New Orleans welcomed "beautiful and rich merchandise in vast quantities and of all kinds, to the point that commerce here has started entering its period of intense movements," which makes residents "hope that celebrations will be very brilliant next winter, when the New Orleans speculators who have gone shopping for that season's clothes in France return, making the shops for rent grow scarce, especially those on the commercial streets." The attachment of New Orleanians to French fashion trends is obvious: those who have returned are already unpacking "their wealth of Parisian luxury, taste, and fashion," and women are competing for the purchase of these luxury goods, in order "to be noticed and shine, in the winter, with much distinction in the societies and with much brilliance and splendor at the fashion evenings of the carnival period" (F 258). France in general and Paris in particular were considered the places of good taste and expertise, and when, for instance, John Davis needed an architect to remodel the Théâtre d'Orléans, he entrusted his son with having plans designed in Paris "to the taste of one of the first-class artists of that capital" (F 269).

Economic ties were extremely close between New Orleans and her former empire. Some New Orleans businessmen went back and forth.[19] The financial links between France and New Orleans were apparently numerous and, several times, French investors were sought for Louisiana. The Banque des Citoyens, for instance, faced with financial difficulties in the spring of 1835, started actively seeking French capital. The bank was in trouble "for the reason that, either in France or in foreign countries, its agents are said to have been unable to find sufficient loans to complete the capital that this bank requires. The agents have not yet returned from their mission," making the people still hopeful for effective assistance (F 252). Capital was eventually secured, as Louisiana was considered as a good place for lucrative investments.

Ties were also maintained by the fact that Louisianans constantly went back and forth between New Orleans and France, either for short visits or longer stays. Mentions of Louisiana families traveling to France are made in virtually every letter and, often, a long list of names is provided. In April 1830, for instance, Boze informs Ste-Gême of the departure for France of Mr. de Marigny, Mrs. Livaudais and her daughter, Mrs. Capet, and the teacher Mr. Charbonnier. Ste-Gême's former doctor, the youngest of the Lemonier brothers, was still in France with his three children, although he intended to come back after a two-year stay, which had begun in the fall of 1829 (F 164). In March 1833, "many families are getting ready to leave for France momentarily" and names are given, along with, most of the time, details about the families: David Urqhuart, Widow Fitzgerald, her son-in-law, Mr. Lompré, and his two children, the family of Dufilho, the pharmacist, Widow Moran, Mr. Ducatel, and Mr. Roc. "There will be, in the expeditions of the vessels bound for Le Havre and Bordeaux, many more passengers, some of them intending to settle and stay there, others intending to return" (F 218). In one single newsletter, the fact that so many of Ste-Gême's acquaintances had departed suggests the significant number of permanent displacements between Louisiana and France and attests both to the continued attraction of France to New Orleanians and to the influences it had maintained in its former colony. French people thus migrated to Louisiana, Louisianans went to France, and, most of the time, Atlantic movements were pendular, with the same people going back and forth across the Atlantic and thus probably maintaining some degree of reciprocity in the exchanges between New Orleans and France. In May 1830, after listing, once again, numerous New Orleanians' departures to France, Boze adds that they generally did not stay long in France, "either because of lack of financial means or because of their taste for the Gumbo filés" (F 166), the last ironical remark suggesting that they had a deep attachment to Louisiana, which had, by then, become their home.

In spite of their attachment to France, New Orleanians were increasingly American then, and most New Orleanians who left for Paris hoped or planned to return to Louisiana, as was the case of the Canonges, in January 1831. The famous lawyer and his wife were planning to return to New Orleans, when Mrs. Canonge, born Mercier, unexpectedly died in Paris (F 178). Mr. Canonge eventually returned to Louisiana in December 1831, along with several other Louisianans (F 193). In April 1832, Boze refers to about twenty New Orleans residents en route to France "to enjoy their wealth," launch into "commercial speculation," or for health reasons, but, in the fall of 1832, a boat from Bordeaux is said to have capsized, with thirty-four passengers on board, most of them returning from a trip to France, who were all safe, although they had lost everything they had on board (F 211). The newsletters are long registers of names of people leaving, as well as people returning. Recurrently, Boze writes, "several French and American vessels have arrived here, disembarking a quantity of passengers back from their travel to France" (F 232). Several subsequent letters mention the same names and more, giving new details about the reasons for these long and laborious journeys to France and back to Louisiana "after enjoying to the fullest the pleasures of its capital" (F 225).

Along the way, Boze informs his addressee of the reasons why Louisianans went to France. People were often traveling for pleasure, to enjoy the fortune they had made in Louisiana. Others, like Mr. Lamber, who "suffers from the disease of wanting to travel to France," went there out of curiosity or nostalgia for their own or their ancestors' country of origin (F 233). Health problems are also often cited as reasons for these trips to France, with Widow Morand leaving to have her eyes treated and Mr. Peychaud to cure his "ulcer in the throat" (F 236).

Many had business matters in or with France, like Mr. John Garnier or Mr. Marot, who traveled to France for "commercial speculations" (F 232). Davis's son went to Paris "doubtlessly to recruit comedians for the shows of next winter" (F 243). Mr. Hispan left for France, "where matters of interest are calling him" (F 268). Felix Labatut, a merchant in New Orleans, left for France in the fall of 1836, intending "to do business with several European cities" (F 271).

Some travelers also went because they had family members in France, like Mr. Albin Michel, who visited his son in Paris (F 232) or Widow Tremoulet, whose daughter resided in Tarbes, not very far from Ste-Gême's residence, and who visited her daughter from time to time, regularly transmitting news from southwestern France to New Orleans (F 271). Many of the most recently arrived in Louisiana had parents in France, like Mme. Papet, whose mother still lived in Paris (F 232), and even people born in Louisiana still had strong ties in France, like Mme. Bourbon Abat, born Alix Poirée, who was, Boze indicates, "a Creole of this city" (F 245) but was still in close contact with her French relatives.

If people often visited their children in France, it was also because Paris was the logical place to send them for their education. There are many such examples in Boze's letters. Lemonier, the doctor, who had four children, among whom were three daughters, visited "the two youngest [who] are still in Paris for their education" (F 205). He later returned to Louisiana from France, leaving behind two daughters for their schooling. His sister had two sons who were also being educated in Paris (F 233). In June 1833, Mrs. Lecarpentier, née Blache, the wife of the auctioneer, left with her youngest son and daughter for Paris, "where they will get a distinguished education" (F 226). The son of Mr. Marot, a native of Nantes, a dry-goods seller on Rue Royale, was also being educated in Paris, which shows that this was common practice, not reserved for the minority elite of the city, and that upper-middle class people also sent their children to France.[20] Even adults went to complete their degrees in Paris, as, for instance, Dr. Ursain Landreau, who left to complete a medical degree in France (F 243). In 1837, the son of Dr. Lemonier had gone back to France "to complete his medical studies, obtain his diploma from the Academy, and return to his birth country for his practice" (F 283).

People thus went back and forth across the Atlantic. Many French people settled in Louisiana; some returned home; many Louisianans visited France; if some settled in France, most returned home to New Orleans. Interestingly, even when people settled permanently, either in France or Louisiana, they never severed ties with their place of origin. Letters and news were always exchanged, as were goods; people visited whenever they had sufficient financial means to do so. Most of the time, even when people did not expect to return to New Orleans, they left behind some of their possessions, as Ste-Gême had done when he had left in 1818, never to return. For twenty-five years until his death, he apparently never even thought of getting rid of his large Louisiana property.[21] Louisiana remained the place where French people invested their money, in the hope of substantial returns. Dr. Picquet, for instance, left for France in May 1831 "with his whole family by way of New York, taking with him his rich fortune, but still leaving in this country 3 rental houses on the levee" (F 185).

French influence thus permeated New Orleans, even three decades after the end of colonial rule, and the impression Boze gives is that this connection had not abated even a whole generation after the Louisiana Purchase. New Orleans was still very European, and of course, very French, in the late 1830s. Even as New Orleanians looked toward France, however, they were already becoming part of the young American republic.

New Orleans in the Young American Republic

Boze's letters clearly show that the United States was now one of the main interests of the still very French inhabitants of New Orleans. Because of the progressive integration of the city into the young republic, the connections between New Orleans and the rest of the United States became increasingly closer. The city became a gateway to North America, as well as a point of convergence for people and goods from the Northern United States.

The young republic's interests are clearly deemed important by Boze. Often, in the early years of the correspondence, he mentions the territorial interests of his new nation. The question of the possession of Pensacola is many times mentioned between January 1818 and January 1819 (F 19 to 28), and he announces to Ste-Gême the sale of Florida to the United States in May 1819 (F 34). In the same letter, he voices his concern that Cuba could fall into the hands of Britain, thereby jeopardizing American interests in the Spanish colony and also those of New Orleanians, especially the Gallic population. "It is said that the nationals do not see favorably this change, according to the general opinion in Havana. The Spanish regime fits better the interests of the French, in all matters, people say, this English nation demanding exclusive commerce in all respects, they could no longer do business there" (F 34). Interestingly, when referring to New Orleans, Boze still speaks of the "interests of the French," showing that there was relative confusion as to what interests were really at stake in New Orleans. In most cases, however, he seems to resolutely place himself within the perimeter of the young republic, suggesting a progressive feeling of belonging to the young American republic, even from someone who apparently never became a citizen of the United States.

Boze's news is, of course, partial, because he reports only what is connected with both Ste-Gême's and his own interests, which by no means presupposes that the news the Louisianans had access to was limited to what he writes to Ste-Gême. The information he gives is always linked to something relevant to Ste-Gême's past or present interests. Because Ste-Gême was one of the heroes of the Battle of New Orleans, General Jackson, the American hero of the battle, interested him, and Boze constantly mentions the fate of the "savior of Louisiana," as he refers to him several times, although the fact that the battle occurred after the signing of a peace treaty between Great Britain and the United States made this heroic victory more symbolic than really useful. In May 1819, he writes of the well-deserved support of the whole American nation for Jackson, adding that "he was approved of by the president and the absolute majority of the Americans, the true friends of their country" (F 34). During Jackson's campaign for the presidency, in 1828, Boze criticizes some Louisianans for their indifference and for not welcoming him "as necessity commanded and as he deserved on the occasion of his visit to this city," adding that he had saved Louisiana and that the United States "is glorified by this very good choice for the interests of the Republic and for its happiness by the guarantee of its freedom" (F 160). He officially announces the candidacy of "André Jackson from Tennessee [*sic*]" to the presidency of the United States in February 1832, with Martin Van Buren as the vice-presidential candidate (F 198). In a postscript to his fall 1832 letter, he announces that it appears that Jackson will be reelected (F 211). In early November, he comments on the Northern votes, concluding that he is "expecting that end so much desired and with much justice by the grateful Louisianans who wish his triumph" (F 212). In December, he confirms the victory of his hero over Clay, rejoicing over it despite the fact that the defeated candidate was a Southerner (F 215). Later, he expatiates on the policies implemented by Jackson, still defending his favorite president. In early April 1834, for instance, he comments on the 1832 presidential veto to the re-chartering of the Bank of the United States and on the 1833 executive order to remove the deposits of federal funds from the bank and place them in state-chartered banks. Boze explains that "it is difficult to have banks renew credit notes since President Jackson refuses, with the firmness of a good patriot and an honest man, the renewal of the Charter of the United States and, despite the outcries of the opposition party, it will become extinct, Amen" (F 238). And, obviously perfectly well informed about the question, he comments on the local repercussions of these decisions, a sign of the now strongly connected fate of Louisiana to that of its new nation. As so many people were concerned, the other banks refused to discount the credit notes "except at the 60-day term, and only if those who endorse them are acknowledged to enjoy a large fortune in cash, which despairs the creditors in difficulty who are compelled to resort to usurers." Although this sometimes made the situation difficult for Louisianans, Boze later adds a long paragraph in which he stresses "the extreme pleasure with which the Jacksonites of this city have learned, through northern newspapers, of the total victory of the president over the aristocratic partisans of the Bank of the United States who wished its renewal at the expiration of the charter," concluding on the "honorable firmness of this patriotic leader" (F 238). Despite his still extremely strong attachment to France, and even if he apparently never requested to become a citizen of the United States, this Frenchman, who had spent over three-quarters of his long life outside the United States, now connected patriotism with the young republic. His letters also show the importance of symbols to confirm Louisiana's integration in the Union, which is hardly surprising, as this was probably the biggest challenge that New Orleanians of the time had to face. The Battle of New Orleans, in some measure the founding moment of American Louisiana, and its hero, Andrew Jackson, remained a powerful connection with their new nation.[22]

Even if he remains attentive to the interests of Louisiana and if this is where his priority lay, Boze is clearly turning his eyes to the young republic and considering the interests of the new owners of Louisiana. Quite naturally, he is often interested in what is closest to Louisiana, the fate of Florida, for instance, being often discussed, particularly in connection with the Indian question. In the spring of 1830, he dedicates a long paragraph to the arrival of an elite troop of 300 to 350 infantrymen of the United States army who will be deployed to Mobile and the Florida border to fight the Indians (F 169). In April 1836, he again tackles the question, informing Ste-Gême that General Gaines has left Fort King and joined General Clinch on February 27. The latter met a detachment of some fifteen hundred Indians armed with firearms and ammunitions on his way. They opened fire to prevent him from crossing a river, and the U.S. army then routed the Indian forces, killing three hundred and losing four men, with six more being wounded in the fight. He adds that the Indians, counting on their better knowledge of the field, are still organizing skirmishes and expresses his hope for the end of the hostility, for the sake of his new homeland (F 267). As in the example of Florida, the national news reported by Boze is generally of specific interest for Louisiana, which attests to his primary loyalty to his state but also to the connection between the state and its new nation. For instance, while Louisiana was still asserting its rank among the slave societies of the South, news of the Nat Turner rebellion, in 1831, obviously shook the conscience of New Orleans. Long descriptions in Boze's letters detail the rebellion, the arrests, the trial, and the sentences.[23]

Despite the often local consequences of the events he chooses to report, he also, at times, demonstrates that Louisianans had the United States' interest at heart, even when it conflicted with the enduring feelings they had for their old colonial power. Although he is not necessarily pleased with the news, he reports on the celebration in Louisiana of certain American successes that are detrimental to French interests. In June 1835, for instance, he comments on the news received in Louisiana that, on April 18, the French Chambre des Députés passed, with a majority of 152 votes, "the law appropriating the 25 million of the American debt with interest," adding that "the nationals of this city have sounded the cannon all day" and will organize banquets "in acknowledgement of this long awaited payment" promised by Louis Philippe (F 255). Although his heart remains French (he comments on Député Berryer, "who defended the cause of his motherland against the claims of the United States" and who will be hurt if he reads about "the insults of the people of this ungrateful nation"), and although he criticizes Jackson's refusal to respond to the French assembly's request that he explain his announcement that there would be war if the debt remained unpaid, he hopes that it will not jeopardize the peace between the two nations, which would be harmful to business, he says (F 256). Louisianans, who were divided as to whether there would be war between France and the United States, were eagerly waiting for Jackson's State of the Union speech, hoping that he would explain why he threatened hostilities (F 260). In New Orleans, some advocated strong resistance to the French demands, and Livingston, for instance, the former ambassador of the United States to the French court, "keeps filling the newspapers with his complaints for the wrongs against this republic," insisting that Jackson should not demean himself to give the explanations requested by the French assembly (F 257). Louisiana had more difficulty than usual taking a clear position on this matter, torn as she was between her old colonial empire and her new homeland, but Louisianans were obviously moving toward more patriotic sentiments for the young republic.

As the years went by, news concerning the young republic took up an increasing portion of Boze's letters, proving that, even to an old Frenchman, the inclusion of New Orleans and Louisiana in the United States was becoming a reality. New Orleanians were thus obviously conscious of their new national destiny and had integrated the United States into their close mental landscape. Even as this connection to the north of the continent was developing, Louisiana was also becoming a place of reinforced interactions with the rest of the American continent, probably helped in this by the increasing autonomy of the American colonies from their mother countries, particularly during the struggles for independence in the Latin American colonies.

New Orleans in the Americas

Because of all its colonial connections with the region, New Orleans unvaryingly appeared as the northernmost point of the Caribbean. And because of its increased port activities, it became the focal point of exchanges with the West Indies and even with Latin America. In the first half of the nineteenth century, ships traveled regularly from New Orleans to Haiti (Les Cayes, for instance),[24] Cuba (mostly Havana, but also Matanzas),[25] Jamaica, and other places as well. Boze's letters reveal incessant movement between the city and other Caribbean regions, especially Havana, but also Jamaica and Santo Domingo. News, people, and goods circulated freely, especially between Havana and New Orleans, although the heyday of exchanges came slightly later, with the development of regular steamboat lines, like that of the U.S. Mail Steamship Company in 1848.[26] Havana was a regular stop on the way from France (F 201). These connections between Cuba and New Orleans occasioned the maintenance of links between the Cuban and Louisianan communities, especially for Saint-Domingue refugees who resided in New Orleans but still had friends and acquaintances from their temporary residence in Cuba. The arrival of a ship from Havana, in April 1830, bringing to New Orleans people Boze knew from Cuba, conveyed to him the news of the death of "several French and Spaniards," including Ste-Gême's debtor Don Augustin de la Terrera y Oliva, as well as his friend (and debtor) Juan Cavallero (F 163). In May 1832, he informs Ste-Gême of the death of Captain Couapé, whom Boze had met in Santiago at the time of the evacuation from Saint-Domingue. Boze gave details of Couapé's whereabouts (in Jamaica first, then back to Santiago) and of his life in Cuba until his death, showing that he had had precise information from Cuba, through letters or from eyewitness reports from travelers to Havana returning to New Orleans or from Cubans visiting the Crescent City (F 204). Boze often mentions "captains and passengers" (F 222), "people arriving from Havana and Matanzas" (F 226). He lists people arriving ("Mr. Theodore, aeronaut" [F 205], "Jean-Baptiste Laporte from Bayonne" [F 280]) and others departing for the Cuban capital ("Senor Don Francisco Sentmante y Sayas with his spouse, born Marigny" [F 226]). In October 1832, he mentions the shipwreck of a schooner, the *Berice*, bound for Havana and carrying several New Orleans residents (F 211). At the time, people were trying to flee the Louisiana cholera epidemic, and a certain number thus migrated to the West Indies (F 212).

There were also links with Haiti. In the spring of 1831, the remains of corsair captain Cadet Liguet, who had died in Port-au-Prince two years earlier, were brought back to Louisiana by his widow, with the permission of the Haitian government (F 161). In October 1833, Captain Lauminé returned from the Windward Islands (F 232). In more anecdotal pieces of news, Boze's reader understands that these movements took place throughout the Caribbean. In May 1832, Captain Lauminé is said to be heading for St. Thomas "to settle, according to what people say, some interests linked with his latest travels for trade in blacks" (F 204).

News from the Caribbean also came easily to New Orleans through letters, and the local newspapers regularly kept people informed about what was going on in all areas of the region. In March 1831, we thus learn, from a letter written in February by a certain Mr. Revé from Cuba and quoted by Boze, the prices of various products on the Spanish island. Among other less important products, the "coffee from the Siera [*sic*] Maestra" sold for ten dollars per quintal, while the price of white sugar had gone down to five dollars per quintal (from eight or nine dollars the previous years), around three dollars for brown sugar, and two dollars for unrefined sugar; Boze concludes that "if things go on like this, in a few years, sugar planters will be in the same position as coffee planters" (F 181). The knowledge of, and interest in, the life of what had been, for many, a temporary asylum was clearly important for New Orleanians, essentially for the Saint-Domingue refugees—although not exclusively, for the various French-speaking communities had intermarried. Regularly, as in March 1833, Boze tells Ste-Gême that he received news from Cuba through the arrival of a ship from Havana (F 218). In March 1832, word of the Christmas slave rebellion in Jamaica reached New Orleans through Jamaican newspapers (F 201). In August 1832, Boze also details at length the fire that ravaged Port-au-Prince on July 8, thereby indicating that news not only traveled but that it traveled relatively fast (F 208).

The same can be said of news between New Orleans and Hispanic America, mostly Mexico, but other countries in Latin America as well. Movement was incessant among the Spanish colonies, the future independent Latin American nations, and Louisiana, for reasons that varied greatly from one case to another. The main destinations were Mexico (Galveston [which was Mexican until the independence of Texas in 1836], Tampico, and Vera Cruz) and Rio de Janeiro.[27]

From what Boze writes, people who left Europe to settle in the Americas were sometimes unsure of their exact destination in the Western Hemisphere, and some migrants to the Americas decided to stay at one of their first stops on the continent, never reaching their originally planned destination. Interestingly, contacts were so frequent between the various zones of the continent that Boze manages to learn about these unforeseen halts. Some of these migrants stayed in Cuba, others went to the southern continent, to Mexico, Venezuela, or French Guiana. In the summer of 1836, for instance, Boze tells Ste-Gême that Mr. Chaton, a watchmaker who had been recommended by Ste-Gême, had not reached New Orleans, "having first left board in Cayenne, where he stopped for the settlement of some interests that have been entrusted to him, people say" (F 271). Although Mr. Chaton had seized American opportunities other than Louisiana, Boze knew about his original plans and followed the details of his journey from France to America. Other migrants pursued their original plans and first came to Louisiana before moving on, sometimes eventually returning to Louisiana and sometimes not. Boze also regularly mentions people traveling to and from Latin America

(F 164). Three grinders from Sauveterre, the town where Ste-Gême lived in southwestern France, are seen circulating among Haiti, Cuba, Louisiana, and Mexico. Boze mentions their arrival, in February 1832, by way of Saint-Domingue (interestingly, he never says Haiti, even after France had officially acknowledged the Haitian republic) and Havana (F 198). After keeping Ste-Gême updated on their whereabouts in Louisiana and the state of their business, Boze informed him that they had left for Tampico, in late April (F 202), confirming the extreme mobility of people within the Caribbean—and American—space. Let us also remember the example of Dr. Antommarchi, the hero of the city, who, after residing in New Orleans for a while, decided to set sail for Mexico, in the fall of 1835, "to practice his skill, as well as because he was curious to roam and get to know the land of the new world" (F 238). He settled for a time in Veracruz before moving to Santiago de Cuba, where he practiced until his death from yellow fever in 1838. People were often on the move in the Atlantic world of the early nineteenth century. They were acutely aware of the opportunities offered by the Greater Caribbean and were ready to seize them all.

Sometimes, Boze's letters suggest general information from apparently anecdotal events. Because of an isolated episode, the reader learns about constant movements in the Gulf. In August 1829, for instance, a military flotilla composed of four ships, with 3,300 men on board, departed from Cuba. Louisianans interpreted this as an attempt to give military assistance to the Mexican government by "attacking with armed forces the republican insurgents of that country." At the time, the still unsettled Mexican government was facing more bloodshed and was involved in what is known as the Cristero War. The flotilla was caught in stormy weather and one boat was damaged, which led it to try to find shelter in New Orleans to get its masts repaired. Louisiana authorities did not accept so easily the arrival of a military vessel belonging to a foreign country, and the governor commissioned a staff officer to warn the captain to leave his boat at anchor. After some negotiations, the men were allowed to land, albeit with many restrictions placed on their movements. The Spanish authorities expressed gratitude to the Louisianans and then promised that all of the regulations would be respected, to prove "they deserved their trust." Boze then comments on the final mission of the flotilla against "the revolting Spaniards who have not had siesta! And for many years!" (F 144).[28] Although somewhat anecdotal, this episode reveals the interest of the Louisianans in what was occurring in the Southwest. Mexico, through Texas, was a short distance away from New Orleans (at least until 1836) and whatever happened there could not but impact the Louisiana capital, which was already at the center of a complex web of economic exchanges. Mexico was a refuge for the privateers of Barataria, who had settled in Galveston when they were no longer *personae gratae* in Louisiana, and many Mexican residents found refuge in Louisiana when their lives were threatened by continual conflict between the autonomists and the Spanish authorities. Several Louisianans even took part in the Mexican War of Independence, in the late 1810s and early 1820s. A few remained involved in activities, including military ones, in the early years of the new Mexican nation.

In the summer of 1829, for example, Boze discusses the assistance given to the Mexicans by some Louisiana "sailors," citing the example of Senor Beluche, known for his involvement with the Lafitte brothers, who was then "employed in the navy of the Mexicans" (F 147). Some of the Baratarians,[29] after moving to Galveston in the late 1810s, offered their services to the Mexicans, to counter the Spanish attempts at reconquest, in the late 1920s. Boze expatiates at length on what Louisianans thought the outcome of the ongoing—or, rather, resuming—revolution would be, showing by this mere mention not only that New Orleans residents were informed of what was going on in Mexico but also that they were interested and closely scrutinized the events unfolding there, two steps away from their border. Their intuition proved wrong, since they thought that Spain would win, because of "the little courage of Mexico's inhabitants to defend it" and the military superiority of Spain (F 147). Their interest in the topic and discussion of the events showed that Louisiana kept close connections with the rest of the continent. Clearly, newspapers were circulated widely throughout the Greater Caribbean space. In September 1829, "the public papers of Veracruz have given us the official news that the Mexicans had fought, on 20 August, a victorious battle against the Spanish army and that their success had occasioned an enthusiasm that gave them hope that they would manage to throw them out of their territory as promised by the newsletters that reach us relatively often and detail their war movements" (F 148). Information about the involvement of the United States is also regularly given, such as when news reached Louisiana that a terrible hurricane in the Gulf of Mexico on September 10 had destroyed several schooners bound for Tampico (F 150). The *Hornet*, a U.S. vessel, and three merchant ships carrying food for the Spanish troops in Tampico were all lost, as well as a French ship, which was carrying away 400,000 gourdes belonging to Mexican residents who were trying to get their money out of the country while the revolutionary events were unfolding (F 150).

People apparently traveled widely on and around the American continent. In the spring of 1830, the already cited Renato Beluche, the former second of the Lafitte brothers in Barataria, was no longer involved in Mexican military operations and had become an admiral in the Colombian army. He was navigating the southern seas while his wife was in Caracas after leaving Porto Cabello, which was no longer safe, Boze tells us (F 161). In early July, Boze reports that Commodore Beluche of the Colombian army has arrived in New Orleans from Pensacola and was accommodated by Mr. Sauvinet (F 170). Later that month, Boze expresses his ignorance of the continued military status of Beluche in Colombia "now that his leader, Bolivar, had lost sovereignty over the army, according to what the papers published in that country say" (F 172). In 1830, Bolivar, who had been ruling over Greater Colombia since 1828, was faced with increasing internal divisions and had indeed offered his resignation to try to save Colombia from dissolution. His resignation was accepted in May and marked the end of Bolivar's political career, a few months before he died of tuberculosis. This could only mark the end of Beluche's military career in Colombia, which explains Boze's questioning of his activities and whereabouts. He also indicated, however, that Beluche's wife was still residing in Caracas and that Beluche intended to go to St. Thomas and bring her and their two children there (F 172). This clearly meant that not only was Boze informed about the political events in Latin America but also that he had more personal news from Beluche. Although Boze had earlier announced rumors that Beluche, "one of the creatures of late president Bolivar" had been executed, in May 1832, he was back in New Orleans, although "spoilt of all his titles of the navy" of Colombia, while his wife was still in Caracas with her children (F 204). In late June, Beluche was en route to Caracas to join his family. In August, he was said to be with his "dame mézelle," which could indicate that the mother of his children was a woman of color (F 231). In the summer of 1833, Beluche was at Porto Cabello and intended to return to New Orleans, after a long period of inactivity, only on half pay, following the death of his protector, Bolivar (F 231). Clearly, both Boze and Ste-Gême knew Beluche from his Barataria days, and this explains the numerous mentions of him in the letters. The extremely precise details Boze gives, however, prove that New Orleanians had a keen knowledge of what was going on in the Americas and of the whereabouts of the people they knew. The narration of Beluche's movements is also a very good example of New Orleans's close connections to Latin America and of the porosity of the various nations and empires of the Americas. A Louisiana privateer, originally from Saint-Domingue, could get involved in the Mexican War of Independence before becoming one of the leading figures of the Colombia navy, under direct command of El Libertador, Simon Bolivar, the hero of the Latin American struggles for independence. That a foreigner could become a high-ranking officer of the army or navy and the symbol of a nation reveals how easily people could circulate in the Americas and how connected New Orleans was to the Latin American world.

The news regularly brought to New Orleans from—sometimes remote—parts of the continent also attests to this. In June 1833, Boze informs Ste-Gême that cholera had reached Tampico and that the son of Widow Blondeau, who had a commercial establishment in Matamora, had died of it (F 227). For months, Boze gave Ste-Gême news of the three grinders he had recommended, who had left for Mexico after a short stay in Louisiana. In March 1833, he tells Ste-Gême that they are still there (F 218). In the midst of the cholera epidemic of the summer of 1833, they were still doing well (F 229), as again they were in September of the same year (F 231). In November, one of the grinders had returned to Louisiana, bearing news that a second one had died of yellow fever in Tampico and that the third was still "busy grinding in another area of that country" (F 233). In July 1834, Boze informs Ste-Gême that the letter he had transferred from Mr. Jacques d'Estoup from Sauveterre for his son Jean, a "grinder, roaming through the cities of Mexico with his grindstone," would most certainly reach its addressee "after my recommendation to a passenger who knows him and is bound for that land" (F 243). In May 1835, good news came from Mexico about the grinder through travelers who had settled in Tampico (F 253). In February 1836, Boze writes that he has not had news from Jean D'estoup [*sic*] Junior directly but that the latter has now settled in Tampico and that, through people originating from the same region as him, he knows that he is still alive and conducting business there (F 265). In the summer of 1836, we last hear of Estoup [*sic*] coming from Saint-Gaudens when Boze informs his friend that he has returned from Tampico, where he earned a good living (F 269).

These are only anecdotal pieces of news to any reader other than Ste-Gême, but they give good measure of the degree of preciseness of the information that circulated and of the close connections New Orleans maintained with Latin America. Giving the same impression of an uninterrupted flow of information between New Orleans and the rest of the Americas, Boze sometimes also comments on more public events. In February 1830, for instance, he discusses the fall of Generals Vicente Guerrera and Antonio Lopez de Santa Ana, who supported the Mexican government, and adds that "Mexico has entered a state of anarchy" and that the outcome of the troubles "will be necessarily dreadful to its population" (F 157). In March 1830, news came to New Orleans that the authorities of Venezuela and Colombia had obliged

Bolivar to renounce his title of superior commander, which he did willingly in face of the superiority of his opponents, "who cannot, however, despite their disunion, but acknowledge the bravery of this distinguished warrior, his merit, his enlightenment, and all the great services he has rendered to his country during his reign [*sic*]." Turning his interest from Venezuela and Colombia to Mexico again, he resumes his commentary on events there, repeating that "since the government has lost the warriors Guerrera and Santa Ana, (the country) is in total insurrection, to the point that blood has already started flowing, if we are to believe the newspapers coming from Veracruz" (F 161). He goes on reporting on the troubles in Mexico, expatiating at length on the balance of power between the Mexicans and the Spaniards (F 164). The reports given by Boze to Ste-Gême clearly indicate that news reached New Orleans from everywhere on the continent and attest to his interest in all things American, in the hemispheric sense of the term. Of course, the news Boze reports from Mexico is, like the rest of his correspondence, very partial and mainly concerns topics of mutual interest to his addressee and himself, but from the regularity of the mentions, we may infer the frequency of movement between Latin America and New Orleans.

Commerce was another important connection between New Orleans and the southern areas of the continent. Many actors of this important economic activity are mentioned throughout the correspondence, either individually or in more general conversations. In May 1832, for instance, Boze cites the commercial ventures of Don Francisco Sentmante y Sayas in Mexico (F 204), and he regularly mentions the departure of vessels, to and from Mexico (mostly Tampico and Veracruz), carrying important cargoes (F 239). Some areas of Mexico had apparently known better days. In December 1833, mentioning his vain attempts to obtain the mortuary documents of a seaman, Charles Pommarède, who was killed in Mantilla, Mexico, in a hurricane in 1818, he says that it was difficult in this "foreign country that is no longer busy with commerce today," adding that his failure was to be accounted for "as much by the distance that separates us from this land as by the scarcity of the travelers, Mantilla having long ceased to be busy with commerce" (F 234). Commerce, however, was still very active in other areas, such as Tampico. Boats and travelers thus connected Louisiana with many very distant places at a frequency that is beyond the imagination of the present-day reader. The Gulf of Mexico was a very busy place, as was the Atlantic Ocean, and news came frequently through travelers' accounts and letters and newspapers. The American world was an open space of circulation and exchange, in which people negotiated their place to the best of their ability.

In the 1830s, Jean Boze was still clearly very French and part of his heart had remained in France, although he had spent more than fifty years, two-thirds of his life, in the Americas. As an old man, who had lived in New Orleans the last thirty of his ninety years, he probably felt too old to give his total loyalty to another territory, and he never seems to have given up his French citizenship, even if the last forty years of his life were spent in non-French territories—Cuba, first, and then Louisiana. In the fall of 1835, fifty-five years after leaving France forever and twenty-five years after coming to New Orleans, he wrote: "I was born French and I love my homeland,[30] which makes me wish for its happiness, its prosperity, its peace, and its liberty," wanting to "see her once more superior to all others without any alliance" (F 258). A few months before, apologizing for trying to discuss politics when he was by no means a specialist, he had accounted for his wish to do so as follows: "an excess of love for my homeland which will always be my religion," using the word religion more in an ethnic sense than a religious one (F 256). Notwithstanding this strong emotional attachment and the loyalty and love he still displayed for his homeland, Boze, despite his old age, was resolutely looking toward the Americas, attesting to the progressive integration of Louisiana into the young republic and the Western Hemisphere. Although it is, of course, impossible to ascertain that his example is representative, the many mentions he makes of the reactions of New Orleanians to national and foreign events strongly suggest that the rest of the Gallic population often shared his point of view and analyses.

What is obvious, at any rate, is that New Orleans was a frequent passage within the Americas and between America and Europe. Its connections to the rest of the United States were rapidly improving while it retained special relations with France. The primary exchanges were economic, and the Crescent City was a favorite place of transit for products from the northern and western United States, from Europe to the east, and from Latin America and the Caribbean to the south. But it was also a meeting place for people who came from the four cardinal points, which accounts both for New Orleans's diversity and for its extraordinary cultural wealth.

5

Cultures

The confluence of people coming from Europe and the Americas gave New Orleans a very specific flavor in the early American decades. The dramatic increase in the population also made for extreme diversity and wealth in the Louisiana capital. Different racial and ethnic groups mingled, as in the other Atlantic cities of the United States. In New Orleans, however, the proportions were unusual and the context very different from the rest of the young republic, and race, ethnic, and class factors interplayed in a unique way. The confrontations and alliances among various groups were the backbone of the social and political construction of the city, producing an original blend that explains many of New Orleans's various evolutions in the nineteenth century.

Boze's testimony is, in this respect, invaluable, for many reasons. As an old man, writing between ages seventy and ninety, he was, to some degree, an outsider. He did not play any political or economic role in the city. He was nonetheless a privileged observer of what was going on in New Orleans. As a Frenchman who had been a colonial, had lived in French, Spanish, and Dutch colonies of the Caribbean, and had chosen to settle in Louisiana, his loyalties still lay with France, even as he proved deeply attached to the American world. Even though he admits that his advanced age and lack of resources prevented him from seeing Europe again, he was in the Americas by choice, and in New Orleans by preference, having, after some early hesitation in the late 1810s, decided against a permanent return to Cuba. Because he settled in the Americas when he was past thirty, and because he still maintained close contacts with his daughter in Germany and with Ste-Gême in France, he had remained very interested in Europe, particularly in his motherland. He was thus a man of the Americas, but with clear Gallic leanings, a man of in-betweenness, or rather, maybe, dual belongingness. Whatever his national interest, however, his primary loyalty unsurprisingly was to those who had twice been his companions of misfortune, during the flight from Saint-Domingue and then from Cuba: the Saint-Domingue refugees, who constituted his first circle of relations and his main focus of interest.

Boze thus observed the city from a privileged place. A man of the Americas, with still strong French connections and a specific loyalty to the Saint-Domingue refugees, he informs the reader about New Orleans society from a unique vantage point, if not in an unbiased way. Clearly on the side of the French speakers in their struggle for influence with the Anglo-Saxons, he is a privileged informant about the community of the Saint-Domingue refugees, long neglected in the historiography of New Orleans. His depiction of New Orleans society is thus unequaled by most other narratives of the period.

The reader will follow him in his depiction of the varied, rich, and often confrontational society of early American New Orleans, going from his evaluation of and relationship with the three-tiered racial system to his assessment of the Creole versus American fight for supremacy and concluding with his perspective on the city's ethnic diversity.

New Orleans, a Slave Society

Boze's letters are full of information on racial interactions in New Orleans during the early phase of Americanization.[1] His own past naturally influenced his perspective. At the time he observed New Orleans, he was a well-traveled elderly man, who ended up spending two-thirds of his life in slaveholding societies, both in the Caribbean and in New Orleans. When he started writing his letters, he had been living in slaveholding societies for four decades. Throughout his life in the tropics, he had occupied key positions in a world that supported the institution. Being a corsair or a harbor captain in a slave colony, he certainly had no abolitionist tendencies. Moreover, he had married into a Saint-Domingue Creole slave-owning family, which means that he had lived in proximity to slavery. He had thus been acquainted with slavery, although nothing indicates that he had been personally involved in either the slave trade or slave ownership. When in Saint-Domingue, he had apparently never lived on his wife's family plantation; he had been either a merchant or a harbor captain, and his corsair activities bear no trace of the least connection with the slave trade, and there is no documentary evidence, either in the colonial Saint-Domingue archives or in the New Orleans ones, that he ever purchased, sold, or owned a single slave. When managing Ste-Gême's New Orleans property, he was never involved in the management of the plantation; the task was undertaken entirely by Auvignac Dorville, and thus Boze had no business contact with Ste-Gême's slaves. He was apparently never directly involved in the institution, although he was always acquainted with it. His perception of New Orleans's slave system is thus of interest.

After slow beginnings, especially during the initial period of French rule, Louisiana had become, in the Spanish period, an important slaveholding society. American rule further inscribed it among the main slaveholding societies of the Americas.[2] Throughout the antebellum period, enslaved blacks brought from the Anglo-Saxon South increased the slave population of Louisiana, including New Orleans. Even if the largest numbers of slaves peopled the plantations of rural Louisiana, the slave population of the Louisiana capital increased steadily in the first half of the nineteenth century. About five thousand slaves had arrived with the Saint-Domingue refugees, some directly from the French colony, others from their owners' various prior asylums in the Caribbean or on the North American continent, and the majority (more than 3,226 of them) by way of Cuba.[3] The slave population continued increasing in the first four decades of American rule. In 1820, the city counted 7,355 slaves in a total population of 27,178, thereby constituting 27.1 percent of the city's residents. This proportion was still below that of the main cities of the American South (36.4 percent for Richmond and 51.1 percent for Charleston), but if New Orleans's slave population was lower than Charleston's (with 12,652), it came in second, way ahead of Richmond (with only 4,387 slaves), which definitely placed it among the main slaveholding cities of the United States.[4] In 1840, the city counted 23,448 slaves, constituting 22.9 percent of the rapidly growing total population, a low percentage compared with the 50.1 percent of Charleston, the only other Southern city that ranked among the ten most populous cities in the United States at the time. This placed New Orleans far ahead of Charleston in terms of numbers (Charleston had a slave population of 14,673) and made it the slaveholding capital of the United States.[5]

Everything in Boze's letters shows that, to him, as to a large majority of the New Orleans people, the institution was a normal fact of life. There is not a single mention of any questioning of its legitimacy in Boze's mind and almost no reference to any opposition to it, save for a side comment on the presence of foreign criminals defending abolitionist theses. Slaves were, to most, mere property, and if something happened to them, it was to the detriment of their masters. This is clear from Boze's letters, and, recurrently, he mentions these losses, which he considers to be purely material. Writing of a racially mixed runaway slave, for instance, he concludes that it is "a loss to the owner" (F 23). Informing Ste-Gême of the death of one of his slaves, Jean-Louis, he says that "it is a new loss you are experiencing which, once again, will prove your good heart since you could have sold him" (F 23). Later, suggesting the possibility of a cholera epidemic spreading to the surrounding plantations, he exclaims without restraint, "in this unfortunate case, it would bring a total ruin to the owners," without the least consideration for the slaves as human beings (F 211). And indeed he later concludes that the planters "have been very distressed by the losses they have incurred from the cholera epidemic, and several still do not know if they will be able to collect and roll the cane when it is ripe.[6] They are really to be pitied. In the meantime, they spare their workforce to avoid exposing it to danger" (F 226). That slaves were mere chattel was clearly deeply ingrained in Louisianans' minds, although not more than in those of other Southerners or residents of the slaveholding societies of the Americas.

Although historiography has generally postulated that slaves' working conditions were worse in Louisiana than in the rest of the South, this is nowhere apparent in Boze's account. His contacts with plantation life were limited mostly to Ste-Gême's plantation, but he was always in close contact with urban slavery. Despite his general acceptance of the institution itself, he strongly criticizes violent behavior toward slaves. He praises the good masters, and they are the majority in his mentions. As Ste-Gême, who showed his good heart by not selling a slave who was apparently likely to die, the master of a racially mixed runaway slave accused of murdering a white still wanted to save his slave, "having the weakness of saying that he was a good subject" (F 23).

From time to time, however, Boze mentions cruel mistresses and emits very negative judgments against them, such as Widow Lanusse, for "her cruel nature with her slaves," or Widow Blanque, who was reported to be "treating barbarously her slaves against the laws" (F 134). His position was apparently shared by the rest of the New Orleans people (and the authorities), since her slaves, who had been found bleeding, were rescued by the police, who were tending to them, Boze explains. Another famous example, that of Mme. Lalaurie, Boze's neighbor, who became infamous for her cruel treatment of her slaves, is discussed at length in the letters; the narration shows that Boze's view apparently reflected the prevailing position in New Orleans.[7] The story of Mme. Lalaurie is well known, but Boze's firsthand testimony is a rich source. In the spring of 1834, Mme. Lalaurie, who had a "cruel and barbarous character with slaves she has often pitilessly caused to perish, which is said to have sometimes drawn her into criminal procedure, but with her wealth, she had always managed to free herself from it" (F 238), was caught up in scandal. Thereupon, her house was set on fire by angry New Orleanians, and she had to flee her house and New Orleans, to escape justice and "the fury of a population gathered by the thousands, of all classes, nations, and colors, in great number, who had rushed to this fire, all motivated by the wish to punish her at the first sight of her cruelties against her slaves." Her case is not the only one, since Widow Lanusse, who, "by making them perish, [. . .] does not have a single servant left to serve her," also had to flee to avoid a similar fate when accused of the same crime (F 238). Boze's observations, in the cases of Mme. Lalaurie and Widow Lanusse, confirm a couple of features of New Orleans society: there were especially cruel masters, as in every slaveholding society, and women seem to have often been among the cruelest, maybe because their subaltern position in society led them to oppressing those below them, although some cases involving men are also mentioned in the correspondence.[8] New Orleans, however, is represented in Boze's narrative as having fewer of those ruthless masters than is sometimes depicted by historians, and the people were apparently always ready to anathematize those uncommonly violent people, if we are to believe Boze's recollections.

Even though paternalism is often attributed to the American South rather than to Caribbean islanders, most of Boze's remarks describe a paternalistic relationship between masters and slaves. This is particularly perceptible whenever he gives Ste-Gême news of the slaves on his Gentilly plantation. He mentions the health of the individual slaves, births and deaths among them, and describes the care of Auvignac Dorville, the overseer, for all his workforce. Their needs are well met, "despite his rough manners," even though "the lazy ones and the bad subjects always meet the punishment they deserve when they stray from their duty." And he concludes, in his usual flourish, that "the seaman as well as the *nègre* like to complain, even if you give them marzipan for breakfast," a comment that seems to depart from ordinary racism by equating the two categories of workers, the free white seaman and the enslaved black (F 235). Masters are mostly depicted as close to their slaves, even the field hands. General Lacoste, for instance, even when sick, insists on going to his plantation on New Year's Day "to receive the compliments of his slaves and carry out his visit" (F 235). Recounting the visit he received from a certain Ierma, who had become the companion of an American after being a slave on Ste-Gême's plantation, Boze reports that she said she regretted Ste-Gême and her mistresses (most certainly his wife and her daughter), who "liked to lavish her with kindnesses in her unfortunate situation." She sends them her respects, expresses her gratitude for their generosity, and promises "to never cease to address prayers and wishes to the heavens for their preservation and the happiness of [them] all, as well as for [Ste-Gême's] return, together with his family" (F 238). This is a rare occasion, in the correspondence, when Boze gives a voice to a slave and, although no generalization should be made from this individual case, there is little reason to doubt the veracity of the example.

Although slaves are mostly voiceless in this narrative, as is typical of narratives of the period, he occasionally alludes to the resistance of some to their enslavement or their treatment. He cites the example of an enslaved American cart driver who had whipped a white and whose master paid twenty-five dollars to avoid a complaint against his slave (F 161). He alludes to the case of a mulatto slave, William Green, who administered three blows with a dagger to his master, a French merchant (F 249). He also several times mentions maroon slaves, recounting, for instance, the story of a slave belonging to the editor of *L'Argus*, who was found wandering around Faubourg Marigny and who was chased by his master and four members of the municipal guard; this is one of the rare mentions Boze makes to a kind of ad hoc slave patrol. The runaway slave managed to flee again after disarming and wounding one of the guards and was ultimately shot at, wounded, arrested, and was awaiting judgment in jail (F 161). In January 1833, Boze alludes to the dismantling of a network of robbers composed of whites but also of black maroons, who occupied a house near the Cane Bayou. They were arrested and taken to jail, along with the whites, who occupied the neighboring houses (F 216). Some maroon slaves were also, from time to time, accused of committing murders, for instance at Bayou Cochon, on the other side of the lake (F 271).

There are other signs that the slaves did not accept passively their lot, since, beyond citing examples of individuals running away, Boze says that New Orleanians permanently feared that the slaves would rebel. To him, the slaves were "always prone to revolt," especially since many bad subjects had been imported from the United States, to the great anxiety of New Orleans residents, who resented the legislature's lack of response (F 164). Indeed, what Boze criticizes about slavery in New Orleans is certainly not slavery itself but rather the increasing influx of slaves from the Anglo-Saxon United States, as he fears that these bad subjects could bring rebellion and jeopardize the peace. He recurrently mentions those slaves who were being imported, "without thinking of the danger, but the places of the North find it handy to get rid of them" (F 160). He keeps mentioning the arrival of increasing numbers of Anglo-American slaves and, throughout his correspondence, denounces the domestic slave trade, and especially those "speculators in human flesh," who sent slaves to a horrible future "by the cupidity of their inhuman trade" (F 192), an interesting remark coming from someone who considered slavery normal. Again, however, it was not slavery that he denounced but the exportation to Louisiana of these Anglo-American slaves, the bad lots the American South was trying to get rid of, according to him, in keeping with the practice of planters to "sell down South" disobedient slaves. In the winter of 1830, for instance, he writes: "I will not mention those who have already arrived but will only tell you that, over the last two years, more than 20,000 slave *nègres* have been introduced in this state, of the two sexes and of all ages, that the places of the North have vomited here, as much because of the lure for profit as to get rid of that caste." He goes on, describing the way in which those slaves are sold and at what prices, concluding that "this trade that continues without pity, without religion, and without respect for the events, has peopled the countryside as well as the city with subjects born American," criticizing the treatment they get from "several barbarous masters." The French-speaking community was apparently as critical as Boze of this domestic trade, since he informs his reader that "several motions to the legislature have started a movement for the abolition of this trade which begins provoking fears for the future, if no end is put to this introduction which could later become very dangerous" because of the vices that those slaves display; he concludes that "good subjects are scarce" (F 175). The fear of slave revolts, with the memory of the 1811 German Coast Uprising and, of course, the Haitian Revolution, were still fresh in Louisianans' minds.[9]

Indeed, two of Boze's longest entries discussing slavery in other slaveholding societies of the Americas have to do with large-scale rebellions. The specter of Haiti was undoubtedly constantly present in his mind and in those of most of his peers, whether they were from Saint-Domingue or not.[10] In 1831, the Christmas rebellion in Jamaica and the Nat Turner rebellion in Virginia reverberated throughout the slaveholding South, including, of course, New Orleans. The rebellions were headline news in the Louisiana capital. Boze quotes long passages from the newspapers on the topic—for instance, in March 1832, an account from *La Tribune de la Nouvelle-Orléans*, in which he gives all the details of the Jamaican rebellion, insisting on the numerous deaths, both among the planter class and the slaves (F 201). In the fall of 1831, he gives details about the Nat Turner rebellion, insisting on the gruesome aspects of both the rebellion and the trial. In six of the seventeen pages of the letter, he clearly shows that his concern is for New Orleans and that this rebellion should be taken as a warning by Crescent City residents:

> A rebellion occurred in one of the parishes of Virginia which has been really unfortunate with 25 white families slaughtered, men, women, and children; the authorities having been warned too late of this disorder, and

> the inhabitants being too scarce and insufficiently armed to be able to repel them, they managed, however, with a rescue party, to kill and wound several, and have made many prisoners among whom the culprits will be judged and castigated. But as the masters will not want to lose everything, they will offer them to these merchants of human flesh who will probably place them with our planters; the public is so weary of this introduction of American *nègres*, half of whom are but escapees from the galleys and the gallows, which has been confirmed by their criminal actions since their arrival in this territory, that they have once again, seriously and in a unanimous voice, sent representations to the government on this topic. (F 189)

The legislature, however, "prolonged the right to import American slaves to replace those killed by the cholera epidemic" of 1832 (F 218). In December 1833, Boze again deplores the passage of a decree extending this right until July 1, 1835 (F 235).

Boze seems to fear disorder constantly. In the summer of 1835, he mentions, with obvious reprobation and repulsion, the arrival in Mississippi of "robbers and American preachers for the freedom of slaves," adding that they have already started pillaging houses in the city and that the prison is already full of these vagrants (F 257). Later that fall, referring to a mob of Irish people, he adds that the police "have caught and arrested in the faubourgs several foreign[11] white and black abolitionists preaching for the liberation of slaves, who expressed their wish to succeed by sword and fire" and who had tried to incite a civil war among the citizens. The City Guard was threatening to punish the activists harshly when they were arrested (F 258). In a similar criticism of anything that could cause disorder, he praises the organizers of raids against maroon slaves in Gentilly. Mentioning a raid that permitted the retrieval of a *nègre* belonging to Mr. Feuillas Dorville, who had been maroon for five years, and another belonging to Mr. Labarre, he praises the "courage of Mr. Auvignac Dorville (Ste-Gême's overseer) who led this expedition against the camp established in the cypress groves behind the Metairie." He even criticizes those who, in the search party, insufficiently "seconded the good will of their brave leader as their common interests commanded," thereby preventing more arrests (F 286). Neither Boze nor the city's residents and authorities were ready to accept any attempt running counter to the institution, whether by white agitators coming from the North or by slaves challenging the system.

Slavery was thus normal, and the now domestic slave trade was unacceptable only because it brought the seed of rebellion to the good Louisiana slaves. Nothing Boze says is unexpected, considering his past and the society he lived in. Many of his remarks, however, hint at the fundamental perversion and paradoxes of the system, although most of them seem to be included unwittingly. Blacks were convicted and executed for killing whites, of course, but also, sometimes, for killing other slaves (F 211). Boze mentions the case of a slave who killed his mistress because "she often mistreated him and denied him the things that were the most indispensable, as food and clothes" (F 208). The slave was, of course, convicted. When a white man, Louis Donnet, was tried for flogging a *nègre* to death, however, the verdict was not guilty and was delivered with approval from the public (F 204). All this seems to be perfectly normal in Boze's eyes, and he never passes judgment or even comments on such events.

His remarks concerning blacks and the way he mentions them are indeed quite common for the nineteenth century, and his representation of slavery is what would be expected from a French colonial in the Americas. He calls them *nègres*, oftentimes refers to them as "frizzy-haired" (F 135), and occasionally uses other such descriptive qualifiers. These derogatory expressions are, however, more often attached to their status as slaves than to their race per se, since he almost never uses such expressions to qualify free people of color, be they black or racially mixed, while he considers as property any slave, black or racially mixed. There is perhaps a single instance in which he openly makes fun of black people in a racial way, when he mentions that the youth of Louisiana had taken up the French custom of growing a beard, including the "frizzy" free and enslaved, adding that "this ridicule makes you laugh of pity at seeing these caricatures from the mid-eighteenth century" (F 265). In the rest of the correspondence, there is ample evidence that, even though Boze considered blacks inferior, he also acknowledged them, finding it perfectly natural for Lacoste to travel as far as Pointe Coupée to "consult a *nègre*, Caparlata, because of the guarantee his friends have given him that the latter would cure him of his old dysentery" (F 239), or vociferously opposing the passage of "a harsh ordinance" forbidding slaves to own dogs (F 207). When, in his testament, his friend Lambert granted freedom to "his mulatto Manette, the faithful keeper of his household," Boze considers this emancipation an "act of charity and acknowledgment of her services" (F 269).

Interestingly, although some of the people he mentions are, as in the case of Manette, described as mulattoes, he rarely mentions the degree of racial mixing of the people he refers to. Contrary to the city's visitors, who systematically described New Orleans people of color as people of all shades, always insisting on the distinction between the black and the "yellow,"[12] Boze almost never does this. Having lived in Saint-Domingue, Cuba, and New

Orleans, Boze was perfectly accustomed to the great diversity of racial mixing he encountered and seems to have been more sensitive to the status—free or enslaved—of people than to the color of their skin. Whether they were enslaved or free was what really made the difference in Boze's eyes, and his assessment of New Orleans's three-tiered system shows that he found absolutely no fault with it, contrary to the Anglo-Americans who sojourned, resided, or settled in the Louisiana capital. Born in New Orleans under French and Spanish rule, the three-tiered order had been reinforced by the massive influx of refugees of color from Saint-Domingue. The last migratory wave of Saint-Domingue refugees, coming from Cuba in 1809–1810, had itself more than doubled the free population of color of New Orleans, and this fact is ever-present in Boze's letters.[13]

Three-Tiered New Orleans

New Orleans, more than any other city of the American South, closely resembled the societies of the southern half of the American continent, including the Caribbean, where free people of color were concerned. It became still closer to its Latin American and Caribbean counterparts, at least in terms of numbers, in the early American period than ever before in its history. With its 6,237 free persons of color in 1820, it was just below New York (which had 10,368), Baltimore (10,326), and Philadelphia (8,782) and well ahead of the other most populated cities in the Northeastern United States at the time, despite the progressive disappearance of slavery from Northeastern states (Boston had only 1,690 free blacks and Washington, D.C., 1,696; the others among the ten most populous cities in the United States, such as Salem or Albany, had only a few hundred free blacks.) As for the largest Southern cities, Richmond and Charleston (the latter being known in historiography for its sizable free-black community) had 1,235 and 1,475, respectively, which was not only comparatively much lower but represented a much smaller proportion of the total population. While in New Orleans, the free population of color represented 23 percent of the total population, the proportion was only 10 percent for Richmond and 6 percent for Charleston.[14]

In 1840, New Orleans's specificity was still more obvious. With a population of 19,226 free blacks, it ranked first among the ten most populous cities in the United States, just above Baltimore (which had 17,967) and New York (16,358) but way ahead of Philadelphia (10,507) and Washington, D.C. (4,808). The other large Southern city, Charleston, had a free black population that had dwindled to a mere 5 percent, with only 1,558 free blacks (adding only 83 people to the number from two decades earlier).[15] Although the percentage of free blacks among the total population in New Orleans had gone down slightly, to 19 percent, the city still ranked second, just behind Washington, D.C., in the proportion of free blacks in the total population. More importantly, New Orleans was alone in her category in the South, the only city with three significant population classes, since the Northeastern cities no longer had a slave population by then and since Baltimore and Washington, D.C., where slavery had not yet been outlawed, had a numerically insignificant slave population (3.1 percent and 7.3 percent, respectively). With 50 percent whites, 23 percent free blacks, and 27 percent slaves, in 1820, and 58 percent whites, 19 percent free blacks, and 23 percent slaves in 1840, New Orleans remained the only city in the United States with a significant proportion of each of the three categories.

To the Gallic and Spanish people of New Orleans, this distribution was a normal feature of society, and it is, indeed, in a very natural way that Boze mentions the three classes, often in trinity, whether to list the common victims of a disease or in more gossipy ways, as when he mentions a certain Dupuy who suffers from "leprosy" [*sic*], adding, in one of the rare occurrences of the word "yellow" in the correspondence, that it could be expected, since this womanizer went "without restraint with the white, the yellow, and the black" (F 134), for once using the words most travelers to the city also used, possibly because he was quoting other gossipers and thus merely repeating verbatim what he had heard.[16] More often than not, however, what is important to Boze is not the color of people but their status. For instance, when he mentions the cholera epidemics of 1832, he grieves for the many Creoles of color from Saint-Domingue who have lost a large part of their skilled domestic workers "who provided those poor expatriates with a living" (F 229). Boze's vision is not as much a racial one as one based on status, and, whatever their degree of racial mixing, the free Creoles of color, especially those from Saint-Domingue, are worthy of his consideration and sympathy, and even, sometimes, empathy.[17] In Boze's eyes, the loss of their slaves was a crucial loss of property and revenue for them, as it was for white people.

Like the vast majority of his peers, Boze considered free people of color an intermediate class that had rights and duties and that could be assimilated neither among the slaves nor among the whites, whatever their degree of racial mixing. Despite the relative impermeability of the three classes in his eyes, Boze does not seem to disapprove, at least on racial grounds, of relationships between members of different classes. In his letters, he never proves judgmental concerning intimate relations that cross the color line, maybe because he is writing to a man who himself has a family of color. He often mentions lifelong relationships, alluding, in a very casual way, to a man who was married to an unfaithful wife, had filed for divorce, and had "immediately settled with a beautiful girl of color from Saint-Domingue who is now pregnant" (F 188). Such unions were natural to him, even when the white men had several partners among free women of color. Commenting, in 1831, on the death of Mademoiselle Lise Thuet, "Mr Sauvinet's housekeeper," he praises her as "a woman of great merit in all matters," says that she will be missed by her family and friends, and concludes that "this friend will now be free with his second housekeeper, a Creole from Saint-Domingue, who has already given him two children" (F 188). To a man like Boze, white men with free partners of color were no surprise, even if there is no indication that he himself ever followed their example.

Relatively more often than expected, Boze mentions men taking with them their illegitimate families to France, as, for instance, Charbonnier, the teacher, who leaves for France with his "housekeeper" Modeste and their three children (F 164). Surprisingly for the twenty-first-century reader, he even mentions several legal unions that cross the color line: "Mr. Maurice Abat, Antoine's youngest son, left for France several months ago with his housekeeper of color, the mother of two, the daughter of late Mr. Girodeau whom we had found, upon our arrival in this country, justice of peace on Rue Royale, with the intention of marrying her, people say, when reaching this free State" (F 183). This mention is absolutely not unusual in Boze's letters, and there are several other examples, like that of Mr. Delegue, who had married his housekeeper in Santiago to make sure that his children would have an inheritance upon his death (F 189).[18] Later, he mentions Mr. Gilard Sr., a coffee planter from Saint-Domingue who had married his housekeeper, Marie Josephe, née Piron, from Port-au-Prince (F 194), or Antoine Carraby, who married his housekeeper in France (F 223). Although interracial marriage had been banned shortly after the Louisiana Purchase, it seems that New Orleanians still found legal loopholes and married their racially mixed partners long after the takeover of Louisiana by the United States, with the last example coming from a letter of 1833.[19]

If the unions sanctified by marriage were extremely rare, many of the most respected public figures of New Orleans had lifelong relationships with Creoles of color, from New Orleans or Saint-Domingue. Let us cite, among many others, Jean Lana, the baker Lavigne, the justice of peace Lanouville with a Saint-Domingue Creole of color (F 204), Louis Gallaux, "a big property holder of this city, who enjoys here, with his Creole family, well-deserved public esteem for their good behavior" (F 216). The long list continues, with details about the unions with free women of color by the owner of the Café des Réfugiés (F 217), the eye doctor Ladevese, Captain Lauminé, who, upon his return from the Windward Islands, intended "to settle forever in this country with his family of color" (F 232), and, most probably, the already cited Renato Beluche (F 231). More surprisingly, perhaps, but also more interestingly in the context of early American New Orleans, he states in a very matter-of-fact way that there had been a fire at the store of Medelice, "who is said to be the natural son of the late Father Thomas (he is the image of him to the point that he could sign Medelice Thomas) and whose mother is a Creole of color from the Cap," adding that the boy "by his good behavior and honorable ambition is already walking toward fortune" (F 237).[20] A Catholic priest could thus be involved in a union with a woman of color without much direct opposition or even reprobation on the part of at least some of the people. All the details Boze gives indicate that these unions (and the families resulting from them) were perfectly official and conducted in the open, with relatively little hypocrisy. When Gême, Ste-Gême's son, traveled to France, he apparently visited his father in Bagen, in the castle where the latter lived with his entire legitimate white family, suggesting that they not only knew of but accepted this racially mixed family (F 244).

If Boze personally was not threatened by these interracial relationships, he observes, from time to time, the reprobation "of society" for such relationships, suggesting that not everyone in New Orleans condoned them. Interestingly, even he sometimes expresses conflicting opinions and suggests that New Orleans society was evolving to be more racially endogamic. In August 1832, he applauds the fact that more and more whites marry into their racial group, adding that "society sees with pleasure that today's youth takes up this honorable condition with much more willingness than that of setting up house with the color as contrary to morals" (F 208). Holy matrimony was thus preferable to illegitimate lifelong relationships across the color line, although it is impossible to know whether Boze's moral judgment had to do with matters of legitimacy or more race-based concerns. New Orleans society seems to have, at times, been ambiguous on the question. If relationships across the color line were conducted in the open, the situation was not necessarily considered in the same way for prominent public figures, perhaps because, to be elected, candidates needed the American vote, or at least part of it. In December 1833, for instance, Boze assesses Denis Prieur's chances of being appointed governor as poor, because the function requires a life beyond reproach, and Boze adds that he will be unable to fulfill this prerequisite, "because the newspapers have accused him, to his shame, of having been living with a mulatto housekeeper for several years" (F 235). In another letter, he comments that "people say that Mr. Casimir Lacoste shows disrespect to his wife since he continues without blushing his affair with his quadroon" (F 267). This suggests that New Orleans society was changing, probably due to the influence of the increasingly more numerous Anglo-Americans. Open interracial relationships thus started being challenged, at least for the public figures involved in the highest political sphere. To be elected, one had to get at least partial support from the Anglo-Americans and thus to conform, at least publicly, to their vision of public morality.

If interracial relationships were not uncommon for free women of color, endogamous marriages within the free class of color were numerous and seem to have led to a progressive blending among the groups of different geographical origins. As time went by, marriages between free people of color from New Orleans and Saint-Domingue became more common, favoring a progressive amalgamation of the two groups. Ste-Gême's eldest daughter, born in New Orleans to two parents from Saint-Domingue, for instance, contracted, in 1833, a "well-matched marriage" with a Louisiana Creole of color, and his son, Gême, married "a young Creole coming from an honest family of his class" (F 265). References to such unions recurred in the later part of Boze's correspondence.[21]

Quite clearly, New Orleans was an unusual place for free people of color, and they adopted practices that elsewhere in the South were reserved for whites. The case of dueling, a common practice among free people of color there, elsewhere reserved for white gentlemen, has already been mentioned. Very often, Boze refers to very wealthy people of color, such as Philippe Azur, or "the daughter of Luce, from Port-au-Prince, a *placée*,"[22] who had a fortune in real estate and slaves, and whose children were educated in the North (F 189). Whether these relationships had been sanctioned by matrimony—which was extremely rare after the 1808 ban—or not, the illegitimate families mentioned by Boze inherited from their white fathers most of the time.[23] There are many instances of this, such as Mr. Barthelemy Macarty, who had given his housekeeper a piece of property worth about fifty thousand gourdes, and whose two racially mixed sons, ages seventeen and eighteen, were being educated at Northern colleges. Upon his death, the two boys inherited from their father, in a perfectly official way that Boze details, before notary Pitot Jr., the executor, and in the presence of two witnesses, Mr. Bourbon Abat and Mr. Tricou, the eldest (F 203). Illegitimate children and even, often, their mothers were well provided for by the white father and companion, as in the case of Ste-Gême's children of color, the owners of a house and six slaves, who put part of their house and some of their slaves up for rent, or even occasionally sold one of their slaves to supplement their revenues as artisans (F 231). Referring to the late Barthelemy Macarty, a former sugar planter in Saint-Domingue, who had, while still alive, given to his companion, Mademoiselle Cécé, the daughter of Luce, a Creole of color from Port-au-Prince, a sum of sixty thousand gourdes in cash, he writes to Ste-Gême that "he had taken all the necessary precautions to ensure that his legitimate family could not, at his death, fight with this woman over it." She had gone to France with part of her fortune and had enjoyed it there "with splendor," before returning to New Orleans for health reasons. When she died, in the spring of 1834, she left "to her two Macarty natural children, very well educated in colleges in the North, an inheritance which people say is still very valuable" (F 238). When Mr. Le Chevalier Hyacinth Azur died, his natural children paid for the burial, including the erection of a tombstone, and led the procession "with their friends and with the whole body of ministers of the parish" (F 234). Very often, at least in Boze's eyes, little seems to have distinguished an illegitimate family from a legitimate one.

The relative economic weight of free people of color is perfectly clear from Boze's letters, and many of them are said to be of some means. Ste-Gême's son, for instance, travels to Europe, financed by his brother-in-law, a Louisiana Creole of color (F 238). It was not unusual to see, in New Orleans, a house "occupied by foreigners belonging to a well-off man of color" (F 268). The Creoles of color often benefited from good education. In 1834, for instance, "Father de l'Hoste, the former editor of *L'Entracte*, has just established a secondary school for the class of color, for boarders, day students, or students taking school dinners, at 82 Esplanade, between Condé and Royale, in a two-story house. It has already opened, with a great number of pupils" (F 239). Not only does Boze present the school as natural, but he criticizes the attempt, two and a half years earlier, by Senator Antoine Ducros, to fine the teachers who instructed free people of color, whether children or adults, in reading and writing. He adds that "philanthropy having risen with outcries," it was rejected by the majority of the legislators, "animated by a spirit of philanthropy," who took the caution of nullifying it, which "left to this race the freedom of getting, for them and their family, the education they wanted" (F 239). What is interesting in this passage is that Boze shows that the majority rose up against this restriction, including the legislators, but also that the attitude of New Orleanians toward race could be slightly more complex than what the mainstream historiography has long described.[24] In this case, a member of the French-speaking community (and not an Anglo-American) tried to restrict the prerogatives of free people of color, which runs counter to what has long been suggested by many Louisiana historians. And Boze wonders what this "uneducated philosopher may think when he sees the school that this first-class literary ecclesiastic fills up religiously." Giving a very good measure of his contempt for Ducros, he colorfully exclaims: "gazing at this school when he takes a walk on the esplanade probably provokes fits of cholera [*sic*] in him" (F 239). Boze was thus very sympathetic toward free people of color, as were, from what he says, many New Orleanians.

Although the free people of color of New Orleans had relatively better social conditions than elsewhere in the South, there is no doubt that they were considered inferior to whites and that, in the 1830s, the three tiers were even to be kept apart on many public occasions. Equality between the free persons of the two races was clearly inconceivable. In 1830, for instance, the "American editor" of the newspaper *Le Libéral* spent six months in jail for intending to publish pamphlets demanding equal rights for free people of color. Although he was finally acquitted in January 1831,

> He could have been sentenced to death or to the galleys for life, according to the judge's choice, in agreement with the law governing the pamphlets circulated in this state. He did not know the laws established by our legislature on this matter, since he dared to defend so openly the cause of the people of color who would have liberally paid him, had he been successful, in the belief that he could manage to extinguish the prejudice existing in the colony [*sic*] and which humiliates them. He would have inevitably incited a civil war in this country by claiming to make them join the whites' rank and freely enjoy the same rights in all and for all! But he failed, thanks to the police who stopped in time the circulation of his incendiary writings. This will be a good lesson to him and he will never again, in the future, undertake matters of such nature. (F 175)

Boze's reaction is a perfect testimony to his intrinsic belief in the inferiority of free people of color and his certainty that equality of rights was impossible. This belief was shared by most white New Orleanians, since, as time passed, even mere commingling in public places of entertainment or on public transportation was becoming inconceivable. When the railroad started operating, for instance, "among the (railroad) cars to the Lake, there is one especially reserved for people of color" (F 231). Ballrooms were segregated, as shown by the opening of a new ballroom for people of color at the corner of Orléans and Bourbon in 1833. Even if facilities reserved for free people of color were not necessarily of lesser quality, the two groups were kept separate. The new ballroom was "vast and as richly decorated as that of Mr. Davis, to the delight of the lovers of carnival entertainments" (F 234), but while the ballroom was dedicated to free people of color, the opening ceremony was "for the reception of the white people who would like to visit it" (F 235). Whites naturally came first everywhere, and segregation seems to have been increasing among public places in New Orleans. In 1835, for instance, the direction of the Théâtre d'Orléans "sent up to the gods the people of color to attribute to the white families the boxes they occupied, so that, in the first group as in the second, people come in crowds." Boze's conclusion is that "the public has been extremely satisfied by this pleasant change which was long to implement" (F 250). Boze never says which categories of the population were pleased by this change, but his reader understands that by "the public" he means the white audience and that the opinions of people of color mattered little in New Orleans society, not even to him. Although this may be accounted for by the increasing prevalence of Anglo-American principles in racial matters, there is no indication in Boze's letters that the Gallic population opposed the mounting segregation.

When it was built, the new prison was also organized in a way that kept blacks separate from whites. There were quarters "for every class of inmate, civil or criminal, born into a white family" and quarters "destined to the *négraille*," although he suggests that the well-being of all of them is important to the authorities, who are building a new prison "for a very humane stay." Separation of the races was totally natural. He continues commenting on the treatment of the *négraille*, saying that "although they are slaves, humanity has been as strictly observed in the building and distribution since the fact that these unfortunate may find what is necessary to them cannot but alleviate their wretched lot" (F 278).

Occupations were also manifestly segregated, and Boze sometimes cringes upon seeing whites employed in hard labor that should be, according to him, reserved for blacks. When describing the building of the railroad, for instance, he vociferously disapproves of the fact that the company "does not employ *nègres* to fell forests or to make excavations. For this hard work, it uses whites, American and Irish and German." As if expecting some retributive justice against this unnatural employment, he then exclaims: "but watch out for the yellow fever!" (F 164). It is true that, at the time, an increase in European migration tended to create interracial tensions, aggravated by the growing employment of Irish and German people for tasks that had been, until then, reserved for blacks, including free people of color—the building of the railroad or digging of canals, for instance. This led to reconfigurations in the work pattern in New Orleans.

Boze's vision of New Orleans's three-tiered order is thus in perfect agreement with who he was and where he lived, and probably reflects the position of the majority of the French-speaking—and, most certainly, Spanish-speaking—group. There were, in New Orleans, three groups that were clearly separated by sets of sometimes unwritten laws, groups that had different rights and obligations, and the rights of each, starting with the whites,' of course, needed to be respected. Boze's perspective is thus totally infused with the notion of difference, although most of the time, this difference seems to derive, in his eyes, from status, rather than race or color. What also appears clearly in his discourse is that New Orleans society was evolving toward a restriction of the rights and prerogatives of free people of color, but also that society in general was apparently increasingly less open and fluid. Even Boze's tone seems to harden, suggesting that the general atmosphere was becoming tenser. What his discourse also suggests is that social class mattered as much as race, sometimes even superseding racial considerations, a trend that sets New Orleans apart from the rest of the South and probably makes it closer to the northeastern port cities of the United States. Thus, by paying relative attention to the different groups (although with a clear deficit concerning the slave population), Boze gives a rather comprehensive depiction of New Orleans's population.

There is, however, one conspicuous absence in the 1,150 pages of correspondence: Native Americans. From many other sources contemporaneous to Boze's letters, we know that they were present in the urban landscape of New Orleans, particularly in the various markets of the city. The narratives of travelers and sojourners in the city in those years recurrently refer to the presence of Amerindians. Benjamin and John Latrobe, for instance, mention them several times in their narratives. Traveling in New Orleans in the early nineteenth century, Benjamin Latrobe describes "a couple of Choctaw Indian women and a stark naked Indian girl" sitting on some stairs, and later "filthy Indians half naked."[25] In 1834, his son, John, describes a ballgame in the street. Among the "crowd of men and boys," he notes "three Indians, their legs bare and a coarse shirt on their shoulders, which did not cover the seat of honor. A cloth apron of about eight inches scarcely answered to the need of making them absolutely decent."[26] Despite their presence in the city, attested by all narratives, the natives were absolutely invisible to Boze. Only once does he mention them, interestingly also in the context of a ballgame. In May 1830, "80 very hearty Chasta Indians [*sic*], in costume and armed with their rackets, came to the ballgame to play against the 80 Creoles of color—mulattoes and blacks—strongest at this game in this country" (F 166).[27] This almost complete oversight is intriguing. He could not but meet them in the streets, but—maybe because it was a negligible fringe of the population in his eyes, or maybe because they had been absent from his earlier Caribbean scenes—he never paid attention to them. They had no outstanding social, economic, or political role; they were part of the landscape; and his attention was thus probably not caught, not even by their quasi-nudity, which shocked travelers unaccustomed to the relative nakedness of slaves in tropical climates.[28]

Boze thus describes an organized three-tiered order, where the groups were legally—and, increasingly, physically—kept apart, but where a relative racial fluidity existed in social relationships, accepted by the Latin element of society and never kept secret. What is striking is that Boze's discourse often seems to be more socially than racially oriented, as if color mattered less to him than social status and the fixed hierarchy among the three categories. Although this perspective is not entirely surprising coming from an Old Regime Frenchman, it seems to have been shared by many, in a strongly hierarchized society where racial difference was not the only factor that mattered but where class and ethnic origin weighed heavily on the web of social relationships.

A Complex Web of Social Relationships

Boze's depiction of both free people of color and whites indeed shows a strong class consciousness. While this is to be expected from a man of the French *ancien régime,* despite the republican views he sometimes expresses when he deals with matters of European politics, for instance, his perspective seems to have been shared by many in New Orleans. The reasons for this strong class consciousness are probably manifold. It was partly the result of the specific colonial past of Louisiana, where the three-tiered order had progressively solidified. It had most certainly been reinforced by the arrival of the refugees since, in Saint-Domingue, the distinction between *grands blancs* and *petits blancs* had been socially discriminating and free people of color had been similarly distributed along class lines. Another reason accounting for this class consciousness—less specific to New Orleans—was the increasing influxes of migrant populations of lower social classes to the city. In the decades of Boze's correspondence, not only did Anglo-Saxon Americans and French nationals migrate in search of better economic opportunities, but the Crescent City welcomed the first contingents of migrants from Germany and

Ireland, although the large waves of those foreigners did not come until the midcentury, in particular the Irish fleeing the Great Famine of the 1840s. New Orleans was no exception among the port cities of the United States, but it ranked second in number of alien passengers, with more than five hundred thousand between 1820 and 1860, far behind New York (which counted more than 3.5 million) but largely ahead of Boston (with 388,000), as well as Philadelphia and Baltimore (both with figures less than half that of New Orleans).[29] The newcomers, mostly from lower economic categories, often faced economic difficulty, and this immigration brought to the city a white working class that had hitherto been extremely limited, a relatively typical feature of slaveholding societies. Paying special attention to social hierarchy might have been a way, for the more established populations of the city, to retain certain prerogatives and avoid being overtaken by the newcomers.

New Orleans displayed a relatively elitist vision of the social order, a perspective largely present in Boze's letters. Interestingly, this was true among whites but also among free people of color. Speaking of the latter, he often makes remarks about social stratification within the group. When giving Ste-Gême news of his racially mixed children, he writes, for instance, that they only mingle with "the best society of their color." Commenting on the building of two ballrooms reserved for free people of color, he specifies that the one at the corner of Bourbon and Orléans "according to appearances, will be reserved for the second class of that order, or, in other words, for ordinary people" (F 234). The other one, belonging to Mr. Dupuy, located in the theater of Rue St. Philippe, is "very richly decorated and of an extraordinary luxury, to the satisfaction of the *Cordons Bleus* who are impatient to shine there" (F 134).[30] Among people of color there were clearly different classes that did not mingle, and the structure of New Orleans society reinforced these differences.

The white group appears similarly stratified, if some of Boze's remarks are to be taken at face value. Referring to an entertainment establishment, he indicates that the "Gumbo Filés of the first and second ranks" have abandoned it to "the third estate and the *négraille*," in short, to people "of an ordinary class" (F 148), interestingly including both blacks and whites in this category. Boze even sometimes mixes remarks on ethnicity and class. He refers, for instance, to Mr. Pedro Feo as "a Catalan of an ordinary class" (F 150), as opposed to Mr. Domingo Fleytas, "descended from a Spanish family" (F 152), suggesting that their social origins positioned them in different categories within the New Orleans social fabric. At times, he is even quite ferocious about social class, mentioning, for instance, a Spanish widow originally "from the Third Estate" whose new husband has so properly "civilized" her that "she is now distinguished in the societies of her rank," and adding that she is "rich in property" (F 196). This clear class differentiation shows how compartmentalized New Orleans society was, not only in terms of race.

Race and social class clearly mattered in the Crescent City in the early American period. There is nothing extremely new in this. Nevertheless, Boze's vision can also sometimes bring novelty to the depiction of the racial pattern and enable a reassessment of the pattern of race relations in early American New Orleans, more submitted than has generally been represented to class considerations. Although he clearly defends the existing order that reserves the harder tasks for blacks, for instance, the reader is often surprised to see how little this is based on purely racial considerations and how much it really is an expression of social conservatism. All the main cities of the young republic received relatively important Irish and German contingents in the first half of the nineteenth century and, in most cities, the competition this immigration induced between the newcomers and black workers led to unrest and even riots.[31] Disruption occurred in the free societies of the Northern cities, where poor foreign workers were accused of taking jobs from freed blacks, but it was present in slaveholding societies, too, including New Orleans, where blacks, and particularly black slaves, had been traditionally confined to lower and harder tasks. Commenting on a rebellion of Irish workers against the mayor's office and the authorities, Boze says that they have "the pretension of being employed, in preference to the class of the free people of color and slaves, for all that is mechanical, carts, etc." He concludes that the authorities have sent the Legion to "oppose with all their strength this scandalous riot" (F 258).

In addition to all of the usual assumptions about the white/black dichotomy, however, Boze thinks that the prerogatives of free people of color—and even of slaves—must be protected from foreigners. In Boze's eyes, as well as the authorities,' manifestly, the local workers' position had to be secured from outside competition, even if it meant preventing white people from taking some of the blacks' prerogatives. There are thus clear signs, from what Boze writes, that things were not always as simple as they are often said to be: that French speakers could sometimes try to legislate against free people of color, although this kind of legislation is generally attributed to Anglo-Saxons; that New Orleans society was very class-conscious, with class sometimes mattering more than race; and that all Louisianans could sometimes defend "their" Creoles of color when there was any attempt by white foreign migrants to encroach upon their rights. Clearly race relations were more complex in New Orleans than is usually assumed. Ethnic and racial identification and interaction were elaborate, often pitting the more established groups, whether white or black, against the newcomers, whatever their color and place of origin, with ethnic loyalties sometimes superseding racial ones.[32] This can be seen, in particular, in the principal confrontation between the incoming Americans and the established Creole populations, often considered the main battlefield in early American New Orleans, although it was larger than this simple dichotomy.

Creoles versus Americans: The Struggle that Shaped New Orleans?

What the historiography of Louisiana has often remembered of the early American period is indeed the opposition between the Creoles and the Americans, with a focus on the attempted "Americanization" of the New Orleans people by the new American rulers and resistance on the part of the Creole population.[33] This struggle partly structured New Orleans antebellum society, as Louisiana historians have shown, and Boze's depiction is, to some degree, perfectly illustrative of this.

Time and again, he refers to this opposition in the correspondence. "There is a contrast of pride between the Americans and the Creoles that will always take them away from a perfect union. These nationals are the legitimate owners of this beautiful country, which entitles them to ostensibly boast about it freely and aspire, from their enlightenment and their merits, to the honorable positions. Well, the Gumbo Filés, who only have, in majority, a shrunken mind, are jealous of them to the point of hatred because they would like to have a superiority over everything and in everything" (F 164). Although Boze is not always so critical of the Creoles and laudatory about the Americans, the important conclusion from this quote is that they will never manage a "perfect union."

The competition, opposition, and sometimes animosity between Creoles and Americans were obviously permanent. Competition was very often commercial and economic, and also concerned the magnificence of their respective faubourgs. In March 1833, for instance, Faubourg Marigny was said to be improving so that it would soon compete favorably with Ste. Marie, "despite the greed of the Americans who pursue its magnificence with their wealth" (F 218). In May 1835, the "majority of the corporation" decided that the new Mint would be located on Jackson Square, which was, at the time, on the former location of Fort St. Charles, nowadays the Old Mint. This was a clear victory for the Gallic population, and "it annoyed the American party, which had used all possible means to manage to have it located at Faubourg Ste.

Marie" (F 252). The Americans had their own banks and their own stock exchange implanted in the faubourg they mainly peopled, and competition for mastery over financial operations was obviously constant (F 253).[34] Creoles and Americans were also involved in more frivolous competition. When news came of the possible aggrandizement of Davis's ballroom, numerous shareholders decided to be part of the venture "to be able, through the beauty of this new construction in size and rich decorations, to surpass the brilliance of the St. Charles Theater which fills the Americans with pride" (F 267). Competition even concerned fashion, with Boze sometimes commenting on "the American women who nowadays dress themselves with such elegance and humble bearing that they seem to want to fight with our Creoles over taste and richness of finery, doubtlessly with the intent of pleasing. But they are, alas, much less well armed" (F 260). When a new hotel was being built by Creoles, it was with the intent of outshining the hotels completed by "these glorious Americans," "these nationals full of pride" (268). When there was news that the cathedral might be rebuilt, Boze expressed the hope that it would "make its architecture of a beauty, of a solidity, of a taste that will strike people with admiration and will not make them regret that mass of Spanish architecture, of a gothic and grotesque taste, which shows the little knowledge of the workers for the arts, 80 to 100 years ago" (F 268). The communities seem to have constantly attempted to excel in all fields, with this competition aiding in the vitality of the city but also partly shaping the discourse on the structuring of New Orleans's social fabric and subsequent historiography.

There was also often a clear political opposition between the Creoles and the Americans and a struggle for the control over institutions and elected positions. As could be expected, political divisions are constantly observed by Boze. In most elections, American candidates opposed Gallic ones. When, in December 1831, he mentions the victory, in the legislative election, of Duplessis and Hoa, two young Creoles, he says that it is "very advantageous for the state and the city, especially because it opposes the American party which only wishes improvements for the neighborhood of Faubourg Ste. Marie in which they have established their properties and commerce" (F 194). He regularly accuses politicians of showing favoritism, of practicing electoral clientelism (F 201). Mentioning a disagreement among three Supreme Court justices—two Americans and one from Marseilles—he concludes that the two Americans sided against the Frenchman, and "the result is that talk in the society of the city accuses the two judges of having been satisfied" (F 229), ending his remark with a series of exclamation points, as he often does when he gossips or comments on politics. In this case, the reader of Boze's letters starts grasping a new reality: oppositions encompassed much more than the Creole/American division and seem to have formed along linguistic lines, both groups proving less homogeneous than what has long been represented by historiography. The Creoles had allies among the non-Creole Francophones, as did the Anglo-Americans among the non-American Anglophones.

Among the many pages Boze dedicates to Louisiana politics, in which he details electoral campaigns, election results, bills, and oppositions and alliances, sometimes in very detailed paragraphs, the reader gets a full grasp of those Gallic vs. Anglo-Saxon oppositions. In November 1832, the residents of Faubourg Ste. Marie even petitioned the legislature to be separated from the city and become "a particular community" (F 213). Political opposition between the two factions is obvious throughout the correspondence. In 1833, "Mr. J. B. Dawson, American, is, until now, the only candidate for the position of governor in the next election and if he is elected, the Louisianans will never recover [the office] because of their divisions" (F 218). When listing the candidates running for the position of major general of the first division, Boze cites "Bernard Marigny, Casimir Lacoste, Zéphir Canonge, and Sparks, American" (F 249). Sparks is the only one whose first name is not given and is also the only one whose origin is added to his name. Quite clearly, there was a difference, in Boze's eyes, in the status of these men. The second vote saw the arrival of a new candidate, "Mr. William Debuys, Creole of this city, who had replaced Mr. Bernard Marigny after his resignation, in the trust that this new candidate can put a halt to the hopes of the American" (F 249). A candidate could thus be chosen for his ability to defeat the only American, despite the long list of other Gallic candidates, who were less likely to be elected. When listing the candidates for the position of mayor, as late as 1838, Boze still mentions "C. Watt, American," while he does not give such qualifiers when mentioning the other candidates. Sometimes, however, when the candidate elected is a Saint-Domingue Creole, he says so, as in the case of Paul Berthus, reelected recorder (F 280). In his eyes, Americans need to be singled out negatively, in opposition to the French speakers, who are generally included within a single group, except when Boze has a community reflex in favor of one of his fellow refugees. It is also to be noted that, thirty years after the Louisiana Purchase, New Orleanians were still using terms like "American" or "national," or even "foreigner," as seen previously, to designate people from outside Louisiana.

Beyond this constant opposition, Boze shows that confrontation could sometimes even verge on violence and create surprising unity among non-Americans, as when, in April 1835, divisions occurred in the city for several consecutive days, "because the Americans have risen up against the Louisiana Creoles and against all the naturalized foreigners of all nations" who had complained about the practice of Governor White to "appoint to public positions, and lucrative ones at that, mainly naturalized foreigners of various nations, while they should lay no claim to them, not to harm the interests of the American natives and Louisiana Creoles." The governor's defense is that he appointed according to "merit and knowledge," "knowing that, if the Constitution of the United States is favorable by right to the nationals, it is also to the naturalized foreigners." The Americans are said to have petitioned the legislature to forbid the appointment to public positions "of French subjects and naturalized foreigners and even to the Creoles born to families from outside." Beyond a union of the francophone community against the Americans, there seems, in this case, to have been a union of everyone against the Americans. The legislature eventually appointed a committee to deliberate on the question, and the committee ended with a vote of eighteen out of thirty against the Americans' request. They voted, Boze comments, in favor of "the Creoles, the French, and other foreigners, naturalized Spaniards, Germans, etc." As the city was on the verge of a civil war, according to Boze, assemblies were organized in the following days, "composed of great numbers of respectable citizens, chaired by eloquent orators, to try to rally the minds to peace and concord" (F 252). Although the situation seemed to ease, at least for a time, the following summer Boze writes: "division still reigns between the Creoles, the foreign French, and the American population" over the issue of those lucrative public positions (F 257).

The oppositions between Creoles and Americans usually described in the literature were thus no myth, but they were probably more complicated than what people generally believe. The opposition was not necessarily between Creoles and Americans but often between Americans and French speakers or even, as in this case, between Americans and everyone else, including recently naturalized foreigners. In another instance, mentioning the many improvements and embellishments of the Carré, Boze comments on "the great desire this company has to make the city's Carré justly shine, despite the jealousy of the American owners who still cannot be on good terms with the Creoles and the French" (F 258). The Creoles were thus not alone in their opposition to the new American rulers, and the rest of the French-speaking population—composed of "foreign French" (Saint-Domingue refugees and immigrants from France)—generally sided with them. Rather than a Creole versus American opposition, then, the opposition thus fell along linguistic lines. For instance, when Boze describes a "new project by American and French capitalists," without the least specification of who the French were and where they were from, he clearly aggregates all French speakers together as if they could be all taken together in their differentiation from the Americans (F 189).

The traditional representation of the New Orleans population as divided into two main linguistic groups, often interacting more through opposition than social relations, seems then to have been partly grounded in the truth; however, the picture Boze gives of the New Orleans social fabric is slightly more complex than the usual Creole/American binary. If there were thus alliances along linguistic lines, the complexity of the web of relationships was nonetheless enhanced by the great diversity of the New Orleans population, much less binary than the linguistic groups just described.

Ethnic Diversity

What strikes the reader of Boze's letters is indeed the impression he gives of extreme ethnic diversity, evident in the constant attention he pays to the origins of the people he mentions. The best expression of this diversity is systematically given whenever Boze comments on yellow fever epidemics, since he always differentiates among the reactions to the disease of the various ethnic groups, then giving some of the rare instances when all groups are aggregated in a single sentence. In August 1829, for instance, "the yellow fever which, since July, has started wreaking havoc, has taken away from us, every day, a number of 10, 13, and 25 of those Spaniards from Mexico and very few French city dwellers until now, but many Americans and other foreigners, and a few Creoles" (F 144). On October 31, 1832, "Americans, Irish, Swiss, Germans, as well as French nationals, died of cholera and yellow fever" and people "from Northern Europe" easily fell victim to those epidemics (F 212). The inflow of foreigners seemed uninterrupted, except during the dangerous summer season. At the end of the 1833 epidemics, "thanks to God, there comes every day a quantity of new foreigners of all nations to the point that pedestrians find it hard to walk the streets of the city" (F 235). New Orleans was definitely a very cosmopolitan city, much more so than most American cities at the time.[35]

First of all, while, for a long time, the Gallic population has been equated with the Creole community in the literature, Boze's narration indicates, as already suggested, a much greater variety, and his comments sometimes revise some stale assumptions about loyalties. Rather than bipolar, the New Orleans social and political scene was multipolar. Various communities—Creoles, Saint-Domingue refugees, and metropolitan French, Anglo-Saxons, and foreigners—lived side by side, opposed one another, interacted, traded loyalties, and occasionally allied against each other in defense of what they deemed important. The previously cited example of the opposition to the appointments to official positions already suggested this diversity. Every one of Boze's letters confirms it. The Creoles were, of course, central to the francophone group, and Boze always takes pains, whenever he alludes to a Creole, to specify "Creole" after his or her name. For instance, he says "Mr. Eugène Marchand, Louisiana Creole," as if this indication were some sort of passport, enabling a clear ethnic identification to situate the characters he is mentioning (F 148).

Although the Gallic population often appeared as one group to outsiders, people's different origins are constantly mentioned in Boze's narrations. Francophones were Louisiana Creoles, Saint-Domingue Creoles, or French, and this trinity is present throughout the correspondence. Boze even establishes differences among the members of the groups. Mentioning ordinary diseases, for instance, he specifies among the victims "several Saint-Domingue Creoles and colonists" (F 147), thereby making a distinction between the Creoles, born in Saint-Domingue, and the colonists, who had been born elsewhere and, like him, had settled there. Even Louisiana Creoles could be differentiated through their longtime origins, like Mr. Lenes, a "New Orleans Creole originating from a Spanish family" (F 239). The members of the groups were apparently always attentive to the differences that existed within the linguistic groups.[36]

People from France were clearly quite numerous in New Orleans, even a long time after the American takeover. Although their migration is largely understudied, there is proof that the flow of migrants from France was continuous throughout the first few decades of the American period. Migrants came for economic reasons, to benefit from new opportunities at a time when the loss of Saint-Domingue for France had closed the gates of the richest French colony of the Caribbean. Political upheaval, like the fall of Napoleon or the 1830 Revolution, brought new migrants to Louisiana, which was increasingly seen as a favorable American destination for French speakers. French historian Marjorie Bourdelais concludes that the best sign of the persistence of this in-migration is that the Anglophones never managed to surpass the Francophones in numbers until the Civil War.[37]

And indeed the constant mentions of them in Boze's letters are the clearest sign of their numerical importance, although it may be contended that his Frenchness made him especially attentive to their presence. As a very cosmopolitan city, whose inhabitants, like Boze, were often born outside it, New Orleans probably made people more attentive to the origins of others. Everyone seems to have known others' origins, especially within their linguistic group, and Boze never forgets to mention this, giving very precise details about the people from France, part of those so-called "foreign French," who were clearly extremely numerous. Among many others, Boze refers to Mr. Soulé, a lawyer from Toulouse (F 204), but also to a native of Nantes (F 206), Mr. Tuyés from Bordeaux, involved in a duel (F 208), and Aycar, "a Provence native" (F 216). There was Mr. Guérin from Lyon (F 147), Felix Arnaud, "a native of Toulon" (F 152), Cyprien Pottier, "a native of Bagnères, in the department of Hautes-Pyrénées" (F 157), and "Laporte from Bayonne" (F 160). When enumerating the victims of epidemics, he lists "St. George de la Valette, who had been in New Orleans for 11 years, born at Faux, in the department of Dordogne, in France" and "François d'Hebercourt de Pernay, born in Champagne, in France" (F 213). Yellow fever also killed Roumage from Bordeaux, Gustave Douzedebas from Bayonne (F 231), and Mr. Marot from Nantes, married to a young woman from Le Havre (F 232). In his eyes, people never lost the label of their birth city. Even if he had lived in New Orleans for fifty years, when "Mr. Elie Giron, aka Malbroux" died, he was still, in Boze's eyes, "a native of Bordeaux" (F 221). After eighteen years in New Orleans, Mr. Jourdan was still "from France" (F 239). And Mr. Deyson was still, upon his death, "native of Landes, ten leagues from Bordeaux" (F 226). Sometimes the details given are even greater, and Boze's reader learns that Father Benoit Richard was born "in Bourdigue, arrondissement of St-Etienne, department of Loire, in France" (F 228).

The diversity we read about in the letters is already striking, but the most original of Boze's observations about nineteenth-century New Orleans is certainly the close attention he brings to the Saint-Domingue refugees. Long ignored in the historiography of Louisiana, because the refugee group tended to side so closely with the Creoles in the protection of their common interests against any American encroachment that observers merged it into the Creole group, it only reappeared in the historiography of the second half of the twentieth century.[38] As a member of the group, interacting principally with other Saint-Domingue refugees and writing to a member of the same group, Boze is a privileged observer of Saint-Domingue refugees. Again, as with the Louisiana Creoles, he never fails to specify details about their origins. When a fire rages, it burns down three houses, "ruining three unfortunate families of color from Saint-Domingue" (F 150). In the same letter, he mentions Mr. Chabaud, a Creole from Port-au-Prince (F 150).

There are hundreds of such mentions, which often describe the everyday events of people's lives. Boze was apparently one of the finest gossips in New Orleans, helped in the task by Ste-Gême's friend, Arsène Blanc's wife, Azurine Labatut, who also had Saint-Domingue ties. Entire paragraphs are dedicated to amorous relationships, lawful or unlawful, and to marriages, births, diseases, and deaths. When he mentions a marriage involving Saint-Domingue refugees, he generally gives details about the backgrounds of the two spouses. When refugees died, the reader learns where they came from, what they did in Saint-Domingue, who they married, when they came to New Orleans, where they settled, what they did for a living, the children they left behind, here again with details about their degree of instruction, position in the city, matrimonial alliances, etc. Adding up the various notes about all the refugees would probably give a great chronicle of their social circles. More interestingly, from what Boze says about them, we get a good picture of their relocation pattern in New Orleans. We know that they lived mostly in the Carré and in the so-called Creole faubourgs of Marigny and Tremé. Following Boze's intense gossip makes it possible to list the names of hundreds of these refugees, to learn of their family relationships through marriages, and to gain insight into what they did for a living in New Orleans.

The letters, for instance, tell much about their occupational patterns. If many successfully managed to fit in, some of them seem to have found it difficult to find their place in New Orleans's socioeconomic world. Telling Ste-Gême of the death of Madame Veuve Cormeau, from Le Cap de Saint-Domingue, at age eighty or ninety, he says that she "lived from the assistance of her good lady friends, who supported her to her last hour" (F 258). On another occasion, Boze reported the death of Widow Mounier, born Chloé Desongar de la Salle, aged about fifty, a Creole from Les Cayes St-Louis, in Saint-Domingue, a former planter, "raised in France with distinction," who left five penniless orphan daughters. Boze adds that no one wants to marry them because they have no dowry, although they were raised in the best manner, "with a very good education," and have been managing a "boarding school for young ladies for several years" and are "beautiful, good-looking, amiable, and full of wit, with a slender waist" (F 268). There are dozens of such examples, giving the measure of the difficult reintegration of the refugees in their new asylum. Even Martin Bonseigneur, who was captain of the City Guard, a sign of a good social integration in his new home, and who was receiving a pension of eight hundred dollars when alive, left, upon his death, his family so destitute that they needed financial assistance. Boze adds: "People think that the city will bring some assistance to his widow and children who are no longer happy after this loss" (F 269). Even Major Savary, the brave refugee of color who was major of a battalion of free refugees of color in the Battle of New Orleans and was commended for his bravery, did not escape poverty. After trying to return to Saint-Domingue and Cuba, he came back to New Orleans, which is "an asylum more in agreement with his feelings, although he suffers from destitution and also from a bad health in his old days" (F 146).

Despite those cases, Boze also describes many success stories, or at least stories of people who managed to put their expertise to use in their new asylum. It would be impossible to cite them all, and a few examples will suffice. Boze mentions a judge at Parish St. Charles whose father had been a lawyer at the Parliament in Lyon and who had previously been royal prosecutor in St. Marc, in the colony of Saint-Domingue, before keeping this position under Toussaint-Louverture, "this assassin governor" (F 269). He mentions Pierre Dormenon from Jacmel, who was a planter and a judge in the Pointe Coupée parish (F 229); the son of a goldsmith in Port-au-Prince, who had followed in his father's footsteps in New Orleans (F 279); Mr. de Ste. Rome, the editor of the *Courrier de la Louisiane*, who "built a fortune in several beautiful properties to the point that today he is among the rich" (F 279); one of the Courjole [*sic*] brothers "from Cap Saint-Domingue," who had become an architect, while his brother was "a merchant, extremely valued in society" (F 280). Refugees sometimes made fortunes in the entertainment business, such as Davis, who had been an apprentice goldsmith in Saint-Domingue and was the successful owner of a ballroom and gambling academy at the corner of Orléans and Bourbon, and then restored the Théâtre St. Philippe, dedicated to "comedy, balls, and gambling" (F 228).

What is clear from his correspondence is that Saint-Domingue refugees relocated in many economic sectors. It seems that almost all occupations are mentioned. They sometimes pursued whatever occupation had been theirs in Saint-Domingue, such as, for instance, Mr. François Xavier Freyd, who had been a tailor, first in Jérémie and then in Santiago, and had a fabric store in New Orleans (F 230). The refugees were also employed by local authorities. They might be customs officers (F 269), city surveyors, like Pilié (F 230), or work in various city services, like Mr. Duralde, the senior officer of the Bureau des Hypothèques, the mortgage office (F 150). They were also often involved in commerce, where they could be commerce assistants (F 269), bookkeepers (F 258), "treasurers," like Labatut's son "at the fabric" (F 225), or bank cashiers, like Louis Prevot the elder (239). They became merchants, like Mr. Legendre (F 148), the son of Widow Puech from Port-au-Prince, married to d'Aquin's oldest daughter, who had a beautiful iron store on the levee (F 160); Mr. Doublet, or Mr. Ferry, from Port-au-Prince, who were also merchants on the levee (F 230); or Labatut, who had a gun store (F 236). Many did engage in highly specialized services, as goldsmiths and jewelers (F 271) or piano tuners, like Louis Teinturier (F 217). They were also found in the professions: many became (or remained) judges, like Jean-François Canonge (F 162), Louis Casimir Moreau Lislet (F 170), whose virtues were extolled by all citizens of New Orleans upon his death in late 1832 (F 213 and 215), or Jacques François Pitot (F 160); they might also be lawyers, like Damien Augustin (F 150), and notaries, like Mr. Mazureau (F 164). Many of the city's doctors, including very successful ones, were originally from Saint-Domingue or descended from refugees, like Labatut's son, the Lemonier brothers, Trabuc, Fortin (F 134), Berger (F 148), and many others. They were pharmacists, like Ducatel (F 160). Refugees also became bakers (F 226), like the d'Aquins, who had "a big bakery" and were "very wealthy" (F 160), or like Etienne Rousset (F 226). Many also became teachers, like the father of Donatien Augustin, who tutored for several families in the city (F 166), or Jean Nicolas Rochefort, one of the first teachers of the "college, at the beginning of the bayou" (F 153).[39] They were artisans, and they also entertained, like Mr. Brochard, the owner of the Café des Réfugiés (F 34). Some were actors or musicians, like Jean Berthier, a former sugar planter of Jérémie, who had been playing the violin "in the orchestra of the Théâtre d'Orléans ever since our arrival in this country, which has helped him soften his mean existence" (F 236). This last mention is a good indicator that some never recovered from their forced exile but that they managed to find the means to survive, using any talent they had, in music, teaching, fencing, or many other fields. What is clear from Boze's letters, as in the case of the French coming from France, is that the refugees were extremely numerous, played an important economic and social part in the life of the city, and could certainly not be overlooked in a glossed-over depiction of New Orleans as a battlefield between the Creoles and the Americans.

This is all the truer in the case of the Saint-Domingue refugees, because they became involved in the political life of the city and even the state. Besides the most famous examples of Derbigny and Prieur, who became governor and mayor, respectively, many lesser-known people also became involved. They occupied several elected positions, like Paul Berthus, elected (and reelected) recorder of the city (F 280), or Peychaud, "who obtained an official position thanks to his relationships" (F 148). Labatut's son, Felix, who was "merchant and treasurer of the church and of the fabric," was also "alderman at the corporation, churchwarden, and justice of peace," and was later elected to the legislature (F 240).

The very numerous refugees from Saint-Domingue, who represented about half the city's population in 1810 after the arrival of the last wave from Cuba, thus added up to the Creole population in all matters of society, occupying important positions in the city's economic and political spheres. When looking closely at Boze's letters, the reader gets a good measure of the complexity and diversity of the French-speaking population. Whether they came from Saint-Domingue, Provence, Bordeaux, or elsewhere in France, many members of this Gallic community were thus not Creoles.

If the French-speaking community was thus more varied and more complex than what has long been thought, the English-speaking group was similarly less monolithic than what has often been said. Of course, the Americans represented the majority of the English speakers. Every letter mentions an American, sometimes with precise details as to where he originated, like the "three Kentucky Americans selling strong liquors to slaves on a boat in front of Mr. Andry's plantation" (F 172). The predominance of Americans was clear. Sometimes, however, Louisianans seem to have found it difficult to differentiate between British and American English speakers, and occasionally, Boze writes "English" and then crosses out the word to write above it "American." Regularly, he says of someone that he is "an Englishman or an American" (F 223, for instance), or, in some cases even, an English speaker, like Mr. Thomas Miqueen, "is *said to be* an Irish national" (my emphasis) (F 170). Boze thus shows that there were not just Americans among the Anglo-Saxons, and the same generalization seems to have been made about English speakers as about French speakers. According to Bourdelais, and although she thinks that Berquin-Duvallon's assertion that English people were more numerous than Anglo-Americans in the early American period is impossible to prove (or disprove), the Anglo-American presence was probably less important than has long been thought, at least up to the midcentury. What is certain is that their presence was manifest, probably because of their economic vitality and because their competition with the Gallic population made them more visible targets of the people of French descent, whether they were Louisiana Creoles or foreign French.[40]

Even though Americans represented a large part of the city's English speakers, there are many mentions in Boze's letters of already large numbers of Irish migrants. In the fall of 1831, two thousand Irish and German people are said to have been brought over for the construction of the new canal. They came in several waves—two boats, for instance, coming with a load of three hundred to four hundred Irishmen on November 13 (F 189). In May 1832, Boze refers to these "indefatigable Irish who pursue, with great courage, and despite a blazing sun, this gigantic venture" (F 204). Although they were far from his social group, for linguistic reasons but also, most certainly, because they belonged to the lower strata of society, from time to time, one appears in his gossip and news, like "Daniel Gillen, Irish," a conductor, who was accidently killed while exploring the remains of a fire (F 238), or Edouard Cullen [*sic*], an Irishman who was executed (F 160). Most of the Irish reached New Orleans after the end of Boze's correspondence, in the 1840s and 1850s, but some were present in the city in the first three decades of American rule. It is difficult to make out their numbers, because they very often tend to be aggregated within the Anglophone group, comprising the Anglo-Americans and the English. When studying Catholic marriages in New Orleans in that period, Bourdelais shows that the Irish ranked tenth in the 1806–1810 period, but fourth (behind people born in France, Louisiana, and Germany) in 1836–1840.[41] Even if the total figures are still difficult to assess, the Irish were indisputably an important part of the anglophone population before midcentury.

The two largest groups were clearly the heterogeneous anglophone and francophone ones. The population of New Orleans at the time, however, was multicultural rather than bicultural, and more variegated than anyone could imagine today. Boze's permanent attentiveness to the origins of people gives a good measure of this diversity. It is clear, from what he writes, that New Orleans constantly received immigrants. In December of 1835, he writes that migration has been continuous since the first of November and that "every day, large numbers of foreigners of all nations and French people" have been arriving "through the North or French cities, after hearing that New Orleans was salubrious" (F 258).

Some categories of non-Gallic, non-Anglo-Saxon populations are more regularly mentioned. There were, in New Orleans, Hispanics, either from Spain or from the American continent, mainly Cuba and Mexico. The Spanish-speaking group seems to have constantly increased, although in much lesser proportions than the two main linguistic groups. The few Spaniards that had come to settle during the colonial period were no longer counted among the Spanish-speaking group in the early American period, since they had mostly amalgamated with the largely francophone majority in New Orleans. There are, however, signs that some Hispanics still arrived in the city in the early nineteenth century, even if the percentage of the total population progressively dwindled from 3 percent in 1820 to 2 percent in 1830, and to only 1 percent in 1840, due to the parallel increase of the other linguistic groups.[42] Many Spaniards came from Mexico, in the wake of Mexican independence, and Boze sometimes refers to them as "expelled from Mexico"

(F 166). Many times, Boze cites "Spaniards out of Mexico," or even "a great quantity of Spaniards coming out of Mexico" (F 147, among many others), indicating that the Mexican Revolution had sent small but not insignificant numbers of migrants toward Louisiana. He even pities those "Spaniards expelled from Mexico" who arrived with money, gambled, and lost everything: "from rich that they were when they got off the boat, many are destitute," and he even says that he saw one who arrived with fifteen thousand gourdes and who, after a month, was trying to sell his coat (F 166).

If these were apparently the majority of the group with Spanish origins, one could also meet in New Orleans the previously mentioned Mr. Pedro Feo, "a Catalan of ordinary class" (F 151), Spaniards like Simeon Cucullu (F 237), "Don Rodriguez of Spanish nation,[43] age 68, the most senior lawyer of this jurisdiction (F 239)," or the "Catalan Barba, running a cabaret" (F 283). There were also Havana Creoles, like Diego Morales, pharmacist, chemist, and medical doctor (F 236), or the son-in-law of Bernard Marigny. Although they were a small minority, there are signs that the group had some leverage in New Orleans society. Mentioning the death sentence of three Spaniards, he adds that a petition for their grace was made by "a Spanish commercial establishment," which shows that Hispanics were in sufficient numbers and still sufficiently influential to try to intervene when some of their compatriots were in trouble (F 201). This also shows that there was a good measure of ethnic support among the various communities present in the Crescent City.

Next in the non-francophone, non-anglophone group came German people, who were among the main immigrant groups at the time, although this was not new, with colonial Louisiana having already been a place of settlement for German immigrants, as the toponymy of Louisiana indicates.[44] The more massive contingents of German migrants reached the city after 1840, representing, in 1850, 11 percent of the total population. The German population was not negligible, however, in the early decades of the American period, with German speakers representing 5 percent of the total population in 1820 and never falling under 3 percent in the next two decades, despite constant francophone and anglophone immigrations.[45] Like the Irish, the Germans worked on constructing the city's infrastructure. In March 1833, for instance, improvements resumed in the city after a pause consecutive to "the death of the Irish and German workers that the cholera pitilessly sent to the grave last November" (F 217). As in the case of Irish people, mentions of individual German people infrequently appear in the letters: a criminal (F 231), a "passenger of German nation" (F 232), Becktel, a "former merchant of German nation" (F 237), or Frederick Fogat's widow, a German national, who lives in Gentilly and sells her goods at the market (F 208).

There were also, more generally, people from elsewhere in Europe, and Boze often mentions the "foreigners recently come to this country" (F 147, for instance). These foreigners are, sometimes, an undistinguishable group, as when Boze tells Ste-Gême about the arrest of four criminals first described as "foreign individuals," who are then "said to be Spanish" (F 194), or when he defines a certain Mr. Gentil as "European" (F 244). From time to time, however, Boze refers to individuals whose origins he gives, showing the presence (if only anecdotally) of a variety of people in the city. The bishop, Leon de Neckere, was Belgian (F 231). New Orleans also had "a Polish doctor" (F 147), and you could meet "Italian-born" Baptiste Alzaret (F 170), the first pilot of the Balize (the entrance of the New Orleans harbor), and Antonio Silva, "a Portuguese national," there (F 243). "Mr. Pandely, a small planter downriver," was a Greek national (F 187), and Theodore Nicolet, "born in Saint-Gall, Switzerland, the consul of the Helvetian Confederation," was a figure of the city, where he owned a commercial establishment, Boze adding that he had owned it for eighteen years, thus confirming his firm implantation, way beyond the diplomatic representation alluded to (F 275).

Since every time Boze mentions someone he gives an indication of his origins, his reader gets a clear depiction of the extremely cosmopolitan population of the Crescent City. There were very few cities as cosmopolitan as New Orleans at the time. The proportion of foreigners was, throughout the first half of the nineteenth century, always very high, even reaching, in 1850, 47 percent of the total white population, which put New Orleans in a close third place in the United States, after St. Louis and Milwaukee.[46] The influx of foreigners was apparently uninterrupted, with peaks of immigration, as in the winter of 1829, when there were "so many unfortunate foreigners who took refuge in this city" (F 150) that Boze seemed concerned. It was apparently relatively easy for foreigners to fit in in New Orleans, and many of these relatively recent New Orleanians seem not to have suffered from their original estrangement. Even if he had been born in Italy, for instance, Alzaret "had made a fortune by running a cabaret" and he was "a sapper, leading the National Guard Corps" (F 170).

New Orleans was thus, in the early American period, and increasingly so as time went by and as population fluxes increased and diversified, a highly cosmopolitan city. There was clearly much more than the typically depicted Creole versus American dichotomy. The anglophone population was extremely varied, as varied as the Gallic one, and there were large groups of foreigners who enriched the city with their work and their diversity. People from various nations coexisted and even interacted, and, although they were often loyal to their group, Boze's description of relationships in the "Babel of the South"[47] is much more ambiguous than a mere loyalty to one's ethnic group, and his letters definitely hint at a complex web of ethnic loyalties.

A Complex Web of Ethnic Loyalties

There was an obvious tendency to support one's own community. Boze's loyalty to the Saint-Domingue refugees was nonnegotiable. Because he socialized with those with whom he shared a specific history, Boze was often critical of Creoles and quick to defend Saint-Domingue refugees, but this Gallic loyalty did not mean that he categorically opposed Americans or Anglo-Saxons. Often, however, he seemed to criticize the advantages granted to Americans, occasionally exclaiming: "If a similar misfortune had occurred to an American, he would have been absolved in principle, whatever might have happened" (F 166). But he was also ready to complain about the advantages Creoles had. When a struggle occurred among three Americans trying to sell liquor to the slaves of the Andry plantation and the owner's son, the latter (age twenty) shot at the Americans, who had refused to leave, killing the owner of the barge, Boze concludes, "but as he is a Creole with rich parents, this unfortunate matter will eventually subside in its pursuits" (F 172).

In the early years of the correspondence, Boze's reader gets the impression that people's origins determined their interactions with others, and endogamic trends seem to have been the norm in New Orleans. Creole society was closely knit; French people stayed within their group and Americans interacted in Ste. Marie, mostly with each other, as Saint-Domingue refugees did in the Carré or the Marigny. Obviously, most of Boze's interactions were with his fellow refugees, and he constantly describes them as socializing together. He also had, for obvious linguistic reasons, but probably not only because of those, constant interaction with other French speakers, to the point that he seems to suggest that he knew most of the francophone group. At one point, he mentions duels "whose actors are unknown to me, even though they are French" (F 208).

People seem to have been constantly attentive to their own linguistic group. Whenever he informs Ste-Gême of something pertaining to the Gallic population, he gives many details about the people, whereas his mentions of Americans are, most of the time, very succinct. He clearly knew more—and cared more—about the French speakers. To give a single meaningful example, in one page, he informs Ste-Gême of the death of three persons. In the first case, the death of a Frenchman, he gives the name (Mr. Derault), the origins ("Bordelais," meaning from Bordeaux), the amount of time spent in New Orleans ("25 years"), the area of residence (Faubourg Marigny), and the occupation (owner of "a firewood shop where he also sold water"). The death of a Saint-Domingue refugee is announced with the name of the deceased (Joséphine Althée Puech), her birth name ("born d'Aquin"), and the name and origins of her husband's family (he was "the son of Widow Puech from Port-au-Prince"). If Boze seems to give less detail, it is most certainly because Ste-Gême knew the families, as he had been a prominent figure of the Saint-Domingue group in Santiago de Cuba and New Orleans for some fifteen years. Finally, mentioning, in the same letter, the death of an American, Boze only mentions that he was murdered and that his assassin had been arrested and jailed. No name is given, nor are the origins and occupation of the deceased mentioned (F 252). The reader can assume that Ste-Gême was interested in the Frenchman, although he might not have known him, and that he knew the Saint-Domingue refugee and her husband's family, but that there was no need to inform him of the identity of the American. The care Boze takes to inform Ste-Gême of the details whenever members of the Gallic community are concerned, on the other hand, indicates that his acquaintances could be described in concentric circles, with more proximity with the refugees, more distance but still interest in the larger French-speaking community, and a relative lack of interest for the Americans as individuals, although he was interested in them as a group.

This schematic concentric structure seems to have been true of larger New Orleans society as well. This is discernible through the marriage pattern that Boze's letters describe for the Gallic group. Creoles essentially married Creoles and Saint-Domingue refugees and their descendants married into the refugee community, and most of the gossip Boze includes demonstrates this—a pattern confirmed among free people of color as well.[48] The son of Judge Pitot married the daughter of Mr. Montegu Jr., whose family was related to the D'Aquins from Saint-Domingue (F 160). Michel Forcisi, "a former Saint-Domingue colonist," was married to a Saint-Domingue Creole (F 222). Even second-generation Saint-Domingans still married each other, such as Luma Augustin, the younger brother of Donatien Augustin, who married "Mathilde Thibault, the older daughter of the late Thibault, deceased in Santiago de Cuba" (F 223). The letters are a long list of such unions, which apparently were the norm for a long time in the early American period.

Interconnections between the various French-speaking groups, however, became more frequent as time went by, especially through intermarriage. When they did not marry into their group, people contracted unions with others from the same linguistic community, as was also the case among English speakers.[49] A few examples will suffice to give the measure of this. Louisiana Creoles married Saint-Domingue refugees, like "Mme. Tournade, née Blache, a Louisianan," who is the older sister of the wife of Lance Lecarpentier, who managed auctions, a Creole from Les Cayes in Saint-Domingue" (F 213). Mr. Augustin married Mlle. Labranche, and their union was celebrated "on the 9th to the satisfaction of the young, pretty, sweet, and kind Louisianan with the Saint-Domingue Creole who triumphed by his constancy, despite those who were jealous of his fate" (F 237). Louisiana Creoles and French people also regularly intermarried, like Mr. Bell, from Savoie, married to a Louisiana Creole (F 222); Miss Félicie Zenon Cavelier, a Creole, to "Mr. Girard, the youngest, from Languedoc, broker in this city" (F 252); Mr. Bernard "from France" to Miss Manette Tricou "from this city," whose brother was also married to a Tricou woman (F 238); and a "woman from Plaquemine, the widow of Lacoste and Cocrane," who was wed to "Doctor Chauvau, a native of Tourraine, aged 40 to 50" (F 283). Many more examples of unions between Louisiana Creoles, Saint-Domingue refugees, and French nationals appear in the correspondence, and there were thus many intersections among the various groups.

There was also, apparently, solidarity among people of the same geographic group. Boze takes pains to find jobs for French people coming from southwestern France recommended by Ste-Gême. He contacts several acquaintances, asking for their help. For a certain Bon, for instance, he writes that he has asked Bringier, the architect, and then his "friends who own a large bakery who have promised to give him the first vacant position." He adds that Bon was also assisted by "people coming from the same region, who help each other" (F 260).

The different groups apparently tended to help their own, and the previously cited examples of the Irish or Spaniards trying to put forward the claims of their group also show the solidarity that existed within most ethnic groups. Boze goes on expatiating on the determination of the Irish, who, after the first conflict with the Legion, went, in arms, to Faubourg Ste. Marie to try to free their jailed compatriots. After sounding a warning bell, the Legion dispersed the mob. City authorities apparently feared such demonstrations, since Boze insists on the means deployed, even mentioning the recall from Baton Rouge and the lake of two hundred men of the regiment commanded by Colonel Twiggs (F 258). They had been sent away for fear of the late-summer epidemic of yellow fever, but the risk generated by the Irish was apparently considered greater than that of the terrible Yellow Jack.

Friction and animosity were doubtlessly frequent among the various groups. The so-called Gumbo Filés occasionally opposed the Saint-Domingue refugees (F 161), the Irish and French Catholics sometimes fought, even physically, including inside the premises of the church (F 161), and there could be animosity and jealousy between the Creoles and the foreigners (164). As a member of the Saint-Domingue refugee group, Boze was even sometimes perfectly ready to side with the Americans against the "narrow-minded Gumbo Filés," who were jealous of the success of the new rulers of Louisiana. Although he was clearly closer to the Louisiana Creoles than to the Americans—if only for obvious linguistic reasons—he often ironizes about the "locals," occasionally using the derogatory term Gumbo Filés to designate them (F 147 and 148, among many others).

In the first forty years of American rule, a medley of races and ethnic groups characterized New Orleans, to the extent that travelers and sojourners noted that New Orleans was the "Babel of the South," a society of many races, ethnic groups, cultures, and languages. Until now, the depiction of New Orleans drawn from Boze's letters has emphasized the confrontations that occurred among the various communities. This confrontation was real in these early American years, and it partly shaped the city. Economic competition, for instance, led to the incredible economic development of the city. Political rivalry enriched the debates. Conflicts over race relations, legislation, or other social and political issues gave New Orleans a specific mode of functioning in the young American republic. Continuing to focus on the confrontational aspect would, however, be overly simplistic, since, while the numerous groups interacted through opposition, they also progressively mingled and gave birth to a very specific society, making New Orleans the "Creole capital" of the United States.

6

The Creole Capital

New Orleans was thus, in the early American era, an extremely cosmopolitan city, where racial and ethnic groups met and new immigrants from Europe cohabited with long-established Louisiana families and seasoned colonials from Saint-Domingue. Catholics coexisted with Protestants; speakers of French, German, and Spanish lived among Anglophones coming from Europe and Anglo-Saxon North America. Such a variegated juxtaposition of racial and ethnic groups could only be productive of a new society. Confrontations and alliances were the main modes of interaction of the various communities, whether they were white, racially mixed, or black, and with Creole, European, Anglo-American, or Saint-Domingue roots. If Boze interacted primarily with Saint-Domingue refugees—whites and free people of color alike—his letters show how the community progressively became acquainted. It happened through amalgamation and acculturation with the other main groups—primarily the Louisiana Creoles, as shown in the previous chapter, but also, as time went by, the Anglo-Americans. What his letters also show is how, in early American New Orleans, economic, social, and cultural segregation progressively gave way to interacting and intermingling, and how the various groups evolved toward a cultural continuum, making New Orleans a North American city with a special flavor, or, as it is often called, the Creole capital.

Creole was always an important denomination in New Orleans, definitely in the colonial period, but also, and maybe increasingly so, in the early American era, because it was used to designate the established residents of Louisiana, as opposed to all the newcomers—mainly Anglo-Americans, the new owners of the territory, but also all the foreigners, French or otherwise, who had come to settle.[1] When used to qualify the city, however, it takes on a specific meaning, suggesting an island of cultural difference in the American South and in Anglo-America more generally, incorporating Louisiana into the Greater Caribbean space and making Louisiana appear as a natural extension of the Caribbean, a different place where a specific cultural syncretism occurred.

While notions of Creoleness or Creolization have been traditionally used to define the cultural processes that occurred in the Caribbean, they are also now considered operational in Louisiana.[2] The processes that, from various cultures (African, European, Native American), created a new blend, unique to a place where the phenomenon occurred, are often a puzzling but also challenging reality that tells us much about the place considered.[3] In the case of Louisiana, while such a process had already undeniably taken place in the colonial era, the arrival of the Saint-Domingue refugees, themselves born in a creolized cultural environment, as well as the arrival of Anglo-Americans and European migrants in the early nineteenth century, produced cultural reconfigurations and gave the city a unique culture.

If Boze's letters tell us little about these processes and if his correspondence seems like a very partial source of information on the phenomena of mutual acculturation with adaptation to a specific context, many of his remarks do suggest the progressive hybridization of various cultures and, surprisingly, show how the Anglo-Americans participated in the transformation of New Orleans into the "Creole capital" of the young republic.

Examining the cultural interactions and hybridizations he describes gives insight into the city's persisting distinctive character throughout the nineteenth-century United States and even beyond. Boze presents the city as a rich religious, linguistic, and cultural center, where initial confrontations seemed to ease after some years and where cooperation progressively prevailed over opposition. He also shows New Orleans evolving from residential segregation to an original urban mix, progressively becoming a city where the different groups, principally the Gallic and Anglo-American ones, of course, but not only them, mingled and interacted. His assessment of New Orleans society also attests to the process of social and cultural Creolization that gave the Crescent City its singularity within the United States.

Showing how diversity made for a specific cultural wealth, but also how reconfigurations occurred among the main groups comprising New Orleans society, and how, through progressively increased interaction and a lessening of cultural segregation, the groups influenced each other and produced a unique cultural blend, will enable a reassessment of New Orleans's distinctiveness in North America.

Religious, Linguistic, and Cultural Wealth

In the early American period, travelers and sojourners who came to New Orleans for the first time were struck by the diversity they encountered in the city. Their descriptions are fed by the sensory overload they immediately felt when they reached the city. Upon arriving in the city in the fog, Benjamin Latrobe heard it long before he ever saw it: "A sound more strange than any that is heard anywhere else in the world astonishes a stranger. It is a most incessant, loud, rapid and various gabble of tongues of all tones that were ever heard at Babel. It is more to be compared with the sounds that issue from an extensive marsh, the residence of a million or two of frogs, from bullfrogs up to whistlers, than anything else. It proceeds from the market and levee, a point to which we had cast anchor."[4] Travelers all describe the variety of sounds, coming from the different languages heard in public places, and many conclude, like Harriet Martineau, that "the groups of foreigners make a Babel of the place with their loud talk in many tongues."[5] Babel is the metaphor that recurs in most of the works, showing the linguistic diversity of the city, found nowhere else in the Americas, at least in comparable proportions, by all these widely traveled visitors. If the variety of languages first struck the ears unaccustomed to such diversity, the cultural mix was always the second thing travelers mentioned, and the sounds of the various musical styles heard everywhere in the city were another source of amazement. From waltzes played in the ballrooms to African music played in Congo Square, a wealth of musical performances left visitors invariably flabbergasted. Reaching the colony in 1803 to hand it over to the Americans, the French prefect Pierre Clément de Laussat marveled at the diversity of musical styles heard in the ballrooms: "boleros, gavottes, English dances, French and English quadrilles and gallopades,"[6] hinting at, if not yet a syncretism, at least a relatively peaceful juxtaposition of the various cultural specificities of the Europeans that peopled the city.

If visitors first marveled at the sounds of the city, sight was the next sense that was challenged. Travelers and sojourners continually recollected the racial and ethnic variety they encountered the minute they disembarked on the levee. The multitudes, Martineau writes, "are conversing in all the tongues and gay in all the costumes of the world."[7] Benjamin Latrobe describes what he sees at the market: "White men and women, and of all hues of brown, and of all classes of faces, from round Yankee to grizzly and lean Spaniards, black negroes and negresses, filthy Indians, half naked, mulattoes curly and straight-haired, quadroons of all shades, long haired and frizzled, women dressed in the most flaring yellow and scarlet gowns."[8] With ethnic variety came varied colorful clothes, but also the goods each group had brought to the city, which, like the musical styles in the ballrooms, mingled in the marketplace. Benjamin Latrobe marvels at "the articles to be sold [which] were not more various than the sellers" before enumerating the wide range of products he sees in the market: "Innumerable wild ducks, oysters, poultry of all kinds, fish, bananas, piles of oranges, sugarcane, sweet and Irish potatoes, corn in the ear and husked, apples, carrots, and all sorts of other roots, eggs, trinkets, tinware, dry goods, in fact of more and odder things to be sold in that manner and place than I can enumerate."[9] Juxtaposed here, in Latrobe's description, are goods commonly found in European and North American markets, but also exotic ones linked with tropical areas of Africa and the Caribbean. All newcomers were struck by what was first juxtaposition, but also, little by little, came to be part of a syncretic culture typical of New Orleans.

Boze was much less amazed by this diversity, because, when he reached New Orleans, he had been living in tropical colonies of France, Spain, and the Netherlands for more than thirty years. He was thus accustomed to areas of intense racial, ethnic, linguistic, and cultural contact. His meandering through the city, however, often gives this sense of diversity. The coexistence and interactions of black, white, and racially mixed people is, of course, one of the varieties described by Boze, as is the juxtaposition of the various ethnic groups. As the previous chapter showed, he met and described people from all regions of France, but also German, Irish, and Spanish people, among many others, representing a good cross section of Europe. People coming from the eastern United States, Mexico, Latin America, and the French and Spanish Caribbean, and representing the whole Western Hemisphere, are seen coexisting, interacting, and finally mingling in his correspondence.

The coexistence of these groups made for the rich cultural development of the city. Because of its linguistic diversity, the city probably had more cultural and entertainment centers than the rest of the young republic, although other port cities of the Atlantic had some measure of such diversity. In New Orleans, the French had their opera, their theater, and their ballrooms. The Americans progressively opened their own theater, ballrooms, and entertainment facilities in Ste. Marie. New Orleans had both French and "American" theaters, as the French speakers called them.[10]

Similar diversity was seen in religion. The first four decades of the national era were marked by an increasing diversification of religious representation in the city. With the arrival of the Americans, mainly, but also of some new European migrants, Catholic churches were no longer the only religious institutions in New Orleans. Very early on in the correspondence, the encroachment of Protestant denominations is obvious. From the late 1810s on, Boze notices increasing religious diversity, evident in the exponential multiplication of Protestant churches, regularly ironizing on the fact, saying that only a synagogue was missing in the city. In 1829, he writes that Faubourg Ste. Marie has grown so much that it will soon be a new city and that he has counted in it "several beautiful churches, Lutheran, Calvinist, Protestant, etc. and now only a synagogue is missing there!" (F 144, F 194). In 1830, many Protestant churches had already been built, among which were "Lutheran and Calvinist" ones, and there is "no doubt in the expectation that the Catholic religion will be outshone by the Anglican one." In February 1832, again, Boze exclaims that "the only thing missing now is a synagogue! Because we see everywhere churches of all religions and all sects and, despite their numbers, Protestants, Lutherans, or Calvinists have lately petitioned our Governor to allow them to open a lottery to dedicate this sum to the building of a new church, but he refused this request, observing that if they wanted to have it built they could do it but with their own money" (F 196). Each community had its church, and Boze bore witness to the "satisfaction, humility, and respect with which the Irish and Germans" went to churches where they could find "in turn for their belief, preachers of their own language" (F 161). The existence of separate Catholic churches, so the various communities could pray and find priests who spoke their own language, is a sign that the early years of the American period saw more juxtaposition than interaction among the various ethnic groups.

In some instances, religious and ethnic diversity gave way to confrontation either among or between various denominations. In 1830, "a slightly serious brawl" occurred "between Irish and turbulent French Catholics" at the Ursulines' Church (F 161). On rare occasions, Protestants and Catholics were also opposed. The celebration of the Fourth of July, in 1835, was such an occasion. Whereas the celebration was supposed to occur at the cathedral, as usual, the colonel of the American Legion decided that he would take his troops to the Lutheran Church of Faubourg Ste. Marie and "deviate from the very ancient custom enjoyed by the Cathedral of the Apostolic Roman Catholic Church in public celebrations." When they reached Rue du Canal, however, all the soldiers decided to turn around and return to the Place d'Armes for the Te Deum. Smith, left alone on Canal, placed his soldiers under arrest. What the anecdote teaches us is that the variety of religions in New Orleans could sometimes lead to conflict, although, in this case, Smith's reaction seems more political and cultural than purely religious. It also teaches us that traditions—like the celebration of the main events at the cathedral—were strong enough to reconcile the sometimes opposed members of the various communities. What is relevant to the present discussion, in any case, is that these anecdotal episodes were sufficiently rare to attract the attention of the residents and receive full coverage by the press, as indicated by Boze (F 257).

Most of the time, in the early decades, the impression is thus that the different churches coexisted alongside one another in harmony and that people effaced their differences in order to pray at the same time, if not together. Despite increasing religious diversity, celebrations of the main events in the city remained Catholic. The end of the cholera epidemic, in November 1832, for instance, was celebrated with a Te Deum at the cathedral and the Ursulines' convent in the Carré (F 213). All the main celebrations, including the founding event of the young American republic on the Fourth of July, were conducted at the cathedral (F 257). What this tradition indicates is that, beyond pacific coexistence, a certain ecumenism was already developing in the city.

Despite the city's religious diversity, the Catholic Church was thriving, because many of the newcomers to the city—French, German, and Irish—were Catholic, as were the Saint-Domingue refugees. Boze describes the celebration, in late May 1830, of the confirmation and first communion of two hundred young women and thirty to forty boys (F 166). The Ursulines were also prospering and ensuring that many young women became educated. The "religious ladies" were building "a row of beautiful two-story houses with shops downstairs" on their property facing the levee. They had hired the architects Gurle and Guillot for the task and expected great revenue from this venture. They were also building a new housing facility on Rue du Couvent, three miles from the Quarter, in a beautiful place in the countryside, with fruit and vegetable gardens. They still had "a great number of boarders for their education" (F 172). In a similar way, the consecration of a new bishop, Reverend A. Blanc, in July 1835, filled the cathedral (F 257), as did the celebration of Holy Week and Easter, in 1836 (F 267). Despite the religious diversity Boze observed, and despite the relaxing of mores, due, according to Boze, to the increasing religious and ethnic diversity, the Catholic Church remained dominant, including in the celebrations of the founding events of the young American republic. Despite the rare confrontations among or between various religious denominations related earlier, peaceful but separate existence is thus what best defines religious life in the early American era, and this model of cohabitation seems to have been the dominant model in all cultural events at the time.

The different communities had their own customs, languages, and cultures. Anglophones and Francophones went their separate ways, attended their own theaters and organized their own cultural and social events. They interacted, in their private and social lives, mainly within their own group. They often lived in their respective faubourgs, or at least the faubourgs where there was a concentration of people from their own ethnic and linguistic group. They built their own banks, hotels, and commercial places. Even in their local institutional and political involvement, the two main linguistic groups seem to have originally operated side by side, without much mingling, probably because the linguistic barriers were, at least in the early decades, still relatively impassable and because each group could thrive in relative autonomy, as long as the main economic and social infrastructures were duplicated. This was true, for instance, of the various corps of the militia and guard. A single, revealing example will suffice to illustrate this. In 1832, Boze included in one of his letters a long list of the companies of the Legion that celebrated the centennial of George Washington's birthday. Boze notes that, among the 1,060 men in full dress, alongside the different corps of the Legion—including the Casadores espagnols, the Chasseurs à Pied, the Gardes d'Orléans, and many others—was the Louisiana Gards Compagnie [*sic*], a company independent of the Legion, Boze adds, and composed of young Americans, "without New Orleans Creoles" (F 198). The letter does not say whether there were many Americans among the members of the Legion, but the very fact that there was a company composed of only Americans and exclusive of the Creoles denotes the segregation that still existed in New Orleans among the different linguistic groups, even at the level of official companies designed to protect the city's residents. Many other such anecdotes in Boze's letters suggest that the different groups mainly lived side by side without much interaction. Early American New Orleans thus seems to have been marked by the separate development of the various communities, each of them displaying a remarkable cohesiveness in the early years. Reading Boze's letters, however, also reveals that the model seems to have evolved in the two decades of the correspondence and that cultural reconfigurations occurred throughout the period, giving, as the midcentury approached, the impression of a more cohesive cultural development.

Reconfigurations

First of all, as already suggested in the previous chapter, divisive issues apparently led to less cohesion within the groups themselves and also to occasional reconfigurations of alliances between the groups. If there are clear signs that the Creole versus American—or rather Gallic versus Anglo-Saxon—dichotomy generally described in the historiography was a fact of New Orleans life, the communities were not as unified as was long thought. Boze shows how Saint-Domingue refugees sometimes distanced themselves from the Creoles and other groups of the Gallic community. For instance, he regularly criticizes the advantages Creoles often had. For example, a Creole, the son of a Mr. Sarager, involved in a fight in which another young man was killed (Baillé's son), is said to have fled the city and "was probably assisted in his flight because he was Creole and from a respectable family" (F 211). He also mentions, for instance, "the favorite recreation of the Gumbo Filés[11] of the first and second ranks of this city," using what appears as a very derogatory and ironic word to designate the Creoles (F 147). The term Gumbo Filé recurs, especially in the early years of the correspondence, betraying a certain disdain for the native Louisianans on the part of Boze. Regularly, he also echoes the complaint that someone has been appointed to a position "because he was Creole," referring, for instance, to a "bad boy" appointed by the mayor (F 198).

Interestingly, several remarks indicate that this resentment was not solely Boze's and that it was common among the refugee community at large. Very often, he indicates that the Creoles were not necessarily well-considered by the Saint-Domingue refugees, especially if they belonged to the lower classes of society, again suggesting a complex superimposition of divisions along ethnic and class lines. Affirming the refugees' negative assessment of the Creoles, he mentions "Mr. Dorville who is extremely saddened by the dishonorable conduct of several Louisiana Creoles who make him blush, to the point that he sometimes tells me that, today, they equal the Americans with their mischiefs," thereby implying that even a member of the Creole community could occasionally confirm the negative assessment Boze and his fellow refugees voiced (F 239). Even though they frequently sided with each other, the French speakers thus did not necessarily remain unified, even when facing the challenge of competition with the Americans.

Some political decisions also clearly divided the Gallic population—along socioeconomic lines, for instance, or for reasons of political ideology. When New Orleans was informed of the vote by the French Assembly of the payment of France's debt to the United States, in June 1835, the "nationals of this city," that is to say the Americans, celebrated all day by sounding the cannon and organizing banquets, which seems perfectly normal. What is less expected is the reaction of the rest of the city's residents. "As for the French and other foreigners, half expressed satisfaction with this payment, and especially the commercial class which is not patriotic, and the other half shrugged from disapproval," which shows that there was not necessarily unity among the French, even in opposition to the Americans, and that they sometimes had diverging interests that elicited different reactions to the same events, including events connected with France (F 255). This description of "the French and other foreigners" is also interesting. Although Boze was himself a Frenchman, which he repeats several times in the letters, he did not hesitate to consider recent French immigrants to the city foreigners. Sometimes, he mentions a "foreigner" (accused, for instance, of illegally circulating bills of exchange), before adding "he is said to be French" (F 255). That he himself was one of those "foreign French," because he had been born and raised in France and had come by way of Saint-Domingue, made no difference to him, maybe because he considered that his already long residence in the Americas and even in Louisiana had already partly creolized him, making him more a citizen of the Americas than a foreigner to the continent. People apparently chose the group they identified with according to circumstances and to empathic reactions. In Boze's case, the fact that he had lived in Saint-Domingue and experienced the Haitian Revolution and forced flight from the former French colony with the other outcasts of the island, made him one of them, a Saint-Domingue refugee, instead of one of those recently imported "foreign French" whom he sometimes despised and criticized.

The 1830 gubernatorial race, however, made Boze and his refugee friends fear that the choice would be a "Gumbo Filé, because of the jealous spirit of these families against people from the outside, without acknowledging the sciences, industry, or fortunes they have brought over to this country in the year 1809, which gave to its commerce a greater momentum from all the advantages, as well as an increase in enlightenment to their instruction" (F 161). The Saint-Domingue refugees could thus occasionally apprehend the nativist reactions of the Creoles. Still commenting on the elections, Boze indicates several times that there were only two candidates, "French or Creole," Mr. A. B. Beauvais, Labatut's son-in-law, and Mr. A. F. Roman, although two Americans, Mr. W. S. Hamilton and Mr. Randall, also were in the race. What opposed the two "French or Creole" candidates was as much their origins (Creole from Saint-Domingue or Louisiana Creole) as their positioning on the national political chessboard, with the former supporting Andrew Jackson while the latter was in favor of John Quincy Adams. He further indicates that the main newspapers endorsed one or the other candidate, with the editor of *L'Argus*, Mr. Gibson, supporting Roman, while *L'Abeille* was behind Beauvais, to the point that a duel was fought between Gibson and Felix Labatut. Although both combatants were slightly injured, the duel ended without too much damage (F 169). Many details are given concerning the contest, showing clearly that the Louisiana Creoles and Saint-Domingue refugees could engage in violence. A famous former inhabitant of Saint-Domingue, Moreau-Lislet, was defending Beauvais, encouraging "many of our brave Saint-Domingue Creoles and Europeans to avenge, by their vote in his favor, the indecent words of these Gumbo Filés of Roman's party who had called them in their conversations seedy refugees" (F 170). Beyond these insults, Boze clearly attributes the initial antagonism and the refugees' strong opposition to Roman (as well as a certain Ducros who considered declaring his candidacy) to the fact that he was a member of the former legislature and one of the supporters of the "Bill [*sic*] which expelled the free people of color coming from the outside, so that our Saint-Domingue colonists have declared undying hatred of him" (F 170). Interestingly, the French speakers could thus be at loggerheads on the question of free people of color, while people tend to think that it was the Americans who tried to legislate against free people of color.

Boze also often shows the conflicting positions of the newspapers during electoral campaigns, even when two French speakers with similar origins were the main opponents. In the contest of Peyre against Prieur, both from Saint-Domingue, for the position of mayor, *L'Abeille* and *L'Argus* again waged a pitiless war, with the former supporting Peyre and the latter criticizing this support. A few days later, *Le Courrier* in turn took issue with *L'Argus* for criticizing Peyre (F 220).

In some cases, New Orleans also faced situations that required unexpected alliances to be formed. After the Irish violently rebelled, in 1835, demanding preferential occupational treatment over black people, the city organized militia companies of Americans, Swiss, and Germans to maintain order, thus including other Europeans among the American troops formed to fight against Anglophones of different origins (F 258). When an ethnic group organized visible action, as in the case of the Irish, there could be some xenophobic reaction—involving a wide array of different people—against members of the Anglophone community. In the wake of the already described protest, some Irishmen seemed to have fallen victim to assaults, sometimes for merely expressing political positions. The City Guard caught "an Irishman," Dr. Warner, who had published a "virulent pamphlet against the Legion in the *Louisiana Advertiser*." They subsequently "shaved him, undressed him, whipped him to blood, and dismissed him by kicking up his backside" (F 258). In a different case that denoted a similar pattern, when the American Whitaker, sentenced to death for murdering a certain Murphy, committed suicide in jail, "the Irish and German population crowded to the gate of the prison to make sure this was true, with the intent of taking his body away and hanging it." The authorities had to send several companies of the Legion to reestablish order against the unexpected alliance between the Germans and the Irish (F 265). Surprisingly, while the Germans had enrolled to fight with the Americans against the Irish rebels, in this case, they united with the Irish against the American murderer. Wavering loyalties thus marked social relationships in the Crescent City, and these unions, although often temporary, helped New Orleanians of various ethnic origins get accustomed to interacting and get acquainted with each other's cultures.

Cohesiveness within the different groups thus sometimes eased and alliances between groups seemed to shift, according to the specific cases. This was the first sign that the tradition of juxtaposition between the different groups was already less strong. Moreover, as time went on, there were clear signs that the various groups adhered less strictly to the de facto social and cultural segregation rules that had prevented them from mingling earlier on.

The Blurring of Ethnic and Cultural Segregation Lines

From time to time, Boze suggests that there were a few instances of ecumenical moments, when religious or ethnic segregation lines disappeared. Describing the passage through New Orleans of three newly appointed bishops on their way to their dioceses, for instance, he mentions the fact that the one going to St. Louis made a few notable sermons, "which were listened to by a great number of Christians of various nations to the point that the crowd filled St. Louis to its gates" (F 166). Although it is always difficult to determine the motive for choosing a particular word, which might, in any case, be unintentional, the fact that he uses the word Christians instead of Catholics may indicate the participation of non-Catholics in the event. At any rate, because he adds "of various nations," he implies that there were Anglophones, Francophones, and Germanophones, even if they were all Catholics, and that, at least on this occasion, the French, the Irish, and the Germans did not attend separate churches.

Boze even seems to suggest that the different groups sometimes influenced each other. For instance, he strongly suggests that the religious orthodoxy of the Catholics had relaxed with the arrival of new migrants to the city. He adds that people were no longer as zealous as they had been in the past, especially in the celebration of the religious holidays, "Christmas, Easter, Corpus Christi, All Saints' Day, and Holy Week." Deploring the absence of the fervent devotion of the past, which he attributes to the death of Père Antoine and to the increasing diversity perceptible in New Orleans, as well as to the unruliness of the youth—constantly ready to provoke disorder in church—

Boze laments that the Catholics of the city seem to have stopped finding relief and pleasure in attending church, and "it is now only in fear that people go to church." He even predicts that "there is no doubt that, with the passing of time, the Catholic religion will be outshone and that the Anglican religion will remain prevalent." He hoped, however, that the German and Irish Catholics would help restore the religious fervor of the rest of the Catholic Church, since "people see with pleasure and satisfaction the humility and respect with which all those Irish and German families go to our churches" (F 161).

Boze sees other signs that the communities were drawing closer. Both Americans and French-speaking New Orleanians seemed to have progressively become accustomed to taking the best of what the coexisting systems could offer. Gallic people, for instance, went on speaking French among themselves but started speaking English when they conducted business. They went on attending the French theaters but apparently also started attending the American one. They still crowded into the French ballrooms but also went to the American ones, whenever it was more convenient to do so or whenever the events organized there were more attractive.[12] Increasingly, the English section of the newspapers, for instance, advertised social events organized by the Gallic community in the French ballrooms in English, suggesting that the Anglophones and Francophones mingled more often.

Interestingly as well, all New Orleanians seem to have become used to taking the best of the various laws and traditions each group had brought to the city. Someone who could not be married in the Catholic Church, for instance, could choose a civil marriage in the American style. In March 1830, when a Catholic priest refused to marry the major general to a divorcee, they went to the judge of the tribunal of St. Bernard Parish, the major's neighborhood, "who performed the act in the American way" (F 160)—this last expression is clear about the dichotomy between the Gallic and the American ways but suggests a progressive acceptance, when they had an interest in it, by Gallic elements of certain American traditions. Very often, while Gallic people tended to be described by the early historiography on Louisiana as resisting an imposed American way in the early decades of the American period, the reader of Boze's letters gets the impression that New Orleans residents chose the best of coexisting systems and that, instead of clinging to the cultural segregation often depicted in the literature, people went from one system to another according to the situation at hand and with their own best interests in mind.

Moreover, people belonging to the various groups lived in less segregated conditions than what are often described, which also helped them get acquainted with each other and with each other's ways. While the early period was marked by a clear tendency toward residential segregation—for instance, the Americans concentrating in Ste. Marie, from the 1820s on—a degree of residential mixing was obvious, favoring exchanges and reciprocal influence. Bourdelais shows, for instance, that Anglophones lived in the Carré, although often in the areas close to Canal Street, mostly as far into the Carré as St. Louis Street. She concludes her empirical study by saying that there was an important, durable anglophone presence in the Carré until 1850, with the number of anglophone households increasing, between 1810 and 1850, from 156 to 1,633. According to her, the percentage of anglophone households in the Carré increased until 1850, from 8 percent in 1810, to 13 percent in 1820, 14 percent in 1830, and 23 percent in 1840 and 1850.[13] Quite clearly, Canal Street, long considered the border between the anglophone and francophone spheres, was an extremely porous border, if a border at all, and Boze gives much evidence of this. In 1835, for instance, he informs Ste-Gême that Rue du Canal was lined with American and French commercial establishments, thereby showing that commerce was not segregated geographically (F 253). Americans also started purchasing land and building houses in the Marigny (F 185), and in 1833, Americans are said to have purchased one of Ste-Gême's pieces of property in the Carré (F 232). If Anglophones lived in what are traditionally considered the French areas of the city, Francophones also lived in Ste. Marie, which Boze called the "American sector," most certainly because a greater concentration of Americans could be found there, although Bourdelais shows that Ste. Marie remained predominantly French, proportionately, until 1830, when she still counts 768 francophone heads of households compared to 565 anglophone ones.[14] Although relatively infrequently, which certainly does not mean that it did not occur more often than he mentions, Boze indeed attests to this territorial mingling, suggesting that Francophones moved to Ste. Marie, including for commercial purposes, even as Americans were becoming more numerous, proportionately, in the faubourg. In 1834, for instance, a certain Michinard is said to be opening a new pharmacy in Ste. Marie, "where the population is American and, as he perfectly masters the English language, it will greatly help him succeed in this establishment" (F 245). In May 1835, Americans were numerous in Faubourg Ste. Marie, as Boze writes that "they have their Faubourg Ste. Marie," but the population was apparently far from exclusively Anglo-Saxon, since Boze says that they "inhabit it in larger numbers" instead of exclusively, which is how he had described it in earlier years (F 253). It seems that Boze was then revising his earlier assumptions and insisting on the ethnic and linguistic mingling that existed in New Orleans, even though he acknowledges that there were clear patterns in the general distribution of the various populations. This evolution may also indicate that there was, by then, more reciprocal interest between the two main linguistic communities.

With the geographical proximity, there also seems to have been a gradual acculturation of the various population groups in New Orleans, starting with the development of more bridges between the two prevailing vehicular languages. Early in the correspondence, already Boze alludes to the necessity of learning English. In 1819, he informs Ste-Gême that his illegitimate son, Gême, is taking English classes, "for without this language, it is impossible today to find a favorable position either in commerce or in any other field" (F 143). In 1834, he says that he wishes his own granddaughters could have been educated at the Poydras hospice, "all the more because the English language is strictly practiced there, which would have been very useful to them upon entering society" (F 260). He also mentions the difficulty of finding a position for Bon, who, recommended by Ste-Gême, had just come from southwestern France to settle in Louisiana. Boze says that jobs are scarce, even for those who speak English, and "since he does not speak the English language, I still have not been able to place him as sales assistant in a commercial shop" (F 260). "To do commerce, you need to know the English language," he exclaims a few letters later (F 265). English is "the main basis for the progression of the newly arrived," since it is "greatly appreciated by the Americans and the merchants of various nations who have established themselves in this city" and has become "the absolute necessity, principally for merchants" (F 280).

The linguistic situation, however, was apparently more complex and less clear-cut than this and, although the case was becoming more exceptional with time, people who did not master English still could, against the odds, manage to succeed in their commercial ventures, because there were enough Francophones to interact with and because many people could carry on their daily business in more than one language (F 280). New Orleanians were apparently the most polyglot of all Americans at the time. The French and Spanish colonial regimes had prepared them for that. Life was clearly bilingual in New Orleans, in the late eighteenth century already, although Spanish had always yielded to French, due to the absence of a numerically significant migration from Spain to their temporary colony. The French and, to a lesser degree, Spanish linguistic influence, however, was felt for a very long time after the Purchase. Records, for instance, could still be kept in Spanish well into the nineteenth century if the record keeper was of Spanish origin.[15] Louisianans had a relaxed attitude toward plurilingualism, especially given that Anglo-Americans had started migrating a good decade before the Purchase and since there were already small contingents of people from Germany or the Canary Islands during the colonial era.

This general accommodation of foreign languages went on, this time mostly French and English, after the Purchase. The Civil Code of 1808, for instance, was bilingual, as was its 1822 revised version. This is not surprising, as it followed the general precepts of the Louisiana Purchase Treaty. More surprisingly, however, in a new territory, then state, of the United States, in case of contention, the French version of the code was authoritative, as the language of its authors was French. Similarly, most of the newspapers of the early American decades were still in French. The evolution toward anglicization was slow and, for a long time, the French and English languages coexisted in the newspapers. Both languages were thus in use, including in legal and official matters. Boze mentions people who spoke "*the* three languages, French, Spanish, and English," the use of the definite article here being of importance and suggesting the normalcy of the use of these specific languages, in accordance with the unusual history of the city (F 220).

In 1830, foreigners were apparently still learning French, since Boze expatiates on a certain teacher, Charbonnier, the author of a grammar book that enables pupils to study more easily and more quickly "and for foreigners to learn, with his simple method and his good principles, the French language correctly and promptly, so that he has had very important sales in this city" (F 164). French speakers studied English and the foreigners still tried to master French, which suggests that more and more people could shift from one language to the other. People read bilingual newspapers and probably increasingly read the two sections (at least in part), since the two sections covered very different subjects.[16] As time went on, there were thus more bridges between the different communities, and the dividing lines, even on linguistic matters, seem to have been less strictly drawn. Americans learned to speak French, and French speakers willingly studied English to be able to fit in in their new nation and thrive economically in early American New Orleans. If New Orleanians progressively adapted to the various means of linguistic communication available to them and if residential segregation was not always clearly marked, the Crescent City's residents also seem to have been more open to intermarriage between linguistic groups.

Amalgamation

Whereas most of the marriages mentioned by Boze in the early years were endogamic in each linguistic community, even though the various groups of French speakers were already intermarrying, Gallic New Orleanians and Anglo-Saxons amalgamated more easily after the 1830s. There are many examples of those intermarriages, progressively more so as years go by, even among the Saint-Domingue refugees. Delphine Sasmates, for instance, is referred to as James Hopkins's wife (F 213). The Creole elite, from New Orleans or Saint-Domingue, increasingly intermarried with Americans, such as the daughter of the late Dr. Lemonier, Marie-Anne Amérie Lemonier, who married Mr. John Mcready, "American lawyer." The wedding was celebrated at a Protestant church and was officiated by Reverend Marenhaut (F 235). Mlle. Bouligny, a Louisiana Creole, married "an American merchant" (F 265). Other examples give an even stronger impression of the increasing blurring of ethnic divisions. The only daughter of Mr. David Olivier married three times: first, the son of Mr. Destrehan (a Louisiana Creole), then "an American," and then Anatole Peychaud, a Saint-Domingue Creole (F 235). These are but a few examples of the many marriages Boze mentions that cross linguistic barriers, and his remarks give a stronger sense that the communities mingled because of a closer proximity between them, but also, sometimes, for economic reasons (F 245). In the case of Mlle. Bouligny, for example, Boze acknowledges that the American was from a "respectable family" and that the marriage was favorable to the bride (F 265). People apparently grew accustomed to these mixed marriages that crossed ethnic and linguistic barriers. In the fall of 1831, Boze mentions a wedding between a Creole and an American, concluding that "these two establishments are very well matched" (F 189).[17] His remark suggests that the socioeconomic match mattered more than the origins of the newlyweds and that unions between Anglo-Americans and the more established French-speaking group had become a normal feature of life in New Orleans. Gallic people, whatever their origins, also married foreigners, such as one of the Joly sisters, who married a Mr. Villamine, "a Spanish national" (F 226), or Marie Thalie Martin, the daughter of a doctor from Provence, who married, in 1834, Joachim Koun, "a merchant of German nation" (F 240).[18]

Reading Boze's later letters gives a real impression that the years of strict segregation among the various ethnic groups were over and that New Orleans was already evolving to become a complex blend of many different origins, due, of course, to its cosmopolitan character, but also to increasing social interaction among people from different groups, which enabled people to become acquainted and intermarry. It both suggests that the relative segregation of the first years had relaxed and that the New Orleanians knew enough of each other's language to be able to communicate and interact, as well as to court and marry.

The increasing exchanges and communication among the various groups, as well as the progressive amalgamation through intermarriage, already suggest that, in the 1830s, a new type of New Orleanian had been born, of several origins—a possible combination of French, Saint-Domingue Creole, Louisiana Creole, Anglo-American, German, Irish, or Spanish. This New Orleanian of a new era progressively seems to have given birth to a number of new shared traditions and shaped a new identity that was no longer French, Domingan, Louisiana Creole, or American, but that was unique to the city.

Creating a Common Cultural Blend

As time went on, New Orleanians seem to have developed a common culture, or even a common civil religion that unified all of them under the banner of the United States, but with a number of peculiarities that made the city special within the nation. This syncretic culture, for instance, was obvious in the celebrations, which constituted a clear element of unification among the residents of the Crescent City.[19]

While New Orleanians had, in the early years after the Louisiana Purchase, celebrated totally separately, sometimes even in violent opposition to one another, the important events of their respective history (whether the Fourth of July or the Fourteenth of July, according to their origins), they gradually mixed and blended during these celebrations.[20] It is true that they became accustomed to common celebrations very early on in the American period, since, from 1815 on, they had one very important event to celebrate together—the founding event of the French-American cooperation in the early years of statehood, the Battle of New Orleans, which took place in January 1815. Ironically, while peace had just been signed between the United States and England in late 1814, putting an end to thirty-two months of conflict, all New Orleanians united to win the biggest victory of the war a month later. What historians have always highlighted about this battle is the cohesion among the various groups of the New Orleans people. Whites and free people of color, Americans, Louisiana Creoles, Saint-Domingue refugees, and even the Barataria pirates led by Jean and Pierre Lafitte, all joined forces to defeat the English.[21] Their striking victory over the enemy was from the beginning a source of pride and local patriotism. It both unified New Orleanians and was specific to them. Every year, the commemoration of the event thus turned into a grand celebration of Louisiana patriotism and an occasion for unity and brotherhood, with Americans, white and black Louisiana Creoles, and white and black Saint-Domingue refugees all numerous in the ranks of the militia and among the veterans.[22]

In 1835, for instance, all the commanders of the Legion marched with their soldiers in the streets of New Orleans. The procession was headed by the governor, who was followed by those who had been present at the battle. "The state gave them a blue ribbon reading '8 janvier 1816' [*sic*] to be placed in the buttonhole on the left side of their uniforms." Everyone then went to mass at the cathedral, where the Te Deum was sung. The cannon was fired all day long. Then there was a banquet offered by Davis at his theater for all the highest officers and officials of the city (F 249). In January 1836, the event was again celebrated "with all the pomp required by the memory of this great success of the war against that nation full of pride" (F 260). In January 1838, Louisianans celebrated the "victory won over the English army by a handful of brave French et caetera [*sic*]," and "this memorable day is still celebrated with the majesty, the glory, the enthusiasm, and the magnificence it deserves" (F 280). Every year, the celebration was all the more important, as it marked the beginning of the carnival season and was followed by two months of festivities, and, every year, especially in the last years of his life, Boze took great pains to describe the celebration, as if he had finally acquired a Louisiana identity that made him cherish this important anniversary more than any other. It had become a true landmark in his life and in the lives of all New Orleanians.

If commemorating the Battle of New Orleans immediately unified New Orleanians, they all also seem to have increasingly taken part in celebrations that were inherited either from the French tradition or from the Anglo-American one. In December 1834, for instance, all inhabitants, Gallic and Anglo-Saxon alike, joined in the celebration of Sainte-Barbe, the patron Saint of the firefighters, artillery men, gunners, and all the professions connected with fire. Although this was originally a Catholic celebration, it was by then shared by every New Orleanian. That day, a high mass was celebrated at the cathedral, the artillery marched on the Place d'Armes, conducting very difficult maneuvers, the cannon was shot three hundred times, and a huge banquet, attended by most of the New Orleans elite of all origins, was organized, in the presence of Antommarchi, Napoleon's last doctor. The next year, on December 5, volleys of shots were fired all day, ending with fireworks. On Sunday, the sixth, a high mass was celebrated, followed by the artillery banquet, which was a fundraiser, with half of the money collected, according to the choice of the artillery, going to the New Orleans orphanage and half to the Catholic Association for Orphans (F 260). In another sign of this syncretism, in June 1836 the "foreigners gave their best wishes to the captain of their militia company for the Saint-Jean"—a tradition, of course, specifically French and Catholic, in which people wish joy to all those bearing the name of the saint of the day on the Catholic calendar (F 268).

If the Anglo-Saxons joined in the celebration of originally Gallic holidays, all the residents of the Crescent City, whatever their origins, also ended up uniting in the celebration of the founding events of the young American republic, their new nation. George Washington's birthday was, for instance, the occasion for sumptuous unitary celebrations in the 1830s. Every year, in January, Boze describes these celebrations, showing that, with time, they became a real tradition for New Orleanians, whatever their origins. In 1834, for instance, January 22 was the occasion for "many festivities with the Legion armed and in full dress, and with the clergy that officiated with great ceremony" (F 237).

The celebration of the founding of the American republic was another occasion for united festivities, and it seems that the French-speaking community did not balk at joining in the event. In 1834, "the 4th instant, we celebrated, with the pomp that this beautiful day deserves, the birthday of the American republic" (F 240), the use by Boze of the pronoun *we* signified his unconditional inclusion and that of the rest of the New Orleans residents, whatever people's origins, in the celebration. New Orleanians were, by then, a sufficiently cohesive community to be thus united under this common designation. Although 1835 was marked by the incident already mentioned of the attempt by the colonel of the Legion to have mass celebrated at the Lutheran church in Ste. Marie, the refusal of the company to follow him was a clear sign that the city's residents wanted to stick to their traditions and continue celebrating a typically American event in a traditionally French New Orleans way. Despite the brief incident, everyone joined in the common celebration, and mass was followed by "great festivities" (F 257). In 1836, "the same pomp, the same joy, the same recreation" as in the previous years was what struck Boze on the occasion of the Fourth of July (F 268).

The ecumenism was such when patriotic events were concerned, that the death at ninety-six of "this venerable patriot Charles Carroll de Carrollton, the last of the signatories of the act of independence" was the occasion of a solemn service at the cathedral, and that, on the occasion, the funeral oration was delivered in English. The death of a Protestant hero of the American republic was thus an occasion for reverence by the francophone Catholics of New Orleans in their cathedral, but in English (F 215). In December 1835, the Legion, under the command of J. B. Plauché, went in arms to the Place d'Armes for a three-hour "procession for the burial of General Bartholomew Shambury, a former officer of the American Revolution" (F 260).

If heroes of the American Revolution thus united all the residents of New Orleans in reverence, the same was true of the heroes of the Gallic community. When Dominique You, Jean Lafitte's right-hand man and one of the honored combatants of the Battle of New Orleans, died in 1830, "the cannon of our artillery was fired all day every quarter of an hour. After being on view in the upper story of the hall of the Cabildo, he was placed in the mortuary carriage and taken to his grave in the evening." The National Guard "had taken arms and, in full dress, they accompanied him with distinguished and religious pomp to his last abode, where he was laid to rest in a beautiful tomb made of brick." The National Guard accompanied his funeral with "several discharges of" guns, and "an infinite number of citizens of all ranks have followed the procession of the deceased to his burial place which I saw being closed by torch light." The reverence of the city for this "brave warrior," who had done significant services for the city "by fighting courageously the English when they invaded this territory in the year 1814" was such that the city council had tried, in the last years of his life, to alleviate his destitution by "generously providing for all his needs, paying great care not to hurt his sensitivity by entrusting sums of money to his great friends who then offered them to him, and which he accepted as loans in the name of services of friendship" (F 174).

The Gallic population thus celebrated American heroes and vice versa; the Americans took part in typically French celebrations; and the founding events of the young American republic were occasions for general rejoicing. As time went by, the various communities thus increasingly mixed and tended to support each other. This was first true among French speakers, as already seen, and intermarriage among free people of color as well as whites played an essential part in blurring boundaries. Beyond matrimony, many occasional or long-term alliances between the different groups tended to erase differences. This probably explains, in large part, the historiographical dissolution of the Saint-Domingue refugee community into a more general "Creole" blend and its long subsequent neglect by historians. When events made it necessary for the various Gallic communities to join forces, even the newspapers seem to have willingly erased the distinction between Louisiana and Saint-Domingue Creoles. After Denis Prieur's election to the position of mayor, for instance, while there is absolutely no doubt that he was born in Saint-Domingue, the newspaper *L'Abeille* wrote, in March 1833, that he was "born Creole," thereby blurring the division between Saint-Domingue and Louisiana Creoles.

Alliances between French and English speakers, including between Louisiana Creoles and Americans, during electoral campaigns are also often mentioned in the later letters. In April 1832, when the aforementioned mayoral election featured two Saint-Domingue Creoles, Peyre and Prieur, an alliance formed between the "Louisiana Creoles and the Americans" behind Prieur, while the Saint-Domingue refugees seem to have mostly—although not exclusively—supported "the glorious Creole from Saint-Marc in Saint-Domingue," Peyre, who accused Prieur of "favoring Faubourg Ste. Marie, at the expense of the Carré of the city" (F 202). In December 1833, Boze again expresses his hope that his fellow Saint-Domingue refugee, Denis Prieur, will not be reelected, adding that he doubts this will happen, because "this Creole has so many creatures in his hand, and principally the majority of the American citizens that he protects to their satisfaction, that it will be very difficult for the [other candidate Mr. Holland, Sheriff Morgand's deputy] to succeed, thanks to his partisans, in replacing him" (F 235). Later, when Felix Labatut became a candidate for the state legislature, rumors predicted his election, "being liked by the Americans, the Creoles, and the French who will give him their votes" (F 252). Americans could thus ally politically with French speakers, when it was in their interest to do so. Boze also sometimes suggests that there could be a mere absence of opposition from the other communities, as when, in 1832, he writes: "People say that the American party is gaining ground in terms of positions, helped by the indifference of the French and Creoles &c at elections" (F 233). Opposition thus often gave way to indifference and even to objective alliance after merely two decades of American rule over Louisiana.

Increasingly as well, New Orleanians reacted as a community and no longer along ethnic or linguistic lines. To take a single example, in the early fall of 1836, on the occasion of the liberation on bail of a murderer with Saint-Domingue origins, "at 10 o'clock at night, a crowd of about 25 to 30 young citizens of various nations" marched to the judge's house in protest (F 271). People seem to have progressively made no distinction between the communities and ethnicity seems to have often been supplanted by socioeconomic or corporative considerations. To take a single example, when Mr. James Workman, a former judge of the district court, died in October 1832, all the members of the Louisiana bar, whether francophone or anglophone, wore "a piece of black mourning crepe on their left arm for sixty days" (F 211).

New Orleans was thus much less segregated—geographically, socially, and politically—than what has long been said, after about two decades of cooperation among its people, and residents started sharing a number of social commemorative events that were common—and exclusive—to them. Boze's later letters also give an impression of increased cultural unification among the different groups.

The Creole Capital

New Orleans was definitely already a Creole city when the Americans took over Louisiana. Native, African, and European cultural traditions had blended to produce a syncretic culture, already specific to New Orleans. The inputs of the various populations in the early nineteenth century enriched and altered this culture, re-creolizing, so to speak, the city. The massive arrival of thousands of Saint-Domingue refugees, for instance, in the first decade of the century, added new Caribbean elements to the Creole culture of the city.[23] The influx of Anglo-Saxon migrants from the eastern United States—as well as all the new European additions to the New Orleans population after the Louisiana Purchase—diversified the population to such a degree that New Orleans's culture was, once again, progressively modified, although it always remained, in its evolutions, unique to the Crescent City. Boze's correspondence is extremely informative concerning the emergence of new features that definitely made New Orleans different from the other cities of the American South and elsewhere in Anglo-America.

First, it seems that, as time went by, the various languages spoken in the city tended to mix more. In his 1834 narrative, Latrobe comments: "it was curious to hear the Spaniard who cursed, swore and explained in three different languages—English, Spanish and French, and spoke all well." This linguistic proficiency is understandable because of the long coexistence of the various linguistic groups, and also because interactions became increasingly numerous as New Orleans reached a fuller integration in its new nation and as the number of Anglophones grew, making collaborations and interactions more numerous. This proficiency never characterized Boze, since all his closest acquaintances were in the francophone community and since there is no indication that he ever spoke English. This is not surprising, considering that he had lived in French-speaking areas for most of his life and that he was already over seventy years old when the anglicization of New Orleans really took off. This may also be accounted for by his relative isolation from New Orleans's bustling economic world, since the last time he was employed in the city was in 1819, before he left for his last trip to Cuba. Boze is most certainly not typical among the French speakers of New Orleans. The situation of the younger New Orleanians, active in the economic life of the city, was, no doubt, different, and there is ample evidence in the archives that they were more receptive to and more proficient in the English language.[24] It is interesting to see, however, that even he seems to have been affected by the increasingly anglophone environment, and his letters, although written in eighteenth-century French, progressively started becoming interspersed with English words.

These little slips are not numerous, but they seem to indicate a certain contamination of Louisiana French by the English language, probably partly occasioned by Boze's reading the newspapers, which were increasingly bilingual. Most of the time, the words Boze uses without translating them refer to either U.S. legislation or political organization. He uses, for instance, the word "recorder," found in an article published in *L'Abeille*, and Boze speaks of the "recorder de la Mairie" (F 189); he speaks of an "alderman" (F 189, F 202); mentions someone against whom a "warrant" has been served (F 172, F 206, F 233, etc.); and uses the word *résigner* to mean "resign from a position," a use that is probably an anglicism since it does not appear in any old French dictionary (F 166). He also recurrently uses the words "bill" (F 166, F 189, F 221, etc.) and "check" (F 265). In a single sentence, he uses both warrant and check, writing that a warrant was launched ("*on lança un warrant*") against someone who had written two counterfeit checks ("*deux checks*"), suggesting that he either repeated what others had read in the news and had told him or that reading the news had led him to take up the words he found in the English section of the newspapers that were among his sources of information (F 275). All the technological novelties introduced after the beginning of the integration of the city in the United States are also generally named in their English version. He almost never speaks of *bateaux à vapeur* but of "steamboats" (F 202, for instance). He mentions, several times, the building of "wharfs," instead of using the French word "quai" ("de nouveaux wharfs," "des wharfs en charpente" [F 202]). Several times, he mentions the *chemin à coulisse*, immediately adding "autrement appelé Rail Road" (F 189, F 205, F 217, F 220, etc.), and very often even directly says "Rail Road (*chemin ferré*)" (F 208), thereby simply adding the translation in French for his reader unaccustomed to this anglophone environment. When he gives the names of the railroad cars, he does so in a strange mixture of French and English: "tobacco plant, sucre plant, coton plant," using, in the case of cotton, the French spelling, with only one T (F 231).

Much of the historiography of early American Louisiana rests on the idea of permanent confrontation between the Anglo-Saxon and Gallic populations. If confrontation and competition did exist in the political and economic worlds, the process of linguistic acculturation seems to have been less painful and less confrontational than is usually believed, and the idea of a forced Americanization needs to be qualified. If the francophone population indeed stuck to its linguistic and cultural practices in their daily family environment but also in most of their social relationships, their willingness to anglicize seems to have been greater than is usually believed. They apparently understood the necessity of reaching out to the increasingly numerous Anglo-Saxon people sharing their city and of making efforts toward a better integration of their group into the young American republic. If they still cherished their traditions and cultural and linguistic practices, they also increasingly adopted their new owners' practices, conscious as they were that this increased mingling was in their best interest. This anglicization was true of whites and of free people of color, as shown by the example of Ste-Gême's illegitimate son, and it even extended to the slaves, since Boze comments that, since twenty thousand *nègres* have been brought to Louisiana, "we hear English spoken everywhere, since there are some of them in every house among the old domestics who have become familiar with the idiom" (F 175). This process of anglicization was a determinant feature of the progressive acculturation of the various groups and, interestingly, acculturation seems to have been reciprocal, although not necessarily linguistically as a whole. The Americans indeed seem to have willingly adopted some of the cultural specificities of the city they were settling in. And, all in all, the first four decades after the Purchase show a clear progression toward the elaboration of a new cultural continuum, borrowing from both dominant cultures, in which the two main groups often met halfway, building, in the process, a new, original culture.

Social practices indeed seem to have increasingly unified Crescent City residents, and the Gallic community apparently adopted some of the more Anglo-Saxon traditions. Boze regrets the sadness of the city on Sundays, in the years following the American migratory influx. The city is now "sad with the conformity of their devotions on Sundays when the deepest silence is observed." Boze complains that the joyful entertainment that was the rule during Ste-Gême's years, and that deeply shocked the travelers who came from the eastern United States, no longer existed.[25] Now, shops were closed, streets were deserted, and New Orleans looked like "one of those cities of the Levant that the plague ravages" (F 244). Several times, Boze laments the end of "French affability" and recurrently regrets the fact that Sundays had become so sad (F 148).

The Gallic population seems to have yielded to some Anglo-Saxon practices, but, at the same time, the acculturation seems to have been going both ways, since the Americans also gradually embraced French traditions. If the city was deserted on Sundays for reasons of Protestant religious orthodoxy, part of the quietness could also be accounted for by the new habit—inaugurated by the Gallic population—of all New Orleanians, whatever their cultural or religious origins, of going to the railroad for entertainment. In 1831 already, "on Sundays, the city is found deserted because all the city dwellers flock to the railroad to enjoy the view of the high society which goes there for its recreation outings, in rich costume and in attire in the latest fashion. Over about a mile, this road is lined up with cafés, restaurants, outdoor establishments, as well as sellers with tables covered with candy, refreshments, and all kinds of fruit, so that the eye pleasantly wanders over all these objects of curiosity" (F 183). Going to the lake for entertainment also became a habit for all New Orleanians. Boze shows that, following a Creole custom, when the weather was nice, people deserted the city and migrated to the lake, where, according to Boze, they feasted, danced, gambled, or "strolled in the shade of rural groves" (F 269). The Creole elite's tradition of going to the lake for leisurely celebrations, made even easier by the opening of the railroad, was apparently adopted by all New Orleanians. There were many festivities at the lake, where people danced "according to the taste of our beautiful Creole ladies" and where people were all dressed in "very elegant country attire" (F 269).

New Orleanians, whatever their origins, also liked horse races. When the new horse track opened in Carrolton, in March 1837, people flocked there to see the new track, "an oval measuring twelve *arpents*[26] by six, surrounded by wooden planks to prevent people from viewing this entertainment from outside." People enjoyed it, despite the entrance fee of two dollars per person to cover "the high value bets that are made before this exercise." On one of the first Sundays in March 1837, there were "several thousand persons, including the whole class of the regiment of the Merchant Marine and that of the barges and steamboats" and they collected more than fifteen thousand gourdes in four days, "including the table d'hôte, the gambling, and the refreshments" (F 273). People of French origin and Anglo-Saxons thus clearly mingled during these social events.

Celebrating Mardi Gras also gradually became a unifying practice. New Orleans was one of the few places in North America where the carnival tradition was thriving. Describing the carnival festivities, Boze scoffs at the American women who "dress themselves today with such elegance and modest bearing that they seem to want to surpass our Creoles in the good taste and wealth of their attire, doubtlessly in the intention to please." Even though they could never compete, in Boze's eyes, with the beautiful Creoles, the "beauties of various nations" tried to outshine the local beauties in these celebrations, thus attesting to the fact that this typical tradition of colonial New Orleans now belonged to everyone—Creoles, Americans, and foreigners (F 260).[27] This was only the beginning of a long tradition of common celebration of this very New Orleans event in a very New Orleans way that was progressively enriched by new traditions imported from Europe (the tradition of the parades, for instance, starting in 1837) or inaugurated by Anglo-Americans (like that of the krewes and thematic parades, for instance, although later, in the 1850s) or by the people of African descent (like the Mardi Gras Indians), which have survived to this day and make New Orleans's Mardi Gras unique.[28]

Some other surprising cultural mixing also occurred, and the theater built by the Americans in Ste. Marie, long called *le théâtre américain*, becomes, in Boze's late letters, *le théâtre américain et italien*. Describing the building as "extremely imposing, which makes it the first theater in the United States," Boze states that the director, Mr. Caldwell, has recruited "first class American and Italian actors and musicians." The theater, for its premiere, received some 2,300 persons, and could accommodate 3,000, while the biggest theaters in Paris and London could accommodate only 2,500. In the first months, Boze rejoices over the fact that it is too far away to attract "our Creole, French, and foreign enthusiasts accustomed to enjoying this recreation in the Carré" (F 258). In 1837, however, Boze acknowledges that everyone recognizes that the St. Charles theater is much better than the Théâtre d'Orléans, which suggests that people attended both American and French theaters and were able to compare them (F 275). The theaters also seemed to become less ethnically segregated as the midcentury drew closer, probably because of the French-speaking residents' increasing English proficiency. In 1835, a French actress, Céleste, was performing in the American theater (F 260). The Italian company, which was integrated into the American theater of St. Charles, featured Italian operas and attracted increasingly larger crowds, with the opera *Il Pirata*, for instance, being attended by "a crowd of spectators of various nations," to the point that the people at the gate could no longer breathe (F 265). The gradual acceptance of different cultural traditions seems to have become the norm in New Orleans from the 1830s onward.

New Orleans was thus on the path toward becoming a more cohesive society, even though differences persisted for a long time among the various linguistic groups. The first generations of French speakers necessarily had difficulty changing the practices they had been born and educated in, and it took several generations of interacting, intermingling, and intermarrying to blur the greatest dividing lines. Thirty years after the Purchase, however, the creation of a common culture, different from the rest of the American South, and from the rest of the United States, was well on its way. Although this covers a proportionately small part of Boze's narrative, his letters hint effectively at this unification process and give the reader a good measure of what was happening.

There is no doubt that New Orleans's diversity, if it subjected the city to conflict and struggles for influence, also gave it its linguistic, religious, and cultural wealth. In initiating competition among the different communities, it enriched the whole of the city. It also created unexpected alliances, which led to more interaction and thus more contact. People learned about their differences and also became accustomed to different practices and traditions. They progressively adopted some of the new cultural features they discovered.

From the mosaic of races and cultures that characterized the first decades of American New Orleans emerged a unique cultural blend that still makes New Orleans distinctive in the United States, and even in North America. Many observers name New Orleans the northernmost Caribbean city, accounting for this distinctiveness by its unique colonial past, which is partly true. Recent historiography has also accounted for it by the arrival, in the first decade of the nineteenth century, in the wake of the Haitian Revolution, of thousands of refugees from the French Caribbean colony of Saint-Domingue. Although this is definitely a good justification of the cultural wealth and specificity of New Orleans, it is still an oversimplification. One of Boze's legacies to history is to show that the early American decades, too long neglected by historians, were probably still more complex than what the traditional and even more recent interpretations have shown, and that the juxtaposition, and then progressive intermingling, of many population groups with very different cultural origins were also seminal in creating the distinctiveness of the Crescent City. All groups played their part and all made for the singularity of New Orleans.

Conclusion

The two decades in which Jean Boze wrote to Henri de Ste-Gême were a wonderfully ebullient period in New Orleans's history. The city was then the capital of the very young American state of Louisiana. In 1818, barely six years after attaining statehood, it was still negotiating its place within the young American republic. Transitioning, in less than three decades, from the very provincial colonial town it still was in many ways to the largest metropolis of the American South was not easy for the Crescent City. Living conditions were still sometimes like those of a small frontier town. New Orleanians had difficulty protecting themselves from dire climatic conditions and lethal epidemics. Unpolished mores often gave way to bouts of uncontrolled violence. As the city struggled to enter the new capitalist world of the young republic, its economy was extremely sensitive to the vagaries of the weather, to political instability in Louisiana or in the rest of the United States, and to international turmoil. Although New Orleans was well on her way to holding her rank in her new nation, her struggle to reach that position was fierce.

Most of the developing cities in the young American republic were going through the same difficult transition. In New Orleans, contrary to the other Southern cities but in synchrony with the cities of the northeastern Atlantic coast, this came with an extraordinary period of improvement and change. The city's population was increasing at an unheard-of pace. Urban architecture was developing and modernizing. Business centers and residential areas expanded, multiplied, and thrived. Architectural innovations made headway in hurricane- and fire-resistant construction. Houses were both more imposing and more refined. The city's infrastructure kept up with its demographic expansion and modernizing transportation. New Orleanians progressively enjoyed walkable streets and banquettes, railroads, canals, and a sewage system, and New Orleans became a more comfortable and easier place to live, as well as a safer and healthier place. If cities like Philadelphia, New York, or

Boston made similar progress, New Orleans was far ahead of the rest of the urban South (if such an oxymoron may be used here).

In these years, New Orleans society greatly evolved as well. While Louisiana held her rank among the slaveholding societies of the North American continent, while slavery was perfectly integrated in the structures of the city, and while the three main population groups were organized (in a way typical of the French and Spanish three-tiered orders) in a stratified system, New Orleans seems to have offered overall something slightly different from what has long been conveyed by historiography. Relations among the various groups of the population were often much more complex than what has long been thought. Upon the traditional divisions among whites, free people of color, and slaves were superimposed a number of considerations that slightly muddled the dividing lines. New Orleans society was very class conscious and highly hierarchized, and this was true among slaves, free people of color, and whites alike. People identified with the group that shared their geographical origins, and race apparently sometimes mattered less than origin. Belonging to the group of refugees from Saint-Domingue could be more important than racial solidarity, and Boze was often ready to side with free refugees of color against any white attempt to limit their rights and prerogatives. In that respect, New Orleans was very different from her Anglo-Saxon Southern counterparts and from the cities of the North as well, which had abandoned slavery but not racial discrimination.

Moreover, while the traditional depiction of the first few decades after the Louisiana Purchase has long been of a two-sided struggle between the Louisiana Creoles and the Americans, oppositions seem to have been much more complicated. First and foremost, what has long been identified as the Creole group seems to have comprised more than people of French or Spanish descent born in New Orleans. Into the Louisiana Creole group were often aggregated the Saint-Domingue refugees and even the foreign French, which renders the depiction of the political, economic, linguistic, and cultural struggle for supremacy as a Gallic versus American one much more accurate than the traditional Creole versus American one. This was clearly a feature unique to New Orleans among the cities of the young American republic, but there was still more than this opposition between two major linguistic groups.

The New Orleans population was indeed much more varied than this binary, and there were many colonials from the former Spanish empire, but also many non-French, non-Anglo-Saxon Europeans in New Orleans in the first half of the nineteenth century. A close examination of the relationships and interactions in the city shows that if members of one linguistic group generally sided together, here again, loyalties and alliances were often more complex than heretofore thought. Linguistic groups sometimes diverged over political or even social issues, and there were unexpected alliances formed among different ethnic groups, as the example of the American, German, and Swiss alliance against the Irish, or that of everyone against the Americans, have shown. Even if most cities in North America at that time received similar contingents of Germans, Irish, or Italians, the ethnic landscape they found upon arrival was very unlike the New Orleans one, and the interactions between those migrants and the local populations developed very differently. Encountering a population comprising large numbers of people belonging to two different ethnic and linguistic groups was not an experience that those who migrated to other American cities had. New Orleans was thus an exception in the American South and even in the United States.

There was even more than this. If New Orleans seems to have often been divided along linguistic lines but also according to the origins of its inhabitants—with the two major groups struggling for domination being, naturally, the Francophones and Anglophones—these decades were those of the early shaping of the city's identity within the new context of the United States. The divisions and oppositions seem to have become less distinct as time went by. The French seem to have understood the necessity of speaking English, and what has often been depicted as an imposed acculturation of the Creoles by the Americans appears to have been more negotiated than imposed.

Although they still mingled less than they could have, the groups gradually became used to living side by side and sometimes borrowed what they liked from the other's culture and traditions. Americans started celebrating French events and the French-speaking group started adopting some American ways. Residential segregation became less strict, the two sides adopted each other's architectural styles, and people apparently interacted more and even amalgamated through an increasing number of unions across linguistic lines. New Orleanians even started building their own specific identity through the invention of celebrations that could unify all of them, the most famous being, of course, the anniversary of the Battle of New Orleans. They also inflected their cultural traditions to bring about a totally new culture, no longer African, or French, or Anglo-Saxon, or specific to any other place, but a New Orleans culture, different from anything found in the rest of the United States, making New Orleans the Creole capital of the young nation.

Boze's meanderings through the expanding, modernizing city tell us much about early American New Orleans. The reports he draws from news he heard from friends or acquaintances, or from stories he read in the newspapers, tell of relationships and interplay in the city after the end of its colonial era. His proximity to the Saint-Domingue refugees, and the Gallic population more generally, enables the twenty-first-century reader to gain insight into this variegated, complex society. He knew from the inside what was beyond the grasp of outsiders.

Of course, there are silences, hyperboles, and probably even fabricated truths in what he writes. He narrates what he believes, and his reports are thus not always true to the facts. He probably also often tells Ste-Gême what he thinks his friend wants to read. He sometimes complains and rants about the difficulty of living in New Orleans to make Ste-Gême pity him and thus get more assistance than he may deserve. His writings are not historical truths, of course. At the same time, he was a recent New Orleanian. He had roamed the Atlantic world, had known many colonial societies of the various European nations and thus had the position of a relative outsider. But he was also a kind of insider. He knew more than many about the Saint-Domingue refugees. He could observe, from a relative distance, the shaping of American New Orleans. He could compare French, Spanish, English, and Dutch colonies of the Americas. He had experienced the race relations of other slaveholding societies and could shed light on New Orleans society. This is why, even though his narrative is not historical truth, it provides a wonderful occasion to grasp what it meant to live in New Orleans in the first half of the nineteenth century. Boze, through his picturesque descriptions, is an idiosyncratic chronicler of the city.

There is still much to learn about New Orleans from his letters, and the configuration of the present book has left almost untouched many pages dealing with the Saint-Domingue refugees. We can still learn more from Boze about who these people were, how they fit into the New Orleans society, what their occupational pattern was, who they interacted with and how, as well as many other facets of their lives. Summarizing some twelve hundred pages of an incredibly rich correspondence in book form cannot produce an exhaustive treatment of what that correspondence's many pages reveal.

It is hoped, however, that the present work has given a measure of the wealth of this extraordinary correspondence and has triggered the reader's interest and curiosity in it and in the unknown treasures that the New Orleans archives still have in store. There are thousands of unexplored documents, including many items of correspondence, which, once studied, will lead to a better understanding of the singular history of New Orleans and will illuminate some of the many mysteries that the early American period still holds for twenty-first-century readers.

Appendix

Lettre originale:

Monsieur[1]
Le Baron Henri De Ste Gême
Chevalier de l'ordre Royal et Militaire de Saint Louis
Par Toulouse
A Saint Gaudens. Département de
la Haute Garonne.
France

1830 *Nouvelles Diverses*
Mars

Nous avons appris que la bouilloire du bateau à vapeur le Guillaume Tell [. . .][2] le 16 du courant creva à la distance de 3 lieues au-dessus de la Rivière Rouge dans les parages de Natchez et ayant sombré de suite, que la cargaison n'a pu être sauvée et cinq passagers y ont perdu la vie !

Le 24. Un nègre esclave américain charretier cingla à dessein un blanc d'un coup de fouet qui saigna. Mais le maitre de ce premier à cette nouvelle se rendit de suite sur le lieu dans la rue Condé, et compta à ce malheureux 25$ pour l'empêcher d'aller faire son rapport au tribunal d'un juge de paix et pour ce payement il se soumit au silence. Mais dans pareil cas l'Avocat Général devrait en prendre connaissance et poursuivre le coupable pour l'exemple !

Le 25. Un nègre américain très robuste et de haute taille appartenant au rédacteur de la feuille L'argus était marron et rodait dans les savanes du faubourg Marigny. Son maitre avec quatre hommes de la garde de ville marchèrent sur lui et le joignirent, mais par sa force il s'en dégagea en désarmant l'un de la Garde qu'il blessa au bras de son propre sabre et prit la fuite. Le propriétaire tira alors sur lui ses deux coups de pistolet et l'ayant manqué il cria à un chasseur qui se trouvait en vue de lui tirer son coup de fusil qui le blessa suffisamment pour le tenir arrêté, et il fut conduit avec le secours d'une charrette en prison ou il est encore en attendant son jugement.

Le 27. Incendie dans la nuit au faubourg Marigny, qui consuma seulement la maison d'une femme de couleur libre blanchisseuse sans avoir eu le temps de pouvoir sauver aucun effet.

Le 27 mars. Le début d'un bourreau blanc de nation irlandaise pour se soustraire à la peine de mort qu'avait prononcé la loi pour son crime d'assassinat, et de cette manière le sheriff est à présent à son aise pour les exécutions auxquelles on voulait exiger sa propre main.

Le 31 Ct.[3] Incendie à 11 heures du matin a la rue de la Douane entre celles de Chartres et de la Levée, le feu ayant pris dans un grand magasin de meubles à un Américain, qui se communiqua de suite à trois maisons en briques de deux ou trois étages qui furent consumées malgré le secours des pompes, ce qui porta un grand désordre au déménagement des propriétaires des maisons adjacentes en craignant que le feu aurait continué ses désastres, que tous les spectateurs de cet événement malheureux se trouvaient affligés de tant de pertes.

Le 5 avril Ct. Mr Denis Prieur a été réélu maire de cette paroisse qui a tiré du canon dans la soirée, et avec une grande musique toute la nuit, en réjouissance de ce bon choix à la majorité des votes contre Bermudez juge de paix en fonction et le journal de L'abeille a dit à ce sujet ce qui suit.

nos législateurs avec leurs lois verbeuses et incohérentes ont assez fait contre nos libertés civiles et politiques, pour avoir tâché de préserver le peu qui nous en reste contre les nouvelles atteintes qu'on aurait pu leur porter si on avait nommé à cette magistrature cet officier public tout intègre, tout savant et tout estimable qu'il soit, lorsqu'on aurait la certitude qu'il était disposé à faire de son mieux pour introduire chez nous la police des villes du nord. L'incompatibilité de nos mœurs avec un tel système était un motif suffisant pour nous engager à nous élever de toutes nos forces contre son élection et remercier dieu de sa chute au candidat

Mr Denis Prieur a obtenu 1063 votes

Et Mr Bermudez. . . . . 439, ce qui a donné une supériorité de 624.

Le 6 Ct. Assassinat à 7 heures le matin en face de l'église des Ursulines par un nègre esclave de Mlle Lize Soulet contre un mulâtre cocher esclave aussi à une famille créole de cette ville qui est mort sur le coup du poignard porté au cœur, et ayant pris de suite la fuite à toute course qu'il n'a pu être arrêté par la Garde. Mais gare si on l'attrape !

La police arrête toutes les nuits des vagabonds et des esclaves errants.

On attend avec une très vive impatience le premier lundi de juillet prochain qui décidera de la place de gouverneur en faveur du candidat qui aura obtenu le plus de votes, et on craint que le choix ne tombe sur un Gombo filé,[4] d'après l'esprit jaloux que ces familles portent contre les gens du dehors, sans reconnaissance aux sciences, à l'industrie et aux fortunes qu'ils ont apportés dans ce pays en l'an 1809 qui donna à son commerce un plus grand élan par tous les avantages, et un surcroit de lumière aux instructions.[5]

Le chemin ferré se continue à force et avec beaucoup d'activité, mais il ne pourra avoir sa fin et son complet de toute cette année tant les travaux sont grands, pénibles et difficiles. Néanmoins le but de la Compagnie se remplira à son parfait avec le temps, pour entrer au nombre des merveilles; ce qui ne pourra que donner une plus grande valeur aux habitations du voisinage de ce beau chemin public d'une nouvelle invention.

Dans mon précédent bulletin, j'ai oublié de vous dire que le curé de cette paroisse s'était refusé de marier le Major Général avec une femme divorcée pour la raison que la religion catholique, apostolique et romaine rend ce sacrement indissoluble et que sur ce refus, désirant remplir sa promesse à sa gentille maîtresse, ils furent sans plus de délai se présenter au tribunal du juge de la paroisse St Bernard son quartier par en bas, qui remplit cet acte dans les formes américaines à leur satisfaction mais la famille est très mécontente de sa conduite à cet égard qui la mésallie.

Joly au service de la marine militaire de Columbia est passé avec le commandement d'un bâtiment de guerre dans les mers du Sud à la suite de son amiral Beluche.

Ce premier a commandé longtemps la place de Marecaillo côte ferme, où il a épousé la fille d'un général espagnol qui le protège beaucoup auprès des nouvelles autorités de Columbia[6] et de Venezuela qui ont forcé le chef Bolivar à se démettre de son commandement supérieur, et il s'en est désisté de bonne grâce pour ne pas s'exposer à un combat inégal en apprenant la marche de ses ennemis avec des forces très supérieures, et qui ne peuvent cependant pas, malgré leur désunion, s'empêcher de rendre justice à la bravoure de ce guerrier distingué, à son mérite, à ses lumières et pour tous les grands services qu'il a rendus à sa patrie durant son règne.

Mézelle[7] la femme de Beluche est aujourd'hui à Caracas, après avoir abandonné son domicile à Porto Cabelo qui ne lui offrait plus de sûreté avec une famille sur les bras.

Le Mexique depuis que son gouvernement a perdu les guerriers Guerrero et Sta Ana est aussi en insurrection complète, que le sang a commencé d'y couler s'il faut en croire les journaux qui viennent de Veracruz.

Lauminé qui manque de la N^{lle} Orléans depuis environ trois ans, n'ayant pas été heureux dans ses courses corsairiennes, et se voyant ruiné pour ses pertes qu'il se décida d'aller en Afrique y traiter une cargaison de noirs pour St Thomas, dans laquelle il a réussi pour avoir touché à sa part, me dit Sauvinet, une vingtaine de mille gourdes, ce qui l'a encouragé à entreprendre une seconde expédition de cette même nature, et il est attendu dans son retour à St Thomas pour faire espérer à ses amis qu'il ne tardera pas de rentrer au sein de sa famille si toutefois ce nouveau voyage lui est aussi profitable que le premier.

Je crois avoir oublié de vous parler dans le temps que le Cap^ne^ Cadet Liquet était mort dans un voyage fait au Port-au-Prince il y a plus de deux ans mais Mdme sa veuve légitime, à cette nouvelle, expédia de suite une goélette pour aller en retirer le cercueil avec le corps de ce défunt, ce qui lui fut accordé par le gouvernement haïtien, et à son arrivée il fut inhumé religieusement dans ce cimetière, accompagné à sa dernière demeure par tous les frères de sa loge maçonnique et d'une compagnie de militaires miliciens qui saluèrent d'une décharge le repos de ce brave corsairien.

Mais tout en respectant sa mémoire, je puis avancer qu'il n'avait donné aucun profit à ses armateurs dans sa dernière croisière à les faire rappeler de sa vaillance et de son bonheur !!

Lorsque la législature de cette ville ouvrit de votre temps ses premières séances sous la présidence de feu Mr Poidras pour fixer cet Etat dans son gouvernement soit pour rester territorial ou pour passer au rang de ceux de l'union, feu Mr Détréan,[8] l'un des membres de ses représentants rempli de lumières et aimant sa patrie, plaida pour qu'il restât toujours territoire et il voyait très bien que je me trouvais de son opinion à cet égard. Mais hélas ! Les intrigants qui aspiraient aux places à l'envi l'un de l'autre étouffèrent la justice des sages représentations de ce respectable citoyen grand propriétaire et parvinrent par leur nombre à obtenir qu'il était beaucoup plus avantageux pour le pays d'être établi en Etat, et par leur réussite c'est aujourd'hui les mêmes personnes qui nous font des lois à nous faire souffrir !

*[9] La voix publique se plait à dire que jamais sheriffs n'avaient rempli les devoirs de cette charge avec autant d'intégrité et de d'humanité que Mr Morgand, qui n'est point fortuné après environ 20 ans d'exercice, et cela pour avoir exécuté les mouvements de son bon cœur envers ceux que la loi lui commandait de sévir rigoureusement. Mais toujours sensible au malheur que souvent pour ne pas exécuter les débiteurs comme son devoir l'y obligeait, il s'était porté souvent leur caution dont les suites de l'ingratitude de ceux qu'il avait servis avec tant de désintéressement lui ont dévoré jusqu'à ses émoluments et sans jamais se plaindre. On dit même qu'il ne cesse de secourir chaque jour l'indigent qui se réclame de sa bienfaisance que l'on prône avec autant

de raison que de plaisir les vertus de ce respectable officier de justice rempli de probité.

Le marquis M. a été, ces jours passés, indisposé, on dit que c'est par suite des tracasseries que lui fait éprouver le récalcitrant Espagnol qui persiste dans ses amours, pour s'en être suivi des propos et des menaces indécentes sur lesquelles ce premier lui a représenté qu'il était prêt à se mesurer lorsque ce sera d'une manière honorable. Mais ce furieux lui a riposté par ces paroles, dit-on ! Seriez-vous hérissé d'armes et même de canons de la tête aux pieds, qu'elles ne sauraient m'arrêter pour vous bâtonner ! Si vous persistez dans votre refus de ma main pour Mlle votre fille, l'objet de mes plus tendres affections.

Ce sont des on-dit je vous le répète, comme celui qu'il a à faire est un rompu !

La farine à 3$ 5 es. le Bril 54 onces le pain d'un escalin.[10]

Quoique je me reconnaisse sans moyen en politique, il me semble d'après les journaux de France que son ministère est Willingtonien ![11] Et qu'avec ce secours l'Angleterre paraîtrait désirer placer en Grèce un roi sous sa férule, et pousser son ambition jusqu'à faire flotter son pavillon sur Navarin île de Turquie pour y établir sans doute une place militaire pour sa colossale marine à pouvoir au besoin en imposer à la Russie, et toujours à la barbe des autres puissances qui restent assoupies sur la marche gigantesque de cette cruelle et ambitieuse nation, qui peut-être aura un jour l'audace de convoiter la place d'Alger, si la France par les armes parvenait à abattre cette puissance barbaresque, qui quoique pirate insolent est d'un grand secours à la France par l'abondance de ses grains qu'elle livre tous les ans à ses besoins et autres denrées. Car je me rappelle que dans mon enfance, j'entendais toujours dire par les anciens que la France nécessiterait le commerce de trois Alger. Néanmoins il devient urgent qu'elle donne une leçon par le siège qu'elle médite et par terre et par mer avec de très grandes forces pour la convaincre qu'elle peut courir tout comme une autre la chance d'un renversement.

Les fêtes de la Noël, celles de Pâques, de la Fête Dieu, de la Toussaint et de la Semaine Sainte qui jadis donnaient à tous les bons chrétiens de la réjouissance pour se rendre en foule et avec humilité aux respectables temples de notre religion pour y faire leurs prières, et bien ! Elles ne sont plus suivies aujourd'hui avec cette ardente dévotion, ni avec ce même zèle de piété que la sage doctrine de feu le révérend Père Antoine[12] son premier ministre avait inspiré à tous les cœurs de ses paroissiens par ses prônes et son exemple à observer et suivre avec ferveur les commandements de dieu et de l'église. Mais les mœurs sont changés, et même les Créoles avouent cette vérité. A présent, ce n'est plus qu'en tremblant que l'on se rend aux églises, après avoir vu la jeunesse de ce siècle ne porter aucun respect aux célébrations religieuses, mais bien pour s'amuser à critiquer les toilettes, à faire quelques espièglerie, et à ridiculiser la modestie des pénitents et pénitentes, ce qui a occasionné dernièrement un grand scandale à l'église des Ursulines, en troublant les ministres de J. C. même dans leur fonction en chaire, qu'il s'en est suivi une rixe un peu sérieuse entre les Catholiques irlandais et ceux français turbulents, qu'elle se ferma et resta ainsi plusieurs jours, en attendant que par le secours du tribunal de la mairie l'ordre y serait rétabli avec cette décence que les fidèles doivent observer dans les temples chrétiens et auquel l'on promit de se soumettre. Mais il n'est pas moins vrai que les fêtes majestueuses et si agréables ne sont plus célébrées avec autant de joie, de pompe et de respect comme au temps passé et les bonnes chrétiennes principalement ne se rendent à leur dévotion qu'avec tristesse, par la crainte qu'elles ont de rencontrer quelque nouvelle scène pour cette jeunesse d'aujourd'hui très mal élevée.

Depuis l'établissement d'un très grand nombre de temples luthériens, calvinistes, &c, il n'y a pas de doute à espérer que par la suite du temps celle catholique sera éclipsée, et que celle anglicane restera la dominante.

On voit avec autant de plaisir que de satisfaction, l'humilité et le respect avec lesquels toutes les familles irlandaises et allemandes se présentent à nos églises, ou elles y trouvent à leur tour pour leur croyance un prédicateur à leur langue.

Ce 12 avril 1830
[paraphe]

Translation:

Monsieur[13]
Le Baron Henri De Ste Gême
Chevalier de l'ordre Royal et Militaire de Saint Louis
Par Toulouse
A Saint Gaudens. Département de
la Haute Garonne.
France

1830 *Miscellaneous News*
March

We learnt that, on the 16th instant, the boiler of the steamboat Guillaume Tell exploded at the distance of three leagues above the Red River in the vicinity of Natchez and having sunk immediately, that its cargo could not be saved and five passengers lost their lives.

On the 24th. An enslaved American *nègre*, a carter, purposefully lashed with a whip a white who bled. But the former's master, when he heard of it, immediately went where it had happened on Condé Street and gave the unfortunate man $25 to prevent him from reporting it to the court of a justice of peace and through the payment, he agreed to remain silent. But in such cases, the General Attorney should be informed and prosecute the offender as an example.

On the 25th. A very sturdy American *nègre* of great height belonging to the editor of the newspaper L'argus was maroon and lurked in the savannas of Faubourg Marigny. His master with four men of the City Guard went after him and found him but with his strength, he escaped from them, disarming one of the guards whom he wounded on the arm with his own saber, and fled. This owner then fired his two pistol shots at him and, having missed him, he cried to a hunter who was in sight to fire his shotgun which wounded him sufficiently to stop him, and he was driven, in a cart, to jail where he still is, awaiting trial.

On the 27th. Fire during the night in Faubourg Marigny, which only burnt down the house of a free woman of color, a laundress, without giving her time to save her personal effects.

On March 27th. The instatement of a white executioner of Irish nation in order to avoid the death penalty the law had pronounced against him for a murder, and so the sheriff is now more comfortable for executions for which his own hand would have been demanded.

On the 31st inst. Fire at 11 in the morning on Customs Street, between Chartres and Levee, the blaze catching in a furniture store belonging to an American, which immediately spread to three brick houses of two and three stories which burnt down despite the firemen's assistance, which brought great confusion in the moving of the owners of the neighboring houses, for fear the fire might pursue its disaster, so that all the onlookers of this unfortunate event were distressed by such great losses.

On April 5th inst. Mr Denis Prieur was reelected mayor of this parish which fired the cannon in the evening, with much music all night long, rejoicing for this good choice of a majority of votes against Bermudez, justice of peace in office and the newspaper L'Abeille wrote on this topic the following.

Our legislators, with their verbose and incoherent laws, have done enough against our civil and political liberties to try to preserve the few that remain from the new infringements that could have occurred if this public officer, as upright, learned, and respected as he may be, had been selected to this magistrature, when there was certainty that he was prepared to do his best to introduce in our midst the police of northern cities. The incompatibility of our mores with such a system was reason enough to commit us to rise with all our strength against his election and to thank God for the candidate's failure.

Mr Denis Prieur obtained 1,063 votes

And Mr Bermudez. . . . . 439 V^{s}, which gave a superiority of 624.

On the 6th inst. Murder at 7 in the morning across from the Ursuline church, by a *nègre*, one of Miss Lize Soulet's slaves, of a mulatto coachman, also the slave of a Creole family of this city, who died instantly from the dagger blow to his heart, and fleeing immediately at full speed, he could not be caught by the City Guard. But watch out if he is caught!

The police arrest every night vagrants and stray slaves.

We are eagerly awaiting the first Monday of next July, which will settle the governorship in favor of the candidate with the most votes, and we fear that the choice might be for a Gumbo Filé, in conformity with the jealous spirit those families bear against people from outside, without recognizing the knowledge, industry, and fortunes they brought to this country in the year 1809 which gave to its commerce a greater impulse by all these advantages, and an increase in enlightenment to instruction.

The railroad is progressing with force and with much activity, but it cannot be totally completed this year because the work is important, hard, and difficult. The goal of the Company, however, will be perfectly reached in time, to be counted among the marvels, which can only give greater value to the plantations neighboring the beautiful public path of this new invention.

In my previous newsletter, I forgot to tell you that the priest of this parish had refused to marry the Major General to a divorced woman because the Catholic, Apostolic, and Roman religion made this sacrament indissoluble, and that, upon this refusal, wishing to fulfill the promise he had made to his sweet mistress, they went without delay to the court of the judge of St. Bernard Parish, his neighborhood down river, who fulfilled this act in the American way, to their satisfaction but the family is very displeased with his conduct hereof which misallies them.

Joly, in the service of the navy of Colombia, has gone with the command of a warship to the South Seas, following his admiral Beluche.

The former long commanded the place of Marecaillo on terra firma, where he married the daughter of a Spanish general who protects him considerably with the new authorities of Colombia and Venezuela who forced Bolivar to resign from his high command, and he withdrew with good grace so as not to expose himself to an uneven fight when he learnt that his enemies were approaching with very superior forces, who, despite their disagreement, cannot but do justice to the bravery of this distinguished warrior, to his merit, to his wisdom, and to his great services to his homeland during his reign.

Beluche's wife[14] is now in Caracas, after leaving her home in Porto Cabelo which no longer offered her safety with a family on her hands.

Since its government lost its Guerrero warriors and Sta Ana, Mexico is also in total insurrection, so that blood has begun to be shed, if we are to believe the newspapers that come from Veracruz.

Not having been fortunate in his privateering activities, Lauminé, who has been away from New Orleans for about three years, finding himself ruined from his losses, decided to go to Africa to trade a cargo of blacks for St. Thomas, in which he succeeded to the point that he got for his share about twenty thousand gourdes, Sauvinet told me, encouraging him to undertake a second expedition of the same nature, and he is expected back in St. Thomas, making his friends hope that he will soon return among his family if this new journey is as profitable as the first one.

I think I forgot, earlier, to tell you that Captain Cadet Liquet died during a journey to Port-au-Prince over two years ago. But his legitimate widow, learning the news, immediately sent a schooner to retrieve the coffin with the remains of the deceased, which was granted to her by the Haitian government and, upon arrival, he was interred religiously, accompanied to his last abode by all the brothers of his Masonic Lodge and by a company of militia soldiers who saluted with a salvo eternal rest for this brave corsair.

But while honoring his memory, I can venture to say that, in his last cruise, he had brought no profit to his ship owners to help them recall his great courage and his good fortune!!

When the legislature of this city opened, in your time, its first sessions under the presidency of the late Mr. Poidras, to decide if the government of this state would remain a territory or become a state of the Union, the late Mr. Détréan, one of the members of its representatives, full of knowledge and loving his homeland, vividly pleaded, with all his moral and philosophical strength, for it to remain a territory forever and he perfectly understood that I shared his opinion about this. But alas! The schemers who coveted each other's positions stifled the justice of the wise representations of this respectable citizen, a big landowner, and managed, by their number, to obtain that it was much more advantageous for this country to be established as a state, and by reason of their success, there remain today the same persons who pass the laws that make us suffer.

* Public opinion likes to say that never had a sheriff fulfilled the duties of this charge with as much integrity and humanity as M[r] Morgand, who is not at all wealthy after about 20 years in office; this for having listened to the movements of his generous heart toward those the law commanded him to punish rigorously. But continually sensitive to misfortune, to avoid executing debtors, as his duty commanded, he often stood security for them and the result of the ingratitude of those he had served with such disinterest has devoured even his remuneration without his ever complaining. He is even said to succor every day the destitute who appeal to his benevolence so that people praise, with reason as much as pleasure, the virtues of this respectable justice officer full of integrity.

The Marquis M has been unwell these past days. People say it is due to the hassles coming from that recalcitrant Spaniard who persists in his love, so that indecent words and menaces have followed, after which the former informed him that he was ready to confront him as long as it was in an honorable way. But this raving lunatic has responded with these words, so people say: even if you were spiked with weapons and even with canons from head to toe, they would not stop me from thrashing you! If you persist in refusing my hand for your daughter, the object of my most tender affections.

Those are rumors, I repeat, as the rumor according to which he is dealing with someone with a wide experience!

Flour at $3 and 5 cts the barrel 54 ounces the bread at one cent.

Although I acknowledge myself ignorant in politics, it seems to me, from the French newspapers, that the cabinet is Wellingtonian! And that, with this assistance, England may wish to place in Greece a King under its thumb, and push its ambition to fly its flag over Navarin, the Turk island, to establish there, doubtlessly, a military place for its colossal navy, to be able, if need be, to impress Russia, and always under the nose of the other powers that remain sleepy in the face of the gigantic progress of this cruel and ambitious nation, which, maybe, will dare, one day, to covet the place of Algiers, if France managed to put down with arms this Barbary nation which, although an insolent pirate, greatly assists France with the abundance of its grain that it delivers to her every year according to her needs and other commodities. Because I remember in my childhood always hearing our elders say that France would need the trade of three Algiers. It is becoming urgent, however, to give her a lesson, with a siege planned both from earth and sea, with important forces, to convince her that she runs the risk, like any other, of being overthrown.

The celebrations of Christmas, Easter, Corpus Christi, All Saints', and the Holy Week, which in the old days caused all good Christians to rejoice by crowding humbly to the respectable temples of our religion to pray, well! They are no longer respected today with the ardent devotion or the pious zeal that the wise doctrine of the late Reverend Père Antoine, its first minister, had inspired in all the hearts of his parishioners by his commendations and his example to observe and follow with fervor the commandments of God and of the Church. But the mores have changed so much, and even the Creoles admit this truth. Now it is only trembling in fear that people go to church, after seeing the youth of this century show no respect for religious celebrations, but only enjoy criticizing people's outfits, committing pranks, and making fun of the modesty of the penitent men and women, which recently occasioned a big scandal at the Ursulines' Church, by disturbing J. C.'s ministers even in their office at the pulpit, so that a rather serious brawl ensued between the Irish Catholics and the turbulent French ones, after which the church was closed and remained so for several days, waiting for the assistance of the city court to reestablish order, with the decency that all the faithful must observe in Christian temples and to which people promised to submit. It is nonetheless true that the majestic and very pleasant celebrations are no longer carried out with as much joy, pomp, and respect as in the past and the good Christian women, in particular, go to their devotions sadly, fearing to encounter a new spectacle by the ill-mannered youth of today.

Since the establishment of a great number of Lutheran, Calvinist, &c temples, there is no doubt that we can expect, with the passing of time, that the Catholic one will be eclipsed and that the Anglican one will remain predominant.

We observe with as much pleasure as satisfaction the humility and respect with which all the Irish and German families come to our churches, where they find, in turn, for their beliefs, a preacher in their own language.

12 April 1830
[flourish]

Notes

Introduction

1. The *Oriente* is the region of the east coast of Cuba located between Santiago de Cuba and Baracoa, right across from the west coast of Saint-Domingue.

2. In less than a year, between May 1809 and January 1810, ten thousand refugees from Saint-Domingue found asylum in New Orleans. All of them were former inhabitants of the French colony of Saint-Domingue. All of them had fled the Haitian Revolution at the turn of the nineteenth century and rebuilt their shattered lives in the neighboring island of Cuba. For more information on the Saint-Domingue refugees in Cuba, see Debien in Brasseaux and Conrad, 31–112.

3. See Poland and Pederson; Bruneton-Governatori; Gerber, "Epistolary Ethics" and "Acts of Deceiving"; Jones; Decker; and also Frenette, Martel, and Willis.

4. See Gerber, "Epistolary Ethics," 6.

5. Probably mostly completed by the Civil War.

6. Historians of Louisiana have focused most of their works on colonial and post–Civil War Louisiana. Although some groundbreaking works have been published in the late-twentieth and early twenty-first century, books on antebellum American Louisiana are still scarce. Since the pioneering work of Fossier, and although some works partly bridge the colonial and American eras (see, for instance, Ingersoll or Spear), few books have been produced on early American New Orleans (save for Tregle, Hirsh and Logsdon, Cossé Bell, Dessens, and a few others).

7. See Spear, for instance.

8. This notion will be developed in chapter 6.

9. Quotation extracted from his article entitled "The South," published in the May 9, 1954 issue of the *New York Times*.

10. Interestingly, in his book *Another City: Urban Life and Urban Spaces in the New American Republic*, Dell Upton mainly studies four cities—Philadelphia, New York, New Orleans, and Boston, with New Orleans being the only one among these located in the South.

11. It will be essential, for instance, to focus on the networks involving whites and free people of color in New Orleans, Cuba, and the commercial hubs of Mexico, like Tampico. This will reveal much about human and commercial exchanges, cultural influences, and

the constitution of the Greater Caribbean as an increasingly dynamic part of the Atlantic space. Examining the way in which the independences, in Anglo-Saxon America as well as Latin America and the Caribbean, tilted the balance of the Atlantic space toward the Greater Caribbean will most certainly reveal unexplored fields of the history of the Americas in the nineteenth century. Although Boze's narrative gives many hints on these topics, there is still much research to carry out.

12. For methodological remarks on the reading of correspondence, see, for instance, Gerber, "Acts of Deceiving," 315.

13. Translation of "porte d'entrée dans un univers mental," Frenette, Martel, and Willis, 8.

14. Many selections from Boze's letters will be used to illustrate the depiction of "his" New Orleans. The translation into English (by me) has endeavored to keep the particular savor of Boze's words. For the sake of clarity, some of the charm of his narration has, unfortunately, been lost in translation.

Chapter 1. Adventure

1. Boze's life has been reconstructed from information found in archival sources, mainly at the Centre d'Archives d'Outre-Mer (CAOM) in Aix-en-Provence, at various archival centers in the Caribbean (Cuba, Curacao) and in the United States (anecdotally, the Rochambeau Papers at the University of Florida, but mainly New Orleans archives). Some material has also been provided by the descendants of both Boze and Ste-Gême. The Sainte-Gême Family Papers (MSS 100 at The Historic New Orleans Collection) has also been a very rich source of complementary information. All further references to this collection will be indicated in the body of the text under F (for Folder) followed by the folder number.

2. Information partly found in his death record at the sacramental records of the New Orleans Archdiocese Archives. At his death, on December 19, 1842, his burial record indicates his birthplace and his approximate age (about ninety). Several of his letters confirm the birth year as 1753, including a letter of 1829, in which he says he is seventy-six. The exact date of birth was sent to the author by Antoine Pagenstecher, Jean Boze's descendant, and is indicated on his birth record.

3. In a brief he wrote to request a position as royally commissioned captain of the port of Jacmel, in Saint-Domingue, in June 1789, he traces his entire career in the French merchant marine. The memoir indicates that he served for fifteen years and enumerates the five campaigns he covered, mentioning the dates, names of vessels, and names of captains, as well as that four of these campaigns occurred "during the war" (with England) and that it was during the fifth campaign that he became "pilot of the King's vessels" when the ship *Le Dictateur*, under the command of Captain Deladries, was disarmed. The memoir is part of the cited document and complements a letter requesting the appointment as Captain of the Port of Jacmel, Saint-Domingue, June 25, 1789. Centre d'Archives d'Outre-Mer (henceforth CAOM), Aix-en-Provence, Inventory of the colonial personnel before 1789, Series E, fm, e50, 217.

4. He served on *La Chimère* in 1775, *Le Montréal* in 1779, *La Gracieuse* in 1780, *La Boudeuse* in 1781, and *Le Dictateur* in 1782.

5. For more on Saint-Domingue before the revolution, see de Cauna, *Au temps des isles à sucre* and *Haïti, L'éternelle révolution*, Laurent-Ropa, or Fick.

6. What Boze was requesting, in 1789, was the Royal Commission, similar to what had been granted to the captains of the harbors of Le Cap, Port-au-Prince, and Môle and Cayes du Fond. His request was not granted, despite the inclusion in his brief of several very warm letters of recommendation, including one by Mr. de Montgrand in October 1780, one by Mr. Delaroque, the captain of the frigate he saved in April 1786, and one by the general intendant who had appointed him captain of the harbor in 1786.

7. His name and signature are found on a set of notarized documents dating from February 1787 to October 1788, attributed to "Boze, Notaire Royal à Castries, Sainte Lucie" (Royal Notary in Castries, Saint Lucia). That it is the same Boze is doubtless, if one compares the signature of the documents and of the letters archived at The Historic New Orleans Collection. The flourish used to initial the documents and sign them is unmistakably that of the Jean Boze living in New Orleans between 1809 and 1842. Moreover, the acts are all initialed by Boze and signed in a different inking, with the mention "Collated" followed by "Nlle Orleans." CAOM, Depôt des Papiers Publics des Colonies (DPPC), Not LCA 1.

8. He was involved in the succession of François Blanc, in Jacmel, in October and November 1792, and in that of Jean-Pierre Gatechan, the husband of Marie Louise Félicité Theuret, a relative of Boze's future wife, in November 1793. The Clerk's Office of Fort Dauphin has him as executor of the successions, in charge of requesting the affixing of seals on the plantation of the late François Blanc and of having them taken off to witness the inventory of the deceased. CAOM, Greffes du Fort Dauphin, October 1792, Succession of François Blanc, DPPC, Gr 151, and CAOM, Greffes de Port-au-Prince, November 7, 1793, Succession of Jean Pierre Gatechan, DPPC, Gr 115.

9. One document, for instance, archived at the Clerk's Office of Port-au-Prince, referring to the sale of two slaves, Jacques and Lise, in October 1792. CAOM, Greffes de Port-au-Prince, DPPC, Gr 227.

10. The whole document—which covers several pages—details the procedure of inventory of the possessions of François Blanc that were stored in Boze's house. François Blanc's succession, October 1792. CAOM, Greffes du Fort Dauphin, DPPC GR 151, 337.

11. Adélaïde was the second daughter of Pierre and Marie-Françoise de Monfray. The 1768 baptismal record of the couple's first daughter, Marie Balsamie, born in 1767, indicates that they were residents at the Marigot, a district of the parish of Jacmel. Adélaïde, born in December 1771 and baptized in 1772, was the goddaughter of Claude Manfret, an attorney at the Parliament of Port-au-Prince. Her father died on his plantation in November 1777. CAOM, Registre de l'Etat Civil, Les Cayes Jacmel, 1714–1778. 85 MIOM 44 AOM, 61 (Pierre Theuret's baptism), 229 (Marie Balsamie's baptism), 285 (Adélaïde's baptism), 301 (Pierre Theuret's death).

12. As indicated in the *Etat détaillé des liquidations*, the register that recorded the indemnification by the French government, at the turn of the 1830s, of the Saint-Domingue

proprietors that had to flee the island during the revolution, leaving all their property behind. France had to abandon any claim on the island when it gained its independence in 1804. But it then negotiated the payment of a debt by Haiti, the prerequisite for its acknowledgement of that independence. After two decades of negotiations, the Haitian president, Jean-Pierre Boyer, under military pressure from France, finally agreed to sign a treaty with the king of France, Charles X. The treaty acknowledges the independence of the colony in exchange for the payment of an indemnity of 150 million francs, later reduced to 90 million, the payment of which crippled Haiti at least until 1888. France used this indemnity to pay back the Saint-Domingue colonists for their lost property on the island. It then instituted a complex procedure of claims, the colonists able to prove that they had owned property in Haiti being indemnified for an amount of 10 percent of their initial property. The indemnification has left detailed records of the property owned by the refugees prior to the Haitian revolution, at least for all those who were still alive (or whose descendants filed a request), had papers documenting their ownership, and did file a request with the French government. These documents provide scholars with an invaluable documentation of property ownership in Saint-Domingue before the Haitian Revolution. For more on the indemnification process, see Jean-François Brière.

13. Boze's property warranted a compensation of 2,510 francs, to be shared between him and his daughter, Marie-Louise Sophie *épouse* Pagenstecher, designated as the sole heir of her deceased mother, her brother Jean-François having died in the meantime. *Ministère des Finances. Etat détaillé des liquidations opérées à l'époque du 1er janvier 1832*, 540. The decision for the compensation was made on January 11, 1831, and paid on March 1, 1831.

14. The whole of the three properties was indemnified for a total of 41,510.45 francs. The plantation of Adélaïde, who was identified as widow Butin from a first marriage and wife of Boze from a second marriage, was compensated for a total of 14,100 francs. The beneficiaries were Marie-Louise Sophie Boze *épouse* Pagenstecher and Jean-François Boze, although he was no longer alive when the payment was made. *Ministère des Finances. Etat détaillé des liquidations opérées pendant l'année 1832 et les six premiers mois de 1833*, 778. The decision for compensation was made on August 28, 1831 and paid on February 1, 1832.

15. For more information on the Haitian Revolution and population movements that ensued, see Dessens, *From Saint-Domingue to New Orleans*, especially chapter 1, "The Saint-Domingue Epic," 6–21.

16. For more on this (as well as numerous references to other secondary sources), see Dessens, *From Saint-Domingue to New Orleans*, 11–14.

17. On that date, he temporarily disappeared from the records in Saint-Domingue.

18. This is when he reappeared in the records of another Caribbean territory.

19. Their marriage, as well as the birth of their children, was recorded in Saint-Domingue, in February 1803 (6 Ventôse an 11, according to the French revolutionary calendar). The act, the last but one in the register of Jacmel, just before the final evacuation of the French from Saint-Domingue, is said to record this marriage and these births, according to the Republican principles set by the *Règlement du vingt-sept messidor an dix* bearing on judiciary organization, in particular articles 174, 175, and 176. The idea was

to officially recognize the children within the judiciary system of the French republic. CAOM, DPPC, Table 55 MIOM 4, Jacmel, 96.

20. This information was transmitted by Antoine Pagenstecher, the descendant of Boze, from the Lutheran registers of Curacao (1757–1825), published by A. A. Lutter in The Hague, in 2000, under the title *Bronnenpublikaties van de Indishes Genealogishe Vereniging* (deel 13). I have not had access to the register. The proximity of the date of birth to the parents' marriage (one month) is surprising. The information, however, seems serious enough to be trusted, considering that the names of the parents totally accord with what we know, and since the names of the godparents are also precisely recorded (François Salinier and Maria Jones). The act recording the births of the children in Saint-Domingue in 1803 unfortunately bears no precise date of birth.

21. The place and date of Sophie's birth were transmitted by Antoine Pagenstecher, as recorded on her death certificate.

22. The birth of the last child is the only one precisely recorded because, like his parents' marriage, it was recorded in Saint-Domingue, on 30 Frimaire an 11 (December 21, 1802). CAOM, DPPC, Jacmel, Record of Deaths, 18.

23. This schooner, as well as the name of her captain, is cited twice in the Curacao registers, since she twice apprehended ships navigating under the British flag. On November 24, 1796, she arrested the schooner *Neptunus*, sailing from Tobago to Boston; on November 19, 1796, she seized the brig *Betty and Molly*, en route to Barbados from the island of Madeira (inventory of the seized ships, information collected by Frank Deffes, the Louisiana descendant of Boze, transmitted by Antoine Pagenstecher).

24. When exactly the Boze family returned is unknown, but it was sometime between the recording of their second son's birth in St. Thomas, in 1799, and the little boy's death in Jacmel, in December 1802, as attested by his death record.

25. For more on the Haitian Revolution, see Dubois (*Avengers of the New World*), Fick, Geggus, Ott, and Sepinwall.

26. This is when Boze and his wife had their marriage and the births of their three children recorded. Boze was then forty-eight and his wife, Adélaïde, thirty-one. Their two living children, Jean-François and Sophie, were aged nine and five, respectively.

27. He was appointed head of the harbor movements ("capitaine des mouvements du port") on April 6, 1802, and captain of the harbor on May 13, 1802. *Rochambeau Papers*, University of Florida, 200 and 362, respectively. Information available in *A Calendar of the Rochambeau Papers at the University of Florida Libraries*.

28. On the last months of the Haitian Revolution, see, for instance, Laurent-Ropa, 322–23.

29. The recording of Jean and Adélaïde's wedding is the last official record of Adélaïde. There is nothing in the Saint-Domingue records, since their marriage and birth of their children is the last-but-one event recorded and since, in late 1803, no record keeping was possible any longer. Until Antoine Pagenstecher's communication of his ancestor's diary, the only thing that was known about her was that she had died sometime before her husband's arrival in New Orleans, in 1809, and after February 1803, when she had appeared before the officer of the public records of Jacmel, in Saint-Domingue.

30. The narrative, extracted from the memoirs written by Sophie's son (Jean Boze's grandson), Gustav Pagenstecher, in 1902, is all we have about their precipitated retreat. It is full of historical inaccuracies but explains the sudden disappearance of Adélaïde from the records. Memoirs of Dr. Gustav Pagenstecher (1902), son of Ludwig Pagenstecher (1780–1833) and Sophie née Boze (1798–1869). Translated from German by Antoine Pagenstecher, revised by Nathalie Dessens. Pagenstacher family papers, transmitted by Antoine Pagenstacher.

31. Inaccurate information. As we have already seen, he was already in the Caribbean by the time the French Revolution broke out and had been there for more than five years.

32. He did go to Curacao, as we know, but if he fled there, it was not because of the French Revolution per se but because of the slave rebellion that had started in Saint-Domingue in 1791. His wife indeed owned property in Saint-Domingue, but from the *Indemnités*, we know that she probably did not own more than one plantation, although her family did.

33. Actually, a third son was born to them in St. Thomas, the Danish Caribbean island, but he died in Saint-Domingue at age three.

34. The original, without surprise, contains the German word "neger," then used to designate black people. I chose here to use "blacks" in its place, in contrast with translations from the French (see note 52 below), to avoid the confusion that might result from the use of a German word in the text.

35. Of course, this is historically untrue. The free people of color did indeed react, but in 1790, and the slave rebellion spread from 1791 on. What occurred in early 1801 was the attempt by Napoleon to recapture the island, which was, by then, autonomous under Toussaint Louverture and his constitution, although Toussaint had left the former colony under French protection. It is true that, because of the arrival of the French Expeditionary Corps, hostilities and atrocities resumed.

36. The reader of this narrative has to bear in mind that this was transmitted by Sophie, who was only five at the time of the events and who left her father at age six, never to see him again. This is the narration of a very traumatic event experienced by someone who was, at the time of the events, a very young girl and who never benefited from family stories after her youngest age. This narrative, however, explains the total absence of record of Adélaïde's death and is all there is to account for her death. Indeed, while Boze's letters are full of details about his life in Louisiana, he never once mentions any part of his previous life in his 1,200 pages of correspondence.

37. Her son's memoirs read: "Soon hereafter, my grandfather moved with his two children to the island of Cuba and from there, later, with his son, to New Orleans, while he sent his seven-year-old daughter, my mother, in company of a Miss Josephine, to Bordeaux, where she was to be brought up in a convent. On the way to Bordeaux, the ship landed in St. Thomas in 1806, and there, my father saw her for the first time and (as she has often narrated) carried her down from the ship in his arms. When my mother was released from the convent, she lived until her seventeenth year under the personal care of her godmother, Miss Josephine, of whom she has always kept fond memories, and whose miniature portrait is still now in the possession of our family. As the circumstances of this

lady were very limited, however, my mother had to finally leave Bordeaux in 1814 and find shelter in Hamburg, in the house of my father's associate, Herr Muehlenbruck, to whom she had been warmly recommended by her godmother. There, my father got to know her better, and he finally married her, one year after his first wife's death (1818), although she possessed no more worldly goods than her modest clothing, as she often told us, her children." This account is corroborated by the many references to Sophie and her letters to her father in the correspondence.

38. Dessens, *From Saint-Domingue to New Orleans*, 18. For more details about the refugees in Cuba, also see works by Gabriel Debien, Alain Yacou, and Agnès Renault.

39. Boze's activities in Cuba are partly revealed by his presence in the official records and by the very few references he makes to this period of his life in a series of letters he wrote to Ste-Gême when he returned to the Spanish island in 1818 and again in 1820, after his removal to New Orleans. Between June 4, 1820, and September 10, 1827, he wrote from Santiago, where he had returned with the mission of trying to settle Ste-Gême's unfinished business. This is another story that will have to be recounted elsewhere, but in the twenty-six letters, in which he narrates his current activities, we catch a few glimpses of his first stay on the Spanish island.

40. He occasionally cites the names of people who assisted him during his second stay, such as Emile Macdonal [*sic*] then retired but who had been the government's secretary for twenty-five years (F 104). He mentions his friendship with Don Manuel Segundo Risco, the Secretary of the Commander of the Marine (F 174).

41. He regularly gives news of them to Ste-Gême. He informs him that he has refused some business offers to be able to dedicate all his time to settling his friend's matters, suggesting that this was the kind of activity he was involved in when he first settled on the island, which would be in keeping with his being labeled a *négociant* in the official colonial documents of Saint-Domingue (F 65).

42. See, for instance, when he marvels at the number of "nationals whom he has employed to overcome the difficulties astute debtors were raising" against him, and continues to pay tribute to them (F 115).

43. For more details, see Dessens, "Napoleon and Louisiana."

44. This is often the case, psychologists suggest, with very old people who have no future in sight.

45. The real name is important to the family (personal conversation [June 2011] with Manuel de Miquel, one of the living descendants of the family, now Consul of France in Lerida, Spain). For more consistency, however, and to respect the name he had adopted in New Orleans, this book will refer to him as Henri de Ste-Gême.

46. The records are still more profusely full of Ste-Gême's traces than Boze's, mostly because of his noble birth, which gave him access to positions unattainable by a commoner like Boze.

47. Letter from Manuel de Miquel to Professor Harry Redman, Jr., dated June 1, 1997, and communicated by Dr. Redman to me in August 2009. The letter contains all the details of the genealogy over eight generations and origins of the title Jean-François Henri de Miguel, Baron de Sainte-Gême, Marquis d'Ustou Montauban. This is confirmed by

the record of French nobility (D'Auriac and Acquier, in the chapter dedicated to the family, "De Miquel de Saintegème" [part VIII]). The same information was sent by Manuel de Miquel to me in June 2011.

48. This is the birthday indicated in D'Auriac and Acquier in the chapter entitled "De Miquel de Saintegème," (part VIII). Most of his military records confirm this date (see, for instance, F 564). His American passports, however, sometimes place his birth in 1769 (F 612 and F 616), and his certificate of bravery in 1773 (F 576), which is clearly impossible, for it would have had him joining the army at age seven.

49. In 1780, at age 13, he joined the Chasseurs à Cheval des Ardennes, a corps in which he became brigadier in 1782, second lieutenant in 1783, and lieutenant in 1788, a rank he held until 1791. In 1790, in the wake of the revolutionary events in France, he migrated to Germany and became one of the fifty elite personal guards of the Comte d'Artois (later Charles X). In 1792, he became an officer in the French regiment of Saxe, transferred to the service of Austria by authorization of the Comte d'Artois. Three times wounded, he pursued the Austrian campaigns until he was transferred, in 1795, to the Hussars and to the service of Britain. Successively lieutenant and captain of the regiment, he was sent to Saint-Domingue in 1797.

50. Unless otherwise indicated, all the translations of the documents in French were done by me. The translations follow as closely as possible the original text, although some alterations were made, in particular in the syntactic structure, to make them understandable by a twenty-first-century English-speaking reader. Whenever the French version was ambiguous, an endnote was added to explain the translation choices.

51. A recapitulation of his services is found under the title "Etat de service de Jean François Henri Baron de Sainte Gème né à Bagen (Hte Garonne) le 5 janvier 1767," at the Administrative Archives of the French *Ministère de la Guerre*, accompanied by a letter from Ste-Gême dated April 28, 1825, and addressed to the Minister of War. MSS 100 also contains many similar documents. Folder 566 contains a detailed presentation of his services, the campaigns he took part in, and his war wounds. Folder 565 attests to his loyalty during his years of service in the army.

52. Folder 564 contains medical records to justify his discharge from colonial service. Folder 566 declares him permanently invalid for service in the colony. Folder 568 contains a document dated August 1, 1803, giving him permission to leave Saint-Domingue to take care of personal matters, stipulating that he would return to France by way of the United States.

53. Simon Faure, May 31, 1813, F 573.

54. Declaration made in New Orleans before Gallien Préval, October 31, 1819, certified in Spanish by the Spanish Consul, Don Felipe Patio, in New Orleans, on November 1, 1819, F 582. Folder 583 contains a notarized document by Rafael Muñoz, dated February 9, 1821, made in Santiago de Cuba, at the request of Juan Boze, representing Don Francisco Enrique Ste Jeme, and enumerating the contents of the *Masséna* when it was seized, including 140 barrels of powder. The document systematically calls the vessel "el corsario," confirming that Ste-Gême was indeed in service when he conducted his activities in Cuba. Boze's correspondence is relatively detailed on these questions. After Ste-Gême

returned to France, in 1818, he entrusted Boze with attempting to recover the property he had lost in Cuba when the authorities had expelled him in 1809, sequestering his property on the island. Between June 4, 1820, and September 10, 1827, it is indeed from Santiago de Cuba that Boze wrote to Ste-Gême, asking for signatures, documents, and power of attorney, detailing all his whereabouts and attempts at individual and administrative resolution of Ste-Gême's financial situation on the island. During those seven years, Boze mainly tried to settle—sometimes in court—a number of debt matters with individuals (José Lara, M. Vt Dallest, or the Causse heirs), as well as with commercial organizations like the Commercial House of Hardy and Co. of Jamaica (F 69). He constantly attempted to obtain reparation for the seizure of the *Masséna*, its contents, armament, and equipment, also requesting damages for the loss of activity (F 589). The twenty-six letters written by Boze from Santiago are found between Folder 43 and Folder 117.

55. With the documents Boze retrieved for him in Cuba, he managed to apply to the Spanish government, assisted by the French government, and obtain a partial resolution of the matter. In March 1825, Boze writes: "I was happy to learn that your journey to Paris to claim the amounts owed to you by the government of Spain from the sale of your maritime properties, fitted out for war, seized and confiscated in 1808 and 9, was partly successful after much difficulty, trouble, and spending, since they granted you the advance of twenty-five percent, with the hope of saving altogether fifty percent on the main amount of $18,016" (F 96). After fifteen years, Boze managed, with some difficulty, to retrieve many of those debts, although he was not systematically successful.

56. This is the case, for instance, of Mr. Causse's debt of eight hundred dollars that was guaranteed to the *nègre* Laurent that Boze attempts to recuperate during his later stay. Throughout this book, whenever a quotation includes the words "*nègre*" or "*négresse*," the original French word will be kept, for lack of equivalent acceptable wording in English. Translating as "black" or "slave" would be inconsistent with the use Boze makes of the words, as well as anachronistic. No direct translation by the words used in the English-speaking word at that time is possible, hence my choice to leave the original French term.

57. Boze regularly gives him news (and gossip) or transmits their regards to him. When settling the Causse debt matter, for instance, he even mentions the fact the one of the Causse heirs, Henri, the elder son of the debtor, was Ste-Gême's godson (F 96).

58. Mentioned by Boze in his letter of October 1, 1818, F 24.

59. These nine years, however, are still easier to trace in the official records than Boze's entire life.

60. Grace King, in her *Creole Families of New Orleans*, dedicates a chapter to him, in which she quotes two sources, including Charles Gayarré.

61. Folder 572 contains his appointment by Governor Claiborne to the Louisiana militia as captain in the Company of Orleans Dragoons starting December 13, 1812.

62. On April 15, 1816, Andrew Jackson wrote a letter commending Major Ste-Gême for his conduct and bravery while commanding a company in Major Planche's battalion during the campaign near New Orleans in December 1814 and January 1815 (F 17).

63. Letter to the French Minister of the War, April 25, 1825, Administrative Archives of the French *Ministère de la Guerre*.

64. What he really says is "votre ancient capitaine d'un batiment," which would translate literally as "your former captain of a vessel."

65. King, 443.

66. In her marriage contract, however, in February 1833, Joséphine Henriette is listed as a free woman of color.

67. See published Archdiocese of New Orleans Sacramental Records, Volume 10 (1810–1812), 136, and Volume 11 (1813–1815), 391. For the marriage contract, see Maduell, 46 (Files of Theodore Seghers 1829–1846).

68. Boze took material care of the children and regularly reported to Ste-Gême. These relationships will be detailed in the next part of the chapter.

69. For more on the habit of acknowledging paternity of natural children in New Orleans, see, for instance, Clark 101–3. This aspect of the New Orleans society will be examined at length in chapter 5. For more on this, see Clark and Aslakson.

70. *Archdiocese of New Orleans Sacramental Records*, Volume 10 (1810–1812), 150.

71. Louis Leufroy Dreux's death is recorded in the *Archdiocese of New Orleans Sacramental Records*, Volume 11 (1813–1815), 144. The marriage of Ste-Gême and Margueritte is recorded in Volume 12 (1816–1817), 105 and 112. The Notarial Archives bear no trace of a marriage contract between Ste-Gême and his wife.

72. See inventory of Louis Leufroy Dreux's legacy, dated May 24, 1814, transferring ownership of the plantation and all the furniture it contained to his wife and children (F 626).

73. The Ste-Gême Family Papers contain several passports issued in Bordeaux, in 1816 and 1817.

74. As shown by the many testimonies of friendship and affection transmitted by Boze in his letters.

75. D'Auriac and Acquier, chapter dedicated to "De Miquel de Saintegème" (part VIII). In already quoted letter of April 25, 1825, to the French Minister of War to claim a military pension, he even says he is the "father of six small children" ("six enfants en bas âge").

76. The Sainte-Gême Family Papers (MSS 100) also contain correspondence from Auvignac Dorville, the manager of the Gentilly plantation, covering the 1818–1873 period. The folders covering the period of Boze's writings (F 19 to F 286) mostly alternate between letters by Boze and letters by Dorville, chronologically arranged. This allusion to Ste-Gême's renouncing his citizenship is found in Dorville's letter of December 27, 1823 (F 77).

77. In 1832, he writes: "About 23 years ago, I met you in St-Yago," adding that he became attached to Ste-Gême to the point that he followed him in the evacuation (F 209).

78. Evoking the two minor Causse children, one of whom is Ste-Gême's godson, Boze writes that they have become "handsome men, principally Henri." He adds: "I did not recognize them until they talked to me" and concludes that Ste-Gême "would be surprised to see them so advanced in all respects" (F 45).

79. In 1832, Boze writes that Ste-Gême "has, for 23 years, never ceased to honor [him] with his trust and his friendship that flatter [him]) infinitely" (F 200).

80. He thanks Mrs. Ste-Gême "for all she did for [him]) during his stay among [them]" (F 23).

81. This is a literal translation of his words, although the whip allusion is obscure. Considering the context, we immediately think of slave ownership, which was apparently never the case with Boze. He rather seems to refer to a period when he was wealthy, although this does not correspond to any set phrase in French, at least from my research.

82. At the same time, the reader of the letters sometimes feels that their relationship was not as personal as could be expected. When compared to Auvignac Dorville's letters to Ste-Gême, Boze's are often less affectionate and less personal, which might simply have to do with the intrinsic difference between an old *ancien régime* Frenchman and a young Louisianan. Sometimes, however, Boze seems to discover elements of Ste-Gême's family life that denote a relative distance between them. In 1830, for instance, Boze writes: "Only through your last [letter] did I learn that you still have brothers [*sic*] while I thought you were the only one of your family still alive" (F 160) and he later names Ovide and Blandine, Ste-Gême's still living brother and sister (F 254).

83. Chapter 5 will examine this community solidarity.

84. In 1818, for the first time, Ste-Gême sent Boze to Cuba as his representative in financial and judicial matters, a mission that was renewed two years later. He writes a letter from Santiago in January 1818 (F 19).

85. Writing of his filial duty and the financial help he gave to his father, he expresses his regrets for not having given him more "when (he) was in great affluence" (F 236).

86. Concerning this fateful event, Boze says, "I found myself walking by your side without a single available resource to provide for my needs" (F 19).

87. When Ste-Gême offered to arrange for him to come to France, he always replied that his destitution made it impossible, as when he writes, in 1818, for instance: "I would willingly accept such an attractive proposal in the winter of my life but I care about my daughter. She is not settled and needs my assistance" (F 23).

88. He insists on all the efforts he has made in Cuba, requesting a percentage on the business dealt with there. For this reason, he insists that he should be granted the 200 Gourdes he has requested and a pension of 16 Gourdes a month until his death (F 209). He sometimes apologizes for not having completed a task Ste-Gême had asked him to perform: "I still have not gone to visit Mr. Le Chevalier Hazeur but I will fulfill your commission as soon as I see him" (F 160). We learn more about the kind of missions he had from the letters. Ste-Gême asked him to inquire about people, like "Mr. Samson and his worker Jean Boi (or his succession if he has died)." Boze had inquired in vain and thought he might then have to go to Pensacola, Mobile, or other parts of Louisiana (F 160). He was also entrusted, for example, with having Dominique Larey's "mortuary extract" legalized and sent to Ste-Gême (F 181). In 1832, he conducted a similar inquiry concerning a captain, managing to find out that he had died. He details at length all his moves in this inquiry, showing that he did not spare any effort (F 204). Later, he writes Ste-Gême about getting a mortuary extract for Charles Pommarède and concludes "remain assured, Mr. de Sainte-Gême, that I never cease to take care of this matter by the desire I have to fulfill your commission properly" (F 234). He also accepted the job of helping two knife grinders who had come from Sauveterre, a village near Bagen, with a letter of recommen-

dation from Ste-Gême (F 198). Although managing the plantation and Ste-Gême's assets seems to have been placed in Dorville's trust, Boze runs little errands for Ste-Gême for most of the period covered by the letters. In 1834, he still writes: "Consequently, you can entrust me with this commission and also those which will come to your mind, serious and frivolous, easy or difficult, whatever, I will always endeavor to carry them out to your satisfaction" (F 243).

89. In the last years, however, he clearly says he will not enumerate the condition of the plantation "for it is Mr Dorville's role to complete this task, as he is more fit than I am to give you all the details" (F 214).

90. For instance, he sends Ste-Gême greetings from "Dr. Lebeau who says he knew you in Saint-Domingue, in Jamaica, in St. Yago, and here in your hunting parties" (152).

91. Boze expresses his pleasure at the company of these "old and respectable true friends" (F 173), elaborating on their encounters in great detail.

92. During his first stay in Cuba, when he alludes to a counterattack by Pepe Lara, one of Ste-Gême's debtors, he says that the latter is threatening to have him deported from the island, in which case Boze adds: "I would find myself greatly annoyed for not having completed the matters of interests I was entrusted with, nor my own, so that, forced to leave this country, I would find myself on my way back to you without a single gourd available to provide for my needs" (F 19).

93. In March 1830, he wrote Ste-Gême that he had sent the last necessary piece to complete his file (F 160). Boze had still not received his compensation in October 1831, expecting little for himself but 25,000 francs for his daughter on her mother's property, fearing that the problems between the French and Haitian governments might impair settlement (F 190). The indemnification files indicate that he obtained only 2,500 francs in March 1831, while Sophie was granted 14,100 francs for her mother's plantation in February 1832.

94. For more on the integration of the refugees in the economic life of New Orleans, see, for instance, Dessens, *From Saint-Domingue to New Orleans*, 67–90.

95. Boze even wrote to him, in February 1838, requesting a raise in his monthly allowance. Insisting on his "destitution," on his "urgent needs," on the "humiliation" he feels at having to request little sums of money, time and again, he enumerates his most urgent needs: cigars, necessities to treat his ailments, night lights, paper, and having his razors sharpened (F 281). This was clearly not part of his arrangements with Ste-Gême, since Boze indicates it is only an advance and that, upon his death, Dorville will inherit some jewels as reimbursement. In the same letter, he also asked Dorville to honor his debt of two dollars for the payment of one hundred cigars to Mr. Cadillac.

96. Madame Lalaurie was a distinguished member of New Orleans Creole society. Accused of severely mistreating her slaves, she had to flee the city and a mob attacked and partially destroyed her house. See, for instance, Conrad, vol. I, 478.

97. Although it seems unlikely that Judge Canonge was not the owner of the house in which he lived, an examination of Folders 50, 51, 54, and 55 of the Vieux Carré Survey has proved fruitless in locating any property belonging to him in those four blocks. It has thus remained impossible to know the exact address of Boze's residence.

98. In March 1837, Dorville wrote to Ste-Gême: "I will not tell you anything new by

informing you that Boze has been with me on the plantation since 21 January" (F 274). All of his letters dated after March 1837 (F 273) were addressed from there, and his last letter, of August 1839, was also sent from there (F 286). In March 1841, Dorville added: "God has forgotten that Mr. Boze is down here. Everything in him has slightly aged except for his meanness and his ridiculous odd habits that no other man but him has ever had. I assure you he is a difficult responsibility for me, because of the fear I have that he may burn down the house any moment as already almost happened two or three times. I prefer death to the loss of your papers. He almost fell out with me for nearly two months because I took away from him two lamps he absolutely wanted to have at night. I am thus no longer obliged to be up as often as it pleases him to roam his room, candle in hand" (F 288). Boze seems to have suffered from senile dementia, and Dorville complains that "Mr. Boze will witness the end of the world. Several times, he went maroon, and I had to send people after him" (F 283).

99. No testament was ever filed with the Louisiana Court of Probate, probably for want of anything to bequeath, although he mentions writing one when he was in Cuba. The New Orleans Will Books, archived at the New Orleans Public Library, bear no mention of a testament by him. No succession was ever filed, probably because he owned nothing, apart from his personal effects. He had written a will in Cuba, in 1825, explaining that he did it in case anything happened to him while in Cuba, to protect the money he was obtaining from Ste-Gême's debtors, and not for his own assets, since he "had nothing to leave to (his) heirs" (F 97). In 1868, Dorville wrote to Ste-Gême's descendant Anatole, requesting instructions as to what to do with the papers left by Boze after his death (F 440). We unfortunately do not know what the answer was and have not recovered any of his papers. A descendant of Ste-Gême, Nancy Lafonta Ste-Gême, says she has no knowledge of such papers, and one of Boze's descendants, Antoine Pagenstecher, has been unable to retrieve any letter of Boze's or his daughter, Sophie's.

100. In a letter of 1837, he told Ste-Gême that she was fine, as well as her children, that the eldest boy was an assistant in a commerce firm, and that he was perfecting his knowledge of the English and French languages (F 280).

101. Mme. de Ste-Gême's brother, Delmas, lived in Pascagoula (F 190) and took care of convalescents, which made him "enjoy public esteem" (F 203). Delmas's son-in-law, Frédéric de St-Féréol, was a translator at the legislature (F 280). Mme. de Ste-Gême's niece, Mlle Dreux, had married Mr. Roi, "one of the first architects of the city, who has a very good reputation and is in charge of building the Citizens' Bank [Banque des Citoyens] on Toulouse Street as well as the new Exchange" (F 279).

102. Detailed information, however, was always the task of Auvignac Dorville, the manager of the plantation. Dorville's invaluable correspondence to the Ste-Gêmes, comprising two hundred letters (for a total of 399 pages), written between March 14, 1818, and September 12, 1873, is also part of the Ste-Gême Family Papers (MSS 100).

103. This will be detailed in chapter 3, in a more general discussion of New Orleans's economic life.

104. Jean Baptiste Longpré correspondence, MSS 626, Williams Research Center, The Historic New Orleans Collection, New Orleans.

105. Boze was the go-between between father and children, expressing the tender feelings they had for each other. He told Ste-Gême that the children sent their regards "with as much respect as tenderness" (F 146). In September 1832, he wrote: "I enjoy visiting them and giving them news from you. They all send you their tender regards" (F 231). In 1834, he said that he no longer visited them but that he got information from Victoire, the cousin of the deceased Adèle (F 244). The larger interest of this example of a free family of color in early American New Orleans will be discussed in chapter 5.

106. The sacramental records indicate that she bore two more children, whose father is not mentioned in the records, one in 1815, a girl who died just after her birth and who is not even named, which might explain why there was no recording of the father, and Rose Ortence [*sic*], on May 14, 1818, baptized in May 1819, and interred in March 1822. (Published *Sacramental Records*, respectively volume 11, 346; volume 13, 339; and volume 15, 307). There is no indication of the identity of the father, and Rose Ortence's baptismal record mentions Adélaïde Ortence and Louis Henri as her sponsors, and identifies them as her sister and brother. It may be conjectured that she was Ste-Gême's daughter but was not recognized because the latter had left for France two months before her birth and was no longer in New Orleans when she was baptized a year later, or because there could be no mention of this continuing relationship once he had married Margueritte Dreux. This would mean, however, that Ste-Gême still had a relationship with Adélaïde after he married Margueritte, a sign of his attachment to her, even though it did not prevent him from leaving New Orleans forever before her last daughter was even born. The other explanation is that she was not Ste-Gême's daughter, a possibility attested to by Boze's saying that a little girl was born to Adèle "whose father is still unknown to me" (F 23), even though, once again this remark could be a way to deter Ste-Gême's wife's suspicion.

107. Adélaïde Philibert's death is not mentioned in the St. Louis Cathedral burial records of the Archdiocese of New Orleans (neither in volumes 9 (1831–1832) and 10 (1832–1833) of the free people of color's record nor in the 1832–1833 volume for white burials). We know, from Boze's subsequent letters, that she was dead in 1833. Her death is not recorded in the published volumes of the sacramental records that cover the period to 1831, and Adélaïde Philibert's death is not indexed in the archdiocese records. Her death might have been recorded elsewhere, incorrectly recorded, or even not recorded at all, given that it occurred at one of the cholera epidemic's peaks.

108. Close to where the Church of St. Augustine now stands.

109. The contract is recorded in the *Files of Theodore Seghers 1829–1846* at the New Orleans Notarial Archives, under the code MAR 3/315. The marriage between Joseph Firmin Perrault (free man of color) and Henriette Joséphine Fortunée Saint-Gême (free woman of color) took place on February 4, 1833. See Maduell, 46.

110. It is unclear whether he assembled carriages or teams of animals drawing ploughs. The French wording is ambiguous.

111. This was the case, for instance, of Toto, the son of Jean Davis, who "will be able to give (him) news from New Orleans" (F 267).

112. Dorville's letters to Ste-Gême often mention the sending of local products, mostly from the plantation. They had sugar or pecans sent to them, but also hot sauce, for instance.

113. There seemed to be a specific "epistolary pact" between the two men, as defined by Gerber, "Acts of Deceiving," 320.

114. See, for instance, Tregle, *Louisiana in the Age of Jackson*, as well as Hirsh and Logsdon.

115. The seventh city in the United States in 1810, with a population of 17,242 inhabitants, it reached the fifth spot in 1820 (with a population of 27,176, which meant an increase of 57.6 percent), a rank it still had in 1830 (46,082, +69.6 percent), before becoming the third-largest city in the country, with 102,193 inhabitants (+121.8 percent). U.S. Bureau of the Censuses, Population of the 100 largest Cities and Other Urban Places in the United States: 1790 to 1990, http://www.census.gov/topics/population.html (consulted October 2008).

116. Tregle, *Louisiana in the Age of Jackson*, 17.

117. See, for instance, Fossier, Tregle, *Louisiana in the Age of Jackson*, and Crété.

118. See, in particular, Fossier. All of these questions will be dealt with in the coming chapters.

119. See Dessens, *From Saint-Domingue to New Orleans*.

120. Tregle, in *Louisiana in the Age of Jackson*, dwells at length on the tensions.

121. See, among others, Hirsh and Logsdon and Cossé Bell.

122. He had some regular informers, such as Mme. Arsène Blanc, née Azurine Labatut, Ste-Gême's old friend. In early 1838, lamenting that he now lives in Gentilly, far from his friends from the city, he writes: "Knowing of my correspondence with you, she enjoyed giving me news of births, marriages, and mortalities, as well as the anecdotes of the week" (F 280).

Chapter 2. Extremes

1. See Stange, 1–22.

2. The map of the areas not flooded by Katrina roughly corresponds to the map of the city in 1867.

3. It is the only one in the period recorded by Kerry Emanuel on his list of notable tropical cyclones. When it hit Louisiana, it was a category 3 hurricane. The next major hurricane occurred in 1856 and was the topic of Lafcadio Hearn's *Chita: A Memory of Last Island*. Emanuel, 264.

4. Letter from Mayor Denis Prieur to the *Conseil de Ville*, New Orleans Conseil de Ville, Messages from the Mayor, Vol. 14, 01/09/1830–12/31/1831, New Orleans Public Library.

5. What Boze called gourde, from an old French habit, was, in fact, at that time, dollar. No conversion thus needs to be made, but "gourde" was kept from the original to retain some of the picturesqueness of Boze's style.

6. "Banquette" is the word used in New Orleans to designate a sidewalk.

7. Tudor, 2: 64.

8. Carter, 305–7.

9. McNeill counts, for instance, a death toll of 60 to 65 percent among the British troops sent to Saint-Domingue in the early years of the revolution (245–46) and one

of 80 to 85 percent in the expeditionary corps sent by Napoleon to regain control over the colony at the turn of the nineteenth century (252–60), remarking that "yellow fever played a political role as well as a military one" (262) and concluding even more generally on "the role of yellow fever and malaria in shaping human history" (263).

10. Also found mentioned as ENSO, which stands for El Niño Southern Oscillation. For more details, see McNeill, 264.

11. McNeill, 265.

12. As a whole, for instance, yellow fever killed some one hundred thousand people in Spain between 1801 and 1804 (McNeill, 266).

13. McNeill, 265.

14. Warner, 103.

15. Trask, 2.

16. Dilworth, 190.

17. McNeill, 288–94. Trask (2) writes that "New Orleans held the dubious honor as the hub of this deadly activity."

18. Dilworth, 78 and 146.

19. Trask, 8.

20. Fossier, 396.

21. Warner, 103.

22. Fossier, 397.

23. McNeill, 304–14.

24. Fossier, 397–98; Crété, 285.

25. Fossier, 401.

26. Trask, 25.

27. For details about all these measures, see Fossier, 398–99.

28. Fossier, 394.

29. McNeill, 288.

30. Trask, 16.

31. Trask, 31–33.

32. Wolf, 167.

33. Fraser, 211. Also see Dilworth, 190.

34. *Le Courrier de la Nouvelle-Orléans*, August 1, 1832.

35. *Le Courrier de la Nouvelle-Orléans*, August 20, 1832.

36. *Le Courrier de la Nouvelle-Orléans*, September 3 and 5, 1832.

37. Cholera was said to have been introduced in Mobile by the arrival of the brig *Jesse* coming from Liverpool on December 25, 1832. In New Orleans, the first two victims were found on the levee and had just disembarked from a steamboat that had reached the city the day before. See Rev. Clapp, cited in Fossier, 404.

38. Tregle, *Louisiana in the Age of Jackson*, 263.

39. Fossier, 409. Chapter XXXII contains many firsthand testimonies that are so horrendous that they make Boze's appear quite mild in comparison. See Fossier, 404–18.

40. Fossier, 409. This is probably the reason why the death of Adèle, Ste-Gême's former companion of color, cannot be found in the death records.

41. General Lacoste having lost twenty-five slaves to the epidemic.

42. See extracts from *Le Courrier* in Fossier, 407–12.

43. See the June 6 editorial of *Le Courrier* on the measures proposed by the city council.

44. See Fossier, both on yellow fever and cholera, 294–418.

45. This was the case of Charleston, for instance, in 1812 (Dilworth, 113) and 1826 (Fraser, 205), of New York, in 1835, when a fire destroyed part of Manhattan (Dilworth, 146), and of Philadelphia, throughout most of the first two decades of the nineteenth century (Dilworth, 85).

46. The fire of March 1788 destroyed 886 of the 1,100 buildings of the city, while that of December 1794 destroyed about 212 buildings. For more details see the Louisiana Timeline in the online *Encyclopedia of Louisiana*, http://www.enlou.com/ (consulted April 20, 2010).

47. In March 1830, Boze describes a fire that destroyed the house of a woman of color, a laundress, in the Marigny.

48. In April 1830, for instance, a furniture shop on Customs Street, between Chartres and the levee, which belonged to an American, was destroyed (F 161).

49. It is difficult, however, to ascertain whether Boze was, at times, focusing excessively on the subject.

50. In English in the original ("compagnie du Rail Road").

51. Mentioning, for instance, the May 1834 fire at a splendid house with several stories and balconies adorned with beautiful ironwork, belonging to Dr. Fromento, he adds that the owner lost more than 30,000 gourdes and that the house was insured for only half of that sum (F 239).

52. Boze uses interchangeably dollar, gourde, and piastre, the American, French, and Spanish currencies.

53. The letter reads "enveloppés de coupeaux." The word "coupeaux" could not be found in any dictionary. The closest word is "copeaux," wood shavings, which is consistent with the present description. This is the reason why it was used in the translation.

54. Crété, 93.

55. For instance, the city of Baltimore did not create the Baltimore United Fire Department until 1834 (Dilworth, 151). Concerning Philadelphia, see, among others, Weigley, 223.

56. See, for instance, Michael Feldberg's chapter entitled "Urbanization as a Cause of Violence: Philadelphia as a Test Case" in Allen and Haller, 53–69.

57. The first paid City Guard of Charleston, for instance, was constituted in 1806. New York constituted its municipal police force in 1845. See Dilworth, 112 and 146.

58. See, for instance, Crété, 84. She uses the daily reports of Mr. Dutillet, a member of the City Guard, to show that most of the content of the reports is about runaway slaves, drunk sailors, bars open after permitted opening hour, or other such minor crimes.

59. Fossier, 161.

60. Fossier, 162–63.

61. Fossier, 164.

62. Fossier, 165–66.

63. Solanges or Sollange, Boze using the two spellings in F 258 (pages 2 and 9, respectively).

64. A racially mixed person, in the French language of the time.

65. The other correspondence included in the Sainte-Gême Papers (MSS 100, Williams Research Center, The Historic New Orleans Collection), that of the manager of Ste-Gême's Gentilly plantation, on the contrary, often alludes to these patrols, which appear to have been organized especially for individual flights and have been composed of managers and owners of nearby plantations.

66. This will be examined at length in the next chapter.

67. Fossier, 163.

68. Fossier, 165.

69. Fossier, 164.

70. Crété, 86.

71. Fossier, 169.

72. Fossier, 171–72.

73. Fossier, 381.

74. See Holland and see Williams.

75. Williams, 6–7.

76. Williams, 8.

77. Dessens, *From Saint-Domingue to New Orleans*, 104.

78. Williams, 42–43.

79. Fossier, 441. Fossier even adds that "the number of duels rose to formidable proportions" in the 1830s, and he also reports vain attempts by New Orleans citizens at establishing a court of honor to replace dueling. Fossier, 442.

80. Martineau, *Society in America*, Vol. 3, 55–56.

81. On anti-dueling laws, see, for instance, Wells, 1825.

82. Quoted in Fossier, 442.

83. For instance, Williams, 68.

84. Cited in Williams, 5.

85. In today's City Park.

86. For instance, Williams, 51.

87. Fossier, 448.

88. As Boze explains in one of his letters, "in this state we adopted the English custom according to which the person challenged to a duel must have the choice of the weapons" (F 188).

89. At times, he explicitly cites his sources, for instance *Le Courrier* (F 227).

90. Many cases are mentioned in Boze's letters, as that of the duel between Francisco Sentmante y Sayas and Agenor Bosque (F 264).

91. Williams, 35.

92. It might be contended, however, that Boze had more interest in the Creoles, either from Louisiana or Saint-Domingue, which might have led him to mention more often these segments of the New Orleans population.

93. This will be addressed at length in chapter 5.

94. Fossier, 167.

95. Walter Johnson opens his book *River of Dark Dreams* with the narration of such an accident (1–3). For more examples and a good measure of the recurrence of steamboat accidents, see Gudmestad, 111–13 and 120–21.

96. This will be examined in the next chapter.

97. Measures to ensure the safety of the passengers were mostly taken after 1850, starting with the passage by the U.S. Congress of the Act to Provide for the Better Security of the Lives of Passengers on Board of Vessels Propelled in Whole or in Part by Steam, in 1852. See Walter Johnson's *River of Dark Dreams*, 119–24.

Chapter 3. Progress

1. Here are the population figures for the 1803–1840 period: 1803: 8,000; 1810: 17,242 (seventh-largest U.S. city); 1820: 27,176 (fifth, +57.6 percent); 1830: 46,082 (fifth, +69.6 percent); 1840: 102,193 (third, +121.8 percent) (U.S. Bureau of the Censuses, Population of the 100 Largest Cities and Other Urban Places in the United States: 1790 to 1990, http://www.census.gov/topics/population.html, accessed April 2008). On figures and distribution of the population, see Lemmon et al., 296. In 1810, New Orleans ranked behind New York, Philadelphia, Baltimore, Boston, and Charleston. In 1820, its population only slightly exceeded that of Charleston, while in 1840, it left both Boston and Charleston far behind. On comparative figures of the leading seaports of the United States, see Albion and Barnes Pope, 419.

2. Lewis, 37. New Orleans (slightly over 17,000) was behind Charleston (24,000) in population figures in 1810, slightly ahead in 1820 (27,000 vs. 24,000), and was four times more populated in 1840 (more than 102,000 vs. 29,000). For comparison's sake, the population of Philadelphia, which ranked second throughout the antebellum period, doubled between 1820 and 1840. Albion and Barnes Pope, 419.

3. Boston was behind (with 388,195), as were Philadelphia (239,057) and Baltimore (231,314). Albion and Barnes Pope, 418.

4. For more details on this, see Bourdelais. She shows that francophone households still represented 49 percent of the population in 1850, becoming a minority of 39 percent in 1860, the anglophone households then representing 41 percent (Bourdelais, 110–12).

5. For more details on "the American suburbs," see the brief description in Lemmon et al., 298–99, and detailed treatment in Bourdelais, 256–65.

6. On what they call "the Creole Faubourgs," see Lemmon et al., 297; see detailed study of the Marigny by Bourdelais, 266–73. For an overview of the foundation and development of the faubourgs, see Upton, 32–34.

7. See Lemmon et al., 300.

8. Bourdelais, 253–54.

9. Bourdelais, 259–61.

10. To get a full measure of the urban vitality of the city in the first three decades of statehood, see Wilson, 65–95, and Bourdelais, 88–100.

11. Fossier, 17.

12. Wilson, 78.

13. Wilson, 91. For more information on the Batture controversy, see Dargo, 101, and Lemmon et al., 295–96. For a detailed narration of the controversy, as well as a thorough analysis of the motives and legal disagreements, see Upton, 22–92. Upton considers this controversy the epitome of the legal battles between the Creoles and Americans, in particular in terms of use and management of public space (Upton, 284). He writes that the controversy showed "competing conceptions of the urban community and its spatial domain" (Upton, 288).

14. Weigley, 281. On Philadelphia, also see, for instance, Wolf, 159.

15. Weigley, 251–52.

16. Lewis, 39.

17. Urban historian of New Orleans Peirce Lewis aptly writes: "The very fact she is a city, of course, makes New Orleans a foreigner in the South—a region which has been unurban in fact and antiurban in sentiment" (Lewis, 14).

18. Dilworth, 113.

19. Boze even enumerates the material chosen (F 202) and techniques used for the pavement (F 204).

20. Lankevich in Dilworth, 146.

21. Warner, 104. Also see Dilworth, 85, and Weigley, 226. Weigley clearly connects this early development to the fear of diseases caused by the existence of stagnant water in wells and cisterns, but also to the necessity for the city to improve firefighting.

22. On Charleston (1790–1828), see Jensen in Dilworth, 110.

23. All references to this article are excerpted from one of Boze's newsletters (F 240).

24. Warner, 105. The figure of 2,127 out of a total population of 54,000 seems low, but the date is comparatively early.

25. Wolf, 160.

26. On Baltimore (1828–1854), see Crenson in Dilworth, 151.

27. See Warner, 99, and Weigley, 285.

28. On Philadelphia, for instance, see Wolf, 149 and 162, and Weigley, 239.

29. The key position of New Orleans at the mouth of the Mississippi River will be discussed at length in the next chapter.

30. The Balize was the pilots' settlement located at the mouth of the Mississippi, a key location for the surveillance of navigation between the Gulf and the port of New Orleans.

31. To give a few examples, the Baltimore and Ohio Railroad was established in 1828 (Crenson in Dilworth, 152) and "the first passenger steam locomotive in America, the Best Friend, began regular service between Charleston and Hamburg (South Carolina)" (Young in Dilworth, 190). In New York, ambitious plans for railroads were made in the 1830s, although most of the construction was completed in the 1850s (see, for instance, Young in Dilworth, 161).

32. For more on the slow decline of Charleston, a city especially impaired by the absence of infrastructure connecting it to the West, see, for instance, Fraser 198–212.

33. Dessens in Dilworth, 158.

34. Tregle, *Louisiana in the Age of Jackson*, 17.

35. Wellborn, 713.

36. Ibid, 710.

37. Donald Macdonald (1826) cited in McDermott, 47.

38. Thomas Hamilton (1831) cited in McDermott, 52.

39. In the first six months of 1819, for instance, thirty-nine ships transporting flour reached Havana from New Orleans, which was the largest number of ships from a U.S. harbor, even though, in volume of transported products, Baltimore ranked first in flour exportation to Havana from the United States. Wellborn, 773.

40. Ste-Gême's Gentilly plantation is a very good example of this. Located south of Lake Pontchartrain, to the southwest of where the University of New Orleans now stands, it was in the near periphery of the city and could be considered part of the urban environment.

41. For more on sugar production in Louisiana, see Follett.

42. Quantity of sugar whose total weight greatly varied through time. In the French colonies, it was set at 1,000 pounds in 1744, then increased progressively to 2,000, and eventually settled at between 1,560 and 1,600 pounds in 1787. In 1789 Saint-Domingue, it was, on average, between 1,100 and 1,200 pounds. Pluchon and de la Bretesche-Hartman, 215.

43. Sometimes anecdotally, through the story of the murder of a German widow on Bayou Road, the readers of Boze's letters learn about practices that were happening in New Orleans. When she was murdered, indeed, at 4 in the morning, she was on her way to New Orleans from Gentilly to sell the produce from her garden in the market (F 208).

44. On the development of cotton in the Lower Mississippi Valley, see Walter Johnson's *River of Dark Dreams*, especially chapter 6, entitled "Dominion."

45. Wolf, 149.

46. Foster in Dilworth, 86. On Philadelphia, see, for instance, Wolf, 150; Warner, especially chapter 4, entitled "Industrialization," 63–78; and Weigley, 230–39. On Boston, see Yoder in Dilworth, 101.

47. New Orleans accounted for 24.5 percent of the nation's total exports (32.9 percent for New York) and for 26.9 percent of its domestic exports (29.5 percent for New York). Albion and Pope, 389.

48. Albion and Pope, 105.

49. To quote but two such examples, D'Aquin, the owner of a big bakery, (F 160) and Mr. Gauthier, the owner of a hardware store, had both made an honorable fortune (F 169).

50. As, for instance, on Rue Royale "in a beautiful house with several stories" (F 160).

51. In 1833, for instance, the oyster stands were rented for a total cost of $9,455, making the cost of each stand about $450, which means that "they will be expensive to eat" (F 231). Concessions granted by City Hall were renewed every year for the period of oyster consumption, from September 15 to April 15, as shown by the regularity with which Boze gives the yearly cost. In 1834, the total cost was 9,530 gourdes (F 244). Oysters were not unknown in other Atlantic cities of the United States (see, for instance, Plate 14 in Upton, showing an oyster stand in Philadelphia), but they were an important part of New Orleans food culture, more so than other places in the country.

52. Boze does not explain where he gets these figures, but the reader may suppose he

used the city directory or a newspaper article that he summarizes without quoting his source. He is so assured about these numbers, however, that the figures were probably accurate.

53. Boze sometimes cites precise examples, like the late Dr. Trabuc and the pharmacist Ducatel; the latter, after making a fortune with his business, had opened a luxury store on Rue Royale (F 160). This is but one example of the many individual mentions of well-to-do doctors and pharmacists.

54. Fraser, 219.

55. Philadelphia and New York were also extremely active, although New Orleans clearly held the upper hand, some of its companies performing in the northeastern cities, especially in the summer, when epidemics sent them away from the city. See, for instance, Wolf, 174.

56. They invested in certain fields that had been until then underrepresented, as Boze shows by citing such examples as that of a former Creole sugar planter in Jérémie, Jean Berthier, who played violin in the orchestra of the Théâtre d'Orléans (F 236), or another who ran a fencing academy (F 244).

57. Walter Johnson speaks of "a city full of mercantile wonders" (*River of Dark Dreams*, 85).

58. See Fossier, 59–75.

59. As surprising as the scale used by Boze might be, he proves the calm of the market by adding that there were "few woodcocks sold," many less than in Ste-Gême's time (F 147). In the following months, several bankruptcies were mentioned, in slightly more crucial areas of the economy.

60. Boze gives many examples of the consequences of epidemics on people's fortunes. A man in debt, whose daughter had married a Saint-Domingue Creole, was so indebted that he had to sell the house he owned in the Carré for five thousand dollars and would likely have to sell his slaves. Privat (whose son was a doctor who had completed his studies in France) had also gone bankrupt and had had to sell the house he owned at the corner of Royale and St. Louis. The late Nicolas Vallery's house on Toulouse had to be sold as well, for the same reasons (F 148).

61. The French government agreed to make six annual payments to the United States for a total of twenty-five million francs.

62. For a good recapitulation of the whole controversy, see Andrew Jackson's December 1834 and December 1835 messages to Congress, as well as his Special Message of January 1836.

63. See Fossier, 45–58.

64. Lankevich in Dilworth, 148.

65. In Manhattan, for instance, there were five banks in 1815, six in 1819, and seven in 1824 (Lankevich in Dilworth, 80).

66. Also see Fossier, 12.

67. Several times, Boze marvels at this new habit of having carriages follow the funeral processions, the number of carriages being an indicator of the wealth and status of the deceased (F 147). When Dr. Mittemberger was buried, in October 1829, the procession

included all the members of the medical profession, all the surgeons, and the entire masonry, followed by "many empty carriages," all signifying the importance of the defunct and his loss to the community (F 148). Another inhabitant is said to have been "accompanied to his last abode by a great and very great number of citizens [. . .] and an infinity of colors in the wake of about forty empty carriages, according to the new usage established for those ceremonies" (F 188).

68. Celebrations will be examined more at length in chapter 6.

Chapter 4. Crossroads

1. This will be developed and illustrated in chapter 5.

2. For more information on nineteenth-century Europe, see Caron and Vernus and Girault and Borne, or, for works in English, see Gates.

3. See Caron and Vernus, for instance, or Gates.

4. On the War of 1812 and its consequences, see, for instance, Remini, 184–99.

5. Charles X's supporters were called Carlists.

6. Although Charles X had abdicated to the Duke of Bordeaux, it was the Duke of Orleans, Louis Philippe, who succeeded him and, in 1832, an attempt at dethroning Louis Philippe in favor of the Duke of Bordeaux was thwarted.

7. The sole year 1836 saw two different governments (under Adolphe Thiers and Mathieu Louis Molé). Molé was then replaced as president of the Council by Jean de Dieu Soult, in 1838, before the government was returned to Thiers, in 1840.

8. Eleven plots against the king were thwarted between 1831 and 1846.

9. For more on French politics at the time, see Démier and also Adounié, or, in English, Latimer.

10. This was the name of the three days of insurrection in Paris, in July 1830, which overthrew Charles X and terminated the period known as the *Restauration*, inaugurating the July monarchy during which Louis Philippe was King of the French (*Roi des Français*) instead of King of France (*Roi de France*), the title of his predecessor. His reign lasted until the Revolution of 1848 and was the last monarchical episode in French history.

11. In November 1831, the workers of the silk industry—called the Canuts—in Lyon rebelled to protest their working conditions. For over a week, hundreds of silk weavers took up arms and occupied the city after a bloody battle with the police forces had caused about six hundred casualties. This first "Révolte des Canuts" is considered the first workers' uprising of the Industrial Revolution in France.

12. In April 1834, a second Canuts uprising occurred in Lyon. It was regarded by all observers as more politicized than the one in 1831. Boze's analysis is thus perfectly in agreement with the later historiography. See, for instance, Bezucha.

13. Already in March 1820, individual liberties had been suspended and censorship legally restored. In 1830, when opposition increased between the chamber and the king, the prefect of Paris ordered the seizure of opposition newspapers, which probably precipitated the insurrection of the Three Glorious Days. In 1835, the government passed new censorship laws against the press.

14. Republican Fieschi tried to assassinate the king. Twelve people were killed in the attempt. Fieschi and his accomplices were arrested and executed.

15. The French flag.

16. For the whole story, see the Louisiana State Museum website, http://lsm.crt.state.la.us/cabildo/cab4.htm, consulted December 23, 2010.

17. After a complex procedure, if the former colonists had proof of property, they were indemnified for the value of 10 percent of their lost property. See Brière for a detailed study of the Haitian indemnities.

18. Brasseaux, *The Foreign French*, ix–xi.

19. For instance, Mr. Laurens, who is said to be in Paris for his business in October 1833.

20. This did not stop in the 1840s and was even true of the free Creole of color elite, as shown by the example of Louis Charles Roudanez, the leader of the first civil rights movement in Louisiana after the Civil War. Roudanez obtained his medical degree from the Sorbonne in Paris and sent all his children, including his daughters, to Paris for an education. For more information, see Dessens, "Louis Charles Roudanez," 26–38.

21. This was also the case, for instance, of previously cited Longpré, whose letters are also archived at the Williams Research Center of The New Orleans Historic Collection.

22. The importance of the Battle of New Orleans will be examined at length in chapter 6.

23. Boze's discussion of the Nat Turner rebellion will be analyzed in detail in "New Orleans, a Slave Society" in Chapter 5.

24. See the exhibit *Gateway to the Americas* on the New Orleans Public Library website, http://nutrias.org/exhibits/gateway/1822.htm, consulted February 14, 2011.

25. Although it bears on a slightly later date, see, for instance, *Gateway to the Americas*, http://nutrias.org/exhibits/gateway/steam.htm, consulted February 14, 2011.

26. Initially designed to carry U.S. mail from New York to California through the Isthmus of Panama, with stops in New Orleans and Havana, the ships of the company soon started carrying passengers. Rich archives on the company are kept at the New York Historical Society (Series 43).

27. See *Gateway to the Americas*, http://nutrias.org/exhibits/gateway/steam.htm, consulted February 14, 2011.

28. The punctuation is that used in the original. Boze frequently uses the exclamation point when he comments on political events.

29. The Lafitte brothers and their pirates were stationed in Barataria, thus their designation as Baratarians. See, for instance, Davis.

30. He uses the French word "*patrie*," which is very strong and denotes a deep sentimental attachment and feeling of belonging.

Chapter 5. Cultures

1. *Americanization* here means the progressive integration of Louisiana into the young American republic. This involved reformation of the institutional and legal frameworks to fit those of the United States, but also linguistic Anglicization, as well as a progres-

sive adoption of cultural influences exerted by the migrants from the eastern United States.

2. See Hall, in particular her chapter entitled "Re-Africanization Under Spanish Rule," 275–315.

3. The number of slaves coming from Cuba can be found in "Response of the mayor of New Orleans to Governor Claiborne," of January 18, 1810, published in *Le Moniteur de la Louisiane*, January 27, 1810.

4. Dilworth, 75.

5. Dilworth, 143. Interestingly, Upton contends that "the institution of slavery and the southern racial order inflected the urban landscape of New Orleans when compared with northern cities, but it did not create a completely different urban world" (Upton, 39).

6. The rolling of the cane is the collection of the cane and its immediate pressing to extract the juice. The process needs to be completed as rapidly as possible to avoid the natural degradation of the sugar content of the plant.

7. For a complete account of Mme. Lalaurie's infamous barbarity, see Long.

8. In 1831, for instance, Boze mentions "four ruthless masters who have been denounced" (F 192).

9. On the German Coast Uprising, see, for instance, Rasmussen.

10. For more on this, see Hunt.

11. When Boze writes "foreign," he most likely means foreign to Louisiana, American in this case.

12. See, for instance, Benjamin Latrobe and John Latrobe.

13. Dessens, *From Saint-Domingue to New Orleans*, 92–98.

14. Dilworth, 75.

15. Dilworth, 143.

16. Visiting the market, Benjamin Latrobe, for instance, mentions "dry goods sold by yellow, black, and white women," 164.

17. This sympathy for free people of color may also be accounted for by the complex network of alliances that existed in New Orleans, involving common languages, common origins, and cultural connectedness. These will be examined later in the chapter.

18. On questions of illegitimacy and inheritance, see, for instance, Clark 103–28. She gives several examples of men who devised ways to make their illegitimate children inherit, either succeeding or failing to elude the heavy restrictions against the practice.

19. This is in agreement with the thesis ably argued and supported by Jennifer Spear. Although the period covered by her study stops in the very early years of the American period, she demonstrates that there was much more continuity in the practices concerning race relationships than heretofore believed. While legislation changed when New Orleans went from French to Spanish to American, she very convincingly shows that mentalities were slower to change than laws and that practice tended to display more continuity than what the legislation suggests.

20. Father Thomas Khune (sometimes also spelled Koune or Koüne) was a Saint-Domingue refugee, a Catholic priest, and all rumors in New Orleans suggested that he

had natural children with a Creole of color of Saint-Domingue. See Dessens, *From Saint-Domingue to New Orleans*, 103.

21. Clark shows that, in the early American period, there were more weddings among Louisiana Creoles of color than among Saint-Domingue refugees of color, as a means, she contends, to distinguish themselves from the refugees (Clark, 61 and 89). She also shows that Louisiana Creoles of color and free refugees of color rarely intermarried in the early decades after the refugees' arrival (Clark, 62–63). Boze's correspondence suggests that intermarriage occurred more and more frequently as time passed.

22. *Placée* is the word that has long been used to describe women who, in New Orleans, after contracting a non-legal civil contract, lived under the protection of a white man, a situation known as "*plaçage*." The existence of *plaçage* is currently being seriously challenged by some historians, who demonstrate that the interracial relationships observed in New Orleans were more often than not common-law unions (not sanctioned by legal proceedings) that proved longer lasting than what the *plaçage* tradition has long suggested. For a detailed debunking of the *plaçage* myth, see Aslakson. Aslakson contends that it was not a New Orleanian tradition but a custom brought from Saint-Domingue by the refugees. He also shows that the expansion of the myth is to be attributed to Anglo-Americans who expatiated on it in the narratives they wrote after visiting New Orleans. The fact that Boze uses the word does not disprove the thesis—quite on the contrary, since he most likely acquired the word in Saint-Domingue and might be using it simply to describe some kind of interpersonal arrangement, instead of a contract drawn under the supervision of the free woman of color's mother, as the myth has often described. Also see Clark on what she calls the "*plaçage* complex" (for instance, 148–61).

23. For a detailed discussion of illegitimacy and inheritance, see Clark, 103–28. The illegitimate families Boze mentions were manifestly provided for by their white fathers during their lifetime. It is difficult to determine from Boze's testimony if inheritance was common, since he may have mentioned only the non-problematic cases. What is certain is that the examples he cites prove that many illegitimate children did manage to inherit.

24. A historiographical debate has long had historians of Louisiana opposing one another. Most historians side with Gwendolyn Hall's defense that the Francophones showed a more relaxed attitude toward race than the Anglo-Americans. Diverging currents, primarily led by Thomas Ingersoll, contend that Francophone elites were in general agreement with Anglo-Americans with regard to racial attitudes toward black people, whether free or enslaved. Although Boze's writings do not prove or disprove either of the two theses, they suggest that there was no real unified position across ethnic lines.

25. Benjamin Latrobe, 162.

26. John Latrobe, 41.

27. This reference to Chasta is slightly surprising, given that the Chasta (or Shasta) originated in Northern California. It is a probable deformation of Choctaw.

28. For a discussion of silences in correspondence and how to interpret them, see, for instance, Poland and Pederson, 294.

29. Albion and Pope, 418.

30. The *Cordons Bleus* designated, in Saint-Domingue, as well as in New Orleans, al-

beit less frequently and only, apparently, after the arrival of the refugees, the highest class of free women of color. See Dessens, *From Saint-Domingue to New Orleans*, 144.

31. On Philadelphia, see, for instance, Wolf, 149. By 1860, a third of the population of Philadelphia was foreign-born, with ninety-five thousand Irish and forty-four thousand German migrants (Warner, 57). In Boston or Charleston, the main contingents were also Irish. See, for instance, Whitehall and Kennedy, 112, and Dilworth, 82, 88, 95, 114, 149–50, 156, 163–64). In Baltimore, in 1839, 20 percent of the city's residents were German-born (Dilworth, 156).

32. In 1840, half the population of New Orleans was foreign-born, which does not make it very different from the other developing cities of the young American republic. Yet, in New Orleans, the specific ethnic landscape inherited from the colonial past gave an unusual turn to the pattern of the integration of foreigners. As Upton contends, "the clash of legal traditions between the Americans and the Louisianans made language a point of social rupture," at least in the early American period (Upton, 41).

33. See, for instance, Fossier, Hirsch and Logsdon, and Tregle. Hirsch and Logsdon's edited collection, revealingly entitled *Creole New Orleans: Race and Americanization*, gathers articles from Jerah Johnson, Gwendolyn Midlo Hall, Paul Lachance, Joseph Tregle, Joseph Logsdon, Caryn Cossé Bell, and Arnold Hirsch. Published in 1992, it was then groundbreaking and still is the most comprehensive study of the relationship between French speakers and Americans in colonial and early American New Orleans. It has remained the reference on ethnic relations in antebellum Louisiana, complemented, in 1999, by Tregle's *Louisiana in the Age of Jackson*. In recent years, however, historians have been more nuanced in their depiction of this duality, with Ingersoll contending, for instance, that Creoles and Americans had more common interests than reasons for opposition and Peter Kastor, among others, evidencing, although in more nuanced ways, the relative commonality of interests between the two groups in *Nation's Crucible*.

34. Upton cites the arcade constructed by banker, financier, and developer Thomas Banks on Gravier Street in Faubourg St. Marie in 1833, to compete with Maspero's Exchange in the Vieux Carré. See Upton, 163.

35. Only the cities of the Atlantic coast displayed a relatively similar diversity, with, besides the main stock of English population, Saint-Domingue refugees, and migrants from Ireland and Germany. They did not have any equivalent Latin population, however, since the French and Spanish Creole population was specific to New Orleans and since this strong Gallic presence, inherited from the colonial period, attracted new waves of migrants from France, a feature unheard of, at least in such proportions, in the rest of the United States.

36. Also see Clark on the lack of cohesion, at least in the early period, between the free people of color of New Orleans and Saint-Domingue.

37. She shows that it was only in 1860 that the percentage of Anglophone households surpassed that of the Francophone ones, with 41 percent of the total population for the former and 39 percent for the latter. Bourdelais, 112.

38. For more on this, see Dessens, "Anatomie d'un oubli historique" and *From Saint-Domingue to New Orleans*.

39. Most certainly the College d'Orléans, founded in 1811.

40. Bourdelais, 113.

41. Ibid, 380–82.

42. Ibid, 114.

43. The French reads "de nation espagnole," which explains the present translation as "of Spanish nation."

44. With, for instance, Côte des Allemands, now known as German Coast.

45. Bourdelais, 113.

46. Official census figures cited in Bourdelais, 97.

47. The expression was used, for instance, by Benjamin Latrobe (161) and Harriet Martineau, *Retrospect of Western Travel* (262).

48. For more on this, see Clark. Using the sacramental records, she demonstrates that intermarriage was rare in the early years after the massive arrival of the refugees from Cuba in 1809–1810.

49. Although this fact is not present in Boze's letters, most likely because he largely ignores the Anglophones, for lack of interest, and because he never mingled with them, Bourdelais shows a clear propensity of the Irish to intermarry or to marry into the Anglo-American community. Bourdelais, 185.

Chapter 6. The Creole Capital

1. In Hispanic America, where the term originated, Creole designated solely the American-born children of European parents. In the French Caribbean, in the sixteenth and seventeenth centuries, the term was broadened to apply to all people born and raised in the Americas, without consideration of race, and, by extension, to everything that was native to the islands. In the Louisiana capital, the term was subjected to important variations through time, with different definitions sometimes coexisting. From the colonial definition that generally applied to the American-born children of white European parents, the term expanded to take on a larger meaning in the early nineteenth century, most likely due to the influence of the Saint-Domingue refugees, and started designating then all those born in Louisiana, without racial distinction or generational specificity. With the Purchase, and due to the wish of the long-standing residents to set themselves apart, it came to refer to those with European origins born in Louisiana before the Purchase. For more detailed definitions, see chapter 4 ("Shaping a Creole Identity") of Domínguez, 93–132; also see Appendix ("On the Term Creole") in Tregle, *Louisiana in the Age of Jackson*, 337–43.

2. This is evident in the publication of books like Buisseret and Reinhardt, *Creolization in the Americas*.

3. The process of Creolization has been defined in several different ways throughout history. The way in which it is meant here follows the theories of Robert Chaudenson and stands for the process of syncretism that occurs among the various cultural traditions that come into prolonged contact through the process of colonization and settlement, with adaptation to the milieu in which the encounter occurs. See Chaudenson.

4. Benjamin Latrobe, 160–61.

5. Martineau, *Retrospect of Western Travel*, 262.

6. Laussat, 86.

7. Martineau, *Retrospect of Western Travel*, 262–63.

8. Benjamin Latrobe, 162–63.

9. Ibid.

10. We will adopt in this chapter this designation, for the sake of clarity and to avoid anachronism.

11. *Gumbo Filé* is the name of the spicy seasoning made of ground sassafras leaves used in making gumbo in Louisiana.

12. For more details on this, see Dessens, in Dessens and Le Glaunec.

13. Bourdelais, 253. Also see her groundbreaking "Morphology of Royal Street" in her annexes, where she indicates the linguistic and occupational pattern of all people living on Royal Street in 1830. Bourdelais, 399–403.

14. Bourdelais, 259.

15. This was the case of the sacramental records of the Archdiocese of New Orleans, for instance.

16. To cite but the two best-known, *L'Abeille de la Nouvelle-Orléans* and *Le Courrier de La Louisiane* both had sections in French and English, of relatively equivalent length, with the two sections containing their own news, although they shared some of the same information.

17. Boze uses the word "établissements," which is as incongruous as its translation as "establishment."

18. Although she mainly focuses on the early endogamic trends, Bourdelais suggests an increase in more exogamic practices after the 1830s. For more on this, see Bourdelais's chapter III, 129–205.

19. For a more detailed presentation of the celebrations in antebellum New Orleans, see Dessens in Dessens and Le Glaunec.

20. For some anecdotes on these oppositions, see, for instance, Rowland, Vol. I, 249 and 331; or Laussat, 147–50.

21. For more information on the Battle of New Orleans, see, for instance, Remini.

22. For more on this, see Dessens in Dessens and Le Glaunec.

23. See, for instance, Dessens, *From Saint-Domingue to New Orleans*, chapter 6.

24. For more on the linguistic situation, see Cabanac in Dessens and Le Glaunec.

25. See, for instance, John Latrobe, 41.

26. An *arpent* is an old measure generally said to be 180 feet (although it varied from one place to another).

27. For an indication of the progressive involvement of Americans in the Mardi Gras celebrations and subsequent cultural enrichment of the carnival practices, see Domínguez, 127–29; Mitchell, 16–19; and Powell, 358–59.

28. For more on the various contributions to New Orleans's Mardi Gras, see Dessens in Dessens and Le Glaunec.

Appendix

1. The letter has been transcribed as closely as possible to the original. Only some minor grammar or spelling mistakes were corrected, and punctuation and capitalization were altered to be more easily legible.

2. Boze manifestly intended to add the name of the ship captain, since he had written "Cap^{ne} . . ." and left a blank that he never filled in, possibly because he never found the information or possibly because he forgot.

3. Ct stands for *courant*, meaning "of the present month."

4. Derogatory way of referring to Louisianans, by association with the name of the spices that they use in cooking gumbo.

5. Clear evocation of the Saint-Domingue refugees who fled Cuba with Boze and Sainte-Gême and settled in New Orleans.

6. This should be Colombie, the French for Colombia.

7. Mézelle is a corrupted form of "mademoiselle."

8. Probably Destréhan.

9. This is noted as an addition to one of the previous paragraphs. Normally, Boze inserts the asterisk in the paragraph he wants to complete. In the present case, he forgot to indicate where this addition should go, although it seems obvious that he is referring to the paragraph mentioning the executioner, the second entry of March 27.

10. He probably means that the barrel of flour is three dollars and five cents and that bread costs one cent.

11. He meant "Wellingtonien," of course, that is to say a partisan of Wellington. He often criticizes the French government for its pro-British positions.

12. Father Antonio de Sedella.

13. Translation by Nathalie Dessens. The translation remains as close as possible to the original, trying to reproduce Boze's style. A few alterations have been introduced to make the English version intelligible.

14. It is impossible to translate the «Mézelle», which may suggest that she was racially mixed, despite the fact that Boze wrote, a few lines above, that she was the daughter of a Spanish officer who protects him.

Bibliography

Primary Sources Archival Material

Archives Administratives du Ministère de la Guerre, Paris

Lettre au Ministre de la Guerre, 25 Avril 1825

Archives of the Archdiocese of New Orleans

Sacramental Records

Centre d'Archives d'Outre-Mer (CAOM), Aix-en-Provence

Dépôt des Papiers Publics des Colonies (Archives des Notaires, Greffes de Fort-Dauphin, Greffes de Port-au-Prince, Registres de l'Etat Civil de Les Cayes Jacmel, Indemnités de Saint-Domingue)

Inventaire des personnels coloniaux avant 1789 (Serie E)

The Historic New Orleans Collection, Williams Research Center, New Orleans

Jean Baptiste Longpré correspondence, MSS 626

Ste-Gême Family Papers, MSS 100

Vieux Carré Survey

New Orleans Notarial Archives

Files of Theodore Seghers 1829–1846

New Orleans Public Library

Conseil de Ville, Messages from the Mayor

Naturalization Records

New Orleans Will Books

Private archives

Communication with Manuel de Miquel, June 2011

Letter from Manuel de Miquel to Professor Harry Redman, Jr. of June 1, 1997 (communicated by Dr. Redman)

Pagenstecher Family Papers (transmitted by Antoine Pagenstecher)

Printed Primary and Literary Sources

A Calendar of the Rochambeau Papers at the University of Florida Libraries (compiled by Laura V. Monti). Gainesville: University of Florida Libraries, 1972.

Bronnenpublikaties van de Indishes Genealogishe Vereniging. The Hague: A. A. Lutter, 2000.

L'Abeille de la Nouvelle-Orléans

Latrobe, Benjamin. *The Journal of Latrobe: The Notes and Sketches of an Architect, Naturalist and Traveler in the United States from 1776 to 1820.* Carlisle, Mass.: Applewood Books, 2007.

Latrobe, John. *Southern Travels: Journals of John H. B. Latrobe 1834.* Samuel Wilson, Jr. F.A.I.A, ed. New Orleans: The Historic New Orleans Collection, 1986.

Laussat, Pierre Clément de. *Memoirs of My Life to My Son During the Years 1803 and After.* Transl. and ed. by Sister Agnes-Josephine Pastwa. Baton Rouge: Louisiana State University Press, 1978.

Le Courrier de la Louisiane

Le Moniteur de la Louisiane

Maduell, Charles R. *New Orleans Marriage Contracts 1804–1820, Abstracted from the Notarial Archives of New Orleans.* New Orleans: Polyanthos, 1977.

Martineau, Harriet. *Society in America.* 3 vols. London: Saunders & Otley, 1837.

———. *Retrospect of Western Travel.* New York: Harper and Brothers, 1838.

McDermott, John Francis, ed. *Before Mark Twain: A Sampler of Old, Old Times on the Mississippi.* Carbondale and Edwardsville: Southern Illinois University Press, 1968.

Ministère des Finances. Etat détaillé des liquidations opérées à l'époque du 1er janvier 1832, Par la Commission chargée de répartir l'Indemnité attribuée aux anciens Colons de Saint-Domingue, en exécution de la Loi du 30 avril 1826, et conformément aux dispositions de l'Ordonnance du 9 mai suivant. Paris: Imprimerie Royale, 1832.

Ministère des Finances. Etat détaillé des liquidations opérées pendant l'année 1832 et les six premiers mois de 1833. Par la Commission chargée de répartir l'Indemnité attribuée aux anciens Colons de Saint-Domingue, en exécution de la Loi du 30 avril 1826, et conformément aux dispositions de l'Ordonnance du 9 mai suivant. Paris: Imprimerie Royale, 1833.

Nolan, Charles E., ed. *Sacramental Records of the Roman Catholic Church of the Archdiocese of New Orleans.* Volumes 5 to 16 (1791 to 1825). New Orleans: Archdiocese of New Orleans, 1990–2002.

Rowland, Dunbar. *The Official Letter Books of W.C.C. Claiborne 1801–1816.* 4 vols. Jackson, Mississippi: Printed for the State Department of Archives and History, 1917.

The New York Times

Tudor, Henry. *Narrative of a Tour in North America.* 3 vols. London: James Duncan, 1834.

Websites

Archives of the Archdiocese of New Orleans: http://www.archdiocese-no.org/archives

Encyclopedia of Louisiana: http://www.enlou.com

Historic New Orleans Collection: http://www.hnoc.org
Louisiana State Museum: http://lsm.crt.state.la.us
New Orleans Notarial Archives: http://www.notarialarchives.org
New Orleans Public Library: http://nutrias.org
Saint-Domingue Special Interest Group, New Orleans: http://freepages.genealogy.rootsweb.ancestry.com/~saintdomingue/
U.S. Bureau of the Censuses: http://www.census.gov/topics/population.html

Secondary Sources

Adounié, Vincent. *De la monarchie à la république (1815–1879)*. Paris: Hachette, 1996.

Albion, Robert, and Jennie Barnes Pope. *The Rise of New York, 1815–1860*. New York: Scribner's, 1939.

Aslakson, Kenneth. "The 'Quadroon-*Plaçage*' Myth of Antebellum New Orleans: Anglo-American (Mis)interpretation of a French-Caribbean Phenomenon." *Journal of Social History* 45, issue 3 (Spring 2012): 709–34.

Babb, Winston C. "French Refugees from Saint Domingue to the Southern United States: 1791–1810." Unpublished PhD Dissertation, University of Virginia, 1954.

Barbé-Marbois, François. *The History of Louisiana*. 1830. Baton Rouge: Louisiana State University Press, 1977.

Bezucha, Robert. *The Lyon Uprising of 1834*. Cambridge, Mass.: Harvard University Press, 1974.

Bourdelais, Marjorie. *La Nouvelle-Orléans. Croissance démographique, intégration urbaine et sociale (1803–1860)*. Bern: Peter Lang, 2012.

Brasseaux, Carl A., ed. *The Foreign French: Nineteenth Century French Immigration into Louisiana, 1840–1848*. Lafayette: University of Southwestern Louisiana, 1992.

———. *A Refuge for all Ages: Immigration in Louisiana History*. Vol. X of The Louisiana Purchase Bicentennial Series in Louisiana History. Lafayette: University of Southwestern Louisiana, 1996.

———. *French, Cajun, Creole, Houma: A Primer on Francophone Louisiana*. Baton Rouge: Louisiana State University Press, 2005.

Brasseaux, Carl A., and Glenn R. Conrad, eds. *The Road to Louisiana: The Saint-Domingue Refugees 1792–1809*. Lafayette: University of Southwestern Louisiana Press, 1992.

Brière, Jean-François. *Haïti et la France 1804–1848. Le rêve brisé*. Paris: Karthala, 2008.

Bruneton-Governatori, Ariane. "Une vaste et riche enterprise: recueillir, rassembler et 'lire' des lettres d'émigrés (XIXe–XXe siècles)." *L'émigration basco-béarnaise aux Amériques au XIXe siècle*. 291–310. Pau: Editions de Gascogne, 2006.

Buisseret, David, and Steven G. Reinhardt, eds. *Creolization in the Americas*. Arlington, TX: Texas A&M University Press, 2000.

Caron, Jean-Claude, and Michel Vernus. *L'Europe au XIXe siècle: Des nations aux nationalismes (1815–1914)*. Paris: Armand Colin, 2011.

Carter, Henry Rose. *Yellow Fever: An Epidemiological and Historical Study of Its Place of Origin*. Baltimore: The Williams & Wilkins Company, 1931.

Cary, Francine Curro, ed. *Urban Odyssey: A Multicultural History of Washington, D.C.* Washington: Smithsonian Institution Press, 1966.
Casey, Powell A. *Encyclopedia of Forts, Posts, Named Camps, and Other Military Installations in Louisiana, 1700–1981.* Baton Rouge: Claitor's Publishing Division, 1983.
Cauna, Jacque de. *Au temps des isles à sucre: Histoire d'une plantation de Saint-Domingue au XVIIIe siècle.* Paris: Karthala, 1987.
———. *Haïti: L'éternelle révolution.* Port-au-Prince: Imprimerie Henri Deschamps, 1997.
Chaudenson, Robert. *Des Iles, Des Hommes, Des Langues. Essai sur la créolisation linguistique et culturelle.* Paris: L'Harmattan, 1992.
Clark, Emily. *The Strange History of the American Quadroon. Free Women of Color in the Revolutionary Atlantic World.* Chapel Hill: The University of North Carolina Press, 2013.
Conrad, Glenn R., ed. *A Dictionary of Louisiana Biography.* 2 vols. New Orleans: The Louisiana Historical Association in cooperation with The Center for Louisiana Studies of the University of Southwestern Louisiana, 1988.
Cossé Bell, Caryn. *Revolution, Romanticism, and the Afro-Creole Protest Tradition in Louisiana, 1718–1868.* Baton Rouge: Louisiana State University Press, 1997.
Crété, Liliane. *La vie quotidienne en Louisiane, 1815–1830.* Paris: Hachette, 1978.
Dargo, George. *Jefferson's Louisiana: Politics and the Clash of Legal Tradition.* Cambridge, Mass.: Harvard University Press, 1975.
Dauphin, Cécile. "Les manuels épistolaires au XIXe siècle." *La correspondance. Les Usages de la lettre au XIXe siècle.* Roger Chartier, ed., 209–72. Paris: Fayard, 1991.
D'Auriac, Frédéric Combes, and Hippolythe Acquier, eds. *Armorial: Noblesse de France.* Paris: Bureaux Héraldiques, 1858.
Davis, Allen, and Mark Haller, eds. *The Peoples of Philadelphia: A History of Ethnic Groups and Lower-Class Life, 1790–1940.* Philadelphia: University of Pennsylvania Press, 1998.
Davis, William C. *The Pirates Laffite: The Treacherous World of the Corsairs of the Gulf.* New York: Mariner Books, 2006.
Debien, Gabriel. "De Saint-Domingue à Cuba avec une famille de réfugiés, les Tornézy (1800–1809)." *Notes d'Histoire Coloniale* no. 74, extrait de la *Revue de la Faculté d'Ethnologie* (de Port-au-Prince), no. 8 (1964): 7–31.
———. "Réfugiés de Saint-Domingue expulsés de la Havane en 1809." *Annuario de Estudios Americanos* 35 (1979): 555–610.
Decker, William Merrill. *Epistolary Practices: Letter Writing in America Before Telecommunication.* Chapel Hill: University of North Carolina Press, 1998.
Deive, Carlos Esteban. *Las emigraciones Dominicanas a Cuba (1795–1808).* Santo Domingo: Fundación Cultural Dominicana, 1989.
Démier, Francis. *La France du XIXe siècle: 1814–1914.* Paris: Seuil, 2000.
Dessens, Nathalie. "Les migrants de Saint-Domingue en Louisiane avant la Guerre de Sécession: de l'intégration civique à l'influence politique. Immigration et citoyenneté aux Etats-Unis." *Revue Française d'Etudes Américaines* 75 (January 1998): 34–46.
———. *Myths of the Plantation Society: Slavery in the American South and the West Indies.* Gainesville: University Press of Florida, 2003.
———. contribution to "1803–1804: Re-Shaping the Atlantic World: Actors and Au-

diences." *The Louisiana Purchase Timeline*. Baton Rouge: Louisiana State University Press and Deep South Regional Humanities Center, 2003.

———. "From Plurality to Singularity: Otherness and Creolization in Nineteenth-Century Louisiana." Ada Savin, ed. *Journey into Otherness*, 29–38. Amsterdam: VU University Press, 2005.

———. "From Saint-Domingue to Louisiana: West Indian Refugees in the Lower Mississippi Region." Bradley Bond, ed. *French Colonial Louisiana and the Atlantic World*, 244–64. Baton Rouge: Louisiana State University Press, 2005.

———. "Anatomie d'un oubli historique: les réfugiés de Saint-Domingue à la Nouvelle-Orléans," Nathalie Dessens and Jean-Pierre Le Glaunec, eds. *Haïti, regards croisés*, 69–94. Paris: Le Manuscrit de l'Université, 2007.

———. *From Saint-Domingue to New Orleans: Migration and Influences*. Gainesville: University Press of Florida, 2007.

———. "Saint-Domingue Refugees in New Orleans: Identity and Cultural Influences." Martin Munroe and Elizabeth Walcott-Hackshaw, eds. *Echoes of the Haitian Revolution, 1804–2004*, 42–54. Trinidad, Jamaica, Barbados: University of West Indies Press, 2008.

———. "Louis Charles Roudanez, a Creole of Color of Saint-Domingue Descent: Atlantic Reinterpretations of Nineteenth-Century New Orleans." *South Atlantic Review* 73, no. 2 (Spring 2008): 26–38.

———. "Napoleon and Louisiana: New Atlantic Perspectives." Christophe Belaubre, Jordana Dym, and John Savage, eds. *Napoleon's Atlantic. The Impact of Napoleonic Empire in the Atlantic World*, 63–80. Leiden and Boston: Brill, 2010.

Dessens, Nathalie, and Jean-Pierre Le Glaunec, eds. *La Louisiane au carrefour des cultures*. Québec: Presses Universitaires de Laval, forthcoming.

Dilworth, Richardson, ed. *Cities in American Political History*. Los Angeles, London, New Delhi, Singapore, Washington D.C.: CQ Press, 2011.

Domínguez, Virginia R. *White by Definition: Social Stratification in Creole Louisiana*. New Brunswick, New Jersey, and London: Rutgers University Press, 1986.

Dubois, Laurent. *Avengers of the New World: The Story of the Haitian Revolution*. New York: The Belknap Press, 1995.

———. *Haiti: The Aftershocks of History*. New York: Picador, 2012.

Eccles, William John. *The French in North America 1500–1783*. East Lansing: Michigan State University Press, 1998.

Emanuel, Kerry. *Divine Wind: The History and Science of Hurricanes*. Oxford: Oxford University Press, 2005.

Encyclopedia of Louisiana. St. Clair Shores, MI: Somerset Publishers Inc., 1999.

Evans, Freddi Williams. *Congo Square: African Roots in New Orleans*. Lafayette: University of Louisiana at Lafayette Press, 2011.

Fick, Carolyn E. *The Making of Haiti: The Saint-Domingue Revolution from Below*. Knoxville: University of Tennessee Press, 1990.

Fitzpatrick, David. *Oceans of Consolation. Personal Accounts of Irish Migration to Australia*. Ithaca: Cornell University Press, 1994.

Follett, Richard. *The Sugar Masters: Planters and Slaves in Louisiana's Cane World, 1820–1860*. Baton Rouge: Louisiana State University Press, 2005.

Fossier, Albert E. *The New Orleans Glamour Period 1800–1840: A History of the Conflicts of Nationalities, Languages, Religion, Morals, Culture, Laws, Politics and Economics During the Formative Period of New Orleans*. New Orleans: Pelican Publishing Company, 1957.

Fraser, Walter. *Charleston! Charleston! The History of a Southern City*. Columbia: University of South Carolina Press, 1990.

Frenette, Yves, Marcel Martel, and John Willis. *Envoyer et recevoir: Lettres et correspondances dans les diasporas francophones*. Sainte-Foy: Presses de l'Université de Laval, 2006.

Gates, David. *Warfare in the Nineteenth Century (European History in Perspective)*. New York: Palgrave McMillan, 2001.

Gayarré, Charles Etienne Arthur. *History of Louisiana*. 1903. New Orleans: Pelican, 1965.

Geggus, David. *Haitian Revolutionary Studies*. Bloomington and Indianapolis: Indiana University Press, 2002.

Gerber, David. "Epistolary Ethics: Personal Correspondence and the Culture of Emigration in the Nineteenth Century." *Journal of American Ethnic History* 19, no. 4 (Summer 2000): 3–23.

———. "Acts of Deceiving and Withholding in Immigrant Letters: Personal Identity and Self-Presentation in Personal Correspondence." *Journal of Social History* 39.2 (Winter 2005): 315–30.

Girault, René, and Dominique Borne. *Peuples et nations d'Europe au XIXe siècle*. Paris: Hachette, 1996.

Girod, François. *La vie quotidienne de la société créole: Saint-Domingue au XVIIIe siècle*. Paris: Hachette, 1972.

Green, Constance McLaughlin. *The Rise of Urban America*. New York: Harper & Row, 1965.

Gudmestad, Robert. *Steamboats and the Rise of the Cotton Kingdom*. Baton Rouge: Louisiana State University Press, 2011.

Guerra y Sánchez, Ramiro. *Sugar and Society in the Caribbean: An Economic History of Cuban Agriculture*. New Haven: Yale University Press, 1964.

Hall, Gwendolyn Midlo. *Africans in Colonial Louisiana: The Development of Afro-Creole Culture in the Eighteenth Century*. Baton Rouge: Louisiana State University, 1992.

Hébrard, Jean. "La lettre représentée. Les pratiques épistolaires populaires dans les récits de vie ouvriers et paysans." *La correspondance. Les Usages de la lettre au XIXe siècle*. Roger Chartier, ed., 279–365. Paris: Fayard, 1991.

Hirsch, Arnold R., and Joseph Logsdon, eds. *Creole New Orleans: Race and Americanization*. Baton Rouge: Louisiana State University Press, 1992.

Holland, Barbara. *Gentlemen's Blood: A History of Dueling*. London: Bloomsbury, 2004.

Hunt, Alfred. *Haiti's Influence on Antebellum America: Slumbering Volcano in the Caribbean*. Baton Rouge: Louisiana State University Press, 1988.

Ingersoll, Thomas N. *Mammon and Manon in Early New Orleans: The First Slave Society in the Deep South, 1718–1819*. Knoxville: University of Tennessee Press, 1999.

Johnson, Sara E. *The Fear of the French Negros. Transcolonial Collaboration in the Revolutionary Americas.* Berkeley, Los Angeles, London: University of California Press, 2012.

Johnson, Walter. *Soul by Soul: Life in an Antebellum Slave Market.* Cambridge, Mass., and London: Harvard University Press, 1999.

———. *River of Dark Dreams: Slavery and Empire in the Cotton Kingdom.* Cambridge, Mass. and London: The Belknap Press of Havard University Press, 2013.

Jones, Bill. "Writing Back: Welsh Emigrants and their Correspondence in the Nineteenth Century." *North American Journal of Welsh Studies* vol. 5, no. 1 (Winter 2005): 23–46.

Kastor, Peter J. *The Nation's Crucible: The Louisiana Purchase and the Creation of America.* New Haven, CT: Yale University Press, 2004.

Kastor, Peter J., and François Weil, eds. *Empires of the Imagination: Transatlantic Histories of the Louisiana Purchase.* Charlottesville and London: University of Virginia Press, 2009.

Kendall, John Smith. *History of New Orleans.* 3 vols. Chicago: The Lewis Publishing Company, 1922.

King, Grace. *Creole Families of New Orleans.* New York: McMillan, 1921.

Lachance, Paul F. "Les vaincus de la révolution haïtienne en quête d'un refuge: de Saint-Domingue à Cuba (1803), de Cuba à la Nouvelle Orléans (1809)." *Revue de la Société Haïtienne d'Histoire, de géographie et de géologie* XXXVII (mars 1980): 15–30.

———. "Were Saint-Domingue Refugees a Distinctive Cultural Group in Antebellum New Orleans? Evidence from Patterns and Strategies of Property Holding." *Revista/Review Interamericana* 29, no. 1–4 (1999): 171–92.

Landers, Jane. *Atlantic Creoles in the Age of Revolutions.* Cambridge, Mass: Harvard University Press, 2010.

Latimer, Elizabeth. *France in the Nineteenth Century.* London: Echo Library, 2007.

Laurent-Ropa, Denis. *Haïti: Une colonie française, 1625–1802.* Paris: L'Harmattan, 1993.

Lemmon, Alfred E., John T. Magill, and Jason R. Wiese. *Charting Louisiana: Five Hundred Years of Maps.* New Orleans: The Historic New Orleans Collection, 2003.

Le Riverand, Julio. *Historia económica de Cuba.* Havana: Instituto Cubano Del Libro, 1974.

Lewis, Peirce. *New Orleans: The Making of an Urban Landscape.* Charlottesville: The University of Virginia Press, 2003.

Long, Carolyn Morrow. *Madame Lalaurie: Mistress of the Haunted House.* Gainesville: University Press of Florida, 2012.

Maduell, Charles R., Jr. *Marriages and Family Relationships of New Orleans 1830–1840.* New Orleans: n.p., 1969.

Martin, François Xavier. *The History of Louisiana from the Earliest Period.* New Orleans: James A. Gresham, 1882.

Martin-Fugier, Anne. "Les lettres célibataires." *La correspondance: Les usages de la lettre au XIXe siècle,* 407–426. Roger Chartier, ed. Paris: Fayard, 1991.

McNeill, J. R. *Mosquito Empires: Ecology and War in the Greater Caribbean, 1620–1914.* Cambridge and New York: Cambridge University Press, 2010.

Mitchell, Reid. *All on a Mardi Gras Day: Episodes in the History of New Orleans Carnival.* Cambridge, Mass: Harvard University Press, 1999.

Ott, Thomas O. *The Haitian Revolution, 1789–1804*. Knoxville: University of Tennessee Press, 1973.

Pearson, Sarah M. S. *Atlantic Families: Lives and Letters in the Later Eighteenth Century*. Oxford and New York: Oxford University Press, 2008.

Pérez, Francisco. *El Café: Historia de su Cultivo y Explotación en Cuba*. Havana: Jesús Montero Editor, 1944.

Pluchon, Pierre, and Sabine de la Bretesche-Hartman. "L'habitation Santo Domingo: Caractères et problèmes des plantations sucrières dominguoises." *Revue d'Histoire Maritime* 2–3 (2001): 163–238.

Poland, Blake, and Ann Pederson. "Reading Between the Lines: Interpreting Silences in Qualitative Research." *Qualitative Inquiry* 4, no. 2 (June 1998): 293–312.

Powell, Lawrence. *The Accidental City: Improvising New Orleans*. Cambridge, Mass: Harvard University Press, 2012.

Rasmussen, Daniel. *American Uprising: The Untold Story of America's Largest Slave Revolt*. New York: Harper, 2011.

Redard, Thomas E. "The Port of New Orleans: An Economic History, 1821–1850." 2 vols. Unpublished PhD dissertation, Louisiana State University and Agricultural and Mechanical College, 1985.

Remini, Robert V. *The Battle of New Orleans: Andrew Jackson and America's First Military Victory*. London: Penguin, 2001.

Renault, Agnès. *La communauté française de Santiago de Cuba entre 1791 et 1825*. Unpublished PhD dissertation, Université du Havre, 2007.

———. *D'une île rebelle à une île fidèle: Les Français de Santiago de Cuba (1791–1825)*. Mont-Saint-Aignan: Publications des Universités de Rouen et du Havre, 2012.

Ripley, Eliza. *Social Life in Old New Orleans*. Gretna: Pelican Publishing Company, 1998.

Scott, Rebecca J., and Jean M. Hébrard. *Freedom Papers: An Atlantic Odyssey in the Age of Emancipation*. Cambridge, Mass: Harvard University Press, 2012.

Sepinwall, Alyssa Goldstein. *Haitian History: New Perspectives*. New York and London: Routledge, 2013.

Spear, Jennifer. *Race, Sex, and Social Order in Early New Orleans*. Baltimore: The Johns Hopkins University Press, 2009.

Stange, Marion. "Governing the Swamp: Health and Environment in Eighteenth-Century Nouvelle-Orléans." *French Colonial History* 11 (2010): 1–22.

Thompson, Shirley Elizabeth. *Exiles at Home: The Struggle to Become American in Creole New Orleans*. Cambridge, Mass: Harvard University Press, 2009.

Trask, Benjamin H. *Fearful Ravages: Yellow Fever in New Orleans, 1796–1905*. Lafayette: Center for Louisiana Studies, University of Louisiana at Lafayette, 2005.

Tregle, Joseph George, Jr. "Early New Orleans Society: A Reappraisal." *Journal of Southern History* XVIII (February 1952): 20–36.

———. "Political Reinforcement of Ethnic Dominance in Louisiana 1812–1845." *The Americanization of the Gulf Coast, 1803–1850*. Lucius F. Ellsworth, ed. Mobile: University of Southern Alabama, 1972, 78–87.

———. *Louisiana in the Age of Jackson: A Clash of Cultures and Personalities.* Baton Rouge: Louisiana State University Press, 1999.

Upton, Dell. *Another City: Urban Life and Urban Space in the New American Republic.* New Heaven and London: Yale University Press, 2008.

Wall, Bennet H., ed. *Louisiana: A History.* Airlington Heights, IL: Forum Press Inc., 1984.

Warner, Sam Bass, Jr. *The Private City: Philadelphia in Three Periods of its Growth.* Philadelphia: University of Pennsylvania Press, 1987.

Weigley, Russel, ed. *Philadelphia: A 300-Year History.* New York: Norton, 1982.

Wellborn, Alfred Toledano. "The Relation Between New Orleans and Latin America, 1810–1824." *The Louisiana Historical Review* 22, no. 3 (July 1939): 710–94.

Wells, Harwell. "The End of the Affair? Anti-Dueling Laws and Social Norms in Antebellum America." *Vanderbilt Law Review* 54, no. 4 (2001): 1805–47.

White, Ashli. *Encountering Revolution. Haiti and the Making of the Early Republic.* Baltimore: The Johns Hopkins University Press, 2010.

Whitehall, Walter Muir, and Lawrence W. Kennedy. *Boston: A Topographical History.* Cambridge, MA: Belknap Press, 2000.

Williams, Jack. *Dueling in the Old South: Vignettes of Social History.* College Station, TX: Texas A&M University Press, 2000.

Wilson Jr., Samuel. *The Vieux Carré. New Orleans, Its Plan, Its Growth, Its Architecture.* New Orleans: City of New Orleans, 1968.

Wolf, Edwin. *Philadelphia: Portrait of an American City.* Philadelphia: Camino Books, 1990.

Yacou, Alain. "L'émigration à Cuba des colons français de Saint-Domingue au cours de la révolution." Unpublished PhD Dissertation, Université de Bordeaux, 1975.

Index

NATHALIE DESSENS, professor of American history at the University of Toulouse-Jean Jaurès, is the author of *Myths of the Plantation Society: Slavery in the American South and the West Indies* and *From Saint-Domingue to New Orleans: Migration and Influences.*

THE UNIVERSITY PRESS OF FLORIDA is the scholarly publishing agency for the State University System of Florida, comprising Florida A&M University, Florida Atlantic University, Florida Gulf Coast University, Florida International University, Florida State University, New College of Florida, University of Central Florida, University of Florida, University of North Florida, University of South Florida, and University of West Florida.

Contested Boundaries

EDITED BY GENE ALLEN SMITH, TEXAS CHRISTIAN UNIVERSITY

Contested Boundaries focuses on conflicts—political, social, cultural, and economic—along the ever-changing territorial boundaries of the American empire to explore the fluidity that characterized these borderlands as they transformed into modern nation states.

The Maroons of Prospect Bluff and Their Quest for Freedom in the Atlantic World, by Nathaniel Millett (2013; first paperback printing, 2014)

Creole City: A Chronicle of Early American New Orleans, by Nathalie Dessens (2015; first paperback printing, 2016)

Entangling Migration History: Borderlands and Transnationalism in the United States and Canada, edited by Benjamin Bryce and Alexander Freund (2015)

Endgame for Empire in the Southeast: British-Creek Relations in Georgia and Vicinity, 1763-1776, by John T. Juricek (2015)

CPSIA information can be obtained
at www.ICGtesting.com
Printed in the USA
LVOW10s2224280518
578746LV00005B/944/P

9 780813 062181